Everyday Architecture of the Mid-Atlantic

Everyday Architecture

CREATING THE NORTH AMERICAN LANDSCAPE

Gregory Conniff, Bonnie Loyd, Edward K. Muller, David Schuyler
Consulting Editors

Published in cooperation with the Center for American Places,
Santa Fe, New Mexico, and Harrisonburg, Virginia

Gabrielle M. Lanier and Bernard L. Herman

of the Mid-Atlantic

Looking at Buildings and Landscapes

THE JOHNS HOPKINS UNIVERSITY PRESS

BALTIMORE AND LONDON

This book was brought to publication with the generous assistance
of the Laurence Hall Fowler Fund.

© 1997 The Johns Hopkins University Press
All rights reserved. Published 1997
Printed in the United States of America on acid-free paper
9 8 7 6 5 4 3

The Johns Hopkins University Press
2715 North Charles Street
Baltimore, Maryland 21218-4363
www.press.jhu.edu

Where no other credit is given, photographs and drawings are
by the authors.

Frontispiece: David Sterrett House, Upper Mifflin Township,
Cumberland County, Pennsylvania. Photographed by David Ames,
Historic American Buildings Survey, 1985.

ISBN 0-8018-5324-9   ISBN 0-8018-5325-7 (pbk.)

Library of Congress Cataloging-in-Publication Data will be found
at the end of this book.

A catalog record for this book is available from the British Library.

For Lania, Jessica, Erica, Amanda, Zachary, Erin, and the memory of Joshua

CONTENTS

ACKNOWLEDGMENTS

Our first note of thanks is to our colleagues and friends at the Center for Historic Architecture and Design (until recently the Center for Historic Architecture and Engineering) in the College of Urban Affairs and Public Policy at the University of Delaware. Without the encouragement, support, and good humor of David Ames, Rebecca Siders, and Nancy Van Dolsen, this project would never have been completed, much less started. David's beautiful photographs enrich the book from start to finish and form much of the visual core for our narrative. We owe a special debt of gratitude to Nancy Van Dolsen for her excellent critical reading of the revised manuscript. Other past and present students and colleagues at the center have also provided suggestions and encouragement at several key points along the way. Bert Jicha deserves a singular note of thanks for his initial enthusiasm and subsequent commentary, which helped shape this project in its earliest stages. Dean Doerrfeld and Wanda Czerwinski produced numerous line drawings for the original manuscript and supplied humor when it was most needed, and Susan Mulchahey Chase and Mark Parker Miller helped procure several critical images. Additional thanks go to Nancy Zeigler, Andrea Marth, Judith Quinn, Stuart Dixon, Carolyn Torma, Margaret Watson, Leslie Bashman Frucht, Meg Mulrooney, Deidre McCarthy, Kirk Ranzetta, Monique Bourque, Sherri Marsh, Caroline Fisher, Allison Elterich, Barksdale Maynard, Anna Andrzejewski, Tracy Myers, Pamela Edwards, Pamela Warner, Susan Mattson, Susan Taylor, Dawn Melson, Julie Darsie, Cindy Gamble, and Alyson Eubank.

Many other colleagues, students, and friends at the University of Delaware, the Winterthur Museum, and the Department of Historic Preservation at Mary Washington College also offered valuable insights and helped this project along in innumerable other ways. Thanks to the editorial skills of Mary Helen Callahan, the original manuscript was improved immeasurably. Carole Hermes and Jane Hoback also provided cheerful support throughout. Additional thanks go to Gary Stanton, John Pearce, James Curtis, Damie Stillman, Doug Sanford, Jack Abgott, W. Brown Morton III, Daniel Rich, Timothy Barnekov, Philip Hayden, Tom Ryan, and Jeff Hardwick.

Several individuals and institutions helped us to locate sources and images, offered a helping hand in the field, or provided commentary at many points along the way. We are especially grateful to Wade Catts, Jeanne Whitney, Lu Ann De Cunzo, Paul Touart, Willie Graham, Edward Chappell, Mark R. Wenger, Marcia Miller, Elizabeth Hughes, Peter Kurtze, and Thomas and Ruth Marshall. Thanks are also due to Bert Denker, Neville Thompson, and Jennifer Munson of Winterthur Museum and Gardens and to Pamela Powell of the Chester County Historical Society. Alice Kent Schooler, a critical resource person for anyone researching Chester County architecture, offered an invaluable commentary on the architectural contributions of R. Brognard Okie. We owe a special debt of gratitude to all of our good friends in the Vernacular Architecture Forum for sharing their insights and continuing to teach us in the field.

This book is an outgrowth of an earlier manuscript, entitled *A Field Guide to Delaware Architecture*, that was written for the Delaware State Historic Preservation Office under a matching funds grant administered by the National Park Service. We gratefully acknowledge the support of Dan Griffith, Joan Larrivee, Carol Hoffecker, J. Ritchie Garrison, and Barbara Benson during the developmental stages of that earlier work. From the outset, its preparation was an endeavor shared with a small and energetic group of local preservation professionals that included Stephen Del Sordo, Valerie Cesna, Alice Guerrant, and Maryanna Ralph. Their happy collaboration made that project a pleasure from start to finish; their suggestions then have significantly enriched the resulting book. If this book has a godfather, it is Lewis Purnell, who has always advocated an architectural history that served the people as much as the academy.

Special thanks are due to Edward K. Muller for his initial suggestion to pursue publication with the Johns Hopkins University Press. We are also grateful to Joe Wood, Peter Roe, Martyn Bowden, and the other members of the Eastern Historical Geographers' Association for their enthusiasm for the project. An anonymous reviewer for Johns Hopkins provided an excellent and perceptive critical reading that helped us to revise and expand the manuscript. George Thompson and Carol Mishler at the Center for American Places have offered encouragement and good advice from the start, and Anne Whitmore at the Johns Hopkins University Press was an excellent editor.

Our debts run deeper than the writing of this book. The patience, love, and encouragement of Rebecca and Lania Herman, Frederika, Paul, and Jessica Jacobs, Frederick and Lucy Herman, Marjorie and Albert Milan, Lynne and Albert Perry, Erin and Steve Lutz, Amanda Swain, and Robert, Virginia, Zachary, Sarah, and Erica Blickens infuse these pages. We wish that Muriel Young and Joshua Swain had lived to see this book. The lessons of our teachers and colleagues also resonate throughout. We extend our heartfelt thanks to David G. Orr, Henry Glassie, Don Yoder, Ritchie Garrison, David Allmendinger, Richard Bushman, Billy G. Smith, Orlando Ridout V, Camille Wells, Cary Carson, Dell Upton, Carl Lounsbury, Catherine Bishir, and Robert St. George.

Finally, our gratitude goes to the many property owners over the years who cheerfully opened their doors and shared their insights and enthusiasm with us. Their gracious stewardship of the built landscape has always made field work a pleasure and insures that there will be an architectural heritage for the future.

Everyday Architecture of the Mid-Atlantic

INTRODUCTION

Buildings, as most students of the subject quickly realize, are the best teachers of ordinary architecture. Books, drawings, photographs, and written descriptions are invaluable, but, inevitably, we learn the most about buildings by taking to the field—by looking, evaluating, measuring, questioning, and looking again. Buildings are best understood not only by careful examination, but also by continual comparison to other buildings and architectural landscapes. Consequently, studying architecture often involves traveling to sites that are widely distant. Because buildings are rarely portable and side-by-side comparisons are often impossible, most people who study buildings try to see as many as they can, to accumulate a visual dictionary. Each building or significant feature viewed in the field extends the individual fieldworker's experience, providing an ever-expanding comparative vocabulary for viewing other structures. But, while knowledge gleaned from fieldwork tends to be cumulative, it also tends to be private. Field research, unless gathered and shared in some way, remains an individual experience, often existing only as rough notes, isolated conversations, or remembered images.

This field guide to common buildings and landscapes from southern New Jersey to Virginia's Eastern Shore grew out of our desire to gather and disseminate some of the observations from our fieldwork. It consolidates and organizes the field experiences of many people who have spent long days measuring and drawing buildings throughout the region, and it continued to unfold during classroom discussions, conversations en route to sites, informal debates about building sequences, and late night discussions at the drafting table. The book is designed to make those experiences accessible to a wide audience, to help people who are not architectural professionals look at, learn from, and enjoy historic buildings and landscapes.

Although this book is intended primarily as an architectural field guide, its interpretive approach can best be described as archaeological. Buildings are viewed, not just as examples of a particular style or time period, but as above-ground archaeological sites, each building expressing its own sequence of historical changes. While traditional historical research utilizes written records, photographs, and drawings, an archaeological approach to architecture begins with the building itself as the primary research source, and involves assessing aspects of form, construction technology, and style as they relate to the broader context of the surrounding architectural and historic landscape. Evaluating a building archaeologically involves "excavating" the structure as if it were an archaeological site: peeling back its layers of occupation and use, assembling the traces of change into some sort of logical sequence, and interpreting or "reading" the evidence.

This book also has another, more pressing goal—to encourage appreciation for, and, by extension, preservation of, the region's historic landscapes. The rate of attrition of historic architecture has climbed dramatically in the past few years, with the result that entire historic landscapes are rapidly being denatured and lost. Development and increased population have wrought profound changes to the built environment throughout the region (Fig. 1.1). The rate at which early buildings are disappearing underscores the need to study and record what remains.

Because the architecture of the mid-Atlantic region is so varied, this book cannot possibly cover all aspects of the built environment. Our primary focus is pre-1940 domestic and agricultural architecture and selected landscapes, although examples of commercial, industrial, and institutional buildings in both rural and urban contexts are also discussed. The buildings included here suggest the region's architectural diversity, ranging from the eighteenth-century single-room "mansions" of Delaware's Cypress Swamp district to the early twentieth-century suburban housing around Philadelphia and Wilmington; from the gable-fronted barns of Virginia's Eastern Shore to the substantial stone bank barns of southeastern Pennsylvania. Topics such as indigenous house forms, regional architectural characteristics, stylistic attributes, and building chronologies are addressed throughout and are illustrated with anomalies as well as with examples of the most typical and the most significant regional forms.

This volume is not intended to be an encyclopedia and does not pretend to

Figure 1.1

Greenlawn Farm Manager's House, Middletown vicinity (original location), St. George's Hundred, New Castle County, Delaware. (*A*) This cruciform plan Gothic Revival house, declared eligible for listing on the National Register of Historic Places, stood on the site of a proposed shopping center. The house and its contemporary stable were documented with photographs and field notes by a team from the Center for Historic Architecture and Engineering in July 1991. The house eventually was moved, while the other structures on the site were leveled. Photographed by David Ames, Historic American Buildings Survey (HABS), 1983. (*B*) Scaled field notes included floor plans as well as elevations and drawings of details like those shown here.

A

B

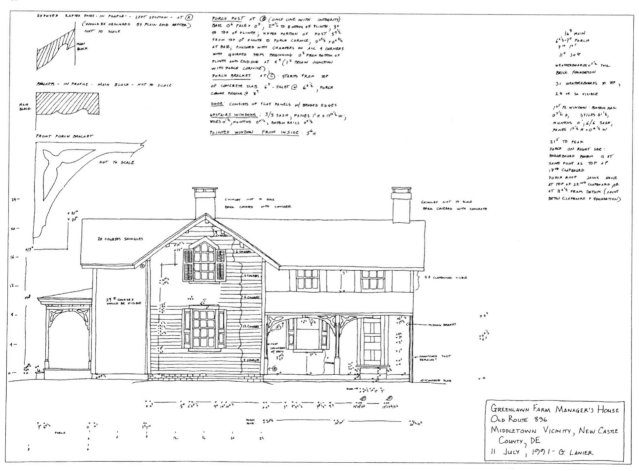

provide a comprehensive catalogue of every building type, construction feature, or stylistic variation in the region. Instead, we offer a way of looking at buildings and a set of tools for approaching architecture archaeologically. Through an examination of architectural form, construction, and style, of landscape issues, and of methods for recording and researching buildings, we introduce a way of viewing and interpreting buildings that can be likened to the way archaeologists interpret the seemingly unrelated bits of evidence that they excavate.

An Archaeological Approach to Reading Buildings and Landscapes

Why study buildings? More to the point, what can buildings—or other objects, for that matter—tell us? Buildings, like landscapes, are cultural artifacts. Like other objects that are made or modified by humans, they are also, according to archaeologist James Deetz, "fossilized ideas." The notion of the proper shape, size, and appearance of an object, whether it is a building or a baseball glove, exists in the mind of its creator. When this idea is given tangible form, a material record of that idea, or an artifact, results.[1]

Architecture, like other material objects, helps people define themselves in the world. Buildings are a form of communication and can be revealing indicators of the ideas and values of the people who built and occupied them. Buildings can be actors as well: their floor plans and room layouts often affect and mold the behavior of their inhabitants. Furthermore, buildings and landscapes continue to suggest patterns of social interaction even when the people who built and occupied them are long gone. (Think, for example, of the evocative sight of an abandoned farm complex, with its house, outbuildings, and close stand of trees, bounded by heavily traveled roads and burgeoning subdivisions.) Buildings express community boundaries as well as individual values, suggesting patterns of community cohesiveness through both their similarities to and their differences from surrounding buildings.

Social values and the ways they are expressed architecturally change through time and from place to place. Architecture that communicated one set of values and ideas in its own time may say something entirely different to us today. We betray our own values even in so simple an act as describing a structure, by making conscious and subconscious choices about what to include, and also what is not important. The picture is further affected by changes to the building itself. Houses are a case in point: Although most

Figure 1.2
Bennett-Downs House, Buena Vista vicinity, New Castle Hundred, New Castle County, Delaware. Photographed by David Ames, HABS, 1991. Despite Victorian changes to the exterior, this house retains much of its original Federal period plan and interior finish. The facade was altered when the mansard roof was added in the late nineteenth century, but the original chimney corbeling is still visible in the attic.

people do not build their own houses, they are continually modifying them. Because each set of owners effects its own changes, the dwelling that has never been altered is rare, if not apocryphal. Changes can be as subtle as a new coat of whitewash or as dramatic as the demolition of an entire wing. Over time, the inevitable accumulation of physical changes renders the original dwelling ever more difficult to see with clarity (Fig. 1.2). Each change to the architectural fabric might be indicative of a subtle shift in individual, social, or cultural values. Such alterations may be the products of widespread improvement or rebuilding, or they may simply be the results of changes in individual circumstances. Nevertheless, most architectural changes leave physical traces. Our task is to find and "read" these traces and make sense of them.

When we read a building archaeologically in search of architectural change, we search for pattern in building history. Of all the techniques that archaeologists use to determine the dates of their sites, the principles of stratigraphy, horizon, and *terminus post quem* are the most useful when applied to architecture.[2] Stratigraphy is based on the notion that, as sites are occupied through time, archaeological remains are layered, with the oldest layers lying deepest in the ground. Layers of occupation are not always orderly or easily determined; still, stratigraphy is a useful tool for dating archaeological sites. Buildings can also be viewed stratigraphically. Individual bits of evidence that seem unrelated at first glance can often be linked and placed in the same general time period, suggesting layers of occupation and alteration that are revealed upon closer inspection. By isolating periods of change, we can reconstruct the appearance of the building over time. We can devise a narrative of sorts, an

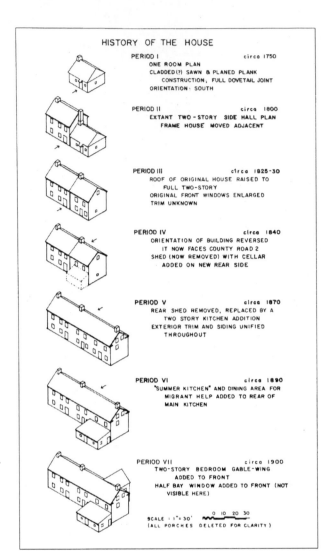

HISTORY OF THE HOUSE

PERIOD I   circa 1750
ONE ROOM PLAN
CLADDED (?) SAWN & PLANED PLANK
    CONSTRUCTION, FULL DOVETAIL JOINT
ORIENTATION : SOUTH

PERIOD II   circa 1800
EXTANT TWO-STORY SIDE HALL PLAN
    FRAME HOUSE MOVED ADJACENT

PERIOD III   circa 1825-30
ROOF OF ORIGINAL HOUSE RAISED TO
    FULL TWO-STORY
ORIGINAL FRONT WINDOWS ENLARGED
TRIM UNKNOWN

PERIOD IV   circa 1840
ORIENTATION OF BUILDING REVERSED
    IT NOW FACES COUNTY ROAD 2
SHED (NOW REMOVED) WITH CELLAR
    ADDED ON NEW REAR SIDE

PERIOD V   circa 1870
REAR SHED REMOVED, REPLACED BY A
    TWO STORY KITCHEN ADDITION
EXTERIOR TRIM AND SIDING UNIFIED
    THROUGHOUT

PERIOD VI   circa 1890
"SUMMER KITCHEN" AND DINING AREA FOR
    MIGRANT HELP ADDED TO REAR OF
    MAIN KITCHEN

PERIOD VII   circa 1900
TWO-STORY BEDROOM GABLE-WING
    ADDED TO FRONT
HALF BAY WINDOW ADDED TO FRONT (NOT
    VISIBLE HERE)

SCALE : 1"=30'   0 10 20 30
(ALL PORCHES DELETED FOR CLARITY)

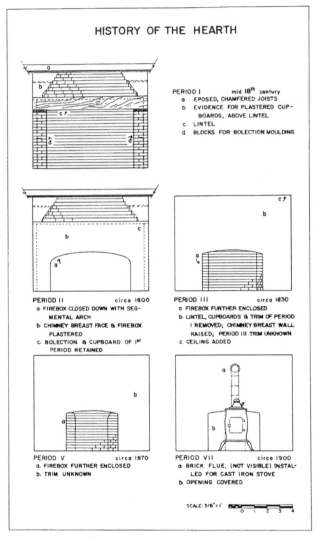

HISTORY OF THE HEARTH

PERIOD I   mid 18th century
a EPOSED, CHAMFERED JOISTS
b EVIDENCE FOR PLASTERED CUP-
    BOARDS, ABOVE LINTEL
c LINTEL
d BLOCKS FOR BOLECTION MOULDING

PERIOD II   circa 1800
a FIREBOX CLOSED DOWN WITH SEG-
    MENTAL ARCH
b CHIMNEY BREAST FACE & FIREBOX
    PLASTERED
c BOLECTION & CUPBOARD OF 1st
    PERIOD RETAINED

PERIOD III   circa 1830
a FIREBOX FURTHER ENCLOSED
b LINTEL, CUPBOARDS & TRIM OF PERIOD
    I REMOVED; CHIMNEY BREAST WALL
    RAISED; PERIOD III TRIM UNKNOWN
c CEILING ADDED

PERIOD V   circa 1870
a FIREBOX FURTHER ENCLOSED
b TRIM UNKNOWN

PERIOD VII   circa 1900
a BRICK FLUE, (NOT VISIBLE) INSTAL-
    LED FOR CAST IRON STOVE
b OPENING COVERED

SCALE: 3/8"=1'   0 1 2 3 4

Figure 1.3

Vandergrift-Biddle House, Biddle's Corner, St. George's Hundred, New Castle County, Delaware. Drawn by Charles Bergengren, HABS, 1983. (*A*) Begun in the mid-eighteenth century as a one-story, hall plan dwelling and repeatedly enlarged through the nineteenth century by the Biddle family and subsequent owners, the house passed through seven major building periods during its long and complicated history. In each period of its growth the house was rebuilt as a new and larger structure, increasingly unified on the exterior but retaining much of its earlier fabric. (*B*) The sequence of alterations in the hall hearth clearly demonstrates changing social attitudes toward cleanliness and comfort: the firebox was closed down repeatedly to provide more heat while containing dirt and smoke.

architectural story connected through a series of points in the building's history (Fig. 1.3).

The archaeological concept of horizon, which also helps us identify layers of architectural change, determines how widely certain ideas spread. Horizon is defined as the chronologically rapid and geographically broad distribution of complex cultural traits. It is often evidenced in historic artifacts.[3] Clothing styles, songs, or jokes that suddenly become popular yet fade almost as quickly offer modern examples of the horizon concept. The widespread availability of machine-cut nails in the nineteenth century illustrates a horizon in architectural and historic terms. Cut nails were widely used after their introduction in the very late eighteenth century, but their popularity gradually waned after wire nails were introduced in the third quarter of the nineteenth century. Like stylistic differences in door hardware and molding profiles, the presence of cut nails in historic building fabric suggests dates of construction and alteration and helps to identify building periods.

Dates are also determined by applying the principle of *terminus post quem*. Translated as "the date after which," this archaeological principle is based upon the simple premise that an archaeological layer can only be as early as the newest datable feature found in it. Viewed in architectural terms, each layer of change in a building can date no earlier than the most recent technology with which it was built. Circular saw marks on original ceiling joists, for example, suggest at least a mid-nineteenth-century construction date, even in a braced-frame house, simply because lumber cut with a circular saw was not widely used until after about 1850.

Taken together, these archaeological tools help us to specify building periods and determine sequences of change. Still, buildings, although inherently interesting, cannot be studied in isolation. They are also part of broader contexts that can critically affect our final interpretation of them. Cultural products of the time in which they were built and altered, buildings also exist within the spatial, physical context of their surrounding landscapes. Although good architectural interpretation rests on careful examination of the building in question, comparison to other building stock in the surrounding community and to historically similar sites enables us to discern broader stylistic and geographic relationships. These relationships, in turn, help us to refine our architectural interpretations and to view individual buildings as aspects of larger cultural landscapes.

Historic Architecture in the Mid-Atlantic Region

The topography, settlement patterns, extreme cultural diversity, and geographic character of this region have combined to create an uncommonly varied architectural landscape. Historic architecture in and around the mid-Atlantic region ranges so widely that the area can be viewed as an architectural crossroads of sorts, where multiple settlement patterns and subregional building traditions have melded to inform the built environment.

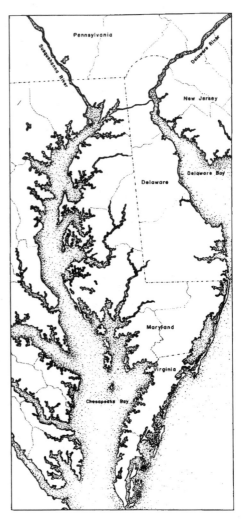

The geographic focus of this book extends from the southeasternmost part of Pennsylvania, lying east of the Susquehanna River and west of Philadelphia—including the counties of Chester, Bucks, lower Montgomery, Delaware, and the eastern fringes of Lancaster—southward to the tip of the Eastern Shore, in Virginia. It includes Salem, Cumberland, and parts of Gloucester counties in southern New Jersey and extends from there westward across the entire state of Delaware to Cecil County and the fringes of Harford County, Maryland (Fig. 1.4). The heavily urbanized landscapes bordering Baltimore and Philadelphia are largely outside the compass of this guide; our focus is primarily on the architecture of towns and rural landscapes.

This region includes several varied and sometimes overlapping building traditions. In the early eighteenth century, the regional house types built in much of southeastern Pennsylvania, northern Delaware, southern New Jersey, and Cecil County, Maryland, consisted primarily of hall, hall-parlor, cross-passage, double-cell, and three-room plan houses. Beginning around the 1740s, side-passage and center-passage plan houses were incorporated into the regional repertoire. Multilevel bank barns also appeared with some frequency throughout part of this region, especially in southeastern Pennsylvania.

Stone and brick were more popular in the northernmost reaches, and stone was especially common where it could be quarried locally, but log remained the favored building material in much of this area as late as the early nineteenth century. The well-known eighteenth-century pattern-end brick houses of Salem County, New Jersey, where early English Quaker settlements took root, survive in considerable numbers, which belies the fact that most early buildings in the area were constructed of wood.

To the south, architectural styles derive from various building traditions. One-story, one-room frame dwellings were the dominant form in lower Delaware and on the lower Eastern Shore of Maryland and Virginia in the eighteenth and nineteenth centuries, although hall-parlor, central-passage, and side-passage plans were also built. Many of these houses lacked excavated foundations. They were erected instead on masonry piers or timber blocks and were sometimes moved from one location to another. Framing traditions associated with the Chesapeake region, such as common rafter roofs, board false plates, and hewn L-shaped corner posts, were also more characteristic of the southern portion of the study area. Early barns in the southern portions of the region were typically crib barns, usually erected on masonry piers or timber blocks.

The diversity of the region's architectural landscape is further evidenced by the timber framing practices present in many early Cumberland County, New Jersey, dwellings, which derive from southeastern New England construction traditions rather than from building practices of the New Jersey area and are the product of a significant early migration from southern New England. Similarly, the Germanic construction traditions common in Lancaster County, Pennsylvania, differ from those that prevail further east.

The wide range of building forms, types, construction techniques, and stylistic features that are evident throughout the mid-Atlantic region precludes an encyclopedic treatment of any one aspect of architecture in this volume. Chapters are organized thematically, each focusing on different aspects of buildings, such as form, construction, or style, or on different types of buildings, such as farm outbuildings or commercial architecture. We hope that, by providing a series of thematic starting points for the study and appreciation of the region's historic architecture, this book will aid all those readers who seek to learn from looking at the landscape.

2

HOUSE FORMS
AND HOUSE LOTS

When we look at buildings in the landscape, we tend to organize what we see into categories based on shared architectural characteristics. For instance, we classify buildings according to construction material and then by construction technique. Thus, we separate log buildings from frame ones, and then we distinguish between the various log buildings on the basis of how the logs are finished and joined. The different methods of finishing and joining the logs define types of log construction. The potential for creating typologies is present in all areas of building design, from siting in the landscape to interior paneled finishes. Once different types have been recognized, they become a valuable tool for evaluating questions of architectural preference and practice.

One of the most important and informative features by which to type architecture is the way in which people define their interior and exterior space. *Form* is the term used to describe the design and division of space, whether it be by house plan, the arrangement of outbuildings in a farm plan, or the placement of residences in a suburban development. This chapter introduces basic house types and common patterns of house lot organization.

Sorting house forms into useful typologies is a procedure common to the study of traditional architecture throughout the world. House types comprise categories ranging from the most basic one-room farm dwelling to the most complex Victorian townhouse. The arrangement of space in and around dwellings reveals the ways people organize and, in a sense, compartmentalize their lives. Changes in household space generally signal larger transformations in lifestyle and social organization. While folks may be quick to embrace the latest fashion in terms of architectural trim, they are far less likely to create fundamental changes in their domestic environment.[1] House types, then, help us see the sociology of architecture: What kinds of domestic spaces did people build and how did they use them? What housing options existed in a given community at a given time? Because houses can be dated through details of construction and ornament, we can also chart changes over time that reveal evolving sensibilities about the kinds of spaces best suited to the expectations and duties of everyday life; we can evaluate how people changed older dwellings in accordance with fashion, convenience, and family fortune. House types also offer insights into questions about class and ethnicity: Do the poor occupy houses fundamentally different in plan from those inhabited by wealthier individuals? Is ethnic identity reflected in the types of houses associated with particular groups, such as British Quakers, African-American freedmen, or Pennsylvania-German farm families? Because no object is simultaneously more public and more intimate than the domestic spaces people build and occupy, we can turn to the organization of space in the house as a means for answering these questions.

House Forms

Our discussion of individual house types begins by describing basic types and then proceeds by establishing general patterns of historical development, based on the kinds of houses people have built and the modifications they have made since the seventeenth century. The time lines suggested here are only approximations based on the rise and fall in popularity of different house types. Some types have endured from the colonial period with remarkably little change; other types enjoyed only brief episodes of acceptance. First, we discuss *open plans,* house plans that provide access from the outside directly into a heated living space. Second, we look at the introduction of *closed plans,* which are characterized by access into the living areas of the house through an unheated stair passage or entry hall. These first two sections refer to distinguishing characteristics of rural, village, and urban housing throughout the eastern United States. Third, from the types of open and closed plans, we consider houses with specialized service wings, where cooking and other "dirty" household functions are placed in kitchen, pantry, and work rooms contained in ells, gable wings, lean-tos, and other types of ancillary spaces. Fourth, we look at the various kinds of additions people made to their houses and how house plans get modified over time. Finally, our overview describes the emergence of the modern living spaces associated with pattern book architecture, late Victorian dwellings, and the appearance of the bungalow and early suburban housing.

Open Plans

Open plan refers to houses designed with direct access from the outside into the heated living areas of the dwelling. Open plan houses are typically associated with the earliest periods of settlement through the mid-1800s. The room connected to the outside was the main living room, generally the site of all the day-to-day functions of the house: cooking, eating, craftwork, sleeping, as well as birth and death. Historically, this primary room had several names—"hall," "common room," "outer room," and "house below." To describe this general living space, we use the term *hall*, a designation also used to describe the main room in postmedieval vernacular housing in Europe and, especially, the British Isles, and a term that distinguishes this general living space from the *passage*, which denotes an entryway usually containing a stair. Open plan variations found in the mid-Atlantic region are relatively limited. The vast majority are only one or two rooms, although some three- and four-room open plans also remain. Although all of these open plans coexisted from the periods of initial settlement through the late 1800s, we will approach them by beginning with the simplest and working our way toward more complex arrangements. Do not mistake this progression in the following discussion for an evolutionary sequence in building.

HALL PLANS

The hall or one-room dwelling contains, in its simplest form, a single door that opens directly into a living space heated either by an open fireplace in older examples and a metal stove in examples that date from the mid-1800s into the twentieth century. One-room houses usually contained at least one window, typically set in the gable end away from the chimney or near the door, and a ladder or stair to a loft or upper story used for sleeping and storage (Fig. 2.1). Hall dwellings were so common that, at the end of the eighteenth century, they housed roughly 85 percent of the inhabitants of southern Delaware and Maryland's lower Eastern Shore; they were similarly common in southwestern New Jersey.[2] Dwellings such as Thomas Sorden's Marshyhope mansion house—"a framed Dwelling house twenty by fifteen feet with a shed to the side"—were typical.[3] Similar dwellings were built throughout the region with a variety of materials, including log, frame, brick, stone, and even "mud" (any of several materials, such as packed earth or cob). The best one-room houses, known as chambered hall plans, were constructed of brick or

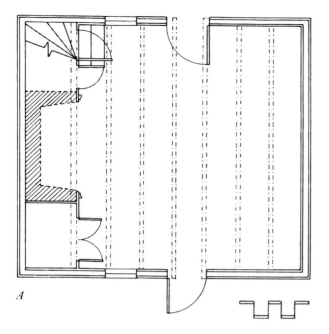

A

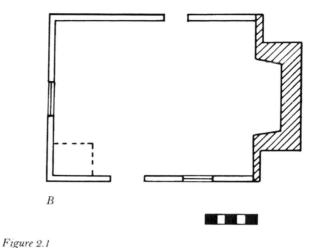

B

Figure 2.1

The simplest form of hall dwelling contained a single door, opening directly into the heated living space, and at least one window. A ladder or stair usually led to a loft or upper story used for sleeping and storage. (*A*) Lowe House, ca. 1800, Laurel vicinity, Little Creek Hundred, Sussex County, Delaware. Drawn by Gabrielle Lanier after M. M. Mulrooney, HABS. (*B*) Pear Valley, built mid-1700s, Machipungo vicinity, Northampton County, Virginia. (*C*) Caesaria River House, ca. 1690, Greenwich vicinity, Cumberland County, New Jersey, drawn by Bernard L. Herman and Gabrielle Lanier, HABS.

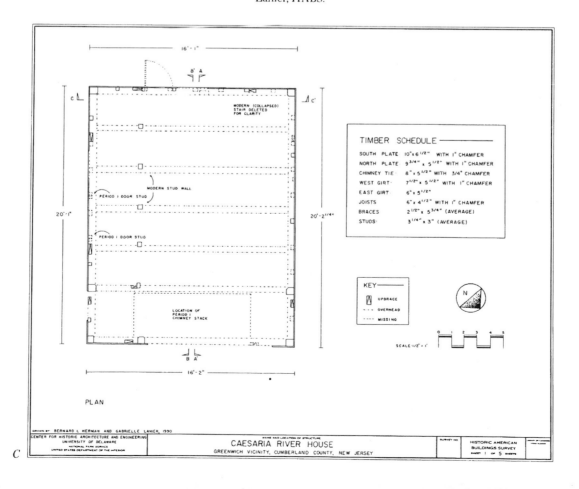

C

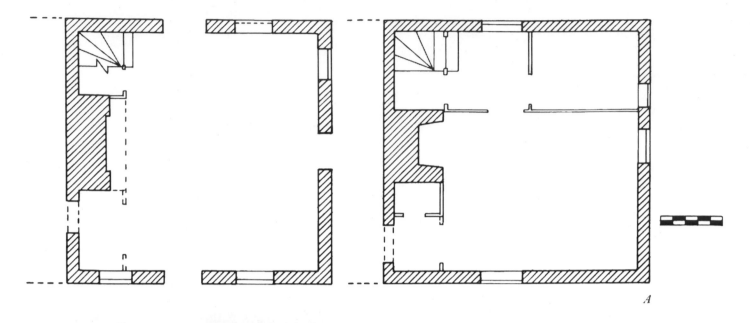

Figure 2.2

One-room plan dwellings with two stories were known as chambered hall plans. (*A*) First floor (*left*) and second floor (*right*) plans of Dilworth House, ca. 1700, Port Penn, New Castle County, Delaware (see also Fig. 7.4A). (*B*) Worker's house, ca. 1800, Bishops Mills, Delaware County, Delaware. Photographed 1976.

Figure 2.3
Cessford, barn and slave house, ca. 1825–35, Eastville, Northampton County, Virginia. Photographed 1975. Slave quarters (*beyond barn*) were most often erected singly or in pairs. Many shared a common, centrally placed chimney pile.

weatherboarded frame and rose a full two stories in height with heated rooms on both floors (Fig. 2.2). Some of these two-story houses, as well as many smaller one-story examples, were elaborately finished, with fully paneled fireplace walls. They were also commonly subdivided on the second floor into two and sometimes three rooms: a heated chamber, a stair landing, and an unheated chamber. While lesser examples were poorly lighted and ventilated, the best one-room dwellings, whether one or two stories in height, tended to have front and back doors and two to five windows on each floor. The standard dimensions for one-room houses were 16 to 18 feet by 18 to 20 feet, with exceptionally small dwellings being as tiny as 10 feet square and large examples as spacious as 20 by 26 feet. While these one-room houses were the most common house form of the 1700s, they became increasingly less popular by the mid-1800s and more closely associated with the lifestyle of the poor. Those constructed in the late 1800s seem almost always to have been built either as farm laborers' houses, millworkers' dwellings, or as urban tenements.

One-room houses also represent the major plan type found in surviving slave quarters in Virginia and Maryland (Fig. 2.3). Where slaves were not housed in the owners' dwelling, kitchen, or some other structure, they were lodged in purpose-built quarters. Quarters were erected most often singly or in pairs and shared a common, centrally placed chimney pile. Even in double quarters, each unit contained its own entry and fireplace. Because slave quarters look much like other one-room houses, surviving examples are generally recognizable only on the basis of their physical association with a principal dwelling or as an outbuilding in a larger agricultural or industrial complex. In the industrial city of Petersburg, Virginia, for example, the same house types provided accommodation for slaves and for white and free black laborers. Comparable housing was erected for millworkers and farmworkers in the Delaware valley. Following the pattern of the one-room house, these small dwellings differed from owner-occupied, one-room residences in their relationship to their surroundings and in the quality of construction and finish. Throughout the region, slave quarters, as well as housing for farm laborers and millworkers, reflected locally preferred building practices in terms of materials and finishes.

TWO-ROOM PLANS

The range of variation in the organization of household space dramatically increases when we deal with houses of more than one room. What two-room dwellings share, though, is the notion of the ground floor hall, replete with all the functions associated with single-room houses but augmented with a second, more private ground floor room, used primarily as a sleeping chamber and sitting room or as a parlor. Two-room dwellings generally fall into one of four categories that are based on the location of the two rooms in relationship to each other and to the overall massing of the house. In each of these categories, the second room holds a different functional and spatial relationship to the hall.

The most common two-room arrangement throughout the region consists of two rooms aligned end to end on the ground floor, with a fireplace at one or each gable end. The main room, or hall, contained the principal fireplace and the stair or ladder to the story above. Popularly known as *hall-parlor* houses, these one-story, one-and-a-half-story, and two-story dwellings were built from the early colonial period through the early 1900s (Fig. 2.4). As with hall plan houses, hall-parlor dwellings were, after 1830 or so, increasingly associated with less affluent households.

The best hall-parlor houses contained a fireplace in each of the two main rooms. The room with the entry from the outside usually held the larger fireplace; the other room typically possessed a much smaller fireplace, either in the center of the gable or, in upper Delaware and adjacent Pennsylvania, in the gable corner at the back of the house. Hall-parlor plans were also built with unheated parlors, especially on the lower Eastern Shore of Delaware, Maryland, and Virginia. These unheated parlors were actually first-floor

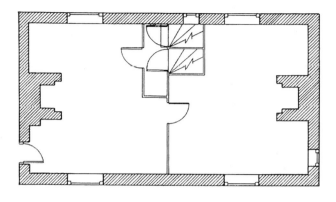

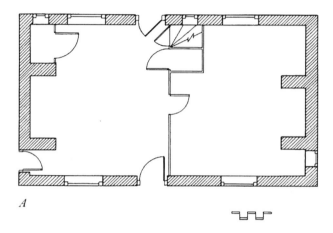

A

Figure 2.4

Hall-parlor plan houses consist of two rooms placed side by side under a continuous ridge line. The best hall-parlor houses had fireplaces at each end. (*A*) Plans of first (*bottom*) and second (*top*) floors of Ashton House, ca. 1705, Port Penn, New Castle County, Delaware (see also Fig. 7.4B). (*B*) Oakford House, built 1764, Lower Alloways Creek Township, Salem County, New Jersey. Drawn by Gabrielle Lanier after L. A. Wiegand, HABS.

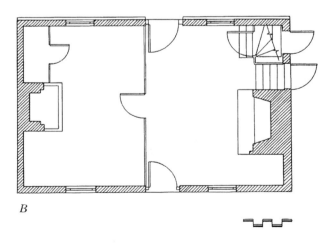

B

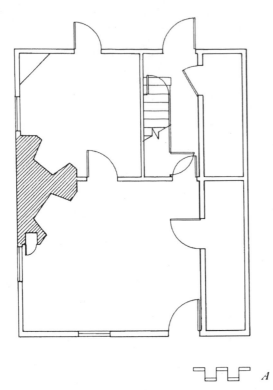

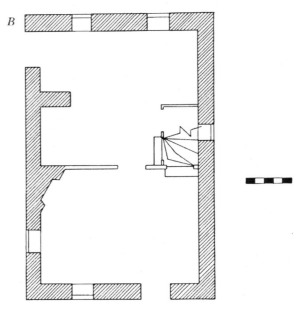

A

B

Figure 2.5
Double-cell plan houses, most often associated with the
Piedmont settlements of northern New Castle County or
with townhousing in Wilmington and other towns through-
out the region, are two-room plans in which the rooms are
oriented back to back rather than end to end. The Hunter
House began life as a double-cell house with a half-passage,
back-to-back corner fireplaces, and a back entry. (*A*) Hunter
House, ca. 1760, Milton vicinity, Sussex County, Delaware.
(*B*) Farm house, ca. 1800, Willistown vicinity, Chester
County, Pennsylvania. (*C*) Plans of first (*left*) and second
(*right*) floors of a house on Lawrence Street (formerly Crown
Street), ca. 1785–90, Philadelphia, Pennsylvania.

sleeping rooms and generally did not serve as formal sitting and entertaining
spaces. Architectural trim in the form of moldings, cornices, and mantel
pieces also served to distinguish the quality and finish of these two rooms;
the better room often contained more elaborate paneling, as well as the best
furniture. The second room, or parlor, has been known by a number of other
names, such as "inner room," "downstairs chamber," and "sitting room." The
presence of a second room in the hall-parlor house led to the use of different
terms, such as "dining room," to label the old hall.

The region's most extraordinary collection of two-room houses surviving

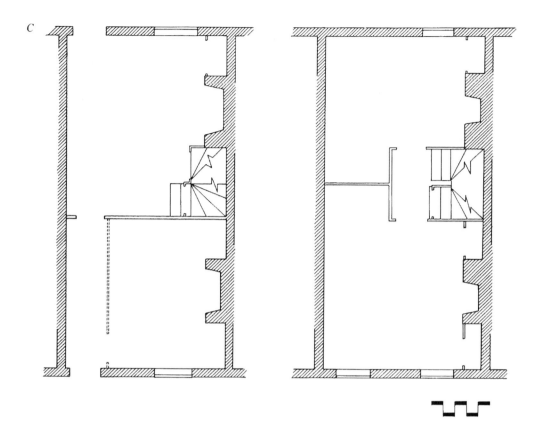

from the eighteenth century remains in southwestern New Jersey. Here, predominantly Quaker builders commissioned elaborate two-story hall-parlor houses throughout the colonial period. The most elaborate examples included decorative brickwork (usually on the parlor end of the house), which contained geometric designs, dates, and initials highlighted with glazed brick (see Fig. 3.33). The interiors of these houses often boasted elaborately paneled fireplace walls, corner winding stairs, and storage closets in the hall. More modest hall-parlor houses, associated with the landscapes of the lower Eastern Shore, made use of single-story frame construction with brick gable ends, while similar dwellings in southeastern Pennsylvania were erected in log, brick, and stone, with locally distinctive pent eaves at the second-floor level.

Another type of two-room house was designed with the interior spaces placed one behind the other, as opposed to the side-by-side arrangement of the hall-parlor house. While there is no historic name for this plan type, architectural fieldworkers often refer to the form as a *double-cell* plan (Fig. 2.5). The heating arrangement in eighteenth- and early-nineteenth-century examples of double-cell houses consists of either back-to-back corner fireplaces or a large cooking fireplace set flat to the gable and a corner fireplace abutting. Late-nineteenth-century examples typically possess a simple stove flue

A

running up a common partition. The principal stair could be placed against the partition dividing the front and rear rooms, in the back corner of the rear room away from the fireplace, or in the space between the back fireplace jamb and partition. Architectural evidence for historic use of rooms in the double-cell house is far from uniform. In some instances, the front room functioned as a common room accommodating all the functions of daily life; in others, the front living space exhibits characteristics associated with a parlor or sitting room. Double-cell houses are generally found in small numbers throughout the

B

region. They tend to be associated most closely with the rural Piedmont settlements of northern Delaware and southeastern Pennsylvania or with urban housing. In urban situations, the front room was almost always a ground floor shop or sitting room, while the room in back served variously as a dining room, kitchen, or work space.

Two-room house plans were also created through the use of original or added *lean-tos*, shedlike wings built against the back or gable elevations of the house and almost always of lesser finish and purpose. Although some lean-tos of the eighteenth and early nineteenth centuries had cooking fireplaces, the majority appear to have been unheated and relegated to purposes such as rough storage, home craftwork, and sleeping. While the interior of the principal room may have been finished with paneling or lath and plaster, the lean-

Figure 2.6
Like double-cell plan dwellings, lean-to plan houses
consist of back-to-back
rooms, but one room is almost always less finished
and less important. The
majority of lean-tos from
the eighteenth and early
nineteenth centuries appear
to have been unheated and
left with exposed framing.
In gable-shedded plans (as
shown in *B*), the attached
one-story shed is typically
not as finely finished as the
main room and is most of-
ten located against the wall
farthest from the chimney
pile. (*A*) Tenant house, ca.
1900, Eastville vicinity,
Northampton County, Vir-
ginia. Photographed 1977.
(*B*) William Percy's House,
Sussex County Chancery
Partition Docket, 1824.

to walls were often left as exposed framing. Evidence for this early lack of
finish in the lean-to is often visible under later interior finishes, appearing as
an accumulation of the smoke stains and scuffings that built up on any exposed interior surface over time.

Gable lean-tos (Fig. 2.6), also characteristically inferior to the principal
living area in space, finish, and construction, are typically found against the
wall farthest from the chimney pile and reach only a single story in height.
Even where architectural evidence suggests that these lean-tos were original
to the building, construction details reveal that they were usually conceived
almost as an afterthought. The gable lean-to is most often attached to the
main block by means of a simple plate spiked to the side of the gable; the
rafters simply slant down to the outer wall. Although some lean-tos were
used for rough storage and work purposes, others could be as finely finished
as the unheated first-floor chamber in a hall-parlor plan.

THREE- AND FOUR-ROOM PLANS

The most elaborate open plan houses contained three or four heated rooms
on a floor and were a full two stories in height, while others were of post-in-
the-ground construction and possessed only a single fireplace heating the
largest room. Building contracts describe the construction and appearance of
buildings in this category as early as the 1640s. For the most part, however,
these larger open plan dwellings seem to date from the 1720s until the early
1800s. By the early nineteenth century, people interested in larger, more
grandiose houses were opting for the classically inspired Georgian house
plans described below. While there are numerous combinations possible for
three- and four-room plans, only two seem to have enjoyed general use. The
most widely built of these was a three-room plan often referred to as the
"Penn" or "Quaker" plan (terms that have caused considerable misunder-
standing about these houses).

The largest room in a typical three-room plan house is a large hall or common room entered directly from the outside and running the full depth of the
house. This room usually contains a large cooking fireplace, although sometimes the cooking fireplace is located in the cellar below. The stair to the
upper loft or second story, as well as built-in cupboards for storage and display, are also customarily located in this room. Adjacent to the hall are two
smaller rooms which seem to have functioned as ground-floor sleeping chambers, offices, or small sitting rooms. Typically these "inner" rooms each contained a corner fireplace and a single window. In some instances, there was
no opening between these rooms, which made it necessary to pass through
the hall when moving from one of the smaller rooms to the other (Fig. 2.7).

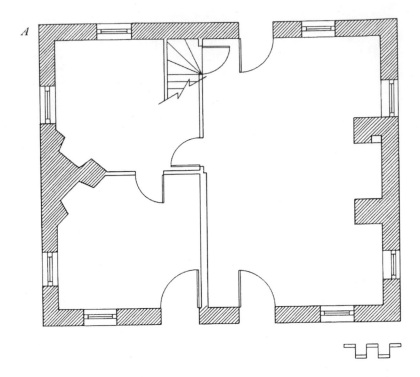

Figure 2.7

Three-room plan houses are typically composed of a large hall or heated common room with two smaller rooms located adjacent to one another on the same side of the hall. The hall is entered directly from the outside and usually runs the full depth of the house. The earliest portion of the Nicholson House (*left half* on *B*) was built on a three-room plan. (*A*) Sawyers House, ca. 1800, Mill Creek Hundred, New Castle County, Delaware. (*B*) Samuel Nicholson House, 1752, Elsinboro Township, Salem County, New Jersey. Drawn by Gabrielle Lanier after E. R. Coutch and C. L. Carroll, HABS.

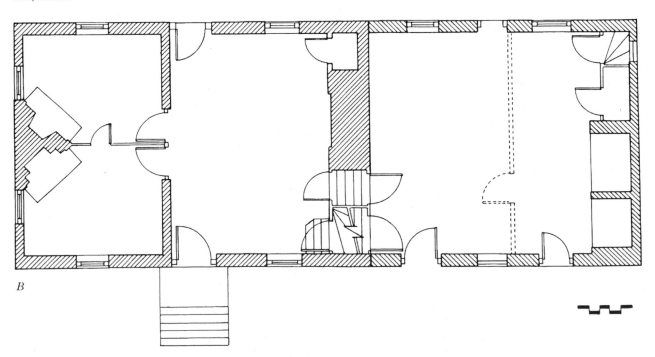

A

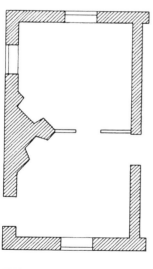
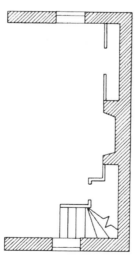

B

Figure 2.8

Townsend House, ca. 1780, Townsend vicinity, New Castle County, Delaware. Photographed 1980. The most elaborate three-room plan houses in the Delaware valley region were often associated with millers or millowners or were used as taverns. They were built of brick or stone and received well-executed interior finishes. The Townsend House contained a fully paneled fireplace wall, a well-designed corner stair, and an array of paneled-door display cupboards.

The grandest three-room plan houses in the region were almost invariably associated with millers or millowners or used as taverns; they were typically built of brick or stone and furnished with well-executed interior finishes. Among the best examples of the three-room plan was the Townsend House near the town of Townsend, Delaware (Fig. 2.8). A two-story, brick structure sited overlooking the associated mill pond, the Townsend House contained a fully paneled fireplace wall with a well-designed corner stair and an array of paneled-door display cupboards. Kensey Johns considered building a three-room plan house of this sort in 1789 on his corner lot in New Castle (see Fig. 2.18). In the end, however, he built a more fashionable Georgian town-house (see Fig. 4.13A). Although houses with comparable floor plans were erected on the lower Eastern Shore, they were typically considerably smaller in size, built of wood, and less elaborately finished. In some instances, the two inner rooms also appear to have been left unheated.

Two less frequently built forms of the three-room house deserve mention. In the eighteenth-century English-speaking settlements of southeastern Pennsylvania and the Western Shore of Virginia, a number of families chose a three-room house with the interior spaces lined up under a common ridge. Sometimes known as *double parlor* houses, these three-room-long buildings enjoyed little popularity in the region, although they emerged as a favored house type in parts of rural England. The second three-room plan type is the continental *Flurküchenhaus*, associated with the German-speaking communities north and west of Philadelphia. Its typical arrangement of an asymmetrically placed center chimney fronting on a kitchen (*Küche*), with a squarish parlor (*Stübe*) heated by a masonry or cast-iron stove and an unheated downstairs sleeping chamber (*Kammer*), bears only the most superficial resemblance to the Anglo-American three-room house and appears to have enjoyed little to no popularity outside the German settlements of Pennsylvania, Western Maryland, and the Valley of Virginia far to the west.

Four-room houses are rarer still. Surviving examples seem to date from the 1760s through the 1820s. The distinguishing characteristics of the plan include direct access into a heated room containing a stair. Behind the entry is a second room, often of similar size. Two comparable rooms adjacent to these complete the plan (Fig. 2.9). We have little sense of how these spaces were actually used except for the entry room, which seems, judging from architectural trim, to have generally functioned as the best room or parlor. Despite its relative rarity, the four-room plan house represented an alternative to the more formal Georgian house plans discussed below. The fact that relatively few builders commissioned such houses indicates that by the mid-

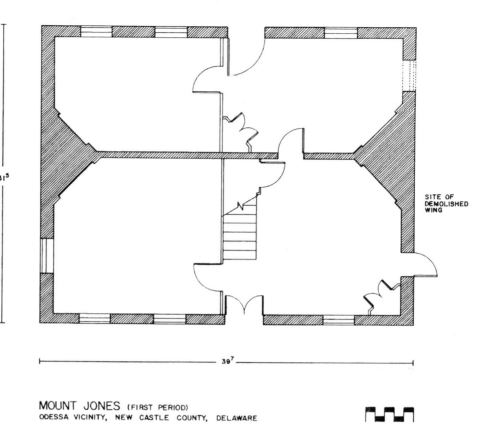

Figure 2.9
Mount Jones, ca. 1790, Odessa vicinity, New Castle County, Delaware. Drawn by Gabrielle M. Lanier. From Herman et al., *National Register of Historic Places: Dwellings of the Rural Elite.* Four-room plan houses are characterized by direct access from the outside into a heated room containing a stair, a second room, usually of similar size, located behind the entry room, and two comparable rooms located along the side.

MOUNT JONES (FIRST PERIOD)
ODESSA VICINITY, NEW CASTLE COUNTY, DELAWARE

1700s, when many affluent families were commissioning major dwellings, they most often opted for one of the Georgian or closed plan types.

Closed Plans

The designation *closed plan* refers to houses that lack direct access into the heated living spaces of the dwelling and accordingly communicate a sense of social distance in the very plan of the dwelling. Closed plans are most closely associated with Georgian houses, which are characterized by symmetrical elevations with centrally placed doors opening into a formal entry or passage that contains the principal stair and provides access to ground floor rooms. Because of the characteristic stair in the entry passage, closed plans are sometimes termed *stair-passage plans.* Access to service wings from this formal passage, however, was indirect. Service wings in closed plans were entered through a separate door, the dining room, or a rear piazza or porch. The key characteristics to note when describing different types of closed plans are the depth of the house and the relationship of the rooms in the main block to the stair passage (Fig. 2.10). The depth of the dwelling refers to the number of

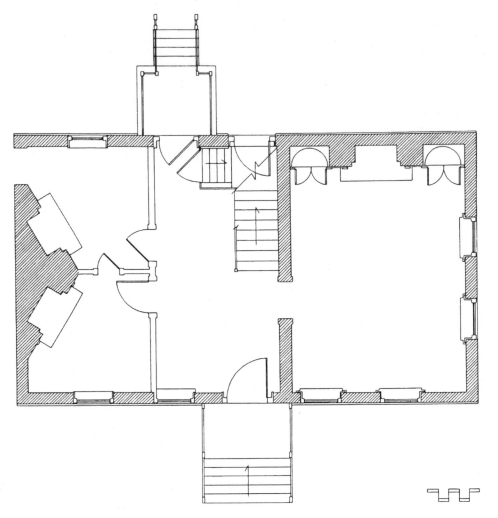

Figure 2.10
John Dickinson Mansion,
1740, Dover vicinity, Kent
County, Delaware. Drawn
by Dean Doerrfeld and Ga-
brielle Lanier. Closed Georgian plan houses lack direct
access into the heated living spaces. Instead, access
is gained through a cen-
trally located passage, from
which doorways lead into
each of the rooms in the
main block of the dwelling.

back-to-back rooms in the main body of the structure. Typically, we refer to this massing as a pile. Thus, a single-pile house is one room deep, a double-pile two rooms deep. The relationship of the rooms to the passage designates the location of interior spaces around the unheated entry and stair. The following discussion begins with the earliest forms of closed plans in the region and proceeds to discuss their later development into the mid-twentieth century.

The earliest form of closed plan house built throughout the lower mid-Atlantic region appears to have been a single-pile house with a center passage containing a stair to the upper stories. Examples as early as the late 1690s have been recorded on the Western Shore of Maryland, but the plan did not gain general currency until the 1740s. These houses typically had five bays, or openings, across the front on each floor, with the doorway into the passage constituting the central element (Fig. 2.11). The next most common

Figure 2.11

Gibbon House, 1730, Greenwich, Cumberland County, New Jersey. Photographed 1995. Drawn by Gabrielle Lanier after C. Cassell and R. F. Coster, HABS. The earliest form of Georgian plan house, which was built throughout the lower mid-Atlantic region, appears to have been a one-room-deep house with a center passage containing a stair to the upper stories. These houses typically contained five bays, or openings, across the front on each floor.

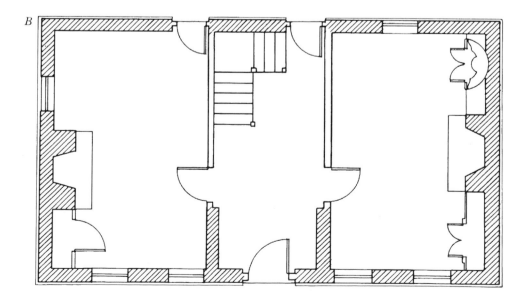

arrangement was a four-bay pattern with an off-center door. Three-bay arrangements tended to be even less frequently built. The basic configuration of the center-passage single-pile Georgian house was the same throughout the region, regardless of building material, siting, styles of interior finish, or local building preferences.

CENTER-PASSAGE PLANS

In a center-passage plan house, access into the house was gained through a centrally placed doorway leading into a stair passage connecting all of the rooms in the main block of the dwelling. In eighteenth- and early-nineteenth-century examples of this plan type, the first-floor rooms on either side of the house seem to have been a parlor and a dining room. We can often determine which of these rooms held which function through two types of detail. First, the quality of finish often serves to identify one room as the "best" room (Fig. 2.12). For example, in a house of the 1760s, one room might be finished with a fully paneled end wall with crosseted overmantels and built-in display cupboards containing butterfly shelves; the other might be less elaborately finished with a plain paneled overmantel and simple flanking storage closets. On the basis of this sort of archaeological evidence we can surmise that the more elaborate room was the parlor, while the less stylish space served as a dining and less formal sitting room. Additionally, the dining room in mid-eighteenth-century and later examples in the lower Delaware River valley typically possesses an original door opening in the rear wall which would have opened into a kitchen wing or onto a small yard leading to a separate cook house. The distinction between parlor and dining room is confirmed further by the direction in which doors swing on their hinges. Typically, the dwelling's front door opens so that the first door opening a visitor sees upon entering is the doorway into the less important room. The door thus creates a barrier or baffle to the best room, setting it apart. The result is the communication of an internal hierarchy in which the parlor is more finished, more formal, and more removed, as opposed to the less important room, which is less finished, less formal, and more accessible (Fig. 2.13).

The second floor of the center-passage single-pile house tends to mirror the first, but with the addition of a small unheated room in the space above the first-floor entry (Fig. 2.14; see also Fig. 3.4). The second-floor spaces also often continue the hierarchical ordering of space found below. This is indicated not only by the quality of trim found in these rooms but also in references found in historic documents, such as room-by-room probate inventories.

Figure 2.12
Baynard House, middle to late 1700s, Harrington vicinity, Kent County, Delaware. Photographed by Courtlandt Van Dyke Hubbard, HABS, 1961. Despite twentieth-century intrusions such as the stove pictured here, the quality of the interior finish still identifies this room as the more elaborate or "best" room.

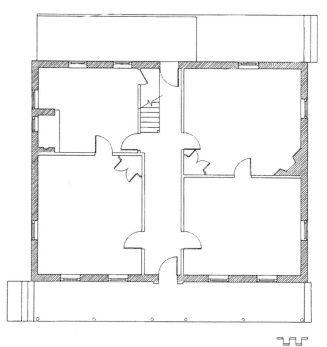

Figure 2.13
John and Elizabeth Pfautz House, Warwick Township, Lancaster County, Pennsylvania, 1813. The direction of door swings in a dwelling can suggest the hierarchy of interior spaces. In this example, the direction of the front door swing subtly directs traffic toward the less formal rooms located to the left of the passage.

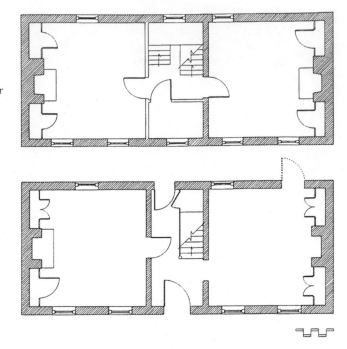

Figure 2.14
Crossan House, late 1700s, Bear vicinity, New Castle County, Delaware. As in this example, the second floor plan (*top*) of center-passage single-pile houses usually resembles the first floor plan (*bottom*). In the space above the first floor entry there is a small unheated room, often described in period documents as "the little room over the entry."

Although the second-floor configuration of these houses usually conforms to the first, there are notable exceptions. The second floor may be subdivided into as many as five rooms plus the second-floor passage. The result is a single-pile first floor and a double-pile second floor. Houses are classified according to the first floor plan, while the number and arrangement of upper-story rooms is recorded through additional notes.

Although the attics of center-passage, single-pile houses constructed prior to 1820 sometimes had dormer windows, their interiors were almost always left unfinished. Only in the 1830s did builders begin as a rule to finish their attic rooms as sleeping rooms. Evidence that finished attics are actually subsequent improvements usually appears in the form of later construction techniques and materials, such as circular sawn lath or molding profiles not in use during the original building period.

The center-passage single-pile plan gained ascendancy during the 1800s, and by the 1840s, the neatly balanced five-bay elevation expressing the internal arrangement of rooms was a common sight from the Pennsylvania Piedmont to Virginia's Eastern Shore. Also, throughout the nineteenth century, people inhabiting older open-plan houses upgraded their dwellings with additions and inserted partitions to create more stylish and liveable Georgian houses. As succeeding generations built and occupied these houses, they changed the types of ornament that distinguished them. In the 1840s, for example, builders constructed Greek Revival and Italianate versions of the plan without actually altering the arrangement and use of space on the inside (see Chapter 4 for a fuller discussion of architectural styles). In the early 1900s, center-passage single-pile houses were still being built from North Carolina to New Jersey. While these late examples no longer contained chimney stacks with open fireplaces and had long ago abandoned the idea of fully paneled walls, they still incorporated the same provisions for domestic living.

By the later decades of the 1700s, builders were erecting two-room-deep center- and side-passage plan houses as well as a variety of other types of side-passage houses. Although center-passage double-pile plans, sometimes referred to as full-Georgian plans, had been built in the countryside around Philadelphia and Annapolis early in the eighteenth century, the type does not seem to have been introduced generally until the 1760s (Fig. 2.15). One of the most pretentious of these mansions was the Corbit-Sharp House of Odessa, Delaware, which was designed and raised by Philadelphia master builder Robert May (Fig. 2.16).[4] The hallmarks of the Corbit-Sharp house plan and its later counterparts remain the centrally placed entry passage containing a prominent stair with turned balusters, and two more or less equal-sized rooms flanking the entry. To one side was the first-floor parlor— the "best" room; to the other stood the formal dining room. The back rooms functioned variously as office space, workroom, and downstairs chamber. The Corbit-Sharp house represents an urban interpretation of the Georgian plan. Two features in particular reflect this urban quality. First, the best room in the house, a large front drawing room, was on the second floor. Second, the original kitchen was located in the cellar. In more rural Georgian houses, the allocation of interior space was handled differently. By the 1780s, rural center-passage double-pile houses were erected with cooking segregated into a rear wing, placed in the back corner room farthest from the first-floor parlor, or housed in a separate kitchen building. Also, rural houses of this type were far less likely to have the best room situated on the second floor; and by the 1820s, almost all recorded examples of the full-Georgian mansions typically had their upper story rooms devoted to sleeping spaces.

Center-passage, double-pile houses continued to be commissioned by prosperous agriculturalists and townfolk throughout the 1800s. In the mid-nineteenth century, for example, the image of the imposing, boxlike Georgian house became the symbol of agricultural success and polite society on the rich farmlands of the region. Italianate, Greek Revival, and Colonial Revival versions of the plan line the streets of Eastville, Virginia; Chestertown, Mary-

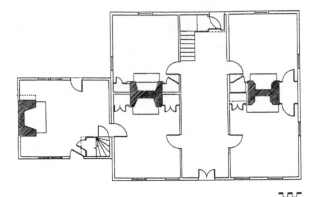

land; and Salem, New Jersey. Today we see those same houses being built in the suburbs of Philadelphia, Wilmington, and Salisbury.

SIDE-PASSAGE PLANS

Side-passage double-pile plans also made their debut in the region's landscape near the end of the colonial period. Side-passage plans are distinguished by a stair passage that runs along one side of the structure, usually for its full depth, and is flanked on one side by two nearly equal-sized rooms (Fig. 2.17). Houses based on the arrangement of a long passage with a stair against the gable wall and two back-to-back rooms opposite were built earlier in the eighteenth century for Philadelphia's wealthy merchant class. In these early urban examples, the ground floor typically contained the stair passage, front office, and rear dining room placed over a cellar kitchen. Upstairs, the front room overlooking the street enjoyed the status of a drawing room and served for more formal entertainment and dining. Other upstairs rooms were furnished as sleeping chambers. In the developing towns, like New Castle, Delaware, and Chestertown, Maryland, these houses tended to be infrequently built prior to the American Revolution. By the 1780s, though, the compact yet impressive arrangement of the side-passage double-pile plan became a mainstay of the region's townscapes. For example, in 1789, Kensey Johns, chancellor for the state of Delaware, living in the town of New Castle, decided to design his new townhouse around a plan of this type; his plan included an original office wing (Fig. 2.18). Like many builders who initially contracted for a cellar kitchen, Kensey Johns quickly moved his household cooking operations and everyday dining into a rear service wing. For the most part, side-passage double-pile houses were not widely built as farmhouses until the early 1800s and later. The greatest concentration of early nineteenth-century plantation seats built on the side-passage double-pile plan are the neoclassical plantation houses on Virginia's Eastern Shore (Fig. 2.19).

A

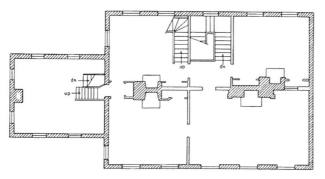

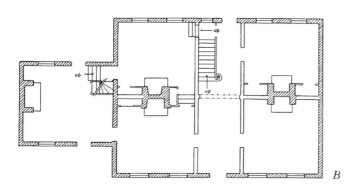

B

Figure 2.16
Corbit-Sharp House, built 1771–72, Odessa, St. George's
Hundred, New Castle County, Delaware. Photographed
1981. Drawn by Gabrielle Lanier after John A. H. Sweeney,
Grandeur on the Appoquinimink. One of the first full-Georgian
plan houses constructed in New Castle County. In the floor
plans (*B*), first floor is at bottom, second floor at top.

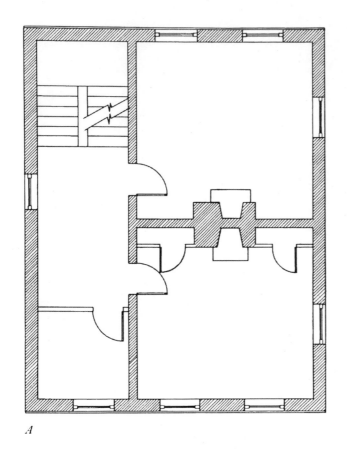

A

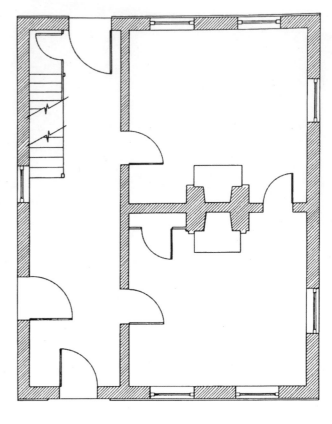

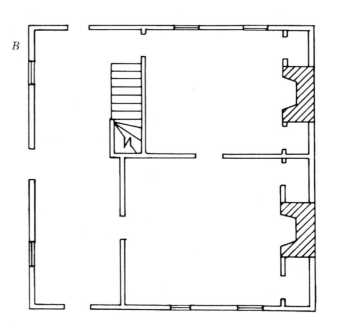

B

EVERYDAY ARCHITECTURE OF THE MID-ATLANTIC

Figure 2.17

These four house plans follow a side-passage double-pile plan. (*A*) First (*right*) and second (*left*) floor plans of Locust Grove, late 1700s, Mt. Pleasant vicinity, St. George's Hundred, New Castle County, Delaware. Drawn by Wanda Czerwinski. (*B*) Elkington, middle to late 1700s, Eastville vicinity, Northampton County, Virginia. (*C*) Al Wise House, late 1700s, Plantation Crossroads vicinity, Northampton County, Virginia. (*D*) 306 Cypress Street, 1808, Philadelphia, Pennsylvania.

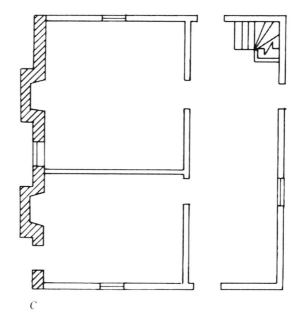

C

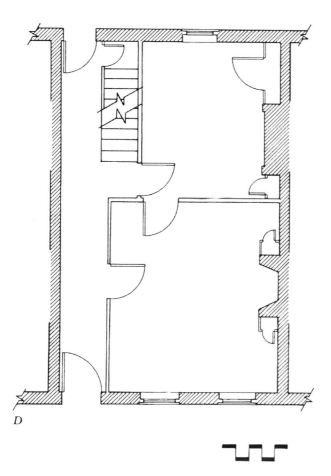

D

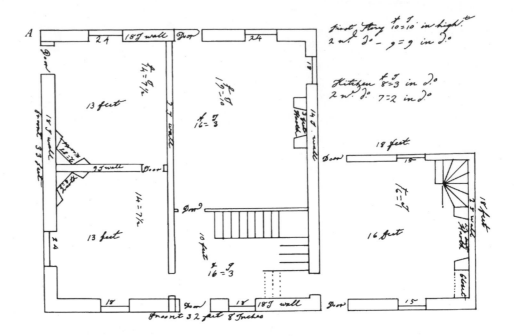

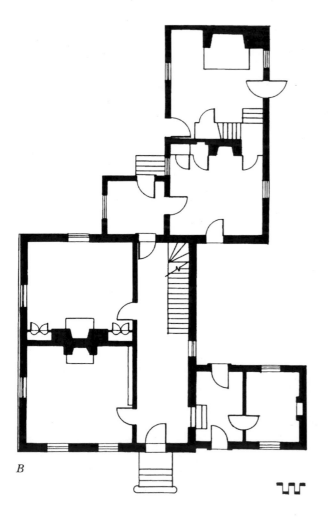

Figure 2.18
Although Kensey Johns considered building his house in the form of a cross-passage plan, he decided to design his new townhouse on a side-passage, double-pile plan that also included an office wing. Johns developed as many as eight plans for his new house before finally settling on one. (*A*) Original plan for the Kensey Johns House, 1789, Kensey Johns Papers, Historical Society of Delaware. (*B, C*) Chancellor Kensey Johns House, 1790, New Castle, New Castle County, Delaware. Plan drawn by Gabrielle Lanier after Robert P. Livergood, HABS. Elevations drawn by Edward M. Rosenfeld, HABS, 1934.

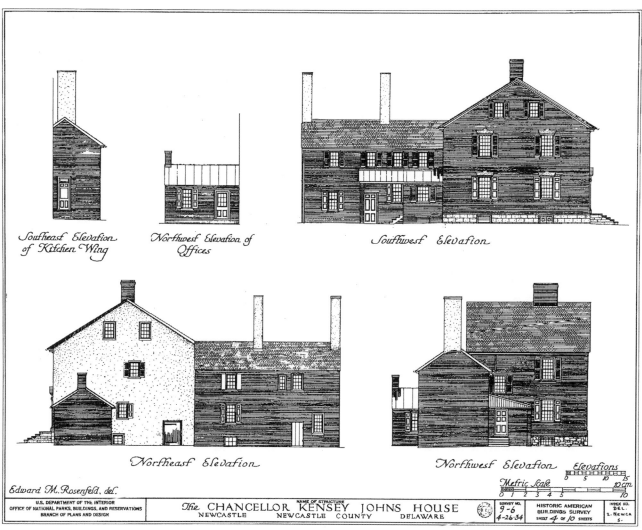

Southeast Elevation of Kitchen Wing

Northwest Elevation of Offices

Southwest Elevation

Northeast Elevation

Northwest Elevation

Elevations

Metric Scale

Edward M. Rosenfeld, del.

U.S. DEPARTMENT OF THE INTERIOR
OFFICE OF NATIONAL PARKS, BUILDINGS, AND RESERVATIONS
BRANCH OF PLANS AND DESIGN

NAME OF STRUCTURE
The CHANCELLOR KENSEY JOHNS HOUSE
NEWCASTLE   NEWCASTLE COUNTY   DELAWARE

SURVEY NO.
9-6
4-26-34

HISTORIC AMERICAN
BUILDINGS SURVEY
SHEET 4 OF 10 SHEETS

INDEX NO.
DEL.
2-NEWCA
5-

C

Figure 2.19

Elkington, Northampton County, Virginia. Photographed 1977. The neoclassical plantation houses on Virginia's Eastern Shore are built on a side-passage, double-pile plan.

In town settings, the first-floor front room served either as a commercial room or downstairs parlor, while the back room seems almost always to have been set aside as a dining room, with the kitchen located either in the cellar or a rear wing. In rural examples, the first-floor front room functioned as a downstairs parlor and the back room served as the dining area. The second-floor front room served either as the best chamber or, in town and city, as upstairs parlor. In nearly all cases, the second floor back room seems to have been a sleeping chamber, as were any third floor and attic stories. The upper-most stories also sometimes contained a small unheated room over the entry, in a pattern consistent with the center-passage plans described above. Later rural examples, dating from the late eighteenth through the mid-nineteenth centuries, also typically contained a front parlor and back dining room on the first floor, while the upper floors were given over to sleeping chambers with varying degrees of finish. Another quality usually associated with rural examples of this type is the placement of cooking, washing, and other domestic work functions in a rear service wing. As in center-passage single-pile plans, the evidence of architectural finishes, coupled with documentary evidence, permits us to establish more precise room functions. By the 1850s the side-passage double-pile plan began to lose favor as a building choice in rural areas, although the type (including half passage and vestibule entry varia-tions) remained popular in the towns and cities through the 1940s.

Less frequently encountered are side-passage single-pile, and half-passage plans. Although rural examples of side-passage single-pile plans have been recorded, this plan type appeared most often in villages and towns and was constructed from the 1780s throughout much of the nineteenth century. Be-side the characteristic relationship of the passage to the principal first-floor room, many of these side-passage single-pile dwellings show evidence of some sort of rear service wing. The principal first-floor room often served simultaneously as parlor, dining room, and chamber.

FURTHER VARIATIONS

The category *half-passage plan* refers to variations of either the center-passage or side-passage plans in which the passage penetrates only half the depth of the house (Fig. 2.20). This form was favored by builders in the mid-1800s who sought ways to maximize interior living space without relinquish-ing the social buffer offered in closed plans. The most common arrangement includes location of a parlor at the side of the passage, with a wider dining room directly behind it. In a few examples, the passage is separately parti-

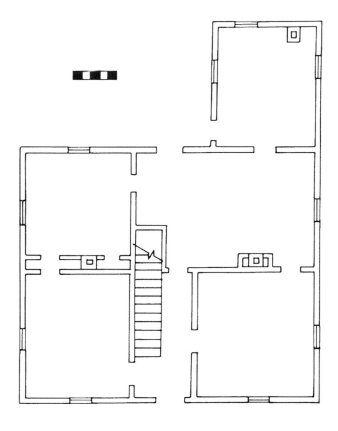

Figure 2.20
Elkennah Brackett Cobb House, late 1800s, Oyster vicinity, Northampton County, Virginia. In half-passage plans the stair passage penetrates only half the depth of the house. Commonly, the parlor was to one side or the other of the passage and had a wider dining room directly behind it.

tioned and the rear of the house is divided into heated rooms, creating what we might call a corner-passage plan.

Finally, a particular variation on the stair-passage plan was built primarily from Virginia's Eastern Shore and down into northeastern North Carolina (see Fig. 4.17). It used a three- or five-part composition with a gable-fronted central block flanked by two smaller wings placed at right angles on either side, forming a T-shaped plan. The entryway of these houses was an unusually wide passage, often termed a salon, which contained the stair and provided access to a parlor behind as well as a dining room and other spaces on either side. Buildings of this type were unusual when they were built and survive today in limited numbers.

Service Wings

The incorporation and segregation of service functions, such as cooking and laundry, into houses through the device of a service wing or addition represents a major change in the development of house types in the mid-

Atlantic region. Although original service wings have been documented from the early 1700s, we generally do not see kitchens and workrooms as common features until well after 1750. Service wings take several forms, including sheds or lean-tos, ells, and gable additions extending the length of the dwelling. Early service wings are associated with dwellings of mid-eighteenth-century rural and urban elite families. In cities, such as Philadelphia, and in the countryside of southeastern Pennsylvania, builders often placed service functions in a cellar or in a lower floor built into the side of an earthen embankment. By the early to mid-1800s, however, service wings on the principal floor of the house were common features on rural and town houses throughout the region. Service wings also represent one of the most imperiled elements in the historic house. Working spaces like nineteenth-century kitchens are unlikely to survive contemporary renovations, even where modern houseowners are engaged in thoughtful and sensitive restoration projects. The threat to domestic service spaces results directly from their role as the workrooms in the house; from the late 1700s to the present, these are the rooms that most often have been the focus of modernization projects.

When we categorize service wings, we typically specify the plan of the main block and then note the position of the wing, the number of rooms it contains, and its height. For instance, we would describe the Kensey Johns House as a two-story side-passage plan with a two-and-a-half story, two-room service ell containing a first-floor dining room and kitchen (see also Fig. 4.13). A very different solution to the problem of incorporating service into the house while segregating it from other spaces appears on the Eastern Shore of Virginia. Houses like Willowdale (Fig. 2.21) in Accomack County, Virginia, contain rooms strung out in a long, attentuated plan locally known as a "big house, little house, colonnade, kitchen," under an irregular roof line, with the best room at one end and the kitchen at the opposite. Similarly, on the Eastern Shore of Maryland, builders erected "telescope houses," which presented a silhouette descending from the tallest section, containing the most formal living spaces, through a series of sections of descending size, culminating in the cooking and storage rooms.

Service wings typically contain one to three rooms aligned front to back or side by side in an ell or gable wing. In the more southern landscapes of Virginia and Maryland, however, the practice of housing service in a separate structure, such as a kitchen standing near the house, remained current into the mid-nineteenth century. The functions of these rooms in relationship to the main body of the house vary according to their number and proximity. One-room service wings usually contain a first-floor kitchen and upper stories

A

Figure 2.21

Builders in Maryland and on the Eastern Shore of Virginia, rather than
building a service wing, often strung out the rooms of the house in a long
attenuated plan known as a "big house, little house, colonnade, kitchen."
The best room was at one end and the kitchen at the opposite. (*A*) Willowdale, early 1700s, additions through early 1800s, Accomack County, Virginia. Photographed by David Ames, HABS, 1984. (*B*) Farm house displaying connected farm plan, Eastern Shore of Virginia. Photographed 1977.

B

given over to sleeping chambers. In the 1800s these chambers housed domestic servants and may have been little more than unheated and unfinished lofts. In other instances and more recently, the rooms over the kitchen have served as family bedrooms or storage spaces. Two-room service wings are usually divided into a dining room and kitchen or kitchen and pantry. In the 1800s the dining room and kitchen arrangement was the most common. Three-room service wings incorporated everyday dining (and sometimes a nursery), cooking, washing, and pantry space. In all cases, the service wing abutted or was nearest to the least formal first-floor room of the main block. In the eighteenth and nineteenth centuries this would have been the dining room, and access to the service wing would have been by a door leading directly from the dining room or across an open porch or piazza. Where cooking occurred in a structure fully detached from the house, the dining room connected to the kitchen across a stretch of open workyard. Sometimes this expanse was covered with an open colonnade or subsequently linked to the house through a series of infill additions such as those seen at Willowdale.

Especially from the mid-1800s onward, service wings often appear as part of the original house plan, but some are upgrades to older dwellings. There is no typology for additions to existing houses that extends much beyond noting the presence of a lean-to, ell, or gable wing. Houses evolve over time, and, as they pass through the hands of succeeding owners and occupants, they are subject to a full range of add-ons (and removals) that reflect a wide variety of solutions for increasing or changing household space (see, for example, Fig. 1.3). The creation of new interior spaces draws on all sorts of architectural strategies, almost all of which can be recognized only through the close examination of construction and decorative details. Sometimes new spaces are created by removing and/or adding new interior partitions. In other instances houses are raised one or more stories in height. The most subtle additions are those which take older unfinished space within the house and, through the application of plaster and lath or other finishes, create an improved room.

Although there is no real workable typology for additions at present, most houses after the construction of add-ons still conform to one of the several house types described above. One-room houses may become hall-parlor or Georgian plans by receiving wings or being incorporated into the larger fabric of a major remodeling. Still, there are the occasional oddities which defy classification. When describing the truly idiosyncratic house, often made up of one addition piled on top of another, it is generally easiest to follow your best sense of the house plan by first identifying the core plan and then describing numbers of rooms, stories, and wings—the essential spatial details that capture the final arrangement.

Tracking the history of additions to houses engages us as house archaeologists. All the tools provided here come into play. Construction materials and technologies testify to building periods and offer insight into the sequence of construction. Similarly, evidence of finishes suggests whether new best rooms or new service rooms were created. But be careful in reaching conclusions. Multiple overlays often mask complicated sequences of change. A single example of a Sussex County, Delaware, house will illustrate how involved the pattern of additions (and subtractions) can become and how complicated writing an individual house history can be.

The Hunter Farm House (Fig. 2.22) began in the eighteenth century as a double-cell, double-pile, half-passage plan house. Two bays across the front and two stories tall, the house had back-to-back corner fireplaces with fully paneled fireplace walls in the front and back rooms. A stair in the rear of the passage provided access to the second floor. A one-story, two-room shed that was attached to the gable wall farthest from the chimney stack was accessed by a low door leading from the front room. During the course of its complicated history, the house was altered at least three times. The first rebuilding significantly reorganized the previous spatial arrangement. During the early nineteenth century, the lean-to shed was removed, and a two-story, single-pile, two-bay house was moved up and attached to the northwest gable of the existing building. The newly attached building had originally been furnished with opposing doors and windows on the front and back walls, a fireplace on the southeast gable, and double windows on the opposite end. When the second building was joined to the first, the fireplace in the newer building was relocated to the opposite gable, the front door in the older house was moved to a more central position, and a center-hall plan was created with a roughly symmetrical front elevation. Subsequent alterations later in the nineteenth century included the addition of a one-story rear service ell, which in turn received a lean-to. While these later additions significantly extended the available space, the major spatial reorganization occurred when the earlier open-plan house was transformed into a closed Georgian stair-passage plan.

Shotgun Houses

An important open plan house type closely associated with African-American settlements in the southernmost landscapes of the mid-Atlantic region is

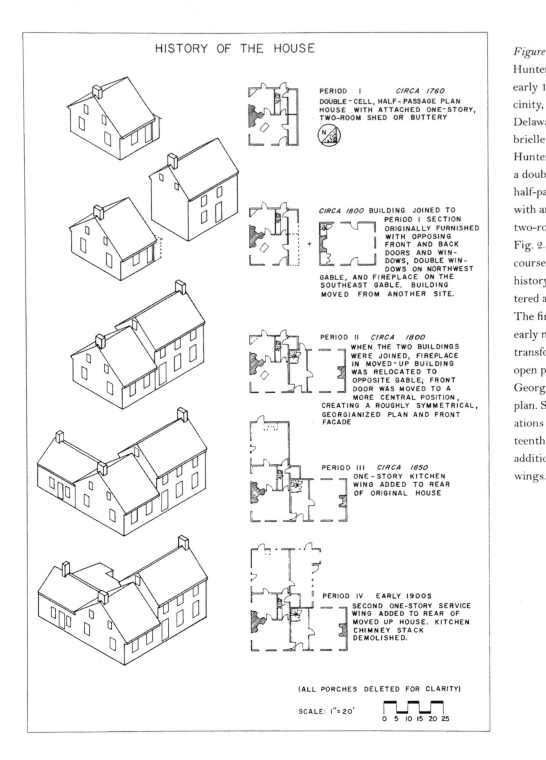

HISTORY OF THE HOUSE

PERIOD I   CIRCA 1760
DOUBLE-CELL, HALF-PASSAGE PLAN
HOUSE WITH ATTACHED ONE-STORY,
TWO-ROOM SHED OR BUTTERY

CIRCA 1800 BUILDING JOINED TO
PERIOD I SECTION
ORIGINALLY FURNISHED
WITH OPPOSING
FRONT AND BACK
DOORS AND WIN-
DOWS, DOUBLE WIN-
DOWS ON NORTHWEST
GABLE, AND FIREPLACE ON THE
SOUTHEAST GABLE. BUILDING
MOVED FROM ANOTHER SITE.

PERIOD II   CIRCA 1800
WHEN THE TWO BUILDINGS
WERE JOINED, FIREPLACE
IN MOVED-UP BUILDING
WAS RELOCATED TO
OPPOSITE GABLE; FRONT
DOOR WAS MOVED TO A
MORE CENTRAL POSITION,
CREATING A ROUGHLY SYMMETRICAL,
GEORGIANIZED PLAN AND FRONT
FACADE

PERIOD III   CIRCA 1850
ONE-STORY KITCHEN
WING ADDED TO REAR
OF ORIGINAL HOUSE

PERIOD IV   EARLY 1900S
SECOND ONE-STORY SERVICE
WING ADDED TO REAR OF
MOVED UP HOUSE. KITCHEN
CHIMNEY STACK
DEMOLISHED.

(ALL PORCHES DELETED FOR CLARITY)

SCALE: 1"= 20'   0 5 10 15 20 25

Figure 2.22
Hunter House, ca. 1760 to early 1900s, Milton vicinity, Sussex County, Delaware. Drawn by Gabrielle Lanier, HABS. The Hunter House began life as a double-cell, double-pile, half-passage plan house with an attached one-story, two-room shed (see also Fig. 2.5A). During the course of its complicated history, the house was altered at least three times. The first rebuilding, in the early nineteenth century, transformed the earlier open plan house into a Georgianized center-hall plan. Subsequent alterations later in the nineteenth century included the addition of two rear service wings.

the "shotgun" house. The single best source on the history of the shotgun house remains John Vlach's study, which traces both the form and the philosophy of the building type from Yoruban culture in Africa to Haitian settlements and finally to New Orleans and the American South.[5] The basic char-

Figure 2.23
Shotgun houses, ca. 1910, Cheriton vicinity, Northampton County, Virginia. Photographed 1995. The basic characteristics of the shotgun house include a gable front and a plan that is one room wide and one to three or more rooms long.

acteristics of the shotgun house include a gable front and a plan that is one room wide and one to three rooms or more in length. Shotgun houses exhibit a range of finishes, from elaborate Eastlake and Italianate detailing to strikingly plain elevations. Shotgun houses in the region discussed here appear most frequently in railroad towns like Exmore and Cheriton, Virginia, where they are arranged in small neighborhoods (Fig. 2.23). The Cheriton shotgun houses are typical of the area: one-story in elevation with gable entries into a plan that extends two or three rooms in length.

Bungalows and Pattern Book Plans

From the mid-1800s on, house plans were influenced by the widespread circulation of pattern books, illustrated manuals that presented architect's designs for new "modern" houses. House types found in the pages of architectural manuals suggested all sorts of irregular plans for people who were ready to build, but just how much spatial innovation builders were willing to incorporate into their houses remains unknown. Pattern books also made use of plan types already favored by builders, simply providing fashionable overlays of architectural trim. Designs of this kind were most apt to appear in the pages of agricultural publications, such as the mid-nineteenth-century *Illustrated Annual Register of Rural Affairs* (Fig. 2.24). Just a few of the house types suggested by pattern book architects are addressed here, while the fashionable characteristics of pattern book designs are dealt with elsewhere in this volume. It is important to bear in mind that, prior to the rapid rise of speculatively built suburbs in the early twentieth century, few builders wholeheartedly accepted pattern book recommendations. In the mid-Atlantic, builders tended to borrow pattern book ideas freely enough to appear modern but selectively enough to avoid suffering the inconveniences of a disruption of traditional lifestyles. The best places to find a wide range of pattern book–inspired houses are the many small towns throughout the region. Because towns typically expanded from a central core outward, it is often possible to get a real sense of the chronological and stylistic progression of pattern book dwellings over the space of a few blocks.

Typical of mid-nineteenth-century pattern book design is the James Lawson House in Woodstown, New Jersey (Fig. 2.25). Based on the design for "Victorian Cottage No. 11" in James Riddell's *Architectural Designs for Model Country Residences*, published in 1861, the James Lawson House is a two-story frame dwelling built on a Georgian plan with an original service ell. The older values of symmetry are evident in the balanced three-bay elevation, which is made modern through the use of Victorian trim and a small square roof-top monitor or cupola. Even houses that present irregular facades, built in the Queen Anne or shingle styles, still adhere to older notions of house form established in the eighteenth century and later modified through service wings. Thus, a house may present a projecting bow-front window or even push the parlor elevation forward in relationship to the main block but on the inside still be a Georgian house.

There are, of course, exceptions to the rule of conservative house types hiding underneath the veil of fashionable trappings. Prosperous clients did choose architect-designed houses that really departed from standard plan options. Auburn Heights in Yorklyn, Delaware (Fig. 2.26), commissioned by an affluent factory-owning family, followed an irregular plan that incorporated a corner turret and large reception hall with fireplace and open stair.

Still, the real revolution in late nineteenth-century plan types associated with the common landscapes of the mid-Atlantic region occurred with the

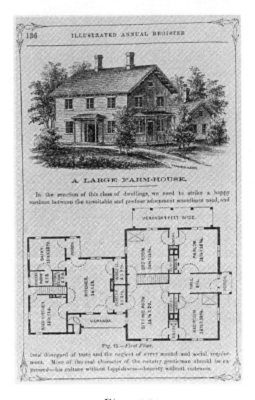

Figure 2.24
Pattern books provided popular and more irregular plan types, as well as designs for fashionable overlays of architectural trim. House plans also appeared in the pages of agricultural publications such as the mid-nineteenth-century *Illustrated Annual Register of Rural Affairs.*

EVERYDAY ARCHITECTURE OF THE MID-ATLANTIC

Figure 2.25

James Lawson House, mid-1800s, Woodstown, New Jersey. Photographed 1995. Typical of mid-nineteenth-century pattern book design is this two-story frame dwelling built on a Georgian plan with an original service ell. Modern features—the Victorian trim and square roof-top monitor or cupola—were added to a traditional symmetrical design.

introduction of two popular house forms: the *bungalow* and the *four-square*. In the last decade of the nineteenth century, architect-authors began to advance more innovative house plans, such as the bungalow. The appearance of bungalows in the mid-Atlantic landscape signaled a major departure from existing house forms. Unlike closed Georgian plans, with their interior arrangement of specialized spaces accessed by an entry passage, bungalow interiors were characterized by a compact, informal arrangement of adjacent rooms with spaces that flowed together. Bungalows rediscovered the notion of the open plan associated with earlier traditional house types. But the spatial arrangement of the bungalow also constituted a fundamental departure from the open plan family by advancing a design solution that could run three or four rooms in depth. The bungalow plan progressed from front to back in a formula that ran from porch to living room and dining room to bedrooms, bath, and kitchen.

Bungalows date from about the turn of the twentieth century through the

Figure 2.26
Auburn Heights, Yorklyn,
Delaware. Photograph, ca.
1902–5, courtesy of Tom
and Ruth Marshall. Auburn
Heights follows an irregular plan that incorporates a
corner turret and large reception hall with fireplace
and open stair.

1930s. Characteristically three-bay, one- or one-and-a-half-story houses with ground-hugging silhouettes and interiors containing five or six rooms, they were built primarily in newly developing suburbs and on the edges of small towns throughout the United States. They also appear in rural landscapes as small progressive farmhouses of the early twentieth century.

The bungalow form characteristically incorporates a broad porch ranging across the front elevation. The porch roof may be one of several styles: shed, cross gable, or pyramidal; but, in all cases, the porch is integral to the overall form of the building. While fenestration and door placement vary among structures, central placement of the entry door, leading directly into a living area or a small vestibule, is most common.

Interiors were typically furnished with fireplaces with rustic hearths and built-in furniture. The bungalow plans published in a Wilmington, Delaware, newspaper between 1910 and 1924, representative of the form, usually contained a living room, dining room, kitchen, and at least two bedrooms plus a bath (Fig. 2.27).[6]

The *four-square* has been described best by Alan Gowans: "Two stories high, set on a raised basement with the first floor approached by steps, a verandah running the full width of the first story, capped by a low pyramidal roof that usually contains at least a front dormer, and an interior plan of four nearly equal sized rooms per floor plus side stairwell—that is the form of house known variously as the box, the classic box, the double cube, the plain

A

Figure 2.27
The appearance of bunga-
lows on the Delaware val-
ley landscape signaled a
major departure from existing house forms. Bungalow
interiors were character-
ized by a compact, informal
arrangement of adjacent
rooms with spaces that flow
together. (*A*) Rickards-
Hudson House, Dags-
boro vicinity, Baltimore
Hundred, Sussex County,
Delaware. Photographed
by Susan M. Chase, 1990.
(*B*) Bungalow plans printed
in *Wilmington Sunday Morning Star,* (*left*) 6 November
1910, p. 14, and (*right*) 9
January 1910, p. 14. Courtesy of Susan M. Chase.

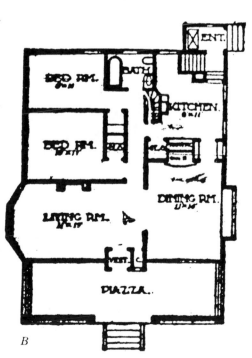

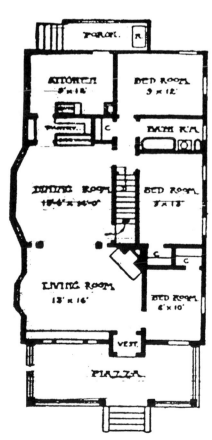

B

A

Figure 2.28
In the four-square house, a new kind of open plan house, entry was usually directly into a large room, termed variously the reception hall or living room, which often contained an open stair in one corner. (*A*) Four-square house, ca. 1920, Capeville vicinity, Northampton County, Virginia. Photographed 1995. (*B*) Four-square house, ca. 1920, Newark, New Castle County, Delaware. Photographed 1995.

B

house, and here as the foursquare."[7] The four-square house (Fig. 2.28) belongs to a new family of open plan houses. Entry into the house was across a porch and into a large room, termed variously the reception hall or living room, which often contained an open stair in one corner. To buffer direct access from the outside, many builders included a small enclosed lobby entry or vestibule in one corner of the living room. Typically, to one side of the living room stood the parlor, and across the back of the house ranged the dining room and kitchen. As with all house plan families, though, there was considerable room for variation. Thus, four-squares with full-width front living rooms are found as well as those with stairs secreted deeper in the body of the house. The key element associated with the four-square plan type is its open arrangement, which was adopted by a largely middle-class clientele, after a century of preference for closed plans. The four-square was accepted into the overall landscape of the mid-Atlantic region, from Pennsylvania Piedmont towns to the flat farm country of the lower Eastern Shore. Wherever four-square houses were erected, though, they retained their distinctive boxy massing capped with a pyramidal roof.

Both open and closed plan dwellings continue to be built today. Middle-class suburban developments from Norfolk to Philadelphia advertise features that have been associated with both plan families from the mid-1800s onward. Subdivisions of closed plan houses built in alternating colonial, Georgian, Victorian, and contemporary styles appear in weekly newspapers. Similarly, sales lots of manufactured homes display an array of dwellings typically affording access directly into a living area which, in the most compact models, joins open kitchen and dining spaces. The most innovative popular plans today appear in the relatively new, invented forms of townhouse and cluster housing development. Even here, however, lobby entries and vestibules continue to articulate patterns of house form and domestic use deeply ingrained in American lifestyles.

House Lots

The character of houses is influenced by the immediate surroundings of their lots or yards. Even in rural areas, farmsteads incorporate a domestic yard, which is spatially and functionally distinct from the farmyard. The organization of the house lot (like the farmstead) can be described by the types of outbuildings and spaces in the yard and the arrangement of those buildings and spaces in relationship to the house.

The relationship between the house and its lot is significant. For example, a type of dwelling-lot combination called the "house and garden" or "garden tenement," based on English models that were known as "cottage-garden" dwellings, is associated with tenant farmers and town development.[8] The house and garden, a dwelling built on a plot of land large enough to include a garden for raising small quantities of vegetables for family consumption, was designed to provide farmworkers with comfortable and convenient housing while simultaneously maintaining a ready supply of seasonal farm laborers. Early-nineteenth-century agricultural reformers such as J. B. Bordley specified that the plots of land on which such houses stood should not be so large that cottagers put more effort into tending their own crops than those of their employers. While the adjacent garden plot was always a significant component of this building type, house and garden dwellings could range widely in value and external appearance. The characteristics of this type of dwelling are based on setting as much as on architecture.[9]

Domestic outbuildings can be divided into three primary categories that are based on their function: food storage and preparation, transportation, and domestic craftwork. In the mid-Atlantic region, outbuildings related to the preparation and storage of food date from the earliest settlement periods and can be subdivided into cooking, processing, and storage functions. Throughout the colonial period, cooking was often done in a separate kitchen or cookhouse located in the yard behind the main house. The tradition of a separate kitchen building began to fade in the Philadelphia backcountry as early as the 1760s, but in the Chesapeake Bay region the practice of cooking, and often eating, in a separate building endured into the early twentieth century.

Kitchens tended to be one-room, single-story structures, often of considerably rougher construction than the main house. Delaware and Maryland orphans' court property valuations taken from the mid-eighteenth century through the 1830s depict a kitchen as an 18 by 20 foot structure on average (Fig. 2.29). The yard between the kitchen and house served as a work area for chopping and stacking firewood, cleaning slaughtered animals, fish, or game, pounding corn in large mortars, and engaging in craft activities such as hooping baskets or repairing household possessions. The interior of early outkitchens was dominated by a large open hearth, but by the mid-nineteenth century the hearth had begun to be replaced with an iron cookstove or range vented through a masonry flue. The interiors of surviving outkitchens dating from the first half of the nineteenth century were typically roughly finished,

Figure 2.29
John Ingram's house and kitchen, Sussex County Orphan's Court document F-194-5, 1796. Throughout the colonial period, cooking was often done in a separate outkitchen located in the yard behind the house, as seen in this period illustration. Separate kitchens were usually roughly constructed, one-room, single-story structures.

with exposed framing, unfinished lofts, and ladders instead of stairs to the attic storage spaces or sleeping areas for resident servants or slaves. Kitchens were sparsely furnished. In addition to basic cooking paraphernalia, the kitchen contained a table and often a loom and spinning wheels. By the late 1800s, however, home textile production had disappeared from the local economy, and cooking was more often contained in service wings of the types described above. Older kitchen outbuildings were often connected to the main house as a direct addition or by building a "hyphen" between the two structures, a practice that produced the distinctive silhouette characteristic of many farmhouses on Virginia's Eastern Shore (see Fig. 2.21).

Smokehouses represent the second most common outbuilding type noted in the documentary record. Smokehouses survive in various forms throughout the region. Regardless of local construction details, smokehouses typically followed a square plan seldom greater than 12 feet on a side; most were capped with a simple gable roof (Fig. 2.30). On the interior the smokehouse was open to the roof. Lightweight poles, sometimes left in the round and sometimes sawn, were nailed to the sides of the rafters and laid across the collar beams. The meats were hung on S-shaped iron hooks attached to the tier poles in the roof. Many smokehouses exhibit evidence of workbenches, where cuts of pork and beef were rolled and packed in salt as part of the curing process. Smokehouses possess only a single, usually outward-swinging batten

Figure 2.30
Townsend smokehouse, Townsend vicinity, Appoquinimink Hundred, New Castle County, Delaware. Photographed 1980. Smokehouses typically followed a square plan seldom greater than 12 feet on a side with an interior that was open to the roof.

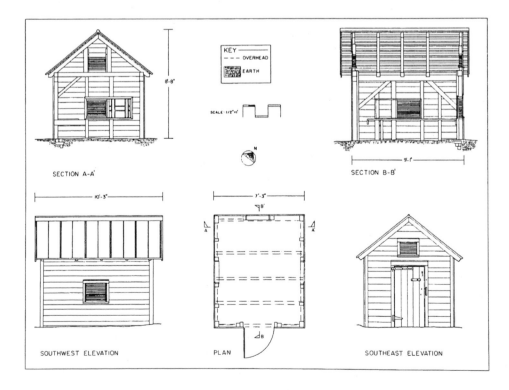

SECTION A-A'

SECTION B-B'

KEY
- - - OVERHEAD
EARTH

SCALE: 1/2"=1'

SOUTHWEST ELEVATION

PLAN

SOUTHEAST ELEVATION

Figure 2.31
Hunter Farm dairy, Milton vicinity, Sussex County, Delaware. Drawn by Nancy Van Dolsen and Dean Doerrfeld, HABS. Milk houses resemble smokehouses in form but are usually furnished with louvered vents to cool the interior.

Figure 2.32
Springhouse, Ridley Park, Delaware County, Pennsylvania. Photographed 1997. Springhouses were generally constructed of stone or log and built directly over a spring, the walls creating a shallow pool of water in which earthenware milk pans, tubs, and jars were placed, resting on barely submerged stone or brick pedestals.

door and no windows. Stone and brick smokehouses typically have ventilation slits or openings in the gables; wood examples do not. Smokehouses decreased in importance with mid-twentieth-century changes in diet and home food preparation. While examples can still readily be identified from Virginia to New Jersey, they tend to survive in recycled form, as everyday storage buildings.

Milk houses and springhouses for storing dairy products were buildings found on nineteenth-century farms, particularly in the Delaware valley. Milk houses resemble smokehouses in form but are generally provided with louvered vents and sliding shutters to cool the interior (Fig. 2.31). Eighteenth- and early-nineteenth-century milk houses found in the Chesapeake region often exhibit pyramidal roofs topped with a small turned or hewn wooden finial. In southern Delaware, milk houses (also known as dairies) were often whitewashed on the interior and situated in a shady part of the yard. In the hottest months, such buildings were periodically doused with water to keep them cool. Later nineteenth-century examples found on the Eastern Shore of Virginia were simple boxlike structures often less than 4 feet square. Mounted on four poles or legs, these tiny and readily movable milk houses were usually placed against the north side of the house or kitchen.

Springhouses and milk houses were far more common on the nineteenth-century landscapes immediately south, north, and west of Philadelphia, where farm butter production constituted a major element of the local economy. Springhouses were generally confined to the Piedmont, where natural springs fed innumerable creeks and streams. Generally constructed of log or stone, springhouses were erected directly over the spring. The walls of the structure created a shallow pool of water in which earthenware milk pans, tubs, and jars could be placed on barely submerged stone or brick pedestals. The lofts of these low-slung buildings were most often left unfinished and used for storage. In some notable Pennsylvania examples, springhouses rose a full two stories in height, with the upper floor being used as a workshop, smokehouse, or storage room (Fig. 2.32).

Domestic shops, like outkitchens, resembled small one-room houses and were situated in the yard, usually in front of the house either at a right angle to the house or parallel to the road (Fig. 2.33). Few domestic shops survive, and the examples that do remain are more readily identifiable by their contents than by their architectural character. A small middle- to late-nineteenth-

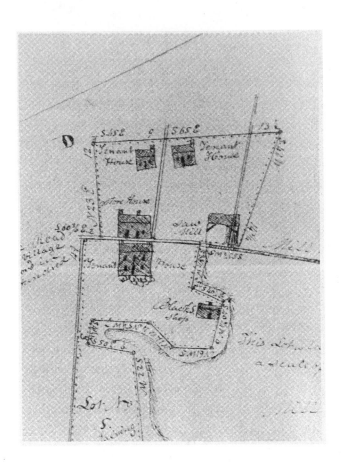

Figure 2.33
Sussex County Orphans' Court document, early 1800s, Division of Dower, Frankford vicinity, Sussex County, Delaware. Shops such as the blacksmith shop illustrated in this period document (*lower right*) resembled small one-room houses and were usually situated in the yard in front of the house.

century blacksmith shop recorded in southwestern Sussex County, Delaware, for example, resembled a small dwelling on the exterior. On the interior, however, an assortment of objects—including a forge, anvils, and other smithing tools—revealed the real function of the building. In the Piedmont, shops were often built as gable wings attached to the dwelling. Typically found in towns, these shops appear to have served both retail and crafting needs. These town workshops were usually built by people engaged in a specific trade that required specialized work space and equipment not readily accommodated in the house. The most common shops mentioned in the documentary records of the region are those of blacksmiths, coopers, cordwainers (shoemakers), weavers, wagonbuilders, and furnituremakers and joiners. Documentary evidence also suggests that shops were most often associated with smallholdings, parcels of land usually smaller than 20 acres, and tended to be concentrated in the landscapes close to Philadelphia.

Transportation-related outbuildings of the eighteenth and nineteenth centuries included chair houses and an occasional one- or two-horse stable. The chair house provided shelter for the riding chair or carriage, which was drawn

Figure 2.34
Privy and storage building, possibly a smokehouse, late 1800s. Photographed 1982. Fairview, Odessa vicinity, Appoquinimink Hundred, New Castle County, Delaware. Privies were increasingly built in urban and village settings after about the mid-nineteenth century.

by one or two horses. Chair houses also sometimes incorporated stable functions. Little is known about the appearance of early examples of these structures, but by the mid-1800s, carriage house builders were raising functionally complex structures that stabled two to six horses, garaged one or two carriages, stored riding gear, and provided hay lofts and feed bins. The grandest examples of mid- to late-nineteenth-century carriage barns are associated with the more elaborate residences in towns throughout the region. In the Piedmont, house lots sometimes contained wagon houses instead of carriage houses. These buildings possessed gable-end openings fronting the public road and provided space for parking wagons below and often shop or storage space above. Horses appear to have been kept in separate stables. Beginning in the early twentieth century, carriage and wagon houses were increasingly replaced by garages.

The final major types of house lot outbuildings are privies and wells. Privies were commonly built in urban and village settings beginning in the colonial period and continuing well into the nineteenth century but seem to have been rare in rural areas until the middle of the nineteenth century (Fig. 2.34). Usually constructed as hand-dug pits, the below-grade sections of privies might be lined with wood, unmortared brick, or barrels. Numerous brick-, wood-, and barrel-lined privies have emerged from archaeological excavations in Philadelphia, Baltimore, and Wilmington. Barrel privies were inexpensively constructed, easily maintained, and frequently abandoned when the oc-

Figure 2.35
"Leaving Home" from Robert B. Hopkins, *Life and Adventures of Andrew Jackson Pettyjohn*, 1887. A well sweep is visible in the center of this illustration of a farmstead in the forest district of Sussex County, Delaware. Wells were most often located close to the house in an accessible spot in the yard. Note also the conical haystacks heaped around central poles, the outbuildings ranged behind the house, and the worm, picket, and post-and-rail fences.

cupants of the property changed. Most barrel privies excavated in Wilmington, for example, were single barrels set in hand-dug pits; some were fitted with removable bottoms that probably facilitated cleaning. The barrels were closely packed on the outside with dense grey clay to prevent contaminants from leaching into surrounding soil and entering the groundwater.

Wells were most often located in an accessible spot in the yard, but they were sometimes housed in the kitchen or under a porch. Occasionally built of wooden cribbing, wells were typically brick- or wood-lined constructions or, like privies, were sometimes quickly and economically lined with barrels. Water was drawn with a well sweep, a lifting device consisting of a long timber pivoted on a tall post (Fig. 2.35). Later in the nineteenth century, sweeps and open wells were replaced with wooden and metal water pumps.

The placement of outbuildings on the house lot also displays pattern. Kitchens, smokehouses, and privies were usually arrayed behind the house. In Sussex County, Delaware, for example, the Steve Hudson Farm (see Fig. 5.25) illustrates a regionally characteristic arrangement: the house fronts the road across a modest yard, with the household support buildings facing the rear service wing. In the Hudson example, these outbuildings include a smokehouse, pump house, and storage shed. The space between the outbuildings and the rear of the house functions as a work yard. Behind the outbuildings, as in the case of the Hudson farm, were the family garden and various pens for hogs and farmyard fowl. If the site included a privy, it was typically located far behind the house and away from the dwelling's water supply.

Urban house lots generally contained fewer outbuildings. The late-eighteenth-century Thomas Mendenhall lot in Wilmington, Delaware, contained the house, at the corner of Front and Walnut streets, and behind the house a kitchen, which appears to have been a freestanding structure prior to 1830. At the inside back corner of the property, Mendenhall built a brick-vaulted privy. The rest of the lot was a packed-earth or paved yard. By the 1830s the original kitchen and privy had been demolished and a new two-story brick service ell built in their stead. House lots elsewhere in Wilmington and other cities display comparable histories. In the eighteenth century, the lot might have contained a number of support buildings, including dairies, storehouses, workshops, and kitchens. In Philadelphia there is also clear evidence that many kitchens were built first, toward the rear of the lot, and used as temporary dwellings while the houses they would serve were being constructed. This represented a form of speculative land improvement, and examples have been found where construction of the house was not accomplished and the kitchen building became the dwelling. By the mid-nineteenth century, however, almost all the cooking, storage, and lodging functions found on the colonial house lot had been incorporated into the house through the construction of rear ells. Still separated from the main house and ell, though, were privies, bathhouses, and carriage houses.

By the late 1800s urban lots increasingly tended to back on a shared alley. Built along the alleys were carriage houses and stables, which, with the introduction of the automobile, were replaced by garages. The carriage houses and stables for town lots were similar in scale, construction, and fittings to their rural counterparts. Town carriage houses and stables, however, were more likely to be two stories in height with the second floor often serving as a lodging space for servants.

In keeping with the need to find housing in congested urban settings, such as Philadelphia and Baltimore, back lots were subdivided for the construction of alley housing and rear yard tenements. Flickwir's Court in Philadelphia, for example, incorporated two facing rows, each consisting of a series of three three-story, ten-foot-square dwellings. In smaller villages, however, builders tended to use their back lots to extend and segregate the functions of the house.

Although the preceding discussion of house forms and house lots provides one way of looking at and interpreting buildings archaeologically, other features also come into play. Building materials, construction technology, stylistic embellishments, and siting within a larger landscape are all important tools for architectural analysis. In the following pages, we will examine the way that construction features can be used to determine building periods and make sense of complicated architectural histories.

3 CONSTRUCTION

Underpinnings, Walling, and Roofing

Construction methods and materials control the strength and durability of a building; like floor plans and siting, they also have a critical effect on overall appearance. For instance, a steeply pitched gable roof produces an architectural effect quite unlike that produced by a flat one with projecting eaves; similarly, a stone or brick-walled dwelling creates an entirely different impression than the same-sized house constructed of wood frame or chinked logs. Construction features can also help to reveal when buildings were built or altered. Like clothing fashions and popular ideas, building practices and materials tend to change over time. Because methods and materials wax and wane in popularity, their presence—and absence—in a building can be telling indicators of the date or period of construction or alteration.

Throughout the United States, construction methods and materials are inextricably linked with tradition and cultural preference. The mid-Atlantic region, an area that has historically been known for its cultural diversity, might more appropriately be described as a region of regions. The material expression of this cultural variety is still visible in the range of building methods and traditions that survive. Although much of this variation is due to building type and function as well as geographic situation and the local availability of certain materials, much also results from initial settlement patterns and prevailing building practices. Building traditions range from early examples of New England–derived timber-framing techniques that still survive in parts of Cumberland County, New Jersey, to the Chesapeake traditions of the lower Eastern Shore of Maryland and Virginia, and from the Dutch-related practices that still exist in parts of New Jersey to the traditional Germanic architecture of Lancaster County, Pennsylvania. This chapter deals with construction by examining materials, methods, and building traditions, including framing and masonry systems, roof construction, and interior and exterior finishes. The chapter is divided into sections relating to the three basic layers of a building: foundations or underpinnings, walling, and roofing.

Underpinnings

Foundations

The foundation supports the entire building. It is the part of a building that is in direct contact with the ground and carries the weight of the walls and roof. Sometimes a foundation is all that remains of a historic house, and it provides the only evidence of the original floor plan. Foundations can generally be divided into two categories: those that continuously underlie the main walls of a building and those that take the form of piers or pilings. Foundations for pre-1940 buildings range from fully excavated coursed stone or brick walls to rectangles of brick piers, simple arrays of carefully placed log sections, stumps, or concrete blocks.

Foundations, their associated elements, and the spaces they enclose form the substructure, or the lowest story, of most buildings; "earthfast" and pier-set buildings, discussed in greater detail later in this chapter, lack excavated masonry foundations and are instead constructed on ground-set piers or wooden posts. Constructed beneath both wood and masonry buildings, foundations must be seated far enough below grade to be unaffected by freezing and thawing, and they must be thick enough to support the weight of the walls and roof above. Foundations also create other rooms; their walls enclose cellars or crawl spaces in addition to supporting the parts of a building that are above grade. Often used as storage spaces, fully excavated cellars might extend the entire length of a building, or cellared sections may be combined with crawl spaces or uncellared foundations. Combinations of partial cellars and crawl spaces are common in the Delaware valley and on the Eastern Shore, especially in buildings with later additions. Full foundations are typically built of a variety of materials, including rubble or coursed stone, brick, concrete or cinder block, or poured concrete.

Most early foundations are seated on natural footings of clay or natural stone outcroppings. Foundations of cellarless buildings were usually begun by leveling the site and excavating a builder's trench. Dug for the purpose of seating the foundations, builders' trenches were wide enough to accommodate the footings of the building (Fig. 3.1). Builders' trenches remained open throughout construction; consequently, building debris and other objects frequently collected or were dropped in them. Because these trenches were usually completely backfilled with soil once construction was finished, they often lay undisturbed for years. Archaeologists often find in builders' trenches reliable evidence of construction dates, since they typically contain objects that date to the original period of construction. Buildings with full cellars usually lack large back-filled builders' trenches. Such buildings were constructed from the inside out, by digging the cellar first and then laying the foundation wall up against the earthen sides of the excavation. In these cases, if a builders' trench was present at all, it was more likely to be a very narrow trench running along the outside perimeter of the cellar wall. Builders' trenches are not visible above grade.[1]

Sometimes buildings that lack true excavated foundations are supported instead by piers. These are, in effect, interrupted foundations. Piers conserve building materials and can be constructed quickly, eliminating the extra work involved in extensive foundation excavation. Piers are typically placed at the corners and at regular intervals under sills and floor joists to raise the building a few feet off the ground; they may consist of stumps, stacked bricks, stones, concrete blocks, cast cement pilings, or combined materials. In the lower Delaware valley, especially in southern Delaware and the Chesapeake region, piers are utilized as foundations for dwellings. More frequently, they are found supporting small outbuildings, such as granaries, sheds, and dairies (Fig. 3.2).

Pier foundation supports are closely tied to early colonial building traditions in the Chesapeake region. The first dwellings erected there in the seventeenth century were built on posts set directly into holes in the ground, rather than on fully excavated masonry foundations. This "earthfast" construction was generally quicker and less labor-intensive than building a more durable foundation. Still, the wooden posts, which were structural members of the building itself, tended to deteriorate, compromising the entire structure. Most early earthfast buildings have disappeared from the landscape, leaving few traces except the discolorations in the soil where the wooden posts stood (Fig. 3.3).[2] After about 1740 or so, durable buildings began to appear in increasing numbers, and these buildings gradually replaced the earthfast houses of previous generations. Still, post building persisted in the colonial Chesapeake and neighboring parts of southern Delaware and

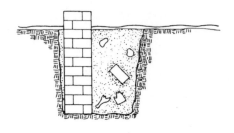

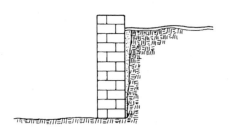

Figure 3.1
Cross-sections of foundations of a typical cellarless building (*top*) and of a cellared building (*bottom*), showing builders' trenches. Drawn by Dean Doerrfeld. Builders' trenches were excavated to seat the foundation. For buildings without cellars, the trench needed to be wide enough for the builders to stand and work in it. Buildings with full cellars had very narrow trenches, if any. Trenches were left open during construction and collected building debris and other objects. They can, therefore, provide archaeologists with a fairly reliable construction date.

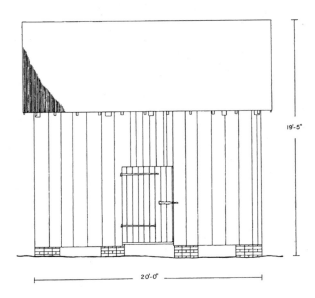

19'-5"

SOUTHWEST ELEVATION

20'-0"

SCALE : 3/8" = 1'   0 1 2 3

Figure 3.2
Cider barn, Hunter Farm, Milton vicinity, Sussex County, Delaware. Drawn by Wanda Czerwinski and Dean Doerrfeld, HABS. In the Delaware valley, especially in southern Delaware and the Chesapeake Bay region, small outbuildings, like the one illustrated here, are frequently built on piers.

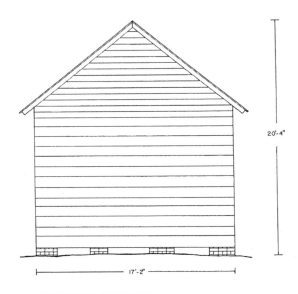

20'-4"

17'-2"

NORTHWEST ELEVATION

A

Figure 3.3

Thompson's Loss and Gain site, Rehoboth Beach, Delaware. Photographed 1987. Drawing, 1988, by W. Lenington, courtesy of Alice Guerrant, Delaware State Historic Preservation Office. Traces of early earthfast buildings are largely limited to the discolorations in the soil where the wooden posts stood. Archaeologists excavating this eighteenth-century site near Rehoboth in 1987 (A) found evidence of an early post-in-the-ground dwelling built on a hall-parlor plan (shown in B).

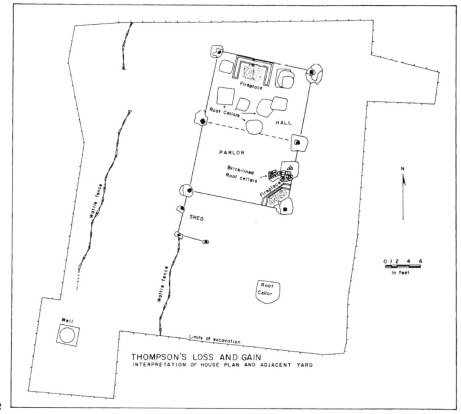

THOMPSON'S LOSS AND GAIN
INTERPRETATION OF HOUSE PLAN AND ADJACENT YARD

B

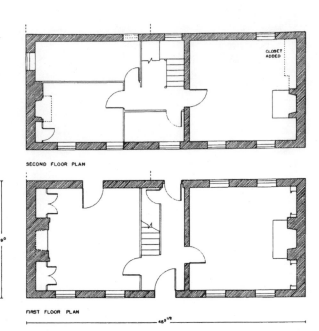

SECOND FLOOR PLAN

FIRST FLOOR PLAN

Figure 3.4
Windsor, Port Penn vicinity, New Castle County, Delaware.
From *National Register of Historic Places: Dwellings of the Rural Elite in Central Delaware, 1770–1830.* Prepared by Bernard L. Herman, Gabrielle M. Lanier, Rebecca J. Siders, and Max Van Balgooy, Center for Historic Architecture and Engineering, College of Urban Affairs and Public Policy, University of Delaware, Newark, Delaware, 1989. The brick bearing wall in this ca. 1760 center-passage dwelling is much thicker than the other interior walls and rises from the cellar to the second floor.

ultimately contributed several important characteristics to later framing traditions in the area.[3] In lower Delaware, where moving buildings from one location to another is a time-honored tradition, the practice of constructing buildings on piers or blocks endured long after post-set buildings declined in popularity. Builders there developed a regionally distinctive construction tradition of setting durable houses on impermanent foundations. This tradition has persisted to the present; pier-set houses are still common throughout Sussex County.[4]

Intermediate Supports

The interior masonry walls and piers associated with foundations provide additional load-bearing support. Common in center-passage and double-pile buildings, masonry bearing walls usually begin in the cellar and extend to the top of the first story, although they sometimes continue through the second floor (Fig. 3.4). Generally speaking, only one of the two hall walls in a center-passage building would be supported by a bearing wall in the cellar. Cellar bearing walls are common in early buildings with three-room plans.

In eighteenth- and early-nineteenth-century buildings, the weight of the chimney stack is often supported by a relieving arch in the cellar. These large, open masonry arches were designed to carry the weight of the fireplaces, hearths, and chimneys above (Fig. 3.5). Earlier relieving arches are usually true arches and were built by setting bricks or stones over arch-shaped wooden forms which were removed once the mortar had set. After the 1820s and 1830s, relieving arches were more frequently constructed as heavy wooden lintels supported by vertical masonry piers. As heating and cooking stoves became more common in domestic spaces and interior fireplaces became smaller and more efficient, chimneys narrowed and massive relieving arches were no longer necessary. In some early buildings from which fireplaces in the main living spaces were removed, the relieving arches in the cellar often provide the only evidence of the original hearth layout (Fig. 3.6). Arches could be built singly or paired back-to-back, depending on the location of hearths and fireplaces in the overall floor plan. Back-to-back corner fireplaces, for example, could be supported by back-to-back relieving arches in the cellar. Relieving arches are occasionally notched inside to hold inset shelves, and early probate inventories confirm that these arches were often used as cellar storage spaces.[5]

Alternatively, corner fireplaces could be supported by a second type of construction, known as corbeling. Corbeling is a technique of cantilevering successive courses of masonry so that the vertical surfaces remain parallel but stairstep outward (Fig. 3.7). The cantilevered stone or brick courses are secured by the weight of the masonry above them. Corbeled fireplace supports are usually keyed into two foundation walls, although corbeling has also been used occasionally on individual foundation walls to support smaller loads, such as stoves. Usually used independently, corbeled supports were sometimes combined with relieving arches (Fig. 3.8). Corbeled supports economize on building materials and occupy less floor space than relieving arches. In addition to supporting hearths and chimney stacks, corbeling is used in other structural and decorative ways, most notably when chimneys are brought to the center of the gable and as a finish for brick cornices and chimney tops (Fig. 3.9).

Some foundation elements were not built of masonry materials. Log joists, found in buildings constructed through the early nineteenth century, are also occasionally used to support the first floor. They can consist of unbarked or partially barked logs, tapered dramatically at either end and set into pockets in the foundation. They might also be tenoned into the sills. Wooden hearth trimmers, timbers that were usually joined to the sills and floor joists, were designed to support the weight of the hearth above. Although log joists and hearth trimmers are technically parts of the house frame rather than the foundation, they are mentioned here because they are usually most visible in cellars and crawl spaces.

Figure 3.5

Thomas Higgins Vansant House, Newark vicinity, Mill Creek Hundred, New Castle County, Delaware. Photographed by David Ames, HABS, 1991. The relationship between the cellar relieving arch and the fireplace it supports is clearly visible in this photograph. The masonry openings gradually narrow from the cellar to the second floor. Some herringbone brickwork appears on the rear wall of the first floor fireplace. This early eighteenth-century building was gutted by fire in 1991.

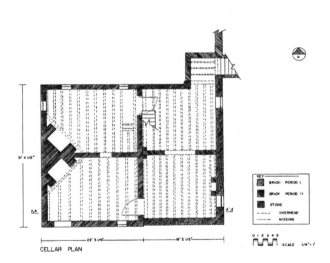

CELLAR PLAN

Figure 3.6

Bellevue Farm, Glasgow vicinity, Pencader Hundred, New Castle County, Delaware. Drawn by Nancy Van Dolsen and Leslie Bashman, HABS, 1991. The relieving arches, visible on the left gable wall at cellar level, were built to support first-floor corner fireplaces, which stood in the original section of this farmhouse. The fireplaces were removed and the masonry stack was reduced in the nineteenth century. This building was gutted by fire in 1992 shortly after it was documented.

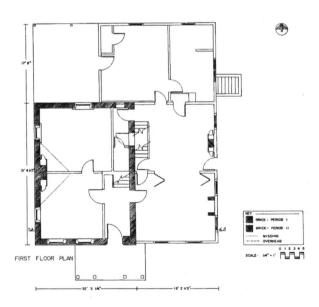

FIRST FLOOR PLAN

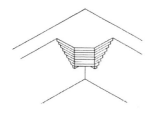

Figure 3.7
Corbeled fireplace supports
are stepped-out masonry
courses that are usually
keyed into two foundation
walls, as indicated in this
schematic diagram. Drawn
by Dean Doerrfeld.

Figure 3.8
Hale-Byrnes House, Stanton vicinity, White
Clay Creek Hundred, New Castle County,
Delaware. Photographed by David Ames,
HABS, 1991. The combination of corbeled
brickwork above a partial relieving arch,
seen in this pre-1775 house, is an unusual
construction feature.

Below-grade Storage Spaces

While many buildings have cellars or crawl spaces beneath them, a few contain other, quite specialized underground storage spaces. Root or potato pits are occasionally seen in eighteenth- and early-nineteenth-century dwellings (Fig. 3.10). Archaeological excavations have revealed the presence of root pits throughout lower Delaware and in much of the Chesapeake region. These semifinished square or rectangular pits were excavated beneath the floor, usually just in front of the cooking hearth. Intended to keep potatoes and other root vegetables from freezing, these spaces could be lined with wood or brick, and some may have been fitted with drains and wooden partitions.

Vaulted masonry cellars, originally intended for food storage, were often built under the most formal room of the classic three-room German plan house found north and west of Philadelphia. These cellars were sometimes furnished with spring-fed troughs and fitted with iron hooks for hanging stored food.[6] Wells, typically lined with brick, wood, or barrels, were sometimes located in kitchens or additions. Cisterns, found in New Castle County, Delaware, and southeastern Pennsylvania, are below-grade water storage spaces and are usually associated with mid-nineteenth-century farmhouses. Barrel-lined, brick, and wooden box–lined cisterns were the most common types.[7] Although most surviving cisterns are capped with a pump head, little evidence of extant cisterns is likely to survive above grade. Most cisterns were located close to the house.[8]

Foundations and their associated elements play the important role of supporting the structure above, but they seldom make particularly dramatic architectural statements. Other features—the overall building form and massing, the shape and pitch of the roof, and ornamental details—play a much more important role. In particular, the materials and methods used for walling, more than any other construction feature, determine the overall appearance of a building.

Walling

Construction systems used in the historic buildings of the mid-Atlantic region fall into three broad groups, based on the type of walling used: masonry or mass construction, frame construction, and log and plank construction. In mass construction, the masonry walls serve a dual purpose: they carry the load of roof and floors to the foundation and also protect the interior of the building from the weather. In frame construction, the walls carry the load of roof and floors to the foundation, but the "skin" of the building—the part that protects it from the weather—exists independently of the frame; although this skin helps to stiffen the frame, it is not load bearing.[9] Log building is used in both mass and frame construction techniques, since the load-bearing walls of log buildings, constructed of sawn or hewn logs, can either be left exposed or clad with an exterior skin of weatherboard or shingle to protect them from decay.

Buildings constructed of brick, stone, and concrete can be seen throughout the mid-Atlantic region, but there are particular areas where masonry construction has historically been more common. Stone and brick have been much more frequently utilized in the northern parts of the region, especially in southeastern Pennsylvania. In parts of Chester and Delaware Counties, for example, stone was a widely used building material by the end of the eighteenth century. Brick buildings were more frequently seen in towns and cities, such as Philadelphia, Baltimore, and Annapolis. By the early nineteenth century, brick had begun to eclipse wood frame as a building material

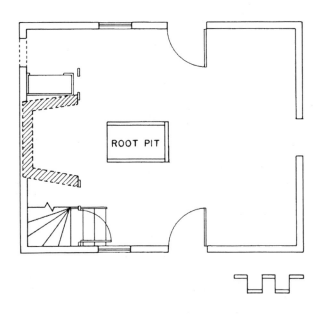

ROOT PIT

Figure 3.10
Potter Mansion, Cedar Creek Hundred, Sussex County, Delaware. Drawn by Gabrielle Lanier after original by William MacIntire and Bernard L. Herman, HABS. Root or potato pits, below-grade storage spaces that were designed to store root crops and protect them from freezing, were usually located just in front of the kitchen hearth, as in this late-eighteenth-century hall plan house.

in several of these more urban areas, due to fire regulations as well as the desire for a more regular urban landscape. On the Eastern Shore of Delaware, Maryland, and Virginia, as well as in southern New Jersey, most early buildings were built of wood, in the form of frame or log. Before 1900, only around one-quarter of the buildings in New Castle County, Delaware, were of masonry construction; in Kent and Sussex Counties, almost all buildings built prior to 1900 were constructed of wood.[10]

Log Construction

Log buildings were a common sight on the nineteenth-century Delaware valley landscape but less so toward the lower Eastern Shore. At times, buildings constructed of logs outnumbered their frame counterparts in many areas. From the Delaware valley to the Chesapeake Bay country, from the first period of settlement until the twentieth century, logs were used to construct buildings ranging from corn cribs, smokehouses, stables, and barns to dwellings, detached kitchens, and tenant houses.

While some architectural historians have argued that Swedish settlers brought log construction techniques with them to the Delaware valley, many other European groups also had longstanding traditions of building with logs. French immigrants to North America reappropriated the vertical log construction techniques that had been practiced in western Europe for centuries. Likewise, German settlers employed a type of horizontal log construction that they had known in Europe, and Scots-Irish immigrants quickly adopted similar building techniques.[11]

Log outbuildings, such as corn cribs and granaries, can still be seen in many parts of the region. While the log walls of a few outbuildings have been covered with siding, many have been left exposed to the weather. Most surviving log houses, however, have been clad with weatherboard, shingle, or aluminum siding, so their original walling material is not always as obvious (Fig. 3.11). In some cases it is impossible to tell if a log building is hiding beneath a sided surface, but occasionally certain visual clues can suggest concealed log walling. Window and door openings that are more deeply set in their jambs than they would be in a typical frame building provide one such clue. Sometimes, an entire building sags through the middle; this "log sag" frequently indicates log walling masked by a later siding layer. Since there are relatively few features that distinguish between eighteenth- and nineteenth-century log work, determining the construction date of a log building is not

Figure 3.11
Because most surviving log houses have been clad with weatherboard, shingle, or aluminum siding, their original walling material is not always evident. The log portion of the building shown in *A* was more clearly revealed when portions of the siding were removed. Although the one-room log house shown in *B* was subsequently clad in vertical board siding, the log walling construction is clearly visible under the window. (*A*) Newark vicinity, New Castle County, Delaware. Photographed by David Ames, 1990. (*B*) Salem County, New Jersey. Photographed 1976.

A

B

always easy. Other building features often provide useful clues. Nail types, saw marks, interior finishes, and other identifying characteristics, such as lap or bridle joints in the rafters at the roof peak, can sometimes help in assigning a construction date.

The most important characteristics of log construction are the treatment of the logs, the way in which the corners are joined (notching), and the way the spaces between the logs are filled (chinking). The final appearance—and sometimes the survival—of a log building depends upon how each of these features is handled. It is important to remember that, since the vast majority of the region's log dwellings were intended to receive exterior sheathing from the outset, these log construction features were not typically visible in a finished house.

Log treatments utilized in the region fall into three groups: logs left in the round, logs hewn square or sawn, and thickly sawn planks. Logs left in the round provided the crudest and least labor-intensive of these methods and utilized unbarked, unfinished round logs or slender poles. Many outbuildings were built this way. Other log buildings were erected using more finished timbers. These included dressed logs hewn flat on the inner and outer faces but left round on the upper and lower sides. The best log buildings employed logs that were first sawn into 2-inch to 3-inch planks, then planed, and finally stacked and joined together at their tops and bottoms with wooden pins. Period documents generally describe log buildings as being composed of "rounds," which refers to the individual courses of logs in a wall (Fig. 3.12).

Notching or cornering, the basic technique used for joining logs at the corners of a building, is a necessary component of all log treatments. Because the entire weight of a log building except the flooring and sills rests on the corners and the notches that form them, and because corner notching also prevents the stacked logs from slipping sideways, the care with which log notching is executed is critical. Delaware valley log buildings were constructed with a few basic notching techniques: V-notching, dovetailing, and mortise-and-tenon joints (Fig. 3.13). V-notching is usually associated with plain and squared log construction, while dovetailing is most often found in the finest sawn log and plank buildings. Mortise-and-tenon joints were sometimes utilized with separate corner posts as an alternative to notching. In this type of construction, logs were sawn into 2-inch- to 4-inch-thick planks that were closely set and tenoned into sawn and mortised or grooved corner posts (Fig. 3.14).[12]

Figure 3.12
Four Square Granary,
early 1800s, Isle of Wight
County, Virginia. Photo-
graphed 1974. Log treat-
ments utilized in the mid-
Atlantic region fall into
three groups: plain, un-
worked logs, logs hewn or
sawn square, and thickly
sawn planks. Period docu-
ments generally describe
log buildings as being composed of "rounds," indi-
vidual courses of logs in
a wall.

The gaps between logs were frequently chinked (Fig. 3.15). Chinking materials varied, typically including rubble stone, brick, clay, wood slabs, construction scrap, and clay or lime-based mortar. Chinking formed of whole
bricks set in mortar was also used; in fact, some buildings seem to be delib-
erately constructed with logs that are spaced exactly 3 inches apart—just
wide enough to receive a course of whole bricks. Wood scrap—shingles,
rough cut slabs, and building debris from the surrounding yard—could be
packed in a clay mortar and used as log chinking. Rubble stone and wood
chinking treatments sometimes received an exterior coating of lime mortar.
In some plank-walled and exceptionally tightly fitted log buildings, the walls
might be chinked with oakum or another similar caulking material. Not all
log buildings were chinked, however. Many agricultural buildings, such as
granaries and stables, were left unchinked; granaries, in particular, were
constructed this way, to promote better air circulation.

Once the walls had been chinked they usually received some sort of exterior finish. If the logs were left exposed, they were often whitewashed. In
some cases the entire surface of a log building was whitewashed, while in
others just the chinking was covered, imparting an overall striped effect to
the exterior wall.[13] While numerous log buildings were left with exposed log
walling, most were intended from the beginning to be covered with weatherboards. Some log buildings, such as smokehouses, were sheathed to keep
them airtight. Others were clad after they were built, to protect especially

Figure 3.13
Log buildings in the Delaware valley were constructed with a few basic notching techniques: V-notching, dovetailing, and mortise-and-tenon joints (see Fig. 3.14). V-notching (*A*) is most often found in plain and squared log construction, and dovetailing (*B*) in the finest sawn log and plank buildings. Photographed by David Ames, HABS.

A

B

vulnerable areas (corner notching, window joints) from moisture and decay or to upgrade their appearance.[14] Many others have been sided repeatedly over the years to improve their appearance as they age. Still, because so many log buildings in the region have been covered over time, we simply do not know how many survive today.

Figure 3.14
Mortise-and-tenon joints were sometimes utilized with separate corner posts as an alternative to notching. Logs were sawn into 2-inch- to 4-inch-thick planks, closely set, and tenoned into sawn and mortised or grooved corner posts.

Figure 3.15
Chinking materials included rubble stone, brick, clay, wood slabs, and lime-based mortar. (*A*) Ross Mansion Quarter, Seaford vicinity, Sussex County, Delaware. Photographed by David Ames, HABS, 1992. The chinking is still visible between the logs of this nineteenth-century slave quarter. Note that the building received a later covering of weatherboard siding. (*B*) Washington County, Maryland. Photographed 1979. Chinking of closely packed stones survives in this log building.

Figure 3.16
Hewn timbers characteristically display a series of regularly spaced check marks, visible on the undersides of these floor joists. Photographed by David Ames.

Joined Timber Framing

Timber-framed buildings, from houses to barns and agricultural buildings, were constructed in the mid-Atlantic region throughout the eighteenth and well into the nineteenth and twentieth centuries. Construction methods varied, reflecting different settlement cultures and carpentry traditions. Most eighteenth- and early-nineteenth-century timber-framed buildings were simple joined box frames built of hewn or sawn members. The type of wood ranged from oak and chestnut to tulip poplar and pine. The manner in which the frame was organized and raised typically provides insight into when a building was constructed and where it stood in the region.

From the period of earliest settlement to the twentieth century, various methods have been used to cut and finish framing timbers. Each method leaves its own characteristic marks, which can be helpful in determining construction and alteration dates. In the earliest timber-framed buildings, logs were hewn square by cutting regularly spaced shallow notches with a felling axe and trimming away the residual pieces with a broadaxe. The felling axe left check marks on the squared timber surfaces during the hewing process (Fig. 3.16). These distinctive hewing marks could be smoothed with an adze,

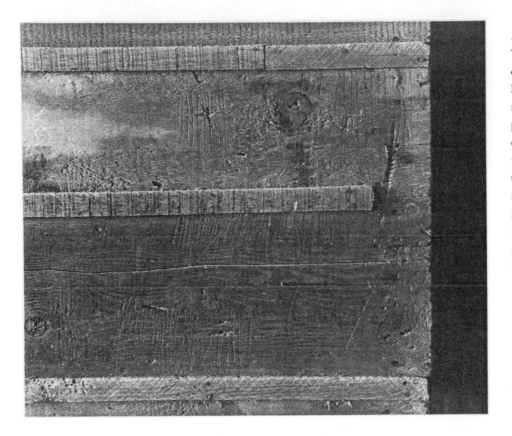

depending on the degree of finish desired, but more often than not they were
left. In much of the region, hewn framing members were utilized through the
early to mid-nineteenth century. Riven framing timbers, such as studs and
braces, are occasionally found in the earliest buildings; riven lath is seen more
frequently. Riving was a method of splitting wood along the length of its
grain with the aid of an axe and a froe, a heavy, thick, dull-edged splitting
tool. Riven timbers can be identified by the rough, parallel split marks that
run along their surface.

Rarely is pit-sawn lumber seen in the earliest buildings, although occasional nineteenth-century examples are found. Pit-sawn lumber is found infrequently in the Delaware valley but is more common in the Chesapeake
region. In pit sawing, an early hand process, a pit was dug in the ground and
a long, double-handled saw was operated by two people, one of whom stood
on the surface of the ground while the other stood in the pit. First, the log to
be sawn was suspended over the pit, then each person alternately pulled on
his end of the saw until the log was cut completely through. Pit saws left
slanting, straight marks that were characteristically irregular and uneven.

Used in the eighteenth century, pit-sawn timbers, like hewn framing members, were gradually replaced by mill-sawn lumber as first water-powered and then steam-driven sawmills proliferated.

The earliest sawmills utilized an up-and-down saw with a narrow, vertical blade to cut lumber. The reciprocal motion of these saws left distinctive marks, a series of closely spaced, parallel lines perpendicular to the length of the timber (Fig. 3.17). Up-and-down-sawn lumber was used through the mid-nineteenth century in the region, until sawmills with circular saw blades became dominant. Mill-sawn lumber is found most frequently in areas where the natural topography lends itself to the establishment of sawmills. In the flat lowlands of the lower Eastern Shore, both the lack of mill seats and the presence of slave labor contributed to the continued use of pit-sawn lumber. Although circular saws were first discussed in Philadelphia agricultural newspapers just prior to 1820, they were not generally used until the mid-1800s. Instead of straight, parallel saw marks, circular saw blades leave a series of arc-shaped marks as they travel through a timber. The presence of these marks can suggest mid-nineteenth-century or later construction or alterations, while buildings containing a range of different types of saw marks may reveal a more complicated construction sequence.

The joints used to link individual timbers were critical to the solidity and flexibility of the frame. Several different types of joints were utilized in an average timber frame (Fig. 3.18). Some of the most commonly found joints include mortise and tenon, lap, and bridle joints. Although more complex examples can be found, these joints form the basic vocabulary of timber framing joints in the area, and most other joints are based on them. A mortise-and-tenon joint is formed by cutting the end of a timber back to form a rectangular projection—a tenon—and fitting it into an equal-sized hole, or mortise. Simple mortise-and-tenon joints and variations on them are used in many places throughout a typical timber frame, especially for joints between posts, sills, and plates. A lap joint, formed by cutting back the ends of two timbers to about half their thickness and overlapping them, is most often used to join sill timbers at the corners of a building and to link rafters at the apex of a roof. A half-dovetail joint, a variant of a lap joint, is formed when one side of the joint receives an angled rather than a straight cut. Half-dovetails are sometimes used to join collar ties to rafters and angle braces to corner posts. A bridle joint is formed when the end of one timber is forked into two sections and fitted over a simple tenon cut into the end of another timber. Bridle joints are sometimes used instead of lap joints to join rafters at

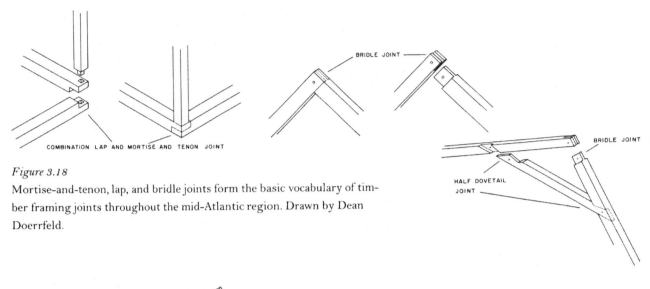

Figure 3.18
Mortise-and-tenon, lap, and bridle joints form the basic vocabulary of timber framing joints throughout the mid-Atlantic region. Drawn by Dean Doerrfeld.

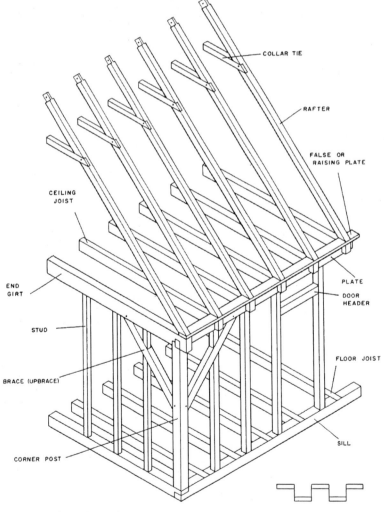

Figure 3.19
The basic elements of a typical timber frame include sills, posts, studs, girts, braces, plates and raising or false plates, joists, collars, and rafters.

the roof ridge. Mortise-and-tenon, half-dovetail, and bridle joints were usually secured with wooden pegs driven through holes drilled in both timbers. Often the peg holes were slightly offset, to create a tighter fit in the finished joints. The joinery in early timber-framed buildings can range from the simplest mortise-and-tenon or lap joints to compound joints that incorporate tenons, lap joints, and other variants. Many buildings contain a variety of joints representing several different levels of complexity.

Sills, posts, studs, joists, plates, girts, rafters, collars, and braces constitute the basic elements of a joined timber frame (Fig. 3.19). Sills, the horizontal timbers that rest on the foundation, are the lowest framing members and were the first pieces to be dropped into place. Because they support the weight of the entire frame and roof, they were also usually among the heaviest sections of the timber frame, typically measuring around 6 inches high by 6 to 10 inches wide. The floor joists, which usually run the width of the building, carry the weight of the floor and were tenoned into the sills. Joists were sometimes very simply made, of heavy, unbarked logs; in other cases, they were more carefully finished, consisting of hewn, squared timbers.

Corner, or principal, posts, intermediate posts, and studs are the vertical elements of the second layer of construction. These elements, which provide the structural support for the walls and help to transmit the weight of the roof to the foundation, were typically tenoned at regular intervals into the sills. Principal posts are the heaviest of these load-bearing vertical timbers. Corner posts are principal posts that were placed at the junction of two exterior walls, forming the corners of the building. In a two-story building, corner posts typically extend to the top of the second story. Additional vertical support is provided by intermediate posts, vertical framing members that are lighter than principal posts. Intermediate posts were usually utilized at either side of door and window openings and between principal posts. Studs are even smaller vertical timbers that were placed at regular intervals between posts to provide extra rigidity to the walls. In the earliest buildings, studs typically were riven; once sawmills became more widespread they tended to be sawn.

Plates, the horizontal framing members that cap the long walls, interlock with the end girts, the horizontal members that top the gable walls, at the corners. Plates and girts are usually fairly heavy hewn timbers and provide additional rigidity for the timber frame. Plates also seat the base of the frame of a typical gable roof, while end girts usually support any vertical studs that constitute the gable wall at the peak. Additional horizontal timbers known as false plates have been common in the lower Delaware valley since the eighteenth century. These are lighter timbers that were placed on top of the projecting joist ends to provide a seat for the rafter feet. Board false plates are relatively thin boards, laid flat directly atop the joist ends. Tilted false plates, which are light, often squarish timbers that were sometimes set into the joist ends at a 45-degree angle, were commonly utilized through the mid-nineteenth century in the Chesapeake region.

Several types of diagonal framing members provide additional rigidity to walls and roof structures. Corner braces, lighter timbers joined diagonally to either posts and sills or posts and plates or girts, help to stiffen the entire frame and prevent the walls from twisting; these were typically placed at 45-degree angles to posts and sills or plates, with their ends located about 3 feet from the junctions of these timbers. Corner braces are often termed upbraces or downbraces depending on whether they are joined to the sills (downbraces) or to plates or girts (upbraces). Downbraces were used more frequently in the Chesapeake region, while upbraces were employed with regularity farther north. Collar ties, which form a triangle with the upper ends of each rafter pair, serve the same function, stiffening each set of rafters and providing rigidity for the roof. Wind braces—framing members that run diagonal to the plate or the roof peak—join several sets of rafter pairs and help provide additional support for the roof.

Rafters, which sit atop the plate or false plate, were fitted together in pairs at the roof peak, most often with simple lap or bridle joints. Rafters are known as common or principal rafters depending on their size. Lightweight horizontal timbers, known variously as shingle lath, roofing boards, or nailers, were secured to the tops of the rafters. These stiffen the roof structure while providing a nailing base for the final covering of roofing shingles.

Purlins—heavy horizontal timbers running the length of the roof—provide additional structural support. Purlin roof frames, fairly common in Delaware valley buildings, are also associated with early colonial roof frames in the Chesapeake, where they are particularly found in roofs spanning double-pile buildings. Roofs in the German-settled parts of Pennsylvania were typically built with a distinctive heavy framing system usually consisting of a combination of purlins and heavier (principal) and lightweight (common) rafters. In some parts of Cumberland County, New Jersey, early timber frame roofs were stiffened with a series of slightly heavier horizontal timbers that were firmly notched into the rafter backs at regular intervals. These timbers, which served much the same purpose as purlins, were usually much lighter than full-sized purlins but more substantial than most nailers.

Timber frames could be constructed with three basic methods: as individual pieces, as completely joined wall units, or as bents, transverse structural units consisting of two or more principal posts joined by tie beams. Most houses were assembled wall by wall, while barns were usually constructed by raising bents. Some small agricultural buildings were built piece by piece.

The wall-by-wall assembly of a typical one-story timber-framed house constructed in the lower Delaware valley and the adjacent Chesapeake region began with the leveling of the building site and the construction of a foundation (Fig. 3.20). Once the foundation was in place, the next step was to place the sills. Sills were usually joined at the corners with lap or mortise-and-tenon joints. After the builders placed and joined the sills, they plotted the placement of the posts and studs along the top surface of the sills and cut blind mortises where these timbers would stand. Floor joists were then secured to the sills with drop-mortise joints, regularly spaced slots cut in the sills and designed to receive offset tenons already cut into the ends of floor joists. When the tenoned ends of the floor joists were dropped into place, their top surfaces were flush with the tops of the sills, and the builders could proceed with the next step—the raising of the walls.

First the long front and back walls were assembled on the ground. The walls consisted of corner posts, intermediate posts, and studs joined and pegged to the plates. With the front and back walls thus preassembled, the builders then raised them into position, sliding the tenons precut at the bottoms of the studs and posts into the matching sill mortises, and temporarily braced the walls into place. Diagonal braces, which helped to stiffen the frame, were usually fitted to posts and plates with half-dovetail lap joints and were most often installed after the walls were raised. With the long front and back walls raised into place and temporarily braced, the builders then positioned the studs and braces for the gable walls. Once the gable studs and braces were placed, the end girts were dropped over the intersections between the corner posts and the plates. As each joint in the frame was fitted together, it was secured with wooden pegs. The attic joists, which extended beyond the face of the long walls, were then laid over the plates, and false or raising plates were laid over the projecting joist ends to form seats for the rafter feet. Finally, rafters and gable studs were raised and pegged into place.

Some houses in Sussex County, Delaware, were built with a framing system known as H-bent construction, a building tradition that is more closely associated with the Hudson Valley "Dutch" traditions of New York and New

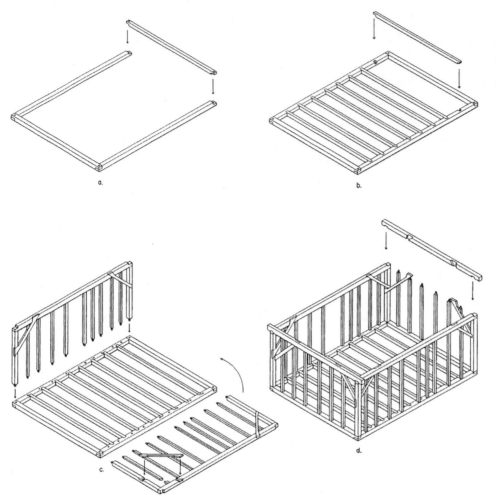

Figure 3.20
This sequence of drawings
illustrates the steps in the
assembly of a typical
timber-framed house.

Jersey (Fig. 3.21). H-bents are transverse, H-shaped structural units consisting of upper-story floor joists tenoned into principal posts. In H-bent construction, the individual H-bents, rather than walls, were preassembled on the ground and raised one by one, usually at fairly widely spaced intervals averaging around 4 feet apart. As each bent was raised into position, it was temporarily braced. Once all of the bents were placed, plates were dropped over the tops of the posts to secure the entire frame. In addition to the H-bent system, timber framing methods in lower Sussex County occasionally exhibited other significant differences. Downbraces were sometimes utilized instead of, or in conjunction with, upbraces. Sussex County builders also favored cased and beaded corner posts. They rarely incorporated the L-shaped corner posts that are commonly found farther south.

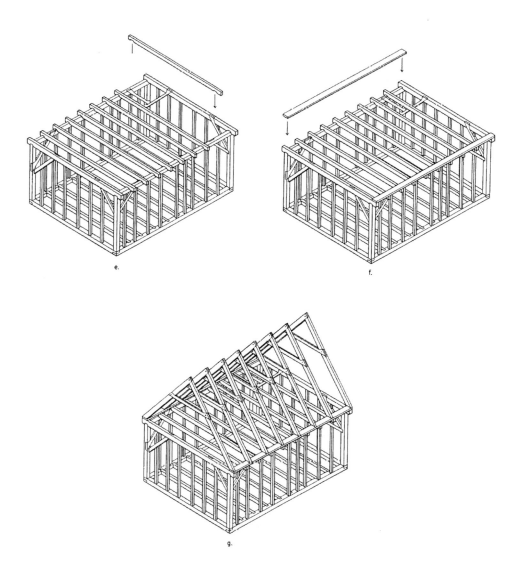

e.

f.

g.

Barns were erected with a similar system in which bents rather than walls were preassembled and raised (Fig. 3.22). Bents were raised one by one atop the foundation and sills. As each bent was placed, it was temporarily braced and secured to the previous bent with light timber rails tenoned into the posts. Once all of the bents were upright, plates were dropped into place over the posts and the roof frame was erected.

While timber frames vary in complexity throughout the region, the type of framing used relates as much to regional preference and cultural tradition as to the nature of the building. Joined timber frames from the first period of durable building in parts of Cumberland County, New Jersey, for example, exhibit characteristics that are more closely associated with early New England architecture and appear to be the result of early migration from Rhode

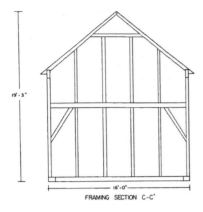

19'-3"

16'-0"

FRAMING SECTION C-C'

Figure 3.21

McGee House, Angola vicinity, Indian River Hundred, Sussex County, Delaware. Drawn by M. M. Mulrooney, HABS. H-bent construction appears in parts of Sussex County, Delaware, as in the McGee House, constructed with a series of H-bents. A typical H-bent is visible in the framing section. The H-bents, seen on end in the longitudinal cross-section, are visible as vertical framing members extending beyond the joists and ceiling to the plate.

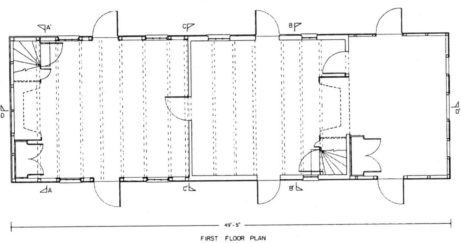

49'-5"

FIRST FLOOR PLAN

SCALE: 3/8"=1'

0 1 2 3 4 5 6

49'-5"

SECTION D-D'

Figure 3.22
Reconstruction of John Dickinson feed barn, Kent County, Delaware. Photographed by David Ames, HABS, 1986. Barns were erected using a system of bents—transverse structural units consisting of two or more principal posts joined by tie beams—which were raised one by one atop the foundation and sills.

Island (Fig. 3.23). A distinctive type of shouldered-and-tenoned corner post joint, which is common on many of the earliest timber framed buildings in this area, is anomalous in the architecture of the broader region. Similarly, there are specific framing traditions that are characteristic of the Chesapeake region. Downbraces tended only to be used south of a line that extends from a point just east of Salisbury, Maryland, and curves northward to include the Chesapeake drainage of the upper Eastern Shore (Fig. 3.24). North and east of this line, joiners used upbraces almost exclusively. Tilted false plates (Fig. 3.25), also associated with Chesapeake building traditions, appear commonly in Virginia and Maryland timber frames, but only two known examples have been found in Delaware, and, as might be expected, both are located in the southernmost part of the state. The practice of notching the exterior face of wall studs to create a firm seating for weatherboards (Fig. 3.26) was utilized on the Eastern Shore of Virginia but is infrequently found elsewhere in the region. More exceptional still are such features as curved principal rafters. These have been found only rarely throughout the region, and have typically been associated with early roof structures. A few examples survive in domestic buildings in western Chester County, Pennsylvania, as well as on the

Figure 3.23
Caesaria River House, Greenwich vicinity, Cumberland County, New Jersey. Drawn by Bernard L. Herman and Gabrielle Lanier, HABS. Early timber-framed buildings in Cumberland County often contain a distinctive type of shouldered-and-tenoned corner post that is anomalous in the architecture of the wider mid-Atlantic region but is characteristic of early New England architecture. Such features appear to be the result of early migration from Rhode Island.

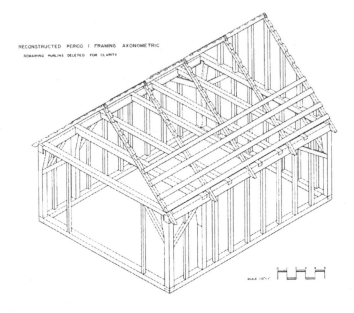

Figure 3.24
Downbraces, braces that extend from post to sill rather than from post to plate, are characteristic of the Chesapeake area. Photographed 1979.

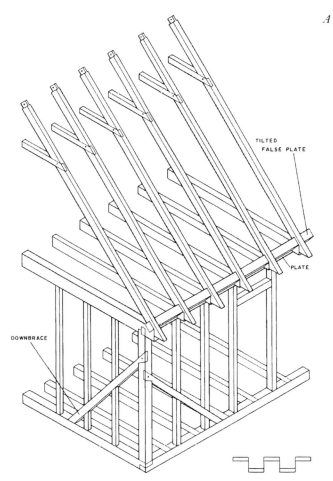

TILTED
FALSE PLATE

PLATE

DOWNBRACE

Figure 3.25
(*A*) Tilted false plates and downbraces are usually associated with Chesapeake framing traditions. (*B*) Fancy Farm Barn, Chestertown vicinity, Kent County, Maryland. Photographed by David Ames, HABS, 1994. The tilted false plate is visible above the main plate at top.

B

lower Western Shore of Maryland and in several churches and meetinghouses in the Philadelphia vicinity.

To the north and west of the region covered by this book are several notable timber framing traditions that appear to draw on seventeenth- and eighteenth-century continental European practice. The two most distinctive of these are those of the Pennsylvania Germans and the Hudson valley Dutch.

Early Pennsylvania-German timber frames were characterized by their unusual bracing, their lack of lightweight studding, and their heavily framed roofs. German timber frames utilized long braces that ran from one horizontal member to another, from a sill to a plate rather than from a sill to a post or a plate to a post. These buildings also typically featured joists that were laid over the tops of supporting beams but not tenoned into them. While German roof systems could vary, many utilized a combination of heavily trussed principal and common rafters and heavily built underframes consisting of purlins supported by flared posts (Fig. 3.27). Ceiling joists were sometimes grooved to receive riven staves or pales that secured mud-and-straw walling. While the original walling material does not always survive, these grooved joists are often still visible in finished as well as unfinished living spaces. Pennsylvania-German bank barns, known for their large dimensions and their cantilevered forebays, had become a hallmark of the German-settled parts of the region by the early nineteenth century. They employed the same framing techniques utilized in domestic architecture.

Dutch framing traditions, primarily apparent in northern New Jersey and the Hudson Valley of New York, resembled those of lower Sussex County, Delaware, and relied on the system of widely spaced H-bents or anchor bents described earlier (Fig. 3.28). Unlike most houses framed in the Anglo-American tradition, in which rooms are typically defined by individual bays measuring between 12 and 16 feet wide, room size in Dutch-framed houses depended on the number of anchor bents present. Most houses employed an odd number of anchor bents; in small houses, five or seven bents were common.[15] Early Dutch-framed buildings also sometimes included walling constructed of straw-and-clay-wrapped staves.

The timber framing traditions that had been present in the region since the earliest days of settlement prevailed through the mid-nineteenth century. Once newer framing technologies were introduced, however, builders could choose from among several different framing methods. For a time, earlier

Figure 3.26
Accomac vicinity, Accomack County, Virginia. Photographed 1977. The practice of notching the exterior face of wall studs to create a firm seating for weatherboards was utilized on the Eastern Shore of Virginia but is infrequently found elsewhere in the region.

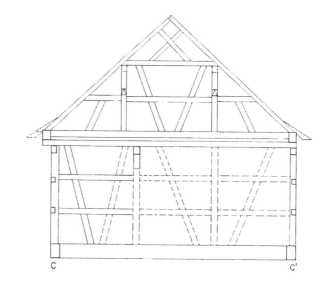

RECONSTRUCTED FIRST PERIOD FRAMING SECTION – 1756

Figure 3.27

Stiegel-Webber House, 1757, Schafferstown, Lebanon County, Pennsylvania. Photographed by David Ames, HABS, 1984. Drawn by Bernard Herman and William Macintire, HABS. Early Pennsylvania German timber frames were characterized by their distinctive bracing, their lack of slightly dimensioned studding, and their heavily framed roofs. They utilized long braces that ran from one horizontal member to another, from a sill to a plate rather than from a sill to a post or a plate to a post.

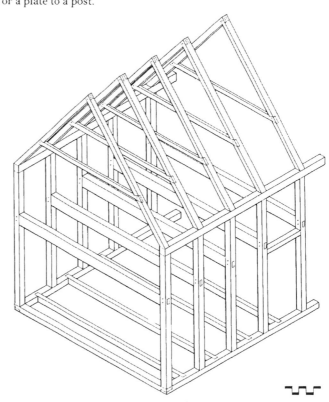

Figure 3.28

Dutch framing traditions, seen mostly in northern New Jersey and the Hudson Valley of New York, resemble those found in lower Sussex County, Delaware. These timber frames used widely spaced anchor bents.

Figure 3.29
Eastville vicinity, Northampton County, Virginia.
Photographed 1977. Com-
bination frames were a
hybrid of heavy timber-
framing and lighter con-
struction techniques. In
this building, lighter,
closely spaced studs appear
together with heavier
downbraces.

timber framing techniques existed side by side with newer methods of building in wood, and many of these earlier techniques persisted in some agricultural and industrial buildings through much of the nineteenth and even into
the first part of the twentieth century. In some cases, different framing systems intersected within a single building. Still, as new ideas and technological
improvements gradually fueled shifts in building practices, earlier framing
methods began to change.

Combination, Balloon, and Platform Framing

As commercially sawn lumber and machine-made nails became more
widely available in the early nineteenth century, joined timber frame construction eventually gave way to newer building methods. The first of these—
known and recognized in pattern books as a combination frame—was a hybrid of heavy timber framing and lighter construction techniques. Like joined
timber frames, these combination frames utilized heavy hewn sills, diagonal
braces, and corner posts, but they also incorporated multiple vertical studs,
slight, dimension-sawn lumber, and nailed joints (Fig. 3.29). In combination
frames, the loads were carried by a series of closely spaced studs generally set
on 2-foot centers between wall posts and horizontal timbers rather than by

Figure 3.30
Balloon framing utilizes light, thin, closely set studs instead
of heavy joined timbers. Drawn by Dean Doerrfeld.

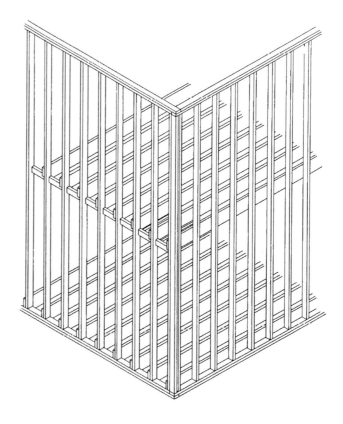

the wall posts and horizontal timbers alone. Load-bearing interior walls constructed entirely of vertical studs also appear in this type of construction.

If the combination frame altered traditional timber construction practices, the balloon frame revolutionized them. Introduced in 1833 in the Midwest, the balloon frame represented a major departure from traditional ways of building in wood. Joined timber frame buildings required large, heavy timbers and carpenters who knew how to cut and fit complex timber joints. Much of the solidity of these buildings depended on the weight of their wooden timbers and the fit of their joints. Balloon-frame building changed this. Instead of heavy wooden timbers, it utilized light, thin, dimension-cut, closely set studs; instead of complicated wooden joints and pegs, it depended upon nails (Fig. 3.30). Because the timbers typically used in balloon frame construction are too narrow to support traditional mortise-and-tenon joints, nails became essential construction components. The widespread availability of machine-made nails helped fuel the spread of balloon-frame construction. Balloon framing was less labor intensive than traditional timber construction, economized on materials, and accelerated the building process. Construction of a typical balloon frame required only a few basic techniques. Strong, light-

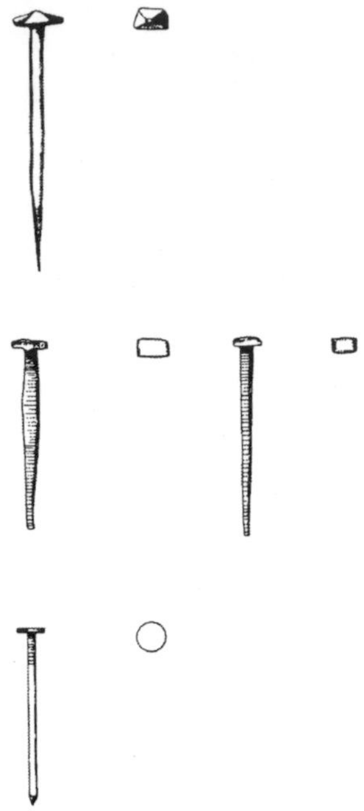

Figure 3.31
Wrought nails (*top*), used in seventeenth-, eighteenth-, and nineteenth-century American building construction, are usually tapered on four sides. The nail shank and head lack uniformity, and the nails are softer and bend or "clinch" more easily than other types of nails. Early cut nails, ca. 1790–ca. 1820 (*middle left*), have shanks that are tapered on two sides. Earlier cut nails were hand-headed; later ones were cut completely by machine and had square, unfaceted heads. Modern cut nails, ca. 1835-present (*middle right*) typically are uniform in size and shape and have heads that are equally convex on each side. Wire nails, ca. 1850-present (*bottom*), are usually manufactured from steel wire and typically have a four-facet point, a round shank, and a flat, round, uniform head.

weight, easily built, and highly adaptable to various floor plans, the balloon frame eventually supplanted earlier framing methods. Balloon framing also encouraged the development of related building technologies, including prefabricated housing. The appearance of balloon framing is most often associated with the rebuilding after the Chicago Fire of 1839 and has been well documented in the mid-nineteenth-century Midwest.[16] Although balloon-frame technology was available in many towns in the middle Atlantic region by the 1850s, balloon-framed buildings did not gain general currency here until after the Civil War, appearing first in the booming railroad towns at mid-century.[17] During the first half of the nineteenth century, the combination frame was much more common.

Platform framing is a more recent modification of balloon framing techniques. Simpler to build than a balloon frame, a platform frame differs primarily in the way the floors are supported. In a classic two-story balloon frame, the studs extend from the sill to the plate and the floors are suspended from the studs. In a platform frame, the studs are shorter, extending only to the height of a single story; they bear the weight of the floors, which are built as separate components or platforms. The floors, in turn, carry another set of vertical studs which then support the next platform or the roof.

NAILS

Cheap, plentiful, machine-made nails fueled the development of modern balloon- and platform-frame construction. Before machine-made nails were common, builders depended on hand-wrought and earlier forms of machine-cut nails. Nails used in most buildings fall into three basic groups: wrought, cut, and wire nails (Fig. 3.31). Because each type of nail was popular for a specific and overlapping period of time, nail types can be used to establish the dates of old buildings. While the presence of a given type of nail does not necessarily fix the date of a building, it can suggest patterns of occupation, alteration, and use.[18]

Wrought nails, handmade nails forged by a blacksmith, were manufactured from the seventeenth to the early nineteenth centuries. Most easily identified by their faceted heads, wrought nails are softer and bend or "clinch" more easily than later types of nails. During the colonial period, wrought nails were scarce and costly; they were made locally in some areas but were also imported in large quantities. After the Revolution, nail-making technology changed, and local nail manufacturers began to supply machine-cut nails in greater quantities. Wrought nails continued to be used for a number of years following the introduction of machine-cut nails, especially for clinching and in other instances where their malleability aided in construction. Wrought nails competed with cut nails until about 1820, after which the former gradually declined in popularity. The development of mechanical nail cutting resulted in a much more plentiful supply of nails in the early nineteenth century. Unlike wrought nails, which were hammered out individually, cut nails were sheared in quantity from a flattened plate of steel. Machine-cut nails generally appeared in urban areas first, gradually diffusing into more rural regions. They became widely available in the Delaware valley region after about 1800, first appearing with machine-cut shanks and faceted, hand-finished heads. Later they were entirely manufactured by machine. Introduced some time around 1850, wire nails did not become widely available in the region until the late 1800s. They replaced other types of nails very gradually, becoming the dominant type only in the early 1900s. Cut nails are still used today in some specific instances, such as flooring.[19]

Masonry Construction

STONE

Stone buildings are concentrated in some parts of the Delaware valley, while in others they are almost nonexistent. Generally speaking, stone construction appears more frequently in the northern and western portions of the region, where locally quarried stone was readily available. In parts of Chester County, Pennsylvania, for example, stone has traditionally been used for foundations and for the walls of dwellings, barns, and outbuildings, such as springhouses and kitchens. By early in the nineteenth century, stone had become the preferred construction material in the county; locally quarried types like schist, limestone, and serpentine were commonly used. Many of these early stone buildings still dot the Pennsylvania landscape today. Further south, in Delaware, southern New Jersey, and on the Eastern Shore of Virginia, stone construction was always much less common than log and timber frame and was typically limited to foundations. Stone foundations, built primarily of fieldstone and river cobbles, can be observed as far south as central Kent County, Delaware, but buildings constructed with stone walls tend to be fewer in number farther south. In the coastal plain of Delaware, building stone—usually granite or schist—was rare enough that it was removed from railway beds or breakwaters and reappropriated as a walling material. Stone houses built as early as 1790 survive in Delaware.

Various types of stone were used for building purposes, including some varieties, like the greenish-colored serpentine quarried in Chester County, that were indigenous to the area. Limestone, granite, and Wissahickon schist are common throughout much of southeastern Pennsylvania; iron-bearing sandstone is used in parts of southern New Jersey; Brandywine granite, an onyx-colored stone, is found in northern Delaware; and a distinctive pinkish sandstone appears in parts of Lancaster and Berks Counties, Pennsylvania.

Stone walling can be categorized as uncoursed or coursed. Uncoursed stone walling is made of stones laid up in a random pattern, without regular horizontal rows or courses. Much of the final appearance of such a wall depends on the shape and size of the available stones. Coursed stone walling is simply stone that has been cut into block shapes so that it can be laid in even horizontal rows like bricks. Stone walling can be further categorized by the degree to which the stones have been finished or "dressed." In most uncoursed walling visible on historic buildings, the rubble fieldstones were roughly cut to shape but their surfaces were not dressed (Fig. 3.32). Even in uncoursed stone walling, however, the stones that were used for corners, thresholds, steps, and sills were often more finely finished. Partially and fully dressed stones, which required more skill and effort to produce, tended to be used primarily in coursed stone walling. Methods of dressing and finishing building stones involved hewing, hammering, chiseling, sawing, and rubbing, and they produced a variety of finishes. The most highly finished building stones were ashlar—a squared, highly finished stone walling characterized by very thin mortar joints.[20]

Stone construction methods, like framing techniques, changed over time. While stone walls constructed in the eighteenth century were rarely finely finished and usually consisted of roughly coursed masonry with raised mortar joints, late-nineteenth-century stonework more often consisted of rubble stone walls built and stuccoed over to look like coursed ashlar (see Fig. 3.43). Alexander Jackson Davis and Andrew Jackson Downing, who helped to popularize the Gothic Revival style in the mid-nineteenth century, recommended building with stone for its naturalistic qualities. By the end of the nineteenth

Figure 3.32
Ephrata vicinity, ca. 1815, Lancaster County, Pennsylvania. Photographed 1991. Most uncoursed stone walling on historic buildings is composed of roughly cut rubble fieldstones.

century, stone tended to be used more decoratively. Mixed stone finishes occurred in some cases. In some early-nineteenth-century urban buildings, for example, the facades were built of coursed and dressed stone while the gables were left as uncoursed rubble. Late-nineteenth-century architecture in the Queen Anne and Second Empire styles often used carved and textured stone for effect, and Romanesque style buildings often made extensive use of roughly dressed or rusticated stone surfaces.

BRICK

Brick construction also tends to be heavily concentrated in some parts of the mid-Atlantic region. Although wood was still the predominant building material in parts of the developing port cities of Baltimore and Philadelphia in the eighteenth century, brick building was also widespread. Many eighteenth-century cities tended to have neighborhoods of intermixed brick and wood construction, but by the 1830s, brick had already eclipsed wood in popularity. Most Delaware valley brick building relates to broader national rather than regional building traditions. By the mid-nineteenth century, especially, brick buildings inspired by nationally popular pattern books became increasingly widespread. Federal brick buildings were erected in urban areas as well as in many smaller towns. Also, while wood has always been a common building material in the area, many frame and log buildings incorporated some brick elements, such as chimneys and foundations.

Figure 3.33
Samuel Bassett House, Pilesgrove Township, Salem County, New Jersey. Photographed 1976. Occasionally bricks were laid in decorative patterns or to spell out dates on the gable ends of buildings, but these special treatments were uncommon and were usually reserved for the dwellings of a wealthy and influential minority. The pattern-end brick houses of Salem County, New Jersey, survive in a concentration that belies their original rarity.

The most expensive and labor-intensive building material used during the late eighteenth and early nineteenth centuries, brick was associated with elite housing and was less common than log and frame. But, because early brick buildings have survived to a much greater extent than have their wooden counterparts, it is easy to assume that brick was used more frequently than it actually was.

The surviving eighteenth-century pattern-end brick dwellings of Salem County, New Jersey, illustrate this point. These houses, usually one-and-one-half to two-and-one-half stories high, are distinguished by windowless gable-end walls that are embellished with vitrified or glazed brick headers laid in patterns ranging from simple letters and dates to elaborate zigzags, diamonds, and figures (Fig. 3.33). Located in several townships throughout Salem County, these dwellings survive there in a concentration that is greater than anywhere else in the country, but they were decidedly rarer in eighteenth-century Salem County than their current numbers might imply, typically constituting just over one-tenth of the houses built at the end of the eighteenth century.[21]

Because of the numerous processing steps required in manufacture, brick was a highly transformed material, perhaps the most "artificial" of all building materials available to many builders.[22] Bricks vary slightly in size, but most average around 8¼ inches on the long face, 4¼ inches on the short end, and 2¼ inches high; they are designed to be small enough to be handled by one person. The long sides of a brick are called stretchers and the ends are known as headers. Because bricks are relatively standardized in size, most brick-walled buildings tend to have similar exterior wall thicknesses, usually measuring 1′1″ thick—the combined width of a single header, a stretcher, and the mortar joint in between. Some brick walls are only 9 inches thick, roughly equivalent to the length of a single brick.

Bricks used in eighteenth- and nineteenth-century buildings were softer and more absorbent than modern bricks. While stories abound of eighteenth-century American buildings being constructed of bricks that had been used as ships' ballast, these assertions are largely undocumented and tend to be the product of local lore. Ships crossing the Atlantic did sometimes carry bricks as ballast, but ballast stones, not bricks, were more commonly used. Usually, brick was manufactured close to the construction site. Early building bricks were made of locally dug clay tempered with sand or straw. They were formed in sand-dusted molds, sun-dried, and fired or "burned" on the building site in earth-set temporary kilns called clamps. The firing process caused some shrinkage; in addition, bricks that were burned at lower temperatures were softer than desired, while those that were overfired often warped. As a result, brickmakers and bricklayers sorted and graded their wares according to quality. Softer, underfired bricks, known as sammel bricks, were used where they would seldom be seen—often on the inside surfaces of cellar walls. Better quality bricks, reserved for the outside face of the wall, were then keyed into the softer sammel bricks. Poorer quality bricks were sometimes utilized along with fieldstone as nogging, a method of filling the spaces between timbers in the walls of frame buildings with rubble masonry. Nogging occasionally filled entire walls from the sill to the plate, but in the more southern sections of the region nogging sometimes reached to a height of only two or three feet above the sills.

During the brickmaking process, the uneven heat in the kiln could produce color variations. Bricks that were stacked closest to the hot center of the kiln were burned to a dark color and often had a salt glaze applied to one

A

Figure 3.34

Glazed headers were sometimes laid up in special patterns on the public facades or gable ends of eighteenth-century buildings. (*A*) John Dickinson Mansion, 1740, Dover vicinity, Kent County, Delaware. Photographed by Jack E. Boucher, HABS, 1982. (*B*) Makepeace, Somerset County, Maryland. Photographed 1980.

B

end. These bricks with glazed headers were culled out for decorative use (Fig. 3.34).[23]

Although machine-made bricks were being manufactured in limited quantities by the 1830s, they did not become widely available until the mid-nineteenth century. Produced by means of power-driven plungers or manual screw presses, these bricks were fired in kilns that could reach higher temperatures; consequently, they were harder, stronger, a darker red, and less porous than their predecessors. They were also more uniform in appearance. Formed in water- or oil-lubricated metal molds, their sharper edges and smoother sides enabled brickmasons to lay them more closely than had been possible with earlier bricks.[24]

Brick types vary. While standard-sized red clay bricks are overwhelmingly used in construction, bricks treated with special surfaces or burned in unusual shapes are also used for decorative or structural reasons. Molded bricks, which are bricks pressed into specific shapes before firing, are most often seen in architectural details such as cornices, window surrounds, and water tables (Fig. 3.35). Bricks have also been molded in cove, chamfered, or bullnosed shapes (Fig. 3.36). Some bricks are cut rather than molded into specific shapes. Rubbed or gauged bricks are soft bricks that have been sawn to a specific shape and then rubbed to a smooth surface. They are used to ornament window and door openings. Bricks with colored surfaces and special glazes are manufactured for use in decorative designs.

Brick walls are constructed by laying bricks in overlapping rows and joining them with layers of mortar. The regular pattern in which bricks are laid is known as bonding (Fig. 3.37). Different bonds produce different decorative results and different strengths. The most popular brick bonds in the early eighteenth century were Flemish bond, produced by alternating headers and stretchers within a course, and English bond, consisting of alternating courses of headers and stretchers. Flemish bond is considered to be more decorative but less stable than English bond; in fact, foundations of eighteenth-century brick buildings were often laid in English bond, while the brickwork above grade was laid in Flemish bond. Glazed headers are frequently seen on eighteenth-century Flemish bond facades.

Common bonds, constructed by laying multiple courses of stretchers interspersed with a row of headers, became more widespread by the second quarter of the eighteenth century. The most widely used types of common bonds were constructed of three, five, or seven courses of stretchers broken by single courses of headers. Header bond consisted of a solid wall of headers and was occasionally used on frontal elevations. Most often used for

Figure 3.35
Kingston-Upon-Hull, Dover vicinity, Kent County, Delaware. Photographed by David Ames, HABS, 1992. Bricks molded into specific shapes before firing were used in architectural details such as projecting water tables like the one shown here.

Figure 3.36
Mayfield, Middletown vicinity, Appoquinimink Hundred, New Castle County, Delaware. Photographed 1983. Sometimes, molded bricks were reclaimed and used for other purposes. In this example, bullnosed bricks have been fitted together to build a wall.

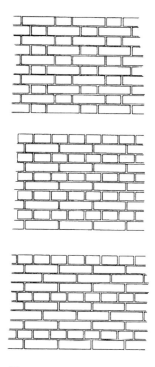

Figure 3.37

The most popular brick bonds in the early eighteenth century were Flemish bond (*top*) and English bond (*middle*). Common bond (*bottom*, a three-course example) became more widespread by the second quarter of the eighteenth century.

decorative effect, header bond is usually associated with eighteenth-century buildings around Annapolis and Chestertown, Maryland. Later in the nineteenth century, American, running, or stretcher bonds—courses with staggered stretchers—became popular. These are the familiar brick bonds visible on later-nineteenth- and twentieth-century buildings.

Other brick bonds are less common but can be found throughout the area. Herringbone brickwork, usually associated with the early-twentieth-century sections of cities and towns, consists of bricks laid diagonally in a herringbone pattern. In the late nineteenth century, more exotic brick bonds became popular. Some of these are variations on Flemish bond. Rusticated Flemish bond, for example, consists of a standard Flemish bond pattern using rough-faced or rusticated headers. Alternating Flemish bond is built of courses of alternate headers and stretchers separated by several courses of stretchers.

Bricks are also sometimes laid in decorative projecting patterns or courses for a more sculptural effect. Water tables, string and belt courses, brick quoins, and corbeled, dentilated, coved, and dog-toothed or mouse-toothed cornices are examples of this type of surface modeling (Fig. 3.38). Water tables are projecting masonry courses that form a sort of base or plinth at the foundation line of a building (see Fig. 3.35). Used primarily on the front elevation, water tables define the division between the cellar and the first floor. String and belt courses, narrow projecting horizontal bands one to three bricks high, often embellish the front walls of eighteenth-century buildings and are sometimes used as flashing for pent roofs. Brick quoins, created in imitation of stone quoins, are groups of bricks projecting from the wall surface at its corners. Used to lock corners together to stabilize masonry walls, quoins are structural features which can also be decorative. Corbeled cornices, which became popular in the 1820s, consist of a series of successively cantilevered brick courses at the top of the exterior walls, just under the roof line (see Fig. 3.9).

Bricklayers employed a variety of arching techniques to span window and door openings. Segmental arches consist of bricks arranged in a curved arching pattern (Fig. 3.39). The arch formation might be roughly created with tapered mortar joints, or it could be more smoothly formed with specially cut, wedge-shaped bricks. Segmental arches sometimes have keystones at their apexes. Formed in squat, truncated wedge shapes, jack or flat arches are constructed by laying a course of bricks on end in a radiating pattern to form the head of an opening. Although jack arches are not arched in a curve, the

Figure 3.38
Choptank-Upon-the-Hill,
St. George's Hundred, New
Castle County, Delaware.
Photographed by David
Ames, HABS, 1995. Bricks
are sometimes laid in patterns or courses that project from the wall, for a
more sculptural effect, as in
this dentilated cornice.

Figure 3.39
Kingston-Upon-Hull, Dover vicinity, Kent County, Delaware. Photographed by David Ames, HABS, 1992. Segmental arches are usually made of brick or stone.

friction from the closely spaced vertical joints provides some of the structural support of a true arch. Rowlock header arches consist of brick headers laid on end in an arch shape.

The sides of brick openings are often defined with partial bricks called closers. Cut or molded to the width of half-headers (queen closers) or half-stretchers (king closers), closers are used to complete the bonding pattern near openings and at the ends of walls (Fig. 3.40). The presence of closers in the middle of solid brick walls can suggest earlier window or door openings.

Brick often follows the same bonding pattern throughout a building, but bond shifts frequently occur for decorative reasons. In some early buildings the bonding pattern on the foundation differs from the rest of the wall. In the nineteenth century, bond shifts occurred more often in walls than foundations. Decorative brick bonds were employed on the front or public facades, while more commonplace stretcher or English bonds were used for side and rear elevations (Fig. 3.41). Sometimes bond shifts were utilized to create intricate patterns on the gable ends of some buildings, but these special treatments were rare. In some cases the bonding on gable walls deteriorates in complexity toward the top of the wall.

Occasionally, masonry walling is composed of mixed materials. Shifts in building material may be original or they may be indicative of subsequent alterations. Close inspection may help to explain the reasons for the changes. Material shifts may occur from the bottom to the top of the foundation, as in the case of a stone foundation topped with several courses of brick. The bricks are used as a device to level or flatten the top course of the foundation wall. Masonry materials may also change from one wall of the building to another, for very different reasons, with the most ornamental—and usually the costliest—materials being reserved for the main facade (Fig. 3.42). In some cases brick has been used to conceal a less costly or less fashionable primary construction material, such as frame or log; in others, brick walls masquerade as entirely different materials, including coursed dressed stone or ashlar (Fig. 3.43; see also Figs. 1.2 and 4.16).

CONCRETE

Concrete walling may be poured or built of block. Poured concrete walling, constructed by pouring liquid concrete into prefabricated forms, is widely used today, especially for foundations. Concrete block walling is constructed of individual concrete units. Walling constructed of "rockfaced" concrete blocks first appeared in the 1890s and is common on domestic buildings

A

B

Figure 3.40
Lower Alloways Creek Meetinghouse, Lower Alloways Creek Township, Salem County, New Jersey. Photographed 1995. The sides of brick openings are often defined with partial bricks called closers, cut or molded to the width of half-headers (queen closers) or half-stretchers (king closers). (*A*) Closers are visible at the seam between earlier and later portions of this brick building. (*B*) A line of closers is clearly visible to the right of this door opening.

A

Figure 3.41

Kingston-Upon-Hull, Dover vicinity, Kent County, Delaware. Photographed by Jack E. Boucher, HABS, 1982. Decorative brick bonds were often used on the front or public facades, while more commonplace bonds were used for side and rear elevations. The front wall and side gable (*A*) of this eighteenth-century building were laid in Flemish bond with glazed headers while the rear, nonpublic elevation (*B*) was laid in common bond.

B

Figure 3.42
York Seat Farm, Little Creek vicinity, Kent County, Delaware. Photographed by David Ames, HABS, 1982. This ca. 1750 frame dwelling was enlarged in the early nineteenth century with a side-passage masonry wing. The addition was constructed of brick with a dressed, uncoursed rubble stone facade.

Figure 3.43
Bennett-Downs House, Buena Vista vicinity, New Castle Hundred, New Castle County, Delaware. Photographed by David Ames, HABS, 1991. During a dramatic nineteenth-century remodeling, the original brick walling of this Federal-style building, visible below the window, was stuccoed and scored to resemble coursed ashlar.

constructed between about 1905 and 1930. Although more than a thousand companies were manufacturing concrete block by 1905, people often bought block-making machines for their own use. Mail order companies like Sears, Roebuck and Company offered consumers inexpensive and versatile block-making machines through their catalogues, and many do-it-yourself builders seized the opportunity to build with this affordable and expressive medium. Concrete block was especially popular because, despite its weight, it was inexpensive and easy to manufacture. When made to simulate broken ashlar, cobblestone, or coursed brick, it could also be ornamental. During the late 1920s and early 1930s, cinderblock gradually replaced concrete block as a common building material.[25]

Concrete block walling is usually coursed in a simple running bond pattern. Rockfaced concrete block is more often confined to foundations and garages, but it was occasionally used to construct entire buildings (Fig. 3.44). Rockfaced concrete block was also used decoratively as quoining and on porches. The Vogl House in Kent County, Delaware, provides one of the most spectacular examples of the imaginative and ornamental use of this material (Fig. 3.45).

MORTAR

Until the late nineteenth century, the lime-and-sand mortar used in masonry buildings was soft, flexible, and characteristically light-colored. Manufactured from clay, sand, and lime derived from burned oyster shells, this mortar created relatively elastic masonry joints. Mortar used after about 1880 was much more rigid. The later mortar contained Portland Cement and was generally stronger, harder, and less absorbent than earlier lime-and-sand mortars. The grayish color of the Portland Cement also made it darker in color. During the late nineteenth century, applying colored mortars in narrow joints became popular on buildings where the appearance of a continuous wall surface was desired. Masonry mortar joints vary in width and surface treatment for both aesthetic and structural reasons. Irregularly shaped stones and bricks require thicker mortar joints to compensate for multiple uneven surfaces. More uniform masonry units can be mortared with thinner joints. Most brick mortar joints average about ⅜ inch thick, while joints for rubble stone walls can be considerably thicker.[26]

Pointing is a process of applying a second layer of mortar to masonry joints after the initial mortar has hardened. Pointing may be undertaken for increased durability, better weather resistance, or to achieve a particular surface appearance. Different pointing treatments produce different effects. Brick walls tend

Figure 3.44
Bridgeville, Sussex County, Delaware. Photographed 1993. This house is constructed of rockfaced concrete block, with contrasting decorative brick banding and red brick segmental arches over the windows.

to be pointed with flush, tooled or struck, and raised joints (Fig. 3.46). A flush joint is produced when the excess mortar is scraped off flush with the masonry surface. Tooled and struck joints are flush joints that are finished by impressing them with a mason's trowel to achieve a concave or angled surface. Raised joints are simply mortar joints that stand above the surface of the wall. Sometimes uneven brick joints were given a more regular appearance by penciling, a method of painting narrow lines directly over the mortar joints. Stone mortar joints vary depending on the type of stone used and how it was laid up. Raised flat or V-shaped joints were often used for uncoursed rubble, while coursed, dressed stone usually received tooled, struck, or concave joints.[27]

Interior Construction and Finish

Floors, interior partition walls, and roofing systems in eighteenth- and nineteenth-century masonry buildings were most often built of wood. Floors were usually constructed by leaving evenly spaced sockets in the exterior masonry walls as they were being raised and laying wooden floor joists into these sockets. Floorboards were then laid on top of and perpendicular to the joists. Alternatively, mortised wooden sills might be laid into the masonry at the first-floor level, to support the floor joists. Material of the joists ranged from partially hewn round logs to fully squared hewn or sawn timbers. Brick walls were usually stepped or built thinner with each additional story, creating ledges to carry the ends of the upper floor joists. The top set of joists was laid atop a plank plate and projected beyond the exterior surface of the masonry wall. Additional partial courses of bricks and mortar were added to make the top surface of the masonry wall flush with the tops of the joists. Brick buildings were usually finished with timber frame roofs; these were constructed of rafters footed on plates or false plates that were laid atop the attic floor joists.[28]

Interior partition walls have been built of a variety of materials, ranging from exposed finished boards, to frameworks of wooden studs or rough-sawn lapped boards overlaid with a finish coat of lath and plaster, to masonry. Partition walls are characterized as load-bearing or non-load-bearing, depending on the extent to which they carry the weight of the upper floors and roof. Load-bearing walls are commonly stud or masonry, while non-load-bearing walls could be simply constructed of boards.

Exposed wooden partition walls appear commonly in domestic buildings dating to the earliest period of settlement and continued to be used through the early nineteenth century. More highly finished board partition walls were

Figure 3.45
Vogl House, Harrington vicinity, Kent County, Delaware. Photographed by Jack E. Boucher, HABS, 1982. Built by Bavarian immigrants in 1915 with the aid of a concrete block machine and molds from Sears, this house provides one of the best examples of the imaginative use of rusticated concrete block.

often ornamented with a narrow bead applied to one or both edges of the boards. Although these board walls were occasionally left plain, they were also frequently painted or whitewashed.

Stud walls were most often constructed of a framework of regularly spaced riven or sawn wooden studs averaging around 2½ to 3 inches by 3½ to 4 inches. Most stud walls were secured to board nailers at top and bottom and finished with a layer of plaster and lath. Stud walls, which usually measure around 5 inches thick, appear throughout the mid-Atlantic region.

Rough-sawn lapped board partition walls, which are not found in the Chesapeake region but were built farther north in the greater Philadelphia area, appeared as early as the mid-eighteenth century and continued in use through the early 1800s. These walls are usually thinner than stud walls; they average around 4 inches thick. They were typically constructed with a core of lapped and staggered, rough-sawn, unfinished boards that usually measured 1 inch to 1½ inches thick and average around 1 foot across the face. Finished on both sides with a coating of lath and plaster, they were usually nailed to the side of a joist and toenailed directly to the floor or to a board nailer.

Masonry partition walls were also built in eighteenth- and nineteenth-century dwellings. Most often associated with stair-passage plan houses, masonry partitions rising from the cellar to second floor level typically defined one but not both partitions in a center-passage house. In double-pile masonry buildings, the load-bearing brick or stone partition wall often divided the front and rear rooms of the house. In all instances, masonry partitions are found in brick or stone buildings and were designed as load-bearing features that were usually related to the construction of the stair or floor joist system.

Whitewash, one of the simplest of interior finishes, was also one of the most widely used from the eighteenth century through the middle of the twentieth century. It was frequently applied directly to exposed wall, joist, and ceiling surfaces. It was also sometimes used on the interior walls of outbuildings. Because whitewashing was often done repeatedly over earlier coats, layers of whitewash could build up over time. These layers can clearly reveal sequences of additions and alterations.

All types of interior walls might also be more thoroughly finished with a coating of plaster—made of varying proportions of clay, lime, gypsum, sand, and hair—that was typically laid over and keyed into a framework of wooden lath. Lath was attached horizontally to studs and posts with short lathing nails or tacks, although lathing subsequently laid on log walls was typically attached vertically rather than horizontally. While the laths used throughout the colonial period were split or riven, mill-sawn lath began to appear toward

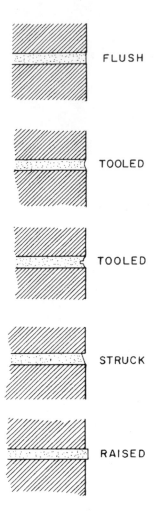

FLUSH

TOOLED

TOOLED

STRUCK

RAISED

Figure 3.46
Types of common masonry
mortar joints include flush,
tooled, struck, and raised.
Drawn by Gabrielle Lanier
after Harley J. McKee in
*Introduction to Early Ameri-
can Masonry: Stone, Brick,
Mortar, and Plaster*, p. 70.

the mid-nineteenth century. Similarly, lathing nails changed as techniques for nail manufacture evolved.

Plaster was also applied to masonry walls, using a base coat of clay mixed with hair or chopped straw or a coarsely tempered lime-based mortar. A finish coat was skimmed over the rough base coat and to complete the wall surface. The walls and ceilings in some early German houses north and west of Philadelphia were formed of a tightly packed layer of straw-wrapped and mud-daubed riven staves finished with a coating of clay plaster. Paled ceilings, another variation on this form of walling, consisted of riven wooden staves, or pales, set into grooved joists; pales typically secured walling material of mud or clay and straw. Early German builders also sometimes used a system of pegs, rather than laths, as a framework to receive wet plaster. Like layers of whitewash patterns, differences in lath and plaster treatments within a building can suggest a chronology of architectural change.

Stucco, a thin layer of plaster made of slaked lime and sharp sand, became fashionable in the early nineteenth century. Although sometimes applied to interior walls, stucco was most commonly used as an exterior finish on many nineteenth century buildings.[29] Stuccoed surfaces might be left plain or scored to simulate the appearance of expensive stone (see Fig. 3.43).

Walls, wainscoting, and ceilings clad in sheets of stamped, pressed metal were popular from the late nineteenth century through the 1920s. Advertisers in trade and builders' journals claimed that pressed metal ceilings were fire-resistant, sanitary, permanent, economical, and decorative. Early-twentieth-century consumers could purchase pressed metal ceilings through manufacturers' trade catalogues and even the Sears, Roebuck catalogue. Although interior pressed metal work appears most often in commercial and public architecture, it was also utilized occasionally in residential buildings. Metal ceiling coverings, which were often modeled on plaster moldings, were usually nailed to furring strips, the joints and nails concealed, and the metal then coated with primer and paint. In the last two decades of the nineteenth century, relief-decorated sheet-metal wall plates were also sometimes used.[30]

Roofing

All buildings, whether their walls are constructed of brick, log, timber frame, or concrete block, require a weatherproof roof for protection. The most numerous types of roofs in the region are common rafter gable roofs, which are built of a series of equally spaced and dimensioned rafters footed onto the framing at the tops of the walls. This type of roof had become the standard roofing system in the region by the end of the seventeenth century and is the most common type built in twentieth-century suburbs. Although common rafter roofs constitute a specific type of roofing assembly, builders have exercised a wide range of construction options within that type. Common rafter gable roofs have been used on buildings constructed of a variety of walling materials, including log, masonry, and frame.

Common Rafter Roofs

During the eighteenth and early nineteenth centuries, construction of a common rafter roof for a timber-framed building typically began with attaching timber plates to the tops of the walls. Attic floor joists were then lapped over these plates (Fig. 3.47). Joists could be trenched into the plate or simply balanced on top of it, and they often, but not always, extended beyond the outside surfaces of the exterior walls. After the attic joists were placed, a false plate, or raising plate, usually consisting of a board or light timber (Chesapeake) or a heavier timber (Delaware valley) that extended the length of the building, was attached to the tops of the joists (Fig. 3.48). False plates joined the roof to the walls at the eaves and provided a seat for the rafter ends; they could be composed of a single piece of wood or several pieces laid end to end. False plates were attached to the joists in a variety of ways: they might be simply nailed to the tops of the joists, or they could be trenched and, occasionally, pinned. Typical false plate construction allowed for numerous adjustments in rafter spacing and created a roof structure that was not particularly dependent upon the condition of the wall below. Because false plates allowed for a certain amount of flexibility during the life of the building, they had traditionally been an appropriate construction choice for post-set buildings that would be subject to settling and rot. Although false plates were widely used, some buildings—usually log structures, barns, and granaries—lacked false plates. The rafter feet in these buildings were seated directly onto the wall plates.[31]

Once the false plates were attached, rafters that had been prefitted, trimmed, and sometimes numbered in their raising order were brought up to the attic floor. There they were reassembled into rafter pairs, hoisted into position, and joined at their apexes with wooden pins driven through precut lap, mortise-and-tenon, or bridle joints. (After 1850, rafters were typically butted and nailed or butted to a thin ridge board and nailed.) As each new rafter pair was raised, positioned, and pinned, it was temporarily stabilized by

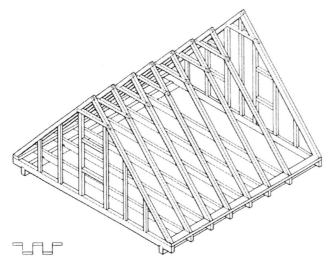

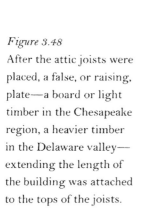

Figure 3.47
Common rafter roofs, which are built of a series of equally spaced and dimensioned rafters footed onto the framing at the tops of the walls, are the most numerous in the mid-Atlantic region. The standard roofing system in the Chesapeake region by the end of the seventeenth century, common rafter roofs remain popular in twentieth-century suburbs.

Figure 3.48
After the attic joists were placed, a false, or raising, plate—a board or light timber in the Chesapeake region, a heavier timber in the Delaware valley—extending the length of the building was attached to the tops of the joists.

nailing it to the others with lengths of shingle lath. Rafters were sometimes notched or birdmouthed at their bases to catch the edge of the false plate and thus check any tendency toward settling and outward movement at the base of the roof.[32]

Collar ties or beams, horizontal timbers that bound rafter blades together in an A-shaped formation, often provided additional reinforcement. In some cases, collar ties were fitted to every other rafter pair; in others, they were employed throughout the roof. Usually placed a few feet below the rafter apex but far enough above the attic floor to allow for adequate headroom, collar ties could be simply nailed or more securely joined with pinned half-dovetail or straight lap joints.[33]

Further rigidity was provided by roofing boards or shingle lath. These were lightweight horizontal timbers affixed to the outside of the rafters; they stiffened the entire roof assembly and provided a surface to which roofing shingles could be nailed. Shingle lath construction was a regional alternative to purlins, the heavier, regularly spaced horizontal timbers that ran perpendicular to the rafters. Typically set into the framing or masonry of the gables, principal purlins are most often associated with principal rafter roofs and usually support the common rafters across their outer surfaces.

Other Roof Types

While common rafter roofs are the most numerous roof type, other types have also been built, including principal rafter, hipped, gambrel, and mansard roofs. Principal rafter roofs are constructed with two sizes of rafters. Larger, heavier principal rafters are widely spaced across the length of the building and give the roof its essential form; smaller, lighter common rafters interspersed between the principal rafters support the skin of the roof, which consists of lengths of horizontal shingle lath or roofing boards. Hipped roofs are similar to common rafter roofs but are double pitched, formed of four pitched surfaces rather than two.

Gambrel roofs are double-pitched gable roofs that are constructed by placing one common rafter roof on top of another; consequently, these roofs are raised in two separate sections. They have two sets of rafter pairs rather than one (Fig. 3.49). The upper set of rafter pairs sits on a second plate, called a kerb plate, which marks the point where the roof pitch changes. The lower section, which consists of more steeply pitched rafter blades attached to tie beams with bridle joints, is erected first, as partially assembled units. The kerb plate, which is laid on top of this assembly, carries the weight of the

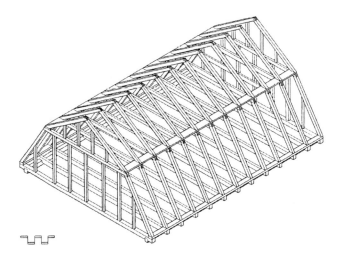

Figure 3.49
Gambrel roofs are double-pitched gable roofs built with two
sets of rafter pairs rather than one.

upper rafters. Then more shallowly pitched pairs of rafters are set atop the
kerb plate and joined at the ridge with bridle joints. Mansard roofs—double-
pitched roofs with a steeply pitched lower section and a very shallowly
pitched and hipped upper section—became popular in the late nineteenth
century.

No matter how a roof is built, the final construction step is to protect the
roof frame and the building below with a water-shedding finish. The roofs
of Delaware valley buildings have been finished and weatherproofed with a
variety of materials, ranging from split wood shingles to corrugated metal,
ceramic tile, and decorative slate, but the original roofing materials have often
been replaced or lie concealed under subsequent layers. Wood shingle roofs
were widely used on houses and outbuildings through the mid-twentieth century. Until late in the nineteenth century, shingle making was an important
component of the lumber trade in the Cypress Swamp region of southern
Delaware.[34] Wood shingle roofs were simply constructed of several overlapping layers of shingles nailed to widely spaced, narrowly dimensioned wooden
supports. These supports, variously termed shingle laths or nailers, ran the
length of the building, parallel to the roof ridge, and were typically nailed to
the rafter backs at roughly one-foot intervals. The individual shingles usually
measured either 2 or 3 feet in length. Shingles were split along the grain of
the wood and tapered at one end to form an extremely narrow wedge shape
in cross-section. The narrow ends of the shingles were then placed side by
side, overlapped for part of their length, and nailed to the shingle lath through
several layers, exposing only part of each shingle to the weather. In this way,
each section of the roof was protected by three layers. Finally, at the ridge
line, the shingles on one side were overlapped for part of their length to pro-

tect the apex of the roof, forming what is called a comb. Roof-wall junctions and areas where the roof was pierced were flashed with a variety of materials, including lead sheathing and wood shingles.

Metal roofing composed of galvanized iron, terne-plate, or tin plate has been used since the mid-nineteenth century and is still present on some buildings. Standing-seam metal roofs are so named because they are characterized by upright seams that run perpendicular to the roof ridge. The seams, which are formed by overlapping and folding the sheets of metal that cover the roof, seal the joints between metal sections to protect against water infiltration. Some modern roofing materials, such as asbestos, asphalt shingle, and rolled asphalt roofing, had appeared by the early twentieth century, and many were commonly used by the 1940s.

Like floor plans and house lots, construction methods and materials provide important clues to dates or sequences of construction, occupation, and alteration. There are many construction practices and features that we have not discussed here. Our goal, as always, has not been to provide encyclopedic coverage. Instead, we introduce the examination of construction methods and materials as one of many overlapping ways to understand and interpret buildings. Just as sequences of additions, evidence of interior finishes, or nail types can confirm building periods, features such as architectural style or landscape treatment can also help to assign construction dates and offer insights into broader historical questions. The following chapters examine some of these features in greater detail.

4

POPULAR
ARCHITECTURAL STYLES

Architectural style, like building plans and construction systems, carries important information. Although stylistic elements are often the features that first catch our eye, interpreting a building on the basis of style alone can be sometimes misleading and often unsatisfying. From an archaeological standpoint, writing about architectural style produces a certain discomfort. Most architectural guides present style as a straightforward linear chronology and provide a checklist of particular stylistic features against which we are invited to compare the buildings we encounter. But as we have already seen, buildings are "messy." The facades of most buildings conceal complex histories, histories which we can begin to unravel by examining style in conjunction with other features, such as form or construction. Style provides only one of several possible clues to a building's past. Archaeologists use style along with the principles of stratigraphy, *terminus ante quem* (the date before which), and *terminus post quem* (the date after which) as a way to date and interpret the assemblages they unearth. Like archaeologists excavating layers of cultural artifacts and making sense of a chaotic jumble of potsherds and terrestrial flotsam, we use style as one of many tools for interpreting architecture.

A helpful concept for using architectural style as a diagnostic tool is *seriation*. In seriation, an approach to artifacts of all sorts, objects are ordered along a time line on the basis of distinctive physical characteristics that include construction, form, and decoration. These same characteristics are also useful for determining the limits of a geographic area where artifacts and specific attributes are found. The New England gravestone studies by archae-

119

ologists James Deetz and Edwin Dethlefsen are excellent examples of the effective use of seriation for object interpretation. Looking at New England gravestones, Deetz and Dethlefsen isolated a number of the decorative motifs they found on the stones, including death's heads, cherubs, willows, and urns. Plotting the incidence of these stylistic motifs against a time line, they established a chronological index to the rise and fall in popularity of different gravestone styles in individual burial grounds. By comparing the chronological profiles of markers recorded in different graveyards, they then addressed questions of continuity and change in regional gravestone style. And by determining where and when these stylistic traits occurred, they began to understand how far, how fast, and how consistently ideas about gravestone fashion traveled. This knowledge in turn established a basis for asking questions about the ways in which people shared ideas about taste and fashion and about how those ideas were connected to changing religious beliefs and attitudes about death.

The principle of seriation, in conjunction with a knowledge of architectural style, similarly yields an important tool for looking at buildings. Take, for example, decorative doorway treatments in a single town. First, organize the doorways by type on the basis of distinctive visual qualities, such as the use of pilasters, fanlights, brackets, or pediments. Second, place these decorative elements in time by dating them on the basis of construction technology, period documentary sources, or established architectural histories. These first two steps, recognizing and grouping objects on the basis of distinctive visual qualities and establishing those groupings in chronological sequence, are the basis of any seriated approach, the final step of which is mapping those same groupings in space. This approach to style allows us to ask questions about what style means and how it is communicated. The stylistic sequence of doorways over time in towns like New Castle, Salem, or Princess Anne ranges from the heavy classicism of mid-eighteenth-century Georgian architecture to the blockier, visually streamlined forms characteristic of mid-nineteenth-century Greek Revival design. We can use this information to ask larger questions about when and why people chose the fashions they did.[1]

Just as buildings can be organized into typologies based on form, siting, or construction materials and techniques, they can also be distinguished from and grouped with one another on the basis of architectural style. Yet the definition of style is slippery. We usually think of architectural style in terms of specific and related ornamental or structural elements that are characteristic

of a particular time period or place. Defined in this way, architectural style—
a collection of building motifs popular in a specific culture at a given time—
is primarily visual. Yet style can also be defined in a much broader sense. We
can think of style as the physical expression of once-popular values—the "fossilized ideas" that offer us a tangible way to find the past. When we look at
buildings that exemplify a certain style, we see more than the ornamental and
structural features associated with that style; we also encounter something of
the philosophy, attitudes, and ideas of a given time and place. By this definition, style, by expressing a set of popular ideas, provides a way of seeing and
an environment for organizing what we see.

Architectural style can be expressed in building elements ranging from
stair balusters to roof silhouettes, yet style can also be carried in broader
features such as room arrangement, shape and massing, or even the way a
building is situated on its lot. Style functions physically as well as socially.
Within a building, ornament can subtly direct movement through space and
define the function or meaning of certain areas. For example, the heavily ornamented front door of a Georgian house calls attention to the entrance and
suggests the center hall that forms the focus of the spatial arrangement
within. But if style can define and lend importance to physical space, it also
serves a social function. Style can unify as well as separate. For instance, architectural ornament that is broadly copied and widely accepted might express the unity of popular ideas by defining buildings as products of a particular era or region. At the same time, buildings of especially high style or that
exemplify the most fashionable ideas of an era may serve not to unify but
instead to set their occupants apart as members of a distinct group.[2]

Style, even in the simplest buildings, is always present—every building
exhibits its own specific shape, size, and set of proportions. Buildings that
represent unaltered examples of particular styles are rare, though, because
almost all buildings begin to be altered in one way or another the moment
they are constructed. While many of these features result from the initial
intentions of the designer or builders, many are also the result of years of use.
Alterations can be subtle or dramatic and can stem from minute adjustments
imposed by everyday use to major changes resulting from a full-scale rebuilding. Time also imposes its own alterations: styles and the ideas they represent
can wear down and lose their currency; architectural solutions that once
seemed appropriate can soon be perceived as excessive or old-fashioned, and
the building that once appeared grandiose may in time seem ordinary. Stylistic features help us identify periods of stasis and change within a single

room, in a whole building, along an entire street, or even throughout a town or region.

There are many more styles and style categories than this book can address. This chapter provides a starting point for identifying architectural style by introducing and describing some of the more common styles evident in the buildings of the region and illustrating some of their most identifiable characteristics. For more in-depth, nationally oriented treatments of architectural styles, many guides can be consulted. Among the most useful are *A Field Guide to American Houses,* by Virginia and Lee McAlester, *Identifying American Architecture: A Pictorial Guide to Styles and Terms, 1600–1945,* by John J.-G. Blumenson, and *What Style Is It? A Guide to American Architecture,* by John C. Poppeliers, S. Allen Chambers, Jr., and Nancy B. Schwartz.

Older towns provide some of the best places to look at buildings for evidence of style. There are excellent examples of specific architectural styles in Dover, Laurel, New Castle, and Lewes, Delaware; Kennett Square, Strasburg, and West Chester, Pennsylvania; Salem, Greenwich, Cape May, Woodstown, and Woodbury, New Jersey; Annapolis and Chestertown, Maryland; and Eastville, Accomack, and Cape Charles, Virginia. One of the best places in the area to view a complete vocabulary of architectural style is the Green in Dover, Delaware. There one can see a full 250-year history of style, including early pre-Georgian buildings, such as the Ridgeley House, as well as elaborate townhouses with Greek Revival, Italianate, Egyptian Revival, and Colonial Revival detailing. Although many stylistic developments reflected national trends, their appearance in the local landscape occurred in the context of regional construction practices and design preferences.

While the earliest houses in the mid-Atlantic region do not fit easily into a particular style category, they can be grouped together on the basis of several identifying features. When viewed together, these features describe a customary or traditional style of building that was common in the region throughout the colonial period (Fig. 4.1). Among the most characteristic features of this building period was the tendency to leave structural members of the house frame—joists, wall plates, corner posts, and tie beams—exposed. Although these timbers were often finished with details, such as beads, chamfers, and scooped, quirked, or lamb's tongue stops, they usually received no further embellishment or covering (Fig. 4.2). In contrast, such structural timbers in houses built after 1740 tended to be concealed. Typical treatments include chamfered and shouldered corner posts, beaded exposed floor joists, and beaded vertical board walls. Other stylistic characteristics of this period were heavy bolection moldings, fireplace surrounds with mantel cornices, closed

A

B

Figure 4.1
The earliest houses in the mid-Atlantic region do not fit easily into a particular style category, but they can be grouped by several identifying features. (*A*) Maston House, Seaford vicinity, Sussex County, Delaware. Photographed by Jack E. Boucher, HABS, 1982. (*B*) Pear Valley, Machipungo vicinity, Northampton County, Virginia. Photographed by Willie Graham, 1986.

string stairs with heavy turned balusters or no balusters at all, and raised-panel architectural furniture, such as chimney cupboards (sometimes with decorative contoured shelves) and storage closets. Plan, as with many stylistic periods, serves as a secondary identifier, and the same finishes appear in one-, two-, three-, and four-room houses as well as in Georgian houses.

Georgian

The Georgian style was popular from 1700 or so until around the time of the American Revolution. Rooted in Renaissance ideals, the Georgian style was spread in America primarily by means of architectural guides or pattern books. The classic Georgian house is a two-story, double-pile, center-passage house that, in its purest form, is characterized by a formal symmetry embellished with robust classical detail, such as a floor plan that emphasizes the specialized functions of rooms. On the main facade, this symmetry most often translates into a central door flanked by two windows on the first floor and five evenly spaced windows on the second floor. Variations on the plan are described in terms of how the principal ground-floor rooms are located relative to the passage. The depth of the house also factors into the description. Thus, a side-passage, double-pile plan is composed of a full-depth stair passage with two rooms on one side and without rooms on the other.

Exterior ornamentation includes corner quoins, cornices with decorative molding and dentils, paneled doors emphasized with classical surrounds, and windows that are aligned both horizontally and vertically. The front entries of the earliest Georgian-style houses in the region lacked the decorative ornamentation that became popular by around 1760. Door surrounds ranged from simple moldings to more elaborate, heavily ornamented architraves flanked by engaged columns or pilasters and topped with classically inspired pediments. Windows might be similarly capped, with projecting stone flat arches or keystone lintels made of dressed stone or even wood. Windows were usually multipaned, double-hung sash characterized by wide, shallow muntins. Decorative cornice treatments included bed and crown molding, dentils, or modillion blocks, but most area examples were either boxed or simply finished with strips of ogee molding. Other exterior ornament, used on masonry buildings, included projecting horizontal divisions such as water tables and belt courses. In the Delaware valley, belt courses tended to function as flashing courses for pent roofs; in the Chesapeake and for higher-style buildings they were more purposely decorative.

Figure 4.2
Christopher Vandergrift House, Port Penn vicinity, St. George's Hundred, New Castle County, Delaware. Interiors in the earliest Delaware valley houses were characterized by exposed structural members, such as joists, wall plates, corner posts, and tie beams, that were often finished with details like beads, chamfers, and scooped, quirked, or lamb's tongue stops. The joist shown here is finished with a simple bead.

The highest-style interior finishes in the Georgian house were usually found on fireplace walls, which were embellished with raised panels and overmantels, some with classical details (Fig. 4.3). Pediments or crosseted surrounds sometimes emphasized overmantels in the most formal room; in less formal spaces, they were more plainly paneled. Fireplaces were often accompanied by symmetrically flanking closets, ranging from elaborate display cupboards with glass doors and butterfly shelves to plain storage closets concealed behind simple paneled doors. Georgian-style architraves, moldings, balusters, and stair handrails were generally characterized by a simple, forceful design and could be composed of a variety of ogees, cymas, beads, and fillets.

Historians and architectural scholars generally agree that the widespread adoption of the Georgian house plan amounted to much more than a transformation in taste or fashion; it marked one aspect of a fundamental change in attitudes—what some have called the shift to the Georgian world view. The Georgian ideals of symmetry, order, specialized room function, and privacy that were embodied in the architecture of the period signaled a movement away from a corporate or collective world view toward a growing emphasis on the individual. This new focus was reflected in other cultural artifacts as well. Like the increasingly private rooms in a Georgian-style house, objects such as dishes and chamberpots that had previously been shared by a number of people now began to be earmarked for individuals.

Similarly, consumer goods such as ceramics and furniture that had once served multiple functions were now designated for specialized purposes; many also began to be manufactured in matched sets.[3]

Numerous Georgian-style houses can be seen in many parts of the region. The Corbit-Sharp house in Odessa, Delaware (see Fig. 2.16), built in 1771–72, provides one of the finest examples of late Georgian architecture in the state. Typically Georgian exterior features on the Corbit-Sharp house include a five-bay, Flemish bond facade, pedimented front door surround with flanking columns, projecting brick water table, stone window lintels with carved keystones, stone belt course, and a modillioned cornice. The interior is arranged in a center-hall, double-pile plan and features a fully paneled drawing room with crosseted window surrounds, a crosseted overmantel topped by a broken arch pediment and flanked by fluted floor-to-ceiling pilasters, crossetted door surrounds topped with broken arch pediments, paneled wainscoting, and elaborately carved chair rails and baseboards (Fig. 4.4).

With a two-story, three-bay brick exterior and fully paneled fireplace walls, Aspendale, near Smyrna, Delaware, built in 1771–73, illustrates an example of mid-level Georgian building (Fig. 4.5). While the three-bay Flemish bond facade is ornamented with typically Georgian horizontal divisions, including a molded-brick water table, double brick belt courses, and modillioned cornice, the front entry lacks heavy ornamentation and is finished instead with a relatively simple molded architrave with overhead transom. Interior finish includes fully paneled fireplace walls, some with flanking paneled display and storage cupboards.

Some fine examples of Georgian dwellings have been extensively altered. The Parson Thorne Mansion in Milford, Delaware, illustrates a Georgian house that was overlaid with late-nineteenth-century stylistic elements (Fig. 4.6). Although remodeled more than once, the current building displays distinctly visible Georgian and Victorian characteristics. The earliest portion of the house, now the rear wing behind the five-bay main block, was a one-room, two-story frame dwelling built around 1730. The main house was constructed adjacent to this structure in the second quarter of the eighteenth century and exhibits several Georgian features, including a five-bay facade with pedimented central entrance, windows capped with splayed wooden lin-

Figure 4.3
Corbit-Sharp House, Odessa vicinity, St. George's Hundred, New Castle County, Delaware. Photographed by W. S. Stewart, HABS, 1936. The fireplace wall in the drawing room of this Georgian-style house is elaborately finished with a broken arch pediment and crosseted overmantel with flanking panels.

Figure 4.4
Corbit-Sharp House, Odessa vicinity, St. George's Hundred, New Castle County, Delaware. Photographed by W. S. Stewart, HABS, 1936. Georgian-style interior detailing includes broken arch pediments, crosseted door surrounds, and fully paneled walls.

tels and keystones, and an elaborate cornice with dentil blocks. When the house was altered in 1879, the remodeling was limited to the exterior of the building. At that time the roof was raised on the main block and the two wings, steeply pitched cross gables were added to each wing, and the gables were further embellished with pointed-arch windows. Although the exterior exhibits both Georgian and Victorian features, the interior retains its earlier Georgian finish; it features an elaborately paneled fireplace wall with a crosseted and pedimented overmantel and flanking fireplace cupboards with butterfly shelves.

The William Brady House, also known as Greenlawn, discussed later in this chapter, illustrates a more dramatic reworking of a later Georgian form. Built in 1810, the house was repeatedly modernized by later nineteenth-century owners who transformed the Georgian facade into a Gothic design. Dwellings such as Greenlawn and the Parson Thorne Mansion illustrate how Georgian stylistic elements can be augmented or absorbed by later changes. Many eighteenth-century examples of Georgian dwellings survive, and the style remains popular today (Fig. 4.7). The traditional Georgian notions of symmetry, balance, privacy, and the distinct functions of separate rooms continue to be applicable to contemporary lifestyles.

Federal

Succeeding the Georgian style, the Federal style became popular along the Eastern seaboard shortly after the American Revolution and remained current in the Delaware valley through the second and third decades of the nineteenth century. Essentially a development of the Georgian style, Federal architecture was largely the result of European architectural ideas. These ideas, promoted most forcefully in England by the architect Robert Adam and in the United States by Asher Benjamin, revolved around a renewed interest in classical Greek and Roman architecture and Renaissance forms. The resulting style, also called Adamesque, combined elements of these forms into a new and distinctive blend that was characterized by an emphasis on verticality, symmetry, delicate and restrained ornamentation, and carefully controlled proportions. Even avowedly "American" architects like Asher Benjamin failed to escape the tyranny of European tastes.

Figure 4.5

Aspendale, Kenton vicinity, Kent County, Delaware. Photographed by
Jack E. Boucher, HABS, 1982. Built during 1771–73 south of Smyrna,
Delaware, Aspendale provides an example of middle Georgian building.
The front entry lacks the heavy ornamentation of the Corbit-Sharp house
(see Fig. 2.16) and is simply finished with a molded architrave and overhead
transom. The interiors of Aspendale are finished with fully paneled fireplace walls, some with flanking paneled display and storage cupboards.

B

C

Figure 4.6
Parson Thorne Mansion, Milford vicinity, Kent County, Delaware. Photographed by Jack E. Boucher, HABS, 1982. The Parson Thorne Mansion, built in two separate stages during the eighteenth century and extensively remodeled in 1879, exhibits both Georgian and Victorian features on the exterior, but the interior retains its earlier Georgian finish.

Figure 4.7
Hockessin vicinity, New
Castle County, Delaware.
Photographed by David
Ames, 1995. The classic
Georgian style has been
widely used and reinter-
preted in modern subdivi-
sions throughout the Dela-
ware valley.

The George Read II House, constructed between 1797 and 1804 on the
Strand in New Castle, Delaware, provides a fine example of the Federal style
(Fig. 4.8). With its smooth, planar facade, Palladian window, and front door
ornamented with a semicircular fanlight and flanking sidelights, the Read
house exhibits all the hallmarks of high-style Federal design. Other notable
features include a low-pitched roof, balustrade with urns, and elongated six-
over-six-light sash windows capped with white stone window lintels ornamented with flat keystones. Like many buildings constructed during the Federal period, the Read house lacks the pronounced horizontal divisions—water
tables, belt courses, and heavy cornices—that were so prevalent on earlier
Georgian buildings. The interior, laid out in a center-hall, double-pile plan
with a side stair hall, is embellished with elaborately detailed center hall arch-
ways with fluted Doric pilasters, classically designed mantels and woodwork
that includes chair rails with punch and gouge detailing, and fanlights over
the double door between the front and rear parlors.

A hallmark of the Federal style was an increased emphasis on windows.
This shift, partly due to the growing availability of larger panes of glass after
the Revolution, translated into exterior facades punctuated by windows that
were often larger and more dominant than their earlier Georgian counter-

Figure 4.8
George Read II House, New Castle, New Castle County, Delaware. Photographed by David Ames, HABS, 1983. The George Read House exhibits all of the characteristics of the Federal style, which deemphasized horizontal elements and increased attention to vertical features.

parts. While both Federal and Georgian style buildings featured double-hung sash, Georgian windows often presented a heavier appearance because of the way they were constructed. Georgian style windows most often consist of many (usually 9 or 12) small panes of glass in each sash secured by broad, shallow muntins. In contrast, Federal-era windows are usually characterized by fewer (most often 6) and larger panes of glass held in place by narrower, deeper muntins (Fig. 4.9). The end result was a larger glazed surface with fewer vertical and horizontal interruptions. Other decorative elements were also employed to emphasize windows on Federal facades. Windows might be set in recessed or blind arches. Alternatively, they might be capped with restrained decorative elements, such as marble or rusticated and painted wood lintels and sills.

In Federal-style buildings, the front door was often accentuated with elaborate surrounds. These might range from single elliptical glazed fanlights to surrounds that incorporated fanlights, sidelights, attenuated columns or pilasters, and small entry porches (Fig. 4.10). The popularity of elliptical fanlights reflected one aspect of the Federal-era preference for incorporating nonrectangular geometric shapes, including octagons, ovals, and circles, into the overall architectural design. Classical motifs, such as urns, swags, and

Figure 4.9

Window muntins (seen here in cross-section) became progressively higher and narrower in profile from the eighteenth to the mid-nineteenth century. The heavier appearance of Georgian windows was due partly to the broad, shallow muntins (*top*, ca. 1780) that were used to secure multiple glass panes in the window sash. Federal-era windows, by contrast, were usually constructed with fewer and larger panes of glass, held in place by narrow, deeper muntins (*middle*, ca. 1790–1810). Muntins from mid-nineteenth century windows are narrower still (*bottom*, ca. 1835–45).

oval paterae or bull's-eyes, were utilized in the highest-style Federal interiors. Joinery techniques expanded to include delicate reeding, punch-and-gouge work, and decoratively edged paneling (Fig. 4.11).

The McGee House, a one-room plan house located in Indian River Hundred in Sussex County, Delaware, presents a more modest interpretation of the Federal style (Fig. 4.12). A number of other Federal-era one-room houses like this one, described as "mansions" or "mansion houses" in period documents, have been identified in Sussex County. These buildings are characterized by an elaborate interior finish housed within a conservative house form.

Examples of less elaborate Federal-period dwellings include the Kensey Johns House in New Castle and the Heller House in Odessa, Delaware. The Kensey Johns House, built in 1790, is a two-story, gable-roofed brick dwelling constructed as a side-hall, double-pile plan (Fig. 4.13; see also Fig. 2.18). Exterior features include a Flemish bond facade, a principal entry flanked by Doric pilasters and topped with a carved frieze and pediment, stone lintels with carved keystones, and a molded brick water table. Interior detailing includes an open-string, bracketed stair with slender balusters and crosseted overmantels as well as window, door, and fireplace surrounds. Interior finish in the Heller House is simpler still, consisting of restrained Federal-style mantels and paneled fireplace walls (Fig. 4.14).

While the George Read and McGee houses provide relatively "pure" and customary interpretations of the Federal style, the Bennett-Downs House in New Castle County illustrates a Federal building that has been extensively modified. At first glance, the house appears to have been built around 1870. In fact, the building dates to a much earlier period and underwent extensive alterations during the late nineteenth century. Closer inspection reveals some Federal elements that provide clues to the building's earlier origin and allow us to peel back the layers of architectural change. Begun in 1815, the house

Figure 4.10
Charles Thomas House, New Castle, New Castle County, Delaware. Photographed by W. S. Stewart, HABS, 1936. In Federal-style buildings, the front door was often accentuated with elaborate surrounds—elliptical fanlights, sidelights, attenuated columns or pilasters, and small entry porches. The doorway in this ca. 1801 house in New Castle is attributable to the shop of carpenter-joiner Peter Crowding.

was originally designed as a two-story, three-bay dwelling with interior chimneys (Fig. 4.15). The plan of the original core was unique in Delaware. When the house was remodeled in the late nineteenth century, a mansard roof was added and the entire facade was altered (see Fig. 1.2). The original brick facade, laid in Flemish bond with glazed headers, was stuccoed over and scored to simulate the smooth appearance of coursed ashlar (see Fig. 3.43). The mansard roof heightened the original main block and added a usable third floor to the interior. During the remodeling, the house was upgraded with such late-nineteenth-century stylistic features as paired brackets, paired round-headed windows, pedimented dormers, and a projecting cornice. Despite these alterations, some Federal features survive. For example, the house retains much of its original floor plan. When the mansard roof was added, the chimneys were heightened. Instead of tearing down and rebuilding the chimneys from the second story upward, the masons simply added to the existing chimney tops. As a result, the original corbeled chimney tops are still visible

A

B

Figure 4.11
Classical motifs such as swags and oval paterae, and joinery techniques such as delicate reeding and punch-and-gouge work
were utilized in the highest-style Federal interiors. (*A*) Sealand, ca. 1800, Northampton
County, Virginia. Photographed 1977. (*B*)
White Cliff, early 1800s, Eastville vicinity,
Northampton County, Virginia. Photographed 1977 (*C*) Geraldville, Port Penn vicinity, New Castle County, Delaware. Photographed 1982.

C

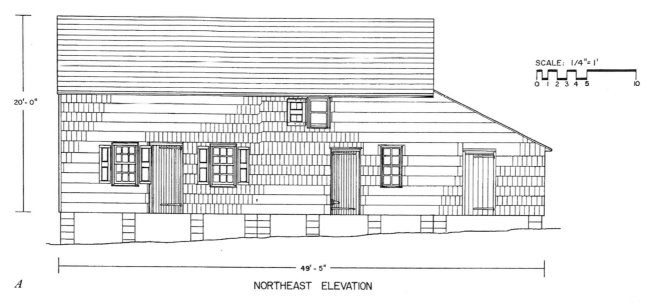

SCALE: 1/4" = 1'

0 1 2 3 4 5   10

20'- 0"

49' - 5"

A   NORTHEAST ELEVATION

Figure 4.12

McGee House, Angola vicinity, Indian River Hundred, Sussex County, Delaware. Drawn by Margaret M. Mulrooney, HABS, 1986. (*A*) The McGee House was originally built as a one-room dwelling. The earliest portion of the house is the center section seen on the northeast elevation (see also Fig. 8.6). (*B*) The house's Federal-period interior finish consists of fully paneled fireplace walls, mantels with reeded panels, boxed stairs, and built-in cupboards with glass-fronted bowfats.

B

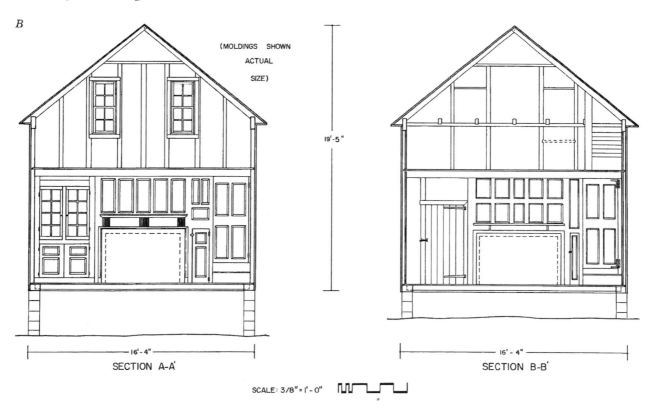

(MOLDINGS SHOWN ACTUAL SIZE)

19'-5 "

16'- 4"   16' - 4"

SECTION A-A'   SECTION B-B'

SCALE: 3/8" = 1'- 0"

A

Figure 4.13
Chancellor Kensey Johns House, New
Castle, New Castle County, Delaware.
Photographed by Edward W. Rosenfeld,
HABS, 1984. (*A*) The exterior of the
Kensey Johns House is furnished with
numerous Federal-style features, including Doric pilasters and a carved frieze
and pediment surrounding the doorway,
and stone lintels with carved keystones
on the windows. (*B*) The interior finish
includes crosseted fireplace surrounds
and fully paneled fireplace walls.

B

Figure 4.14
Heller House, Odessa, New
Castle County, Delaware.
Photographed by W. S.
Stewart, HABS, 1936.
Many Federal interiors
were simple and restrained,
as illustrated in these flat-
paneled fireplace walls and
plain mantels.

in the attic. Finally, the primary entrance on the first floor retains its original
Federal surround, including a space for an elliptical fanlight over the door
(Fig. 4.16).

Builders on the Eastern Shore and in southeastern Virginia and adjacent
North Carolina used a tripartite Federal design for some elite plantation
houses in the late eighteenth and early nineteenth centuries. In its most
common form, the typical tripartite house consisted of a two-story, gable-

fronted central block with flanking one-story wings placed at right angles to the core (Fig. 4.17). In plan, these houses are distinguished by a front passage (also known as a salon) that connected the principal room(s) in the main block to those in the wings. Variations on this plan include five-part designs with the outermost units also built with gable fronts. Similarly, gable-fronted houses based on the plan of the core but lacking flanking wings were built for wealthy merchants in a number of lower Chesapeake Bay cities.

With its emphasis on smooth surfaces, harmonious proportions, and Greek, Roman, and Renaissance forms, the Federal style was but one stage in the ongoing nineteenth-century movement toward a full-blown classical revival. By the 1820s and 1830s this interest in classicism had culminated in the broadly popular Greek Revival style.

Greek Revival

Associated with public buildings as well as domestic architecture, the Greek Revival style became popular enough from the 1830s to around 1850 to become the dominant building style in many parts of the United States. Mid-Atlantic builders did not seize upon full-blown Greek Revival style as enthusiastically as did their counterparts in places like upstate New York or along the southern reaches of the Mississippi River, however. In most of the region, builders tended to use Greek Revival motifs without recourse to the total image (Fig. 4.18). Ongoing archaeological investigations in ancient Greece inspired the classical ornamentation and proportions of the style, and decorative features associated with momumental Greek architecture became popular. The resulting style is characterized by mostly symmetrical principal facades, low-pitched roofs, pedimented gables, classical proportions, and heavy cornices with unadorned friezes. Porches supported by prominent columns were among the most widely repeated stylistic features (Fig. 4.19). Some Greek Revival buildings feature a classic Greek temple front that utilizes aspects of the Doric, Ionic, or Corinthian orders (Fig. 4.20). Temple fronts—either extending the full height and width of the facade or miniaturized as one- or two-story temple-form porticoes—appeared on commercial and public buildings, such as banks and courthouses, as well as on domestic architecture; but many houses instead utilized a rectangular transom over the door, often ornamented with flanking sidelights. In Greek Revival buildings, the arched and fan-shaped windows that were popularized in Federal-style buildings were discarded in favor of such entrances. Other Greek Revival features include gable fronts, raking cornices, tall first-floor windows, friezes with attic story windows, and front or corner pilasters. Exteriors were often painted white in imitation of the white marble of ancient Greek buildings; sometimes brick or stone buildings were stuccoed and grooved to simulate the smooth surface of coursed ashlar. Bold, simple moldings were utilized on the interior as well as the exterior. Greek Revival moldings differ noticeably from the heavier, more forceful moldings popular in Georgian and Federal buildings; Greek-derived moldings present a more elliptical appearance in profile (Fig. 4.21).

The architect Thomas U. Walter used Greek Revival detailing to soften the stark lines of Philadelphia rowhouses. In Portico Row, for example, built from 1831 to 1833, he utilized marble ionic tristyle (three-columned) porches with side-passage plan townhouses.[4] Although most Greek Revival buildings feature largely symmetrical facades with center or side passages, the floor plan, as in many other stylistic periods, is less expressive of the style than are the exterior features and interior embellishments.

Gothic Revival

The Gothic Revival, a romantic architectural style that was popular in the 1840s and 1850s but declined in popularity after around 1865, was in many ways a reaction to the classicism popularized by the Greek Revival. The style, which looked toward medieval antecedents, was the result of a general movement away from the limitations imposed by classical architecture and was popularized by pattern books like those of Alexander Jackson Davis and Andrew Jackson Downing. In the Gothic Revival style, the two separate architectural ideas of Christian symbolism and picturesque Romanticism were blended into a distinctive new style that mixed sacred and secular motifs. Medieval church architecture provided the inspiration for much of the ornamentation characteristic of the style. The Gothic Revival was primarily a rural building tradition and was rarely used in urban settings, largely because it was always promoted as an architectural style that was compatible with the natural landscape, but in part because the multiple gables and wide porches characteristic of the style were not physically suitable for narrow urban lots.

Buildings constructed in the Gothic Revival style are characterized by

Figure 4.15

Bennett-Downs House, Buena Vista vicinity, New Castle Hundred, New Castle County, Delaware. The original two-story, three-bay core, begun in 1815, still remains, despite late-nineteenth-century alterations that added a mansard roof and projecting bay windows. The house retains much of its original Federal floor plan, including a center passage, interior chimneys, and evidence of opposing doors in the hall.

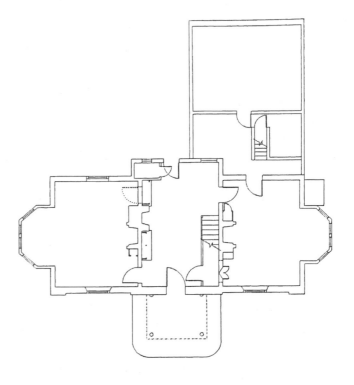

Figure 4.16

Bennett-Downs House, Buena Vista vicinity, New Castle Hundred, New Castle County, Delaware. Photographed by David Ames, HABS, 1991. The main first-floor entrance is another of the original Federal features that survived the house's extensive late-nineteenth century alterations.

Figure 4.17

White Cliff, Eastville vicinity, Northampton County, Virginia. Photographed 1977. On the Eastern Shore and in southeastern Virginia and adjacent North Carolina a tripartite Federal design was employed in some plantation houses built in the late eighteenth and early nineteenth centuries. The most common tripartite house consisted of a two-story, gable-fronted central block with flanking one-story wings at right angles to the core, as illustrated by the structure shown here.

A

B

Figure 4.18

In the Delaware valley, full-blown examples of the Greek Revival style are not as widespread as in other regions. Delaware valley builders typically appropriated individual Greek Revival motifs, such as the triglyphs ornamenting the front of the Boulden House (*A*) and the rectangular transom over the door of the Thomas Lamb House (*B*) and used them selectively. (*A*) George W. Boulden House, Pencader Hundred, New Castle County, Delaware. Photograph, by Richard Jett ca. 1981, courtesy of Delaware State Historic Preservation Office. (*B*) Thomas Lamb House, Blackiston, Kenton Hundred, Kent County, Delaware. Photographed by David Ames, HABS, 1994.

EVERYDAY ARCHITECTURE OF THE MID-ATLANTIC

A

B

Figure 4.19

Columned porches are a Greek Revival feature that shows up frequently. (*A*) Crystal Palace, Franktown, Northampton County, Virginia. Photographed 1995. (*B*) Cleremont, Mt. Cuba vicinity, Christiana Hundred, New Castle County, Delaware. Photographed by David Ames, HABS, 1986. (*C*) Abbott Tide-Mill Farm House, 1845, Salem vicinity, Salem County, New Jersey. Photographed by David Ames, HABS, 1991.

C

Figure 4.20
Woodlawn, Smyrna vicinity, Duck Creek Hundred, Kent County, Delaware.
Photographed by Courtlandt Van Dyke Hubbard, HABS, 1960. Originally
built in the 1700s but extensively altered in 1853, Woodlawn has been described as the most successful example of a Greek Revival temple front
building in Delaware.

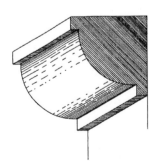 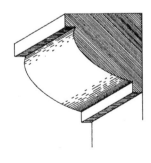

Figure 4.21
Greek Revival moldings (*right*) present a more elliptical appearance in profile than the heavier, more forceful Georgian
and Federal moldings (*left*).

Figure 4.22
Rockwood, Wilmington vicinity, New Castle County, Delaware. Photographed by David Ames, HABS, 1983. The multiple cross gables and asymmetrical massing visible here are hallmarks of the Gothic style.

picturesque, asymmetrical massing and varied building heights and are usually elaborately ornamented, whether they are constructed of wood, stone, or brick (Fig. 4.22). An emphasis on gables is a hallmark of the style. This emphasis often takes the form of multiple steep, narrow gables or central cross gables, which are typically ornamented with elaborately scroll-sawn vergeboards. The pointed arch, present in window openings, door surrounds, dormers, and porch ornamentation, is another feature of Gothic Revival architecture. Other Gothic details typically include towers, crenelations, quatrefoil decorations, angled bay windows, gabled dormers, paired casement windows, leaded stained glass, tracery, finials on gables and dormers, and contrasting colors of brick and stone. Gothic Revival dwellings are often characterized by asymmetrical plans that afforded flexible room arrangements and created the picturesque, asymmetrical exterior massing that exemplifies the style.

Gothic Revival buildings in the region range from full-blown interpretations of the style to greatly simplified examples that exhibit only one or two Gothic features. The Rose Cottage in Dover, Delaware, illustrates a fully developed Gothic Revival dwelling (Fig. 4.23). An Andrew Jackson Downing–style building, the three-bay house stands one-and-a-half stories high and is of frame construction. The house consists of a main block with two wings at the back that extend lengthwise. Typical Gothic Revival details include

A

B

Figure 4.23
Rose Cottage, Dover, Kent County, Delaware. Photographed by (*A*) Jack E. Boucher, HABS, 1982, and (*B*) David Ames, HABS, 1984. This Gothic Revival house was based on the designs of Andrew Jackson Downing and features an elaborately carved vergeboard, second-story casement windows, and a one-story front porch with low pointed arches and modillioned cornice.

a vergeboard that has been elaborately carved in a series of pointed arches; the vergeboard is further ornamented with pendants on the eaves and ridge. Other notable details include an angled bay window, first-floor windows with wooden hood and scrollwork sills, second-story casement windows, a one-story front porch with low pointed arches and modillioned cornice, and a front door ornamented with spade-shaped panels.

While examples of such nearly pure Gothic Revival buildings can be seen throughout the region, there are many instances in which earlier buildings have had Gothic features grafted onto them. In the Piedmont, there are relatively few examples of buildings constructed from the outset in the Gothic Revival style. More typically, a few Gothic stylistic features were applied over an earlier building as part of a remodeling. This method of upgrading was especially popular in many parts of the region. Greenlawn, introduced earlier, offers just such an example of the Gothicizing of an earlier form. The alterations to Greenlawn were heavily influenced by the writings of A. J. Downing, whose *Architecture of Country Houses* proved to be one of the more influential architecture books of the nineteenth century. The first major alterations included a new kitchen and dining room wing in 1830; around 1860, the kitchen wing was extended and refenestrated; finally, the main block of the house was enlarged into a double-pile plan and the grounds were relandscaped in the picturesque style around 1884 (Fig. 4.24). The alterations effected such dramatic changes that the exterior was almost completely Gothicized (Fig. 4.25). Mid-nineteenth-century Gothic features added to the facade included bracketed eaves, a cross gable, a balustraded roof deck, full-length windows, and an elaborate sawnwork and bracketed porch. The only surviving feature of the original circa 1810 Georgian facade was the round-arched paneled doorway on the west elevation (Fig. 4.26).

Greatly simplified versions of the Gothic Revival style appear as traditional house forms—hall-parlor or central-passage dwellings—with no other stylistic embellishments than a centrally placed cross gable or pointed-arch dormer windows (Fig. 4.27). In eclectic architecture, discussed later in this chapter, Gothic Revival details such as pointed arch windows, tracery, and scrolled vergeboards were often appropriated and utilized in combination with features of other nineteenth-century styles.

Italianate

An architectural style that became popular between 1850 and 1880 was inspired by Italian rural architecture. Intended to resemble the rambling villas

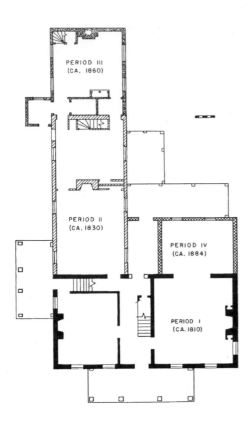

PERIOD III
(CA. 1860)

PERIOD II
(CA. 1830)

PERIOD IV
(CA. 1884)

PERIOD I
(CA. 1810)

Figure 4.24
Greenlawn, Middletown vicinity, New
Castle County, Delaware. Alterations to this
ca. 1810 Georgian-style house included a
new kitchen and dining room wing in 1830,
an extension and reworking of the kitchen
wing around 1860, and an enlargement
of the main block into a double-pile plan
around 1884.

Figure 4.26
Greenlawn, Middletown vicinity, New Castle County, Delaware. Photographed by David Ames, HABS, 1983. The only surviving ca. 1810 feature on this heavily Gothicized Georgian house is the round-arched paneled doorway on the west elevation, visible here beneath the elaborate sawnwork and bracketed porch.

Figure 4.25
Greenlawn, Middletown vicinity, New Castle County, Delaware. Photographed by David Ames, HABS, 1983. The original Georgian facade of this building was transformed into a Gothic design.

of the Italian countryside, the Italianate style originated in the romanticism of the Picturesque movement and was introduced to America primarily through the writings of Andrew Jackson Downing, Calvert Vaux, Samuel Sloan, and others.

While the general hallmarks of the Italianate style include overhanging eaves ornamented with bracketed cornices and an overall emphasis on verticality (Fig. 4.28), interpretations of the style throughout the region, like interpretations of the Gothic Revival style, can range from simple to elaborate. The most fully developed examples are characterized by low-pitched, hipped roofs with wide, projecting overhangs supported by brackets; tall entrance towers with round-topped, sometimes divided, entrance doors; elongated, round-headed, and sometimes paired windows capped with projecting hooded or pedimented and bracketed moldings; as well as by corner quoins, rusticated foundations, balustraded balconies, square cupolas, and arcaded porches (see Fig. 2.25). A less elaborate interpretation might feature only a few of the most essential elements of the style: tall, squarish proportions, a projecting, bracketed cornice, a few elongated, round-headed windows, and a divided front door. Typical interior ornamentation in Italianate buildings

A

Figure 4.27
The Gothic Revival style was utilized at varying levels of intensity, often
appearing as greatly simplified embellishments, such as the centrally placed
cross gables shown here, applied to traditional house forms. (*A*) Quinby vicinity, Accomack County, Virginia. Photographed 1995. (*B*) Burcham Farm
House, ca. 1870, Millville vicinity, Cumberland County, New Jersey. Photographed by David Ames, HABS, 1991. (*C*) Kennett Square vicinity, Chester
County, Pennsylvania. Photographed 1995.

A

B

Figure 4.28
Low-pitched roofs with wide overhangs and bracketed eaves
are characteristic of the Italianate style (see also Fig. 2.25).
(*A*) Padgett Funeral Home, Cedarville vicinity, Cumberland
County, New Jersey. Photographed by David Ames, HABS,
1991. (*B*) Salem vicinity, Salem County, New Jersey. Photographed 1995.

includes cast plaster cornices, ceiling medallions, and corner blocks on door and window surrounds. Because an emphasis on verticality was an important aspect of the style, most Italianate buildings rise at least two stories in height. Still, the Italianate style was flexible enough to lend itself to a variety of interpretations, including both symmetrical and asymmetrical facades as well as gable-fronted and towered examples. Unlike the Gothic Revival style, the tall, slender proportions of the Italianate style were well-suited to narrow urban lots as well as more expansive rural locations, and the style was adapted just as easily to attached rowhouses as it was to freestanding dwellings surrounded by extensive yards.

Like the Gothic Revival style which it eventually supplanted, the Italianate style was partly a reaction to the rigidity and formality of the classicism that had been stylistically dominant for the previous century. The Italianate style proved to be extremely popular in the Delaware valley, in part because it could be executed in a variety of ways. For example, farmhouses built in the Italianate style can be seen throughout Delaware; the largest and most impressive concentrations of them are around Middletown, in New Castle County. Most Italianate houses in the region are essentially Georgian houses with Italianate features such as bracketed cornices grafted onto them.

Monterey, built in 1847, illustrates the way the Italianate style was interpreted regionally (Fig. 4.29). The house incorporates features from the Georgian, Italianate, and Greek Revival styles. Italianate features—such as the low, hipped, standing-seam metal roof with projecting eaves and modillion cornice—and Greek Revival features—such as the single-bay entry portico with Doric entablature—are applied to a building that is essentially a Georgian-style center hall plan.

Second Empire

Like the Gothic Revival and Italianate styles, the Second Empire style was a further reflection of the popular interest in asymmetrical and picturesque forms. Popular from around 1860 to the mid-1880s, the Second Empire style reinterpreted earlier French styles but retained many Italianate features, such as decorative cornice brackets and towers. The most definitive stylistic feature is the mansard roof—a double-pitched roof with a steep lower slope and an overhang less pronounced than that of most Italianate roofs. The mansard roof, combined with other characteristic features—including projecting and receding surfaces, deep classical moldings, and ornamental details that were

A

B

Figure 4.29
Monterey, built 1847, McDonough vicinity, New Castle
County, Delaware. An Italianate roof (*A*) and Greek Revival
entry portico (*B*) were applied to a building with an essen-
tially Georgian-style center hall plan. Photographed by
David Ames, HABS, 1983.

Figure 4.30
Dover Green, Kent County, Delaware. Photographed 1993. The mansard roof is the most definitive feature of the Second Empire style.

emphasized by differently textured and colored materials—creates an overall effect that is ornate and monumental.

Mansard roofs are usually double pitched with a steeply pitched lower section and a low, shallowly pitched hipped upper section that often appears flat (Fig. 4.30). They almost always feature dormers. The lower slopes of such roofs can be built in straight, flared, concave, convex, or ogee shapes. They are often patterned, sometimes with ornamental tile or slate laid in contrasting colors, and are usually bounded by molded cornices above and below and ornamented with decorative brackets. Like the Italianate style, an identifying characteristic of the Second Empire style is the emphatic and often decorative treatment of the junction between the overhanging roof and the walls. Mansard roof tops were also sometimes embellished with ornamental cresting.

Other characteristics of the Second Empire style include solid, boldly ornamented forms. Ornamentation often consists of paired columns, pilasters, projecting towers, and classical pediments. Towers may be placed centrally or asymmetrically and are usually capped with mansard roofs that sometimes feature shapes that contrast with the shape of the main roof. Windows are frequently taller on the first floor than the upper floors and might be bracketed, hooded, or pedimented. Window openings, often round headed and grouped in pairs or threes, are sometimes flanked with pilasters or columns. Typical door treatments include arched double doors with glass upper panels. Finally, exterior wall corners are often decorated with quoins. In Second Empire, as in so many other architectural styles, plan is less of an identifier than is exterior ornamentation.

The Second Empire style shared the flexibility and adaptability of the Italianate style which it closely resembles. Second Empire styling was utilized frequently in public as well as domestic architecture, and the characteristic elements described above appear in both symmetrical and asymmetrical interpretations. While freestanding buildings allowed for the fullest expression of the most monumental and ornate features, many Second Empire elements, most notably mansard roofs, were also utilized in more closely spaced urban settings (Fig. 4.31).

The mansard roof design became especially popular for remodeling earlier buildings because it increased the total usable floor space in an existing house by providing better light and head room on the attic story. Close inspection of a building with a mansard roof can sometimes reveal an earlier

A

Figure 4.31
Freestanding buildings afforded the fullest expression of the most monumental and ornate Second Empire features, but many elements were also applicable to more closely spaced urban settings. (*A*) Ichabod Compton House, Mauricetown, Cumberland County, New Jersey. Photographed by David Ames, HABS, 1991. (*B*) Green Street vicinity, Middletown, New Castle County, Delaware. Photographed by David Ames, HABS, 1989. (*C*) Commercial block, Middletown, New Castle County, Delaware. Photographed by David Ames, HABS, 1985.

B

C

core that has undergone extensive remodeling. The Bennett-Downs House, discussed earlier in this chapter, offers an example of just such a remodeling (see Figs. 1.2, 3.43, 4.15, and 4.16). By the addition of a mansard roof and other prominent stylistic features, such as cornice brackets, paired upper-story windows, and a patterned roof covering, an earlier building could receive an updated look.

Stick and Shingle

The stick style of architecture was nationally popular during the 1860s and 1870s and derived its name from the "stickwork" decoration that appeared on exterior surfaces. Although not structurally significant, stickwork decoration was used to suggest the framework of the building. Stickwork, typically simple and angular, generally consisted of boards applied over a clapboard surface, usually joined at right angles but sometimes placed diagonally to resemble half-timbering. It could also appear as simple projecting bands. Stickwork decoration most often was used near roof gables and upper stories. Roof gables could feature decorative trusses at their apexes, while wide, overhanging eaves often revealed exposed rafter ends or brackets. Wooden wall surfaces might be ornamented with varied patterns of horizontal, vertical, or diagonal boards. To express the notion of structural honesty in architecture, features such as corner posts, roof rafters, purlins, brackets, porch posts, and railings were also exaggerated. Essentially an appropriation of medieval English building traditions, the stick style was characterized by verticality and an angular, asymmetrical silhouette. Other features of the style included a steeply pitched gabled roof, often with cross or steeply intersecting gables, pointed dormers, verandas, one-story porches, and wall surfaces with multiple textures. The stick style was a transitional nineteenth-century style which, with its angularity, asymmetry, and emphasis on surface decoration, resembled aspects of both the earlier Gothic Revival and later Queen Anne styles.

In the Delaware valley, there are relatively few fully developed examples of the stick style. Instead, as with so many other nineteenth-century styles, a few individual ornamental features, such as exposed rafter ends or decorative gable trusses, were utilized sparingly as decorative motifs.

Popular in the 1880s and 1890s, the shingle style was primarily associated with northeastern seaside resort architecture. Because it tended to be a fashionable style associated with architect-designed buildings, it was never as

Figure 4.32
Cape Charles vicinity, Northampton County, Virginia. Photographed 1995. This house exhibits elements of the shingle style, most notably the siding of continuous wood shingles and the asymmetrical massing.

widely adapted as some other contemporary styles. The most prominent feature of the style—and the source of its name—is a wall surface sided with continuous wood shingles and usually lacking corner boards. Other characteristics include steeply pitched or gambrel roofs, cross gables, wide porches, asymmetrical forms, large, open interior spaces, and a movement toward interweaving the interior and exterior spaces.[5] While this style is not particularly common in this area, there are a few examples (Fig. 4.32).

Queen Anne

Popularized in the nineteenth century by a group of English architects, the Queen Anne style began to appear in the United States around 1880. This style is characterized by contrasts of forms, materials, and textures. Asymmetrical massing, steeply pitched roofs, and varied shapes and surface textures contribute to the overall effect (Fig. 4.33). Motifs typical of the style were derived from medieval and Jacobean architecture, and the scale of many Queen Anne buildings was often unusually grand. Good examples of Queen Anne style houses can be seen in and around many towns, particularly Townsend and Middletown, Delaware, Kennett Square, Pennsylvania, and Woodbury and Bridgeton, New Jersey.

A

GOTTHARDT 1890 QUEEN ANNE
189 DELAWARE STREET
WOODBURY, NEW JERSEY

Figure 4.33
Queen Anne–style buildings typically utilize contrasts of
forms, materials, and textures. (*A*) Gotthardt House, 1890,
Woodbury, Gloucester County, New Jersey. (*B*) Lindale,
Magnolia, Kent County, Delaware. Photographed by Jack E.
Boucher, HABS, 1982.

B

Plain flat walls are seldom seen in this style. Instead, walls were decorated with varied textures or their surface planes were broken by towers, bay windows, wall insets, and overhangs. Combinations of surface textures are common. First floors faced with stone or brick typically contrast with upper stories sided with other materials. Plain weatherboards might be mixed on the same building with fish scale or other decoratively shaped shingles. Roofs tend to be gabled or hipped. Multiple gables, as well as high, front-facing gables or roof gables that overhang cutaway bay windows, are common in this style. Window treatments typically vary: key stylistic features are bay windows, beveled and leaded glass, and windows with a mixture of small and large panes, especially a large, central, square pane of glass surrounded by multiple smaller square panes. Stained glass windows, used singly or in groups, are also typical of the style. In contrast, door and window surrounds were characteristically left simple, and doors were often lit with a single large pane of glass at the top. Other decorative features include molded decorative bricks used for accent, carved ornamental wall panels, and turned and carved wooden decoration embellishing gables, cornices, and porches.

Contrast of forms is also typical. Rounded forms, such as towers, wraparound porches, and conical roofs, were juxtaposed with the angular shapes of walls, projecting bays, and hipped rooflines; vertical elements, such as steep gables, turrets, elaborately ornamented chimneys, and roof cresting, contrasted with horizontal features like textured banding or the extended horizontal line of a cornice or balustraded porch. A projecting round or polygonal tower with a conical roof is a common feature. Towers could be built of masonry or wood and were usually placed at the corner of the facade. Chimneys are often large and medieval in design, their masonry surfaces sometimes enlivened with patterns of projecting and receding brickwork. Large, open porches, many with rounded corners and balustrades, figure prominently in the style and are usually asymmetrical, often extending the full width of the facade and continuing along one or both side walls.

Queen Anne interiors are characterized by an openness, freedom, and asymmetry that departed markedly from the symmetry and classicism of the earlier Georgian and Federal styles. Typical floor plans feature a large central living area that contained both a fireplace and the stair to the upper floors; this central room flows directly into adjacent rooms. The projecting bay windows and towers that figure so prominently in this style produce multiple irregular spaces within, many of which flow directly into or provide illumination for larger living spaces (Fig. 4.34).

As in much of the country, the Queen Anne style proved to be popular and relatively enduring in the Delaware valley and appeared in masonry as well as frame and combination examples. While Queen Anne elements appear on attached buildings in urban settings, the style—with its multiple projecting forms, contrast of surface textures, and grand scale—realized its fullest expression in freestanding buildings (Fig. 4.35).

Eclectic

The eclectic style, popular in the late nineteenth and early twentieth centuries, has been defined in various ways. The term is used broadly to describe architecture that exhibits features borrowed from a number of different styles, drawing from all of the colonial American and European architectural styles. Georgian, Italianate, Second Empire, Gothic Revival, and Queen Anne stylistic features are often appropriated and recombined in a single building to create a unique architectural statement. Exterior details such as the paired windows and prominent, paired cornice brackets of the Second Empire style, Gothic-style trefoils or pointed arch windows, Queen Anne wraparound

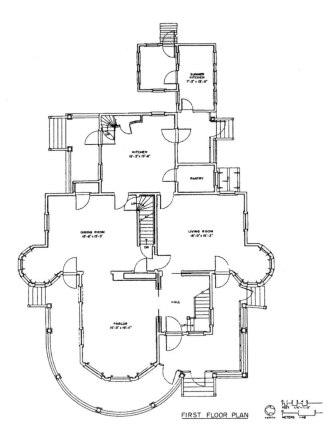

FIRST FLOOR PLAN

Figure 4.34
Lindale, Magnolia, Kent County, Delaware. Drawn by Scott Barnard and Charles B. Tonetti, HABS. In a typical Queen Anne floor plan, a large central living area opens directly into adjacent rooms.

 *A*

 *B*

Figure 4.35

The Queen Anne style, popular and relatively enduring in the Delaware valley, is best expressed in freestanding buildings. (*A*) Holland House, Eastville Station, Northampton County, Virginia. Photographed 1977. (*B*) 201 Delaware Avenue, Bridgeville, Sussex County, Delaware. Photographed 1993. (*C*) Whittington House, Crisfield, Somerset County, Maryland. Photographed 1995. (*D*) Crockett House, ca. 1890, Crisfield, Somerset County, Maryland. Photographed 1995.

 *C*

 *D*

A

Figure 4.36
Eclectic architecture is characterized by the combination of
elements derived from various style periods—Georgian,
Italianate, Second Empire, Gothic Revival, and Queen
Anne—to create a unique architectural statement. (*A*)
Henry Coulbourn House, ca. 1870, Crisfield, Somerset
County, Maryland. Photographed 1995. (*B*) Elkton vicinity,
Cecil County, Maryland. Photographed 1995.

B

porches, and wide, overhanging, Italianate-style eaves might be grafted onto buildings that retain essentially Georgian, central-passage plans (Fig. 4.36).

Bungalow

Bungalows, which contrast sharply with many of the grander and more heavily ornamented Victorian styles, began to appear around the turn of the twentieth century and remained popular through the 1930s. The bungalow, sometimes described as "a house reduced to its simplest form," was designed to harmonize with any landscape. To this end, the style emphasized naturally colored exterior walls, fine craftsmanship, and leaving construction materials as close as possible to their natural state. Characterized by low silhouettes with low-pitched, overhanging roofs and encircling porches, bungalows were originally designed as rustic leisure cottages but soon began to be constructed as permanent homes. While many bungalows throughout the region were built in newly developing suburbs, such as those in and around Wilmington, Delaware, they were also constructed in villages and other more rural areas. Single bungalows are a common sight, although the form was also frequently built in multiples.

Bungalows are typically three-bay, one- or one-and-a-half-story houses and can be constructed of frame, brick, stone, concrete block, or any combination of these materials. Frame bungalows are often shingled, although clapboarding is sometimes found on the exterior. The typical low-pitched, shallow roof terminates in deep, overhanging eaves supported by substantial brackets. The roof can be designed as a side-gable roof with the ridge of the roof parallel to the street or as a front-gable roof with the line of the roof perpendicular to the street. Exposed structural members, such as rafter ends that extend beyond the walls and roof, are common. A broad, deep porch with a flared base and a shed, cross gable, or pyramidal roof almost always extends across the facade and is supported by corner pillars. Porch pillars are often tapered and might be constructed of the same material as the dwelling or of a contrasting material. Other exterior features include bay windows and a centrally placed front door (Fig. 4.37 and Fig. 2.27).

As we have seen, the openness of the bungalow floor plan represented a major departure from earlier, closed house forms. Most bungalows were simply and functionally designed with open floor plans and interconnected rooms. Instead of opening into an entry hall, front doors often opened directly into living rooms; interior rooms were often interconnected or separated only

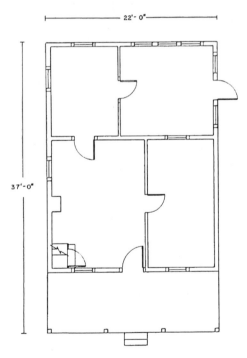

Figure 4.37

McCabe House, Roxana vicinity, Sussex County, Delaware. Photographed by Susan Chase, 1990. Drawing from Susan A. Mulchahey et al., *National Register of Historic Places: Adaptations of Bungalows in the Lower Peninsula/Cypress Swamp Zone of Delaware, 1880–1940.* Bungalows are typically three-bay, one-story or one-and-a-half-story houses. This rural adaptation lacks the built-in furniture usually found in the bungalow style.

by low half-walls. Many interiors had fireplaces with rustic cobblestone or brick hearths. Other features included exposed ceiling beams, stained wooden surfaces, and built-in cupboards, buffets, bookcases, and window seats. Bungalows typically had five or six rooms: a living room, dining room, kitchen, and two or three bedrooms, plus a bath.

The "craftsman bungalow" represents a popular variation on the bungalow form. Adhering to the general principles of bungalow design, the craftsman bungalow is notable for details which emphasize construction elements as decorative features. Often the features that were highlighted reflected antiquated building methods—such as mortise-and-tenon carpentry—that served no real structural purpose in the more modern dwelling. Alan Gowans captures the craftsman style most succinctly, tracing its origins to Gustav Stickley's concept that an "honest home let its materials and structure be frankly and freely expressed." Gowans identifies several craftsman hallmarks, including dramatically projecting rafters, visually assertive wooden elements like canted columns and curved roofs, and ornamental stonework or clinker brick that stresses rough-hewn texture.[6]

Colonial Revival

The Colonial Revival style had a significant and lasting impact on Delaware valley architecture. Popularized in large part by the Philadelphia Centennial of 1876, the style became increasingly popular during the late nineteenth and early twentieth centuries; and, as evidenced by modern subdivisions throughout the region that still feature Colonial Revival–style houses, it continues to be widespread today (Fig. 4.38). Perhaps because Colonial Revival styling seems to impart an air of respectability, it has also been a popular treatment for a wide variety of public buildings, including schools and commercial buildings, even gas stations.

The Colonial Revival style appropriates some features of earlier architectural styles. Typically interpretations of true colonial period buildings rather than exact copies, Colonial Revival buildings borrow stylistic elements from Georgian, Greek Revival, and Federal buildings, especially porticoes, sidelights or fanlights, pedimented doors and windows, paneled doors, dormers, and multipaned windows. These features are often exaggerated, especially in earlier examples of the style. For instance, front entrances are often emphasized with pedimented porticoes, flanking pilasters, and sidelights or fanlights; broken arch or swan's neck pediments over doors and windows are

A

Figure 4.38
The Colonial Revival style, which gained currency in the late nineteenth century, remains popular throughout the region. (*A*) Elkton vicinity, Cecil County, Maryland. Photographed 1995. (*B, C*) Newark vicinity, New Castle County, Delaware. Photographed 1995.

B

C

frequently overstated. These borrowed architectural features are often utilized very differently than they would have been in their original prototypes. Front entries feature sidelights without accompanying fanlights, prominent porticoes are typically finished with curved undersides, multipaned double-hung sash windows are often used in pairs, gambrel roofs are steeply pitched and usually furnished with full shed dormers, and two-story buildings are built with flat-roofed, one-story wings—all features that would have been uncommon in original examples. Builders in the Colonial Revival style also employ hipped roofs, flat arches with large, exaggerated keystones, elaborate windows placed prominently above entrances, and modillioned cornices, sometimes combining them with elements from more modern styles. Symmetry is often associated with the style. While the earliest Colonial Revival buildings were more likely to feature exaggerated "colonial" elements, many later examples are more accurate copies of their colonial predecessors. This change is due largely to the wider dissemination of information about colonial architecture.

While many buildings were designed from the outset with Colonial Revival features, overlays of Colonial Revival styling have sometimes been applied to earlier cores. Belmont Hall, built in the last quarter of the eighteenth century for a wealthy landowner, blends Colonial Revival and Georgian features. A three-story, five-bay brick dwelling with two rear service wings, Belmont Hall was Gothicized in the nineteenth century. Subsequently heavily damaged by fire in 1922, the building was partially rebuilt and restored soon afterward using many Colonial Revival elements (Fig. 4.39).

Early in the twentieth century, several restoration architects fueled popular interest in early architecture and contributed tremendously to the Colonial Revival in the mid-Atlantic region by restoring, remodeling, and in some cases completely reworking earlier dwellings. R. Brognard Okie of Philadelphia was one of the most well-known of these early restoration-preservationists, and the results of his efforts can be seen throughout the region. From 1898 to 1918, Okie worked with the architectural firm of Duhring, Okie, and Ziegler. This firm was responsible for numerous projects, most of which were based on the kind of residential development that was taking place in Philadelphia at the turn of the century. When Okie resigned from the firm in 1918, he continued to practice privately, concentrating his efforts on the restoration and reconstruction of colonial and Federal-period buildings. Most of his projects consisted of alterations and additions to private residences, although he also restored several public buildings. While his work ranged throughout the

mid-Atlantic region and occasionally extended as far afield as Kentucky, most of his projects were based in Pennsylvania. Okie's most famous projects were probably Pennsbury Manor—the reconstructed home of William Penn—and the Betsy Ross House in Philadelphia.[7] Although Okie is generally viewed as a gentlemen farmer's architect, not all of his projects were large and expensive houses. Like many other Depression-era architects who designed for a clientele with memories of a finer life, he was often forced to be pragmatic, and several of his projects were modest suburban dwellings.[8] Many of these "restorations" tended to be rather interpretive, and in some cases disruptive, of the original building fabric. Materials from other houses were often removed and appropriated for use in a different setting, and architectural details that were evocative of the colonial era but not necessarily historically accurate were sometimes utilized. While many of these early restorations may seem inappropriate by today's more exacting standards, architects such as Okie must be credited for promoting popular awareness of and appreciation for

Figure 4.39
Belmont Hall, Smyrna vicinity, Kent County, Delaware. Photographed by Courtlandt Van Dyke Hubbard, HABS, 1960. Built in the last quarter of the eighteenth century and heavily restored after a fire in 1922, Belmont Hall exhibits both Colonial Revival and Georgian features.

Figure 4.40
Merestone, Mill Creek Hundred, New Castle County, Delaware. Photographed 1995. Early-twentieth-century restoration architects such as R. Brognard Okie of Philadelphia fueled popular interest in early architecture and contributed tremendously to the Colonial Revival in the mid-Atlantic region. Okie renovated, enlarged, and modernized the log core of Merestone, and added visually sympathetic wings to either gable.

early buildings, several of which might never have survived in any form without his efforts (Fig. 4.40).

Four-Square Style

The term *four-square* refers to a house type that is often grouped with Colonial Revival buildings but will be treated separately here, because it is encountered frequently enough and is distinct enough to deserve special attention. Commonly seen throughout the region in suburban as well as more rural settings, four-square houses are usually two-story, two-bay dwellings constructed in a cubic shape and topped by a pyramidal or hipped roof (Fig. 4.41). A one-story columned porch extending the full width of the main facade is a common exterior feature. Porch columns were sometimes constructed in closely set pairs, were sometimes tapered, and often stood on substantial masonry pedestals. Front-facing hipped dormers, containing single or paired windows, are often present. Some four-square houses have four dormer windows, one on each slope of the roof. A window or series of windows intended to provide light for the stair is often located midway between the first and second floors on one side exterior wall. Side bay windows on the first or second floor are also typical.

This style of dwelling began to be built in the last decade of the nineteenth century and remained popular until around 1920 or so. Four-square houses were constructed in brick, frame, rusticated concrete block, and a mixture of materials. Almost always nearly square in plan, the first floor usually consists of a living room, dining room, kitchen, and a half-depth side passage; the second floor is typically laid out with four bedrooms and a bath. Architectural detailing in four-square houses can derive from several different styles; readily incorporated are features from bungalows and from the broader range of Colonial Revival architecture.

Manufactured Houses

During the early part of the twentieth century, a new and different type of housing appeared on the American landscape. Mail-order houses from Sears, Roebuck and Company, Aladdin, Montgomery Ward, and other manufacturers made the dream of home ownership a reality for many families. House designs ranging from bungalows and summer cottages to spacious, multistory dwellings were selected by manufacturers to appeal to a wide audience. Mail-order houses offered consumers quality construction at an affordable price and gave homeowners the opportunity to be directly involved in the building process. Manufactured houses usually consisted of a complete package that included plans, building instructions, and precut materials, all shipped by train to the building site. Customers could also purchase the plans alone and construct their houses with locally milled materials (Fig. 4.42).

Mail-order houses came in a variety of floor plans. Available designs ranged from more closed plans, with partial- or full-depth central halls separating the less formal rooms, to open plans, with rooms that were largely contiguous. While some designs offered a clear division between public and private space, others blended public and private spaces. Consumers could select from several different spatial arrangements that offered a range of choice but still reflected the standardization of the construction process.[9]

Other Styles

Other styles or stylistic elements that appear occasionally within the region include French Chateau, Mission, Egyptian Revival, and Eastlake styles. French Chateau dwellings, most visible in northern New Castle County, Delaware, are characterized by large, steeply pitched hipped roofs, upward-flaring eaves, and stuccoed wall surfaces. Arched dormer windows and prominent chimneys are also common features. Identifying elements of Mission-style houses, popular in the last decade of the nineteenth century until about 1920, include red tile roofs, wide overhanging eaves, and porch roofs supported by large, square piers. The Egyptian Revival style is very rare in the Delaware valley but a few examples do exist. The most visible characteristic of this style includes prominent Egyptian columns, usually resembling bundles of sticks tied together at top and bottom and flared at the top. Popular at the end of the nineteenth century, Eastlake stylistic motifs are named for the English architect and furniture designer Charles Locke Eastlake whose book, *Hints on Household Taste*, fueled a demand for simple, tasteful design. Eastlake popularized rectilinear, Gothic-inspired designs characterized by "honest" construction and structural integrity. Eastlake motifs most often include spindlework—consisting of decorative sawn spandrels ornamented with turned beads—on porch balustrades and friezes and incised decorative ornamentation on projecting gables (Fig. 4.43).

After assessing a building in terms of its architectural style as well as its form and construction features, we can begin to reweave all of this information into an integrated architectural narrative that may help to inform broader historical questions. In the remaining chapters, we will shift our attention away from

A

B

Figure 4.42
Mail-order houses from Sears, Roebuck and Company, Aladdin, Montgomery Ward, and other manufacturers made the dream of home ownership a reality for many families. (*A*) Miller-Hudson House, Williamsville vicinity, Baltimore Hundred, Sussex County, Delaware. Photographed by Susan Chase, 1990. From Mulchahey et al., *National Register of Historic Places: Adaptations of Bungalows in the Lower Peninsula/ Cypress Swamp Zone of Delaware, 1880–1940.* The original owners purchased the Sears, Roebuck design "The Westly," and built this house of wood cut from the property and milled locally. (*B*) Another Sears house, Cape Charles, Northampton County, Virginia. Photographed 1995.

Figure 4.43

Woodstown, Salem County, New Jersey. Photographed 1995. Motifs popularized by English architect Charles Locke East-lake often include spindlework on porch balustrades and friezes and incised decorative ornamentation on projecting gables.

the basic tools for looking at buildings and will turn instead to studying particular types of buildings. We will begin with an examination of agricultural buildings and will then briefly address industrial, commercial, and religious architecture. Finally, we will examine the implications of architectural fieldwork for broader landscape studies and will conclude with a discussion of several methods for studying and recording architecture.

FARM OUTBUILDINGS
AND PLANS

Farm buildings write the history of the agricultural landscape. The plans and construction of barns, granaries, stables, corn cribs, wagon houses, and cart sheds remind us of the ways in which farmers tilled their soil, stored their harvests, and organized their work. The discussion of chronology and geography in this brief introduction grossly oversimplifies the complexity of the region's agricultural history and architecture. The historical periods suggested below overlap by decades; the geographical subregions have no hard boundaries but are drawn based on the evidence of standing buildings and documentary evidence obtained from sources ranging from orphans' court property valuations to federal agricultural census returns. Still, the general observations provide enough background for us to seek out, evaluate, and interpret agricultural buildings. Our chronology starts with the oldest generation of surviving buildings. Sadly, there are almost no colonial farm buildings standing anywhere in the region. Thus, our understanding of the earliest farm architecture depends on the painstaking research of documentary historians and archaeologists.

Moreover, there are simply more types of farm buildings representing more local stylistic variations than an introductory field guide can address. As in our discussions on house form and construction, the goal here is to help you learn to look at buildings and recognize functional and formal classifications. Looking at farm buildings through an archaeological lens includes evaluating how form and construction combine with location and chronology to suggest how the barns, granaries, stables, and other structures worked in the context of local farming practice. Once individual buildings have been described and identified, you can build comparative interpretations by looking at functionally similar structures in other settings. Through this strategy, you can look at the range of barn types across the region as well as over time. Through a comparative approach, you can then begin to talk about how barns signify different approaches to farming and how builders employed local knowledge to house those approaches.

Chronologically, surviving barns and farm structures define three major periods in the region's agricultural development. The first of these periods runs from the eighteenth century into the 1830s and is characterized by a grain-based agricultural economy in the Delaware valley and a tobacco-based economy in the Chesapeake. By the mid-1700s, however, Chesapeake Bay country farmers had also switched to grain. In the Philadelphia hinterland, the cultivation of wheat and corn occurred along with the growth of dairying and cattle raising. From New Jersey to Virginia, the most commonly cultivated grain was corn. Other types of agricultural produce included Delaware brandies distilled from local peaches and apples, cow hides for leather, and wool sheared from sheep.

The second extended phase of agricultural development that we can deduce from extant buildings ran from the early 1800s into the early twentieth century, a period which encompassed significant changes in agricultural building design and construction. The excavation of the Chesapeake and Delaware Canal in 1829, the extension of railroad lines from Philadelphia southward, and the development of numerous spur lines throughout the region in the mid-1800s exerted a tremendous influence on how and what farmers cultivated. High speed rail transport made it possible to ship even the most perishable crops, such as strawberries and peaches, out of the local area. The agricultural depression following the Civil War also had a lasting impact on agriculture in the region. It brought a shift toward more diverse crops: fruits, vegetables, and grains. We can characterize this middle period by the industrialization of agriculture, the emergence of strong regional urban markets, and the advent of "scientific" and "mechanized" farming. In the first half of this protracted period, from around 1830 to 1880, what was produced by area farms remained much the same. What changed was the scale and extent of farming as well as farm building size and design. The latter part of the period, after 1880, witnessed a general stagnation in the architecture of agriculture. Economic setbacks during the 1870s, the rise of midwestern and western wheat cultivation, and the subsequent relocation of the national milling industry to the upper Midwest undermined local pre–Civil War agricultural prosperity. Farm buildings in this second phase of the period continued older design traditions, though they tended to be scaled back and to contain a mix of farming activities. The closing decades of the 1800s also saw a rise in the cultivation of more perishable crops, which required rapid transportation to market: peaches grown on the plains of central Delaware, strawberries and melons cultivated in the sandy soils of Virginia, tomatoes from the flat countryside of southwestern New Jersey, and even marine harvests of oysters, wildfowl, terrapins, and fish from the Chesapeake and Delaware bays. While the economics of agriculture seem to have been more volatile in the waning years of the nineteenth century, the design of agricultural buildings remained conservative and familiar.

The third period of agricultural building activity covered here runs from the first decades of the twentieth century to the 1940s. The major changes that occurred during this period involved the introduction of engine-driven tractors and trucks, the electrification of rural areas, the growing importance of hygienic standards (especially for dairying), the introduction of large-scale poultry farming, and the geographic expansion of truck farming. This third phase also brought significant changes in the design and appearance of farm buildings. Older buildings, especially those built to house draft animals or loose hay, became obsolete and were either recycled to other purposes or pulled down. At the same time, farmers erected new types and styles of farm structures. In southern Delaware, for example, farm owners commissioned a number of bow-roofed dairy barns with ground-level milking parlors built of brick or terra cotta block. The first generation of Eastern Shore chicken houses also made their appearance at this time. Often hundreds of feet in length, these ground-hugging structures sometimes included a two-story chickenkeeper's dwelling in the center.

Now, even the comparatively recent farm architecture of the first half of the twentieth century is disappearing with astonishing rapidity. Post–World War II housing developments and industrial ventures have encroached on arable land throughout the region. Similarly, agricultural practices continue to evolve. The primary crops throughout much of the central Eastern Shore and southeastern Pennsylvania are wheat, feed corn, and soybeans. Harvesters thresh the grain as it is cut, and farm trucks haul the crop to weigh stations and large storage facilities. The main crop kept on the farm is hay, which feeds the decreasing number of dairy herds, as well as horses, which are kept for recreation and show rather than work. Fruits and vegetables, including melons, peppers, tomatoes, potatoes, and cucumbers, contribute to the farm economies of southern New Jersey and the Eastern Shore of Virginia. Large canneries, roadside farmstands, and migrant labor housing document the textures of twentieth-century truck farming.

Changes in agriculture translate into changes in the landscape. Farm buildings and the changes made in their design, function, and siting over time remain the best sources we have for learning about the history of agriculture. Documents such as inventories and agricultural census returns tell us about what and how much farmers grew. Farm buildings, however, inform us about how they actually engaged in the business of farming. Barns from the mid-1800s show evidence of how animals were kept, tools stored, and crops processed; annual counts of the numbers of bushels of corn dumped into granary bins are still found carved or painted on granary walls. This chapter describes some of the basic forms of agricultural architecture, and, like the other sections of this book, does not pretend to offer an encyclopedic listing of all the farm buildings standing in the countryside. We offer a core of information. Looking at farm buildings in the field will add to this body of information in ways that will enable the reader to explore the history of farming through the archaeology of these buildings and to reflect on the historic uses of the land.

Early Farm Buildings, 1780–1830

The oldest farm buildings that survive in significant numbers date from the first couple of decades after the Revolution and generally reflect a growing improvement in architecture (a trend also displayed in housing). Our knowledge of agricultural architecture of the colonial period is based almost exclusively on documentary and archaeological evidence, although there remain a handful of exceptional barns and granaries.

Even as we look at surviving farm buildings of the post-Revolutionary period, we must remember just how few of these structures actually remain. At present, for example, no more than a dozen pre-1830 feed barns are known to be standing in the area of Delaware that stretches from the Chesapeake and Delaware Canal to the Sussex County line. Similarly, diminishing numbers of the big Pennsylvania barns remain. The conversion of arable land for housing developments, changing agricultural practices, and the expense of maintenance have doomed many of these monumental barns. Within our study area, it is only in the more heavily agricultural landscapes north and west of Philadelphia that significant numbers of these buildings still stand.

The largest structures and most durable traditions in farm architecture in the region were in the Piedmont of northern Delaware and Maryland and in southeastern Pennsylvania. Here average farm size decreased in the early

1800s even as the amount of acreage in production on any given farm increased. The result was an agricultural landscape operating at greater efficiency. The farm building most closely associated with this process is the bank barn, a large two- or three-level barn with an embanked lower level for animal housing and upper floors for hay mows, grain processing, and storage.

The opposite of the highly developed landscapes of the Piedmont counties were those associated with the heavily forested and swampy areas around the Cypress Swamp straddling the southernmost portion of the Delaware-Maryland line. In Delaware's Dagsborough and Broad Creek hundreds, for example, the typical farm of 1830 remained largely wooded with marketable timber. Farm land was usually adjacent to the house lot or consisted of distant "outfields" that were surrounded by split rail or pole fences for protection from free-ranging swine and native vandals, such as bears. The primary crop in this area was corn, and the most common farm building was the pole-built corn crib. The open lands of the upper Eastern Shore were dedicated to an agriculture based on the cultivation of wheat as well as corn. Dairying and buttermaking, which would grow as a significant segment of the farm economy, were also pursued. Farmsteads in these counties generally possessed numerous barns and outbuildings grouped in courts or ranges. Each of these buildings tended to be functionally specific: the barn held hay and feed, stables sheltered horses, granaries contained the grain, cart sheds protected wagons from the weather. The dominant farm building of this area is the feed barn—a roughly 20 by 40 foot frame barn divided into three spaces for processing and storing hay, grains, and animal feed.

Bank Barns

A bank barn is a two- or three-story multipurpose barn generally sited with one wall built into a natural or manmade earthen embankment (Fig. 5.1). The primary design goal of the bank barn was to incorporate as much stabling, stalling, crop storage, and processing as possible into a single efficient structure. The close identification of this barn with the British and German settlement areas of the Delaware valley led nineteenth-century writers to term this building the "Pennsylvania barn." The bank barn's reputation drew on its close association with images of agricultural productivity and progressive or scientific farming. One author concluded his comments on the plan of a Philadelphia-area bank barn with this commendation: "consider the perfect manner in which this building has been planned and finished, embracing every desirable comfort without any waste of room, and the arrangement of which precludes all waste of labor."[1]

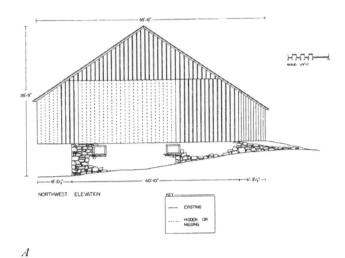

NORTHWEST ELEVATION

KEY
——— EXISTING
····· HIDDEN OR MISSING

A

Figure 5.1

Bank barns are usually two- or three-story multipurpose barns situated with one wall built into a natural or created earthen embankment. (*A*) Fahnestock Barn, Waynesboro vicinity, Franklin County, Pennsylvania. Drawn by Penelope Schaffer Gioffre, HABS. (*B*) Green Meadow Barn, ca. 1809, Appoquinimink Hundred, New Castle County, Delaware. Photographed 1988.

B

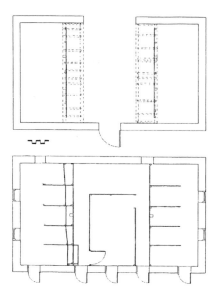

Figure 5.2
Peters Barn, 1810–30, Mill Creek Hundred, New Castle County, Delaware. Drawn by Stuart Dixon. Bank barns were designed for maximal efficiency, the goal being to incorporate as much stabling, stalling, crop storage, and processing as possible into a single structure. The lower story (*bottom*) was usually divided into stalls and pens for housing horses, cows, and calves. Access to the upper story (*top*) was by an earthen ramp that led up to a centrally placed wagon bay and threshing floor.

Bank barns might be of stone construction or built with heavy timber frame or have log upper stories over a stone lower story. Frame bank barns were constructed on a principal post-and-rail system and vertically sided. Log barns were composed of two separate pens divided by a central runway, which was used for threshing. Stone bank barns typically possess a framed, vertical-sided front wall, but the gable and back walls are stone. Regardless of walling materials, bank barns are covered with steep gable roofs carried on heavily framed principal rafter roof trusses.

The interior organization of the bank barn consists of a lower banked story divided into stalls and pens for housing horses, cows, and calves (Fig. 5.2). Access to the stabling areas consists of several doors across the downhill side of the barn (which usually faces south or east). Each door opens onto either a feeding aisle or the stalls. Decades of manure, crushed straw, and dirt often hide the fact that the stall floors were paved with cobbles or fieldstone. Farmers laid straw over the cobbles to protect the hooves of their animals and to provide bedding. Once soiled, the straw and manure were removed and composted for fertilizer. The doors into the lower level of the bank barn are typically divided horizontally into what are popularly known as Dutch doors. The top door can be opened while the bottom remains latched. This arrangement provides light and ventilation without the risk of escaped livestock. The lower level of the bank barn opened onto a paddock or pound. Walled with stone or fenced, the pound contained the general work area of the barn, where horses were groomed and harnessed, cows branded, and manure stored in piles. Few of these pounds survive.

The upper stories of the bank barn are entered by way of an earthen ramp. The interior organization of the upper floor of a bank barn most often follows a three-part plan comprising a central runway or threshing floor flanked on either side by hay mows. The plan was defined by the framing system that rose through the building to carry the heavy roof trusses required to span the 30-foot or greater depth of the building. In some bank barns, the hay mows shared a story with the runway; in others the hay mows were dropped down a full story on either side. The latter arrangement minimized the amount of lifting required of farm laborers engaged in stacking the harvest that fed and bedded the animals below. Barns with drop-away hay mows enabled their builders to incorporate grain bins and threshing operations under the runway. In some instances, farmers extended their barns with bridge houses, small structures that joined the barn to the ramp. Bridge houses were sometimes used as extra grain storage space. The early bank barns associated with English-speaking settlements typically lacked forebays, second-story extensions of the front. Where forebays exist, closer examination reveals them almost invariably to be additions made in the middle to late 1800s.

Delaware valley bank barns have their roots in three traditions. First, many of the British settlers of northern Delaware and extreme southeastern Pennsylvania came from the north and west of England, where a tradition of building bank barns without forebays began to take hold in the middle to late 1600s. Second, a significant number of Pennsylvania's settlers had migrated to the region from Germany and Switzerland, where a tradition of building barns with forebays was well-established long before any outmigration began.[2] This tradition provided the likely antecedents for the Pennsylvania-German bank barn. Third, the majority of surviving bank barns throughout the region date to an early period of agricultural reform when the notion of consolidated farm functions was gaining favor. The effective combination of tradition and innovation found its perfect resolution in the great bank barns of eastern Pennsylvania and adjacent Delaware and Maryland.

Three-Bay Barns

From the coastal plain of New Jersey through parts of Virginia's Eastern Shore, the predominant barn form in the post-Revolutionary period was a three-bay barn. Also known as Yankee, English, feed, or runway barns, these barns were typically of frame construction, measuring 20 to 25 feet deep and 35 to 50 feet long, and were divided on the interior into three spaces structurally defined by the frame itself (or in log examples by the log pens and the space between them) (Fig. 5.3). Entry into the three-bay barn was gained through tall double doors centrally placed in both long walls of the building and opening onto the runway. In terms of overall form, all three-bay barns appear similar, but individually they seem to have been tailored to meet the requirements of particular farm functions. For example, feed barns, the most common surviving form of these barns, sit 2 to 3 feet above grade and are completely floored on the interior. The interior spaces appear to have been dedicated entirely to crop processing and storage. The Davies Barn near Little Creek, Delaware, represented this type of usage (Fig. 5.4). Roughly 24 feet by 33 feet, the framed and wood-floored Davies Barn stood on a full rubble-stone foundation. The central bay served as a threshing and fanning area while the spaces to either side served as hay mows and granaries. The positioning of timbers in the construction of the Davies Barn also allowed for the insertion of temporary loft floors, thereby permitting hay mows to be placed over grain storage spaces.

Documentary evidence and a handful of surviving examples suggest that most three-bay barns served more general functions. In the general purpose three-bay barn, farmers used the central area for crop processing, storage, and to shelter farm wagons and other tools. The spaces to either side were typically designed for housing animals, with cows and horses segregated and facing each other across the runway. Pole joists laid across the nailing rails in the gables, as well as the tie beams defining the runway bents, supported mows of loosely stacked hay. Some barns combined the functions of a feed barn with more general usage. One end of the building might be floored and dedicated to grain storage and threshing, the central runway dedicated for use as a work area, and the opposite end reserved for stalling. Overhead, these barns often incorporated provisions for a temporary hay loft. Still other barns followed the three-bay division but in individual ways. The plan of one southern Delaware example, the Marsh Barn, reveals that the building was designed with a central runway work area, a hay mow, and corn cribs (Fig. 5.5). The corn cribs, however, were built as sheds that were integral to the original barn design, and this produced a barn elevation that appeared to be the result of addition rather than carefully wrought design.

Almost all recorded examples of frame three-bay barns followed the same basic construction pattern. Each barn was raised in four bents, framing units that defined the interior spaces; the basic arrangement included two gable bents and two runway bents. Each bent was preassembled flat on the ground and then raised into place. The siding (usually vertical boards) was fastened to horizontal nailing rails that joined the bents. Usually two nailing rails were

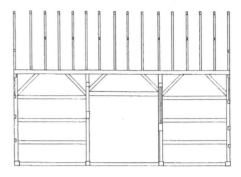

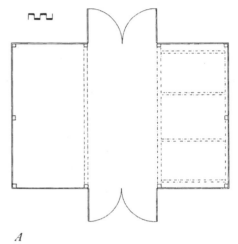

A

Figure 5.3

Three-bay barns, the predominant barn type in the eighteenth century from the coastal plain of New Jersey through parts of Virginia's Eastern Shore. The interior is divided into three bays or spaces (*A*). The Retirement Barn, built sometime between 1800 and 1820, is the last known surviving example of a three-bay or traditional English-style barn in southern New Castle County, Delaware. (*A*) Drawn by Meg Mulrooney and Bernard L. Herman. (*B*) Retirement Barn, Biddles Corner vicinity, New Castle County, Delaware. Photographed by David Ames, HABS, 1982.

B

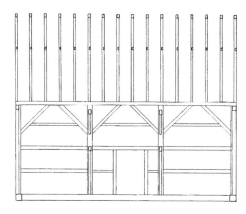

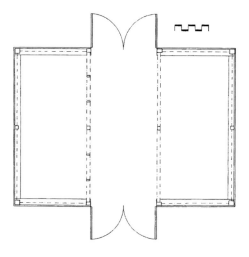

Figure 5.4

Davies Barn, 1800–1820, Little Creek vicinity, Kent County, Delaware. Drawn by Meg Mulrooney and Bernard L. Herman. The Davies Barn, which had a full rubble-stone foundation, was a typical three-bay feed barn.

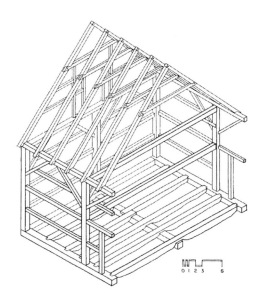

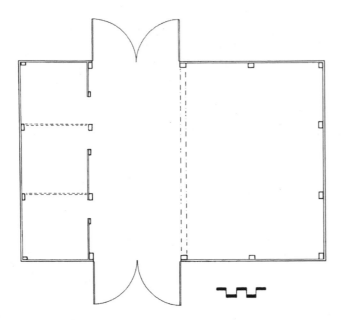

Figure 5.5
Marsh Barn, 1810–30, Indian River Hundred, Sussex
County, Delaware. The original design included a central
but asymmetrically placed runway work area, a hay mow
(*right*), and corn cribs (*left*) that were originally built as a
shed.

placed in each wall panel defined by the bents. Once the bents and rails were in place, the builders lifted the heavy wall plates into position, then set the diagonal corner braces that stiffened the frame. Finally, the rafters were set in position. In the upper reaches of the Delaware valley, most rafters were footed directly to the plate. Further south and west, on the Eastern Shore of Maryland and Virginia, however, the most common arrangement involved spiking the rafter feet to a raising plate carried on loft joists.

Farmers continued to build three-bay barns throughout the nineteenth century. The later examples tended to preserve the variable functions of the type. For example, we know that feed barns were built on raised foundations in the 1840s and 1850s. On the poorer agricultural lands fringing the swamps of southern New Jersey and the Eastern Shore, the three-bay barn remained an exceptional amenity until the mid-1800s, when builders began to erect them for much the same uses as their earlier northern counterparts. The caution here is that, while the three-bay barn should generally be assigned to an earlier period of agricultural development in one part of the region, it remained a desired and current design for other locales well into a later time period.

Gable-Fronted Barns

Associated with the agricultural landscapes of the Eastern Shore of Maryland and Virginia are distinctive gable-fronted barns. In some instances these buildings were designed for use in curing tobacco; in others they were intended as threshing and feed barns. The gable-fronted barns of the lower mid-Atlantic region should not be confused with the Dutch barns of central and northern New Jersey and the Hudson Valley of New York.[5] Although those Dutch barns possess broad gable elevations, they differ from the gable-fronted barns of the lower mid-Atlantic region in two key ways. First, the Dutch barns employ a distinctive framing method that makes use of heavy H-bents with through-tenoned anchor beams that divide the interior into a number of equal-sized, structurally defined bays. While gable-fronted barns also make use of principal post construction, they generally do so in a manner that follows the carpentry practices indigenous to the Chesapeake Bay region. Second, in plan the Dutch barns consist of a broad central unit for threshing and agricultural storage flanked by integral sheds intended for livestock. Gable-fronted barns tend to possess a slightly elevated central element dedicated to threshing and grain storage with the flanking sheds set aside as corn cribs. In tobacco barns the allocation of space is comparable, despite differences in the way tobacco is stored and cured. That there are similarities of form and appearance between these types that derive from different formal, functional, and settlement traditions underscores the central theme of this field guide: only the careful archaeological examination of architectural evidence will enable the fieldworker to separate meaningful from superficial parallels. Begin with the building at hand, then broaden your analysis to compare and contrast it with like structures.

The characteristics of the gable-fronted barn include its gable end front and a typical plan consisting of a wide central work area with an overhead loft flanked on either side by long narrow storage spaces. In some instances the storage spaces are integral to the overall structure of the building, while in others they are obviously added lean-to wings. The earliest surviving gable-fronted barns date from the late eighteenth century and were constructed with heavy timber frames raised on brick piers or timber blocks and floored on the main level. As noted in the following discussion of granaries, gable-fronted barns shared formal characteristics with buildings specifically built for grain storage. Later examples of gable-fronted barns (some built well into the early twentieth century as earthfast structures) often include earthen-floored interiors with central work areas, overhead hay lofts, and flanking shed stables, stalls, and storage spaces.

The Willowdale Barn in Accomack County, Virginia, is an excellent example of the gable-fronted barn form (Fig. 5.6). Raised in a single building episode, the Willowdale Barn may have sheltered several kinds of crops, including tobacco, hay, corn, and wheat. Supported on brick piers and built of

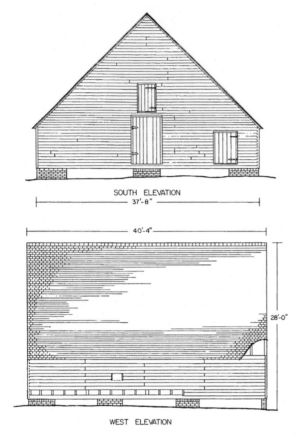

SOUTH ELEVATION
37'-8"

40'-4"

28'-0"

WEST ELEVATION

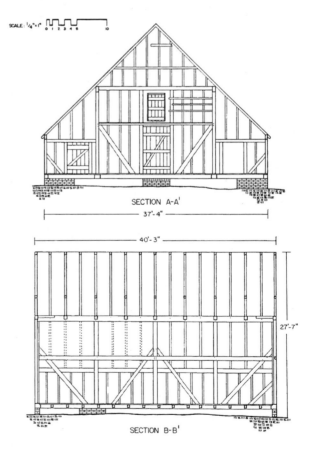

Figure 5.6

Willowdale Barn, ca. 1800, Accomack County, Virginia.
Drawn by Penelope Schaffer Gioffre and Bernard L. Herman.
The Willowdale Barn exemplifies the gable-front barn, a
distinctive form found on the Eastern Shore of Maryland
and Virginia.

SCALE: ¼"=1" 0 1 2 3 4 5   10

SECTION A-A'
37'-4"

40'-3"

27'-7"

SECTION B-B'

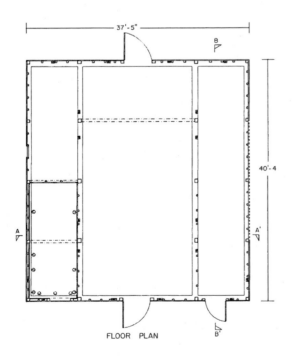

37'-5"

B

40'-4

A   A'

FLOOR PLAN

B'

Figure 5.7

Fancy Farm Barn, 1700s, Chestertown vicinity, Kent County, Maryland. Photographed by David Ames, HABS, 1994. The interior of this oak frame barn was subdivided into four roughly 9-foot bays that show possible vertical division for bilevel storage on the main floor. An overhead loft and flanking sheds provided additional storage space.

hewn and pit-sawn pine, this braced-frame barn dates to the late eighteenth or early nineteenth century. The interior of the roughly 37-foot front, 40-foot deep building contains three structural divisions: a 19-foot wide central bay flanked by nearly 9-foot-wide integral sheds. Evidence in the form of tie beams and robbed mortises (mortises left open after the original tenoned members have been removed) indicates that provision was made to subdivide these spaces horizontally and vertically into a variety of bins, cribs, and temporary lofts. The same strategy was applied to the Fancy Farm Barn in Kent County, Maryland (Fig. 5.7). Built of hewn oak, the central frame presents a 24-foot front and runs 36 feet in depth. Principal posts and tie beams divided the interior into four roughly 9-foot bays that show evidence of possible vertical division for bilevel storage on the main floor. Overhead, the loft provided additional storage for grain and other crops. The 9-foot-wide flanking sheds on either side were similarly divided into a number of slat-sided bins for storing dried ears of corn.

Corn Cribs and Granaries

The ubiquitous farm building for storing corn was the corn crib. But, within that general purpose, these buildings achieved significant variation in

Figure 5.8
Corn crib, 1800s, Broad
Creek Hundred, Sussex
County, Delaware. Photo-
graphed 1988. Corn cribs,
like this one constructed
of notched round logs, or
poles, are often called
stacks in Sussex County.

construction and appearance. We have singled out a few of the most common types among the great variety on the landscape. Corn cribs were long, narrow log or frame gable-roofed structures typically set on wooden blocks, stumps, or masonry piers. Log cribs were left unchinked and frame cribs were slat-sided to provide ample air circulation for the drying of the ears of corn stored inside. The interiors were typically left undivided, although many surviving cribs show provision for the installation of temporary partitions that created two or more discrete bins within the crib. Log cribs tended to be built with either rough V-notched or dovetailed corners, while frame cribs were built with principal posts and rails. In Sussex County, Delaware, corn cribs are also referred to as stacks (Fig. 5.8). The term *stack* suggests the moveable quality of these structures, which range from 7 to 10 feet in width and 15 to 20 feet in length. As recently as the mid-twentieth century, farmers purchased cribs at local farm sales and carted them home for use on their own farms. The localized meaning of *corn stack* also points up the need to talk with people about their buildings and not to make assumptions about terminology. Many of us think of a corn stack as a sheaf of corn stalks.

The uneven progress of agricultural practice is reflected in the size and proportions of log corn cribs throughout the region. Although some early cribs have been recorded in northern Delaware, for example, field observation suggests that small corn cribs were being phased out by the 1800s in favor of more spacious and functionally flexible crib barns (discussed below). Similarly, as late as the 1930s, small cribs of hewn logs, but with roofs of mill-sawn boards joined with wire nails, were being built in the central counties of the Eastern Shore.

A much more elaborate corn crib form is represented by the Woodward-Pennock corn crib in Chester County, Pennsylvania (Fig. 5.9). Built of hewn and mill-sawn oak timbers and sheathed with widely spaced vertical wood slats, the Woodward-Pennock corn crib dates to the late eighteenth or early nineteenth century. The interior of the roughly 5-foot-wide, 29-foot-deep building contains four narrow bays, or spaces. A single door on one of the narrow ends and several slatted openings near the roof line provide ventilation to the interior. Although it is now raised on stone and concrete piers, this building was constructed with timber "legs" tenoned into the underside of the sills.

Granaries, which survive infrequently today, were also not as common on the historic landscape as one might think. The typical granary, like the corn crib, was one-story high, gable-roofed, and of log or frame construction (Fig. 5.10). The plainest form of the granary consisted of a roughly square post-and-rail or stud wall frame tightly sealed with weatherboard or vertical board-and-batten siding. The interior was often wainscoted to a height of three feet with horizontal boards, and overhead the sealed loft typically contained a number of walled bins and grain chests. Granaries were designed primarily to store grain in sacks or bins. Threshing, which involved flailing, treading, and winnowing, took place either in the barn or, more often, according to period sources, in the packed earth yard in front of the granary.

In the highly productive grain-growing areas of the upper Eastern Shore, several granaries anticipated the rise in the mid-nineteenth century of the crib barn. For example, during the 1820s, a New Castle County farmer named Richard Mansfield built a log and frame granary on his farm, Achmester, that contained two log-walled corn cribs, a central work and storage area, and loft storage bins. As built, Mansfield's granary stood on a rubble

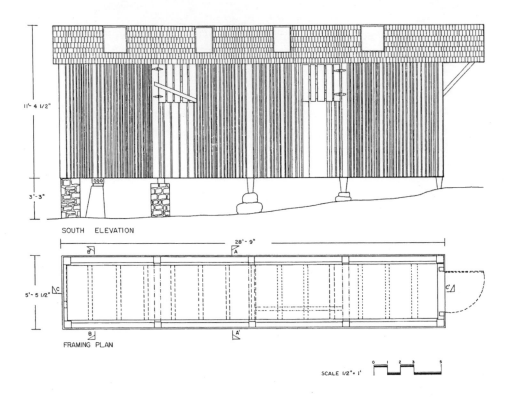

11'- 4 1/2"

3'- 3"

SOUTH ELEVATION

28'- 9"

5'- 5 1/2"

FRAMING PLAN

SCALE 1/2"= 1'

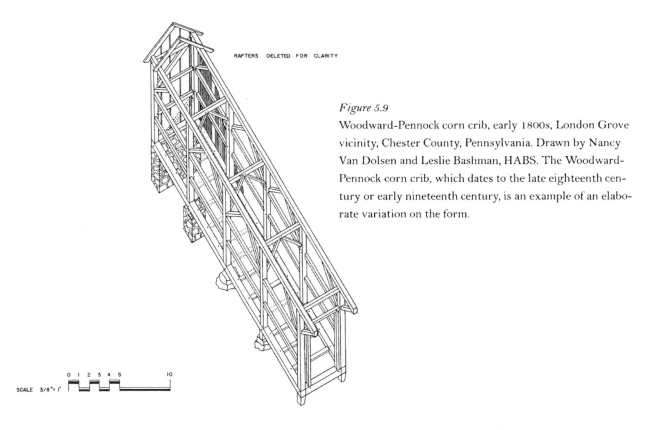

RAFTERS DELETED FOR CLARITY

Figure 5.9
Woodward-Pennock corn crib, early 1800s, London Grove vicinity, Chester County, Pennsylvania. Drawn by Nancy Van Dolsen and Leslie Bashman, HABS. The Woodward-Pennock corn crib, which dates to the late eighteenth century or early nineteenth century, is an example of an elaborate variation on the form.

SCALE 3/8"= 1'

Figure 5.10
Granary, early 1800s, Philips Hill vicinity, Sussex County, Delaware. Photographed 1983. Granaries were typically one story high, gable roofed, and of log or frame construction.

fieldstone foundation, was sided with vertical board, and was floored throughout (Fig. 5.11).

Other Farm Buildings

In the 1780 to 1830 period, farms often included stables. These buildings tended to be of log, frame, or, on occasion, brick or stone construction. They were usually divided on the interior into 4-foot-wide stalls with feed boxes located at the head of each stall.

Certain small barns of the central Eastern Shore possessed a houselike appearance. In the early 1800s these small barns were usually one-story and averaged 16 by 20 feet—exactly like the houses with which they were associated (Fig. 5.12). A great many farms also had workshops, as well as all-purpose "lumber" buildings used for general storage. The vast majority of these work buildings were constructed of wood and, as stables also did, often looked like dwellings. The houselike quality of many early agricultural buildings emphasizes the flexibility of agricultural architecture. Within the 360 square feet of a small one-and-a-half-story frame building, a farmer could store implements and seed, set up a workshop, or lodge a farmhand. The ability to utilize a single building in so many different ways underscores the difficulty of identifying farm buildings by a single function. Only the evidence of use enables us to ascertain how buildings worked on the farm.

Figure 5.11
Achmester log granary,
1800–1820, St. George's
Hundred, New Castle
County, Delaware. Photo-
graphed by David Ames,
HABS, 1983. The Achmes-
ter log granary, one of only
three known surviving pre-
1825 agricultural buildings
in southern New Castle
County, is an early example
of the consolidation of
grain processing and storage functions in a single
building. The structure was
built with two log-walled
corn cribs, a central work
and storage area, and loft
storage bins, and was a pre-
cursor of the crib barn.

More ephemeral in nature were seasonal structures. Almost every farm possessed conical hay stacks heaped around a pole set in the ground. Similarly, during the early winter, many farmers erected "hog gallows" for slaughtering. Built on posts set in the ground, hog gallows supported cross pieces from which to suspend the carcass during gutting, scraping, and butchering. Hog gallows and hay stacks, like the once-common wells built with heavy sweeps carried on a single, ground-set post, have disappeared from the landscape.

The best depictions we have of mid-Atlantic farmyards during the 1780 to 1830 period come from a handful of pictorial sources. An 1880s drawing of the Pettyjohn Farm in Sussex County, Delaware, as it appeared in the 1820s (see Fig. 2.35) shows post-and-rail, picket, and worm fences, hay and fodder stacks, a well with sweep, and other once-ordinary architectural features. Similarly, the Godfrey Gebler Farm in Chester County consisted of a two-story house facing the public road. To the left of the dwelling stood a formal garden surrounded by a picket fence and bordered by an orchard. Across the road were several farm buildings including a second house and two much smaller, nondescript structures which illustrate the most general form of utilitarian farm buildings. Also associated with these structures in their post-

and-rail enclosure is an open frame, water-driven sawmill. Of the Gebler Farm buildings, only the house and main barn are likely to have survived.

Representing two very different landscapes in the larger region, the Pettyjohn and Gebler farms provide clear instruction for modern day fieldworkers. Both views indicate the centrality of the house in the farmstead. At the same time, they illustrate fences, gardens, wells, hay stacks, and orchards—all part of the architectural landscape of the farm. Other buildings include readily recognizable work buildings, such as a mill or tenant's dwelling, and the more anonymous array of small barns, corn cribs, granaries, and storage structures.

Improved Farms, 1830–1920

The agricultural landscape was transformed dramatically and repeatedly throughout these decades. In southern New Castle County, Delaware, and adjacent Maryland and New Jersey, the greatest level of change occurred from about 1840 to 1870. In the forested and swampy landscapes of the central Eastern Shore, the major transformations in the agricultural scene did not take place until after the Civil War. In the Pennsylvania and Delaware Piedmont, by contrast, farmers had begun to incorporate alterations in farm building design and use by the late 1700s.

The evidence of farm buildings shows us some of the agricultural changes that occurred during this nearly century-long period. First, farm buildings built from the mid-1800s into the early twentieth century incorporated the increasingly mechanical or industrialized functions of the farm into their plans and use. Second, barns and other agricultural structures expressed a growing concern with the organization of farm activity. Work and storage spaces were increasingly specific and architecturally distinguished. The popular dictum "a place for everything and everything in its place" encompassed even the most mundane aspects of farm building design. These functionally defined spaces were grouped in carefully designed buildings that included such wonders as the carriage house–stable–poultry house–shop–piggery–pigpen built by J. K. Williams at Woodlawn in St. George's Hundred, New Castle County, Delaware. A third significant change was that farm buildings, particularly in the lower Delaware valley and adjacent Maryland, were built on an increasingly monumental scale, even if they continued to house much the same kinds of functions identified in the 1780 to 1830 period. In the interiors, barn builders often expressed their abilities in the form of overly

complicated framing joints, including paired braces and pinwheel-like shed trusses. The George Farm Barn in Duck Creek Hundred, built in the mid-1800s, illustrates the elaboration of both scale and finish found in mid- to late-nineteenth-century Delaware valley farm architecture. This six-bay oak barn, more than 65 feet long and 35 feet deep, attempted to incorporate all the functions of the farm into a single structure. Lastly, building materials were increasingly likely to come from outside the community, particularly in the case of new farm buildings being erected in an area of intensively used land.

Of all the many types of farm buildings that once stood in the countryside, we typically encounter only a handful of common farm structures in the course of fieldwork. The bank barn, crib barn, cart shed or wagon barn, horse barn or stable, and work shop/storage house represent the most common types and are the ones which will be addressed below.

Other, highly specialized buildings, such as the threshing barn at Cochran's Grange near Middletown, Delaware, or the Wilson Potato House in Queen

Figure 5.12

Figure 5.12
Barn, ca. 1800, Broad Creek
Hundred, Sussex County,
Delaware. Photographed
by David Ames, 1989. The
small barns of the central
Eastern Shore resembled
houses and were usually
one-story buildings averaging 16 by 20 feet, the same
dimensions as their accompanying houses.

Anne's County, Maryland, were both significant and unusual elements in the farming countryside (Fig. 5.13). Although no comprehensive catalog exists for these less frequent building types, it is nonetheless important to recognize and evaluate them. Again, the reader using this field guide is advised to look at the functions associated with more common farm building forms and then attempt to identify those functions in the structure being investigated. Historic farm buildings are voluble informants to students of the agricultural past. Our challenge is to look carefully and systematically, think critically, and interpret cautiously. With close attention, even the most seemingly peculiar farm structure will communicate its history of use and change.

Improved Bank Barns

By the 1830s agricultural writers throughout the United States had identified and promoted the image of the multistoried bank barn as the agricultural building which most closely represented the ideology and spirit of progressive or scientific farming. Bank barns by this time were already a well-established building type on the farms in the Pennsylvania and Delaware Piedmont. Through the middle decades of the 1800s they became increasingly popular on the rich lands of southern New Jersey and the upper counties of the Eastern Shore. The basic intention behind the bank barn was a farm building which incorporated all (or almost all) of the farm's storage, processing, stabling, and other related work functions into a single structure. The ideal bank barn—with basement (first-floor) stables, stalls, and upper-level hay mows, threshing floor, granary, corn cribs, and work rooms—was only partially adopted by most farmers.

The Logan Lane Barn on St. Jones Neck, Kent County, Delaware, and the Redden Barn in Queen Anne's County, Maryland, are representative of the fuller expressions of the improved bank barn. Both contained well-defined spaces for corn and grain storage, threshing, hay mows, and livestock stalling. Still, many farmers throughout the region preferred to place grain processing and storage functions in a building that was separate from livestock housing. In some instances, builders opted for the image of a large bank barn without giving up the internal organization of the old three-bay barns discussed above. Wheatland Barn near Mount Pleasant in New Castle County, Delaware, exemplifies the tension between progressive ideals and customary practice and how farmers could combine the two in a single structure. From the road, one would see a large frame barn with slightly off-center double

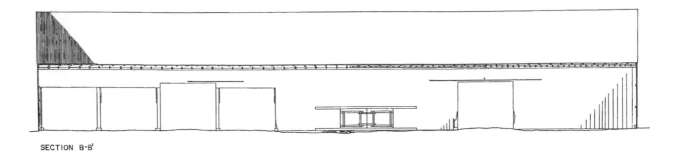

SECTION B-B'

SECTIONAL ELEVATION A-A'

0 1 2 3 4 5   10
SCALE: 3/16" = 1'-0"

doors rising from the ground level to the eaves; from the fields, the barn would be seen to have a clearly defined projecting forebay overhanging the lower livestock level (Fig. 5.14). Despite its size and appearance, Wheatland Barn basically represented the old tripartite division of space associated with an earlier generation. Wagons loaded with hay could be driven into, and through, the barn from either side. Laborers, however, had to lift the hay into mows located on the upper level—an arrangement at obvious odds with a popular literature espousing economy of labor and careful organization of space. Grain, corn storage, and processing were housed in a crib barn located elsewhere in the farmyard. The lower level of Wheatland Barn was divided by the earth floor runway that asymmetrically bisected the plan. Horses occupied box stalls in the west end, while milk cows and other cattle fed and sheltered in the considerably larger east end. Thus, Wheatland Barn, like many of its contemporaries, exhibits the persistence of tradition as a means of organizing innovation. Because farmers throughout the region knew what worked and what had made them rich, they were able to adopt and adapt popular barn design in ways that continue to tell us much about agriculture and creativity in the landscape.

By the mid-1800s, bank barns increasingly tended to be frame buildings

Figure 5.13
Cochran's Grange Threshing Barn, ca. 1835, Middletown vicinity, St. George's Hundred, New Castle County, Delaware. Drawn by Charles Bergengren, HABS. Buildings such as the threshing barn at Cochran's Grange, near Middletown, Delaware, were highly specialized and fairly uncommon.

A

Figure 5.14

Wheatland Barn, St. George's Hundred, New Castle County, Delaware.
Photographed by David Ames HABS, 1990. Like many bank barns, the
Wheatland Barn was built as a large, two-level structure with a forebay,
visible in *B*, but it lacked the earthen bank or ramp to the main floor that
typically characterizes the form. The interior arrangement also reflected a
more traditional use of space.

B

A

Figure 5.15
Bank barns built during the 1800s were increasingly likely to have brick or stone walls at the basement, or first-story, level. (*A*) Lancaster County, Pennsylvania. Photographed 1977. (*B*) Bucks County, Pennsylvania. Photographed 1976.

B

EVERYDAY ARCHITECTURE OF THE MID-ATLANTIC

Figure 5.16
Cochran Grange Bank Barn, mid-1800s, Middletown vicinity, New Castle County, Delaware. Photographed by David Ames, HABS, 1982. The trusses in many bank barns employ a system of diagonal struts bracing canted queen posts; the queen posts in turn support the purlins, to which the rafters are joined.

supported on brick or stone basement levels (Fig. 5.15). The barns stand today as essays on the art and technology of timber construction and are excellent classrooms in which to learn the fundamentals of braced frame building techniques. In the typical three-bay bank barn, the building is composed of four major bents, often rising 15 feet or more from the runway floor. The basic framing technology makes use of heavy post-and-rail construction strengthened with substantial tie beams. Of particular note in many bank barns are the elaborate roof trusses. These trusses employ a system of diagonal struts bracing canted queen posts; the queen posts in turn support the purlins, to which the rafters are joined (Fig. 5.16). When we look at bank barn framing, we are left not only with an appreciation of the completed building, but in many cases, we can also interpret how the building was actually raised. In almost every farm building with exposed framing, numbering on the timbers, the direction of driven pegs, and the relationship of major timbers can reveal just how carpenters erected their works.

Crib Barns

One of the most common nineteenth-century farm buildings left standing in the mid-Atlantic landscape is the crib barn. From the earliest known example, built at La Grange, near Glasgow, Delaware, in 1817, to the latest models, erected further south at the turn of the twentieth century, this building type has remained consistent in form and use. The crib barn in its most common form is a one-story gable-front frame building (Fig. 5.17). The ground floor is divided into three basic units. A broad central runway extends the length of the building and there are most often double doors at each end

Figure 5.17
Crib barn with cart shed
and hayloft attached, ca.
1850, Smyrna vicinity, New
Castle County, Delaware.
Photographed 1985. In its
most common form, the
crib barn is a one-story
gable-front building of
frame construction.

as well as low earthen ramps for driving wagons and farm carts into the building. Farmers used the runway for more than drawing wagons full of corn and other cereals into the building; corn shellers and wheat fans could also be set up there for threshing and cleaning grain. Corn cribs for the storage of corn in the ear extend the full length of the barn on either side of the runway. A winding stair rises from the runway to the loft in one corner. The loft area above is divided into several plank-walled grain bins, which were used to hold loose threshed grain. Bushel counts carved into the planks defining the bin entries still afford us a record of nineteenth- and early-twentieth-century harvests. Holes cut in the floor of the aisle that separates the bins enabled workers to reload wagons in the runway below without the back-breaking labor of hauling full sacks of grain back down the stairs. Although the fully developed crib barn was designed to admit wagons and provide ample work space, there are examples that are scarcely larger than the old style raised granaries of an earlier generation. In these small crib barns we are still likely to find all the requisite spaces (runway, cribs, loft grain bins), but on such a reduced scale that the only vehicle the farmer could have used would be a wheelbarrow.

Crib barns differ from gable-fronted barns in two ways. First, they were built to function exclusively as grain and corn storage buildings, and second, their design was specifically intended to admit wheeled traffic, such as wagons loaded with corn.

While the crib barn emerged as the dominant farm building type in southern New Jersey, Delaware, and Maryland, two other corn and grain storage buildings remained significant at the northern and southern extremes of the region. Log, pole, and lightly framed corn cribs continued to be built throughout the lower Eastern Shore. A group of three such corn cribs was built in the early twentieth century on a farm near Millsboro, Delaware (Fig. 5.18). Each of the cribs stood on four brick piers, located at the corners, and was built of dovetailed sawn logs. Door jambs and rafters were secured with wire nails. In form and design these three cribs were identical to examples described 150 years earlier; in construction they were clearly products of the early twentieth century. Further north, corn cribs were built either as long, narrow, freestanding frame structures sited near the primary barn (Fig. 5.19) or were incorporated into the plan of a bank barn as part of its bridge house, covering the ramp, or as a shed wing. There were, of course, other types of corn cribs and crib barns, such as combination corn cribs and wagon houses (Fig. 5.20). As with most other types of farm buildings, our primary responsibility is to identify the structure's function and the way the building plan is organized to facilitate function.

Horse Barns and Stables

Even as multipurpose bank barns became the architectural ideal for well-ordered farms throughout much of the lower Delaware valley, farmers continued to build functionally specific farm buildings. Horse barns and stables vary in appearance, but they all share a few basic characteristics (Fig. 5.21). Most horse barns contain a lower stabling floor and either a loft or full second story for storing hay and feed. The gable-roofed structures possess several Dutch double doors in both the front and back and usually at least one in each gable. The central door opens onto a feeding aisle from which the farmers replenish the feed boxes. The doors to either side provide the means to bring horses in and out of the building as well as to muck out the stalls. The stalls average four feet in width and are plank-sided to an approximate height of 4 or 5 feet. Diagonal struts footed to partial joists or simply set in the earthen floor run up to the ceiling joists and support the stall partitions. Thus, the overall arrangement on the ground floor of stables built during this period continued an older stabling pattern generally associated with three-bay barns. The hay loft above was filled from wagons parked in the farmyard below. By the late 1800s hay tracks had been installed in most stables and bank barns, with the result that moving hay through the building became much easier. To get the hay from the loft to the stalls and feed boxes below, farmers built hatches in the loft floors and simply pitched the hay down.

Figure 5.18
Corn cribs, Millsboro vicinity, Sussex County, Delaware.
Photographed 1994. These three twentieth-century log and
pole corn cribs were built with circular-sawn logs.

Figure 5.19
Corn crib, 1900–1910, Haycock vicinity, Bucks County,
Pennsylvania. Photographed 1976. Corn cribs in the more
northerly parts of the Delaware valley were long, narrow,
freestanding frame structures placed near the barn.

Figure 5.20
Granary, late 1800s, Haycock Township, Bucks County,
Pennsylvania. Photographed 1975. Some farm buildings,
such as this drive-through granary in Bucks County, Pennsylvania, combined the functions of corn crib and wagon
house.

Figure 5.21
Horse barn, latter 1800s, Woodside, St. George's Hundred, New Castle County, Delaware. Photographed 1980. Like almost all farm buildings erected between 1830 and 1920, stables and horse barns were framed on a post and rail system and sheathed with vertical board siding.

On the increasingly mechanized farms of the middle to late nineteenth century, stables often were large two-story boxlike structures or were built in the form of the three-bay barn. Stalls in both types occupied the ground-level spaces on either side of a runway space that ranged in width from sufficient clearance for a wagon to space enough only for one person with a bucket or wheelbarrow. Like almost all farm buildings erected during this period, stables and horse barns were framed on a post and rail system and sheathed with vertical board siding. Although supported on masonry footings, the buildings were still framed close to the ground, so that their animal occupants could be led in and out without difficulty.

Cart Sheds and Wagon Barns

The rise of mechanized agriculture in the mid-1800s meant that farmers needed buildings that could house their equipment: threshers, mowers, hay wagons, harrows, plows, and other large implements. The construction of cart sheds and wagon barns answered this need. Where these cart sheds survive, we often find them with trucks, tractors, and other modern equipment occupying the spaces that once housed horse-drawn wagons and mowers.

The most common type of cart shed consists of a low frame structure with an asymmetrical gable roof, open front, and sided back and gables (Fig. 5.22). Posts set in the earth or on footing stones support the shed structure by carrying tie beams, which join the low rear wall to the overhanging front

Figure 5.22
Woodlawn cart shed,
1886, Odessa vicinity, St.
George's Hundred, New
Castle County, Delaware.
Photographed by David
Ames, HABS, 1985. This
low frame structure, with
its asymmetrical gable roof,
open front, and sided back
and gables, is typical of the
most common type of cart
shed built in the Delaware
valley.

gable, and by supporting the ridge boards required to carry the roof rafters. The supporting posts are sometimes hewn, sometimes left in the round, and sometimes shaped only at the top, where carpentry demands a regularly worked surface. Lightly framed back and gable walls are typically enclosed with vertical board siding nailed to post-and-rail construction. Cart shed roofs, covered with wood shingle in the nineteenth and early twentieth centuries, are now mostly sheathed with metal. The framing systems employed for open-fronted cart sheds define a structural bay system based on regularly positioned principal supporting posts and tie beams. Each structural bay also provides a single storage unit in the shed.

Functionally, these were buildings designed to garage farm equipment; formally, they helped define the larger plan of the farmstead through their spatial relationship to other farm structures. A courtyard could be created when builders placed two cart sheds facing each other and at right angles to the ridge of a centrally placed barn, a design also popularized in published farm manuals. A single cart shed might be built abutting or near the primary barn or be ranged with other farm buildings in a pattern leading back to the main barn. In all cases, the use of cart sheds is partly understood through the identification of their relationship to other buildings in the farmyard.

Considerably rarer than cart sheds and almost exclusive to the Pennsyl-

vania and Delaware Piedmont are wagon barns. These buildings bridge the functions of crib barns, carriage houses, workshops, and cart sheds. A particularly good example that illustrates the basic characteristics of the building type is the Pyle wagon barn near the Pennsylvania-Delaware border (Fig. 5.23). Built of stone, the Pyle wagon barn fronted the public road and a now-demolished bank barn. Its rear gable was built into an embankment and its front is open and faces the road. The lower floor sheltered wagons and other vehicles as well as tack; the upper floor contained grain bins, corn cribs, and an open work space.

Mixed-Use Barns

Many farmers, especially those tilling less profitable lands or maintaining less specialized farming operations, built themselves a single mixed-use barn. Particularly common on the Eastern Shore and across the Chesapeake Bay in southeastern Virginia, mixed-use barns simply combine many of the storage and stabling functions of the farm into a single structure. Typically erected as gable-fronted, single-story buildings with lofts, mixed-use barns tend to project an informal appearance and are often overlooked by those who study the rural landscape. In terms of design, however, these unassuming buildings

Figure 5.24
Steve Hudson Barn, early
1900s, Baltimore Hundred,
Sussex County, Delaware.
Photographed by David
Ames, HABS, 1991. The
Hudson barn, a mixed-use
barn, consists of a central
runway with animal stalls
on the left and equipment
storage on the right.

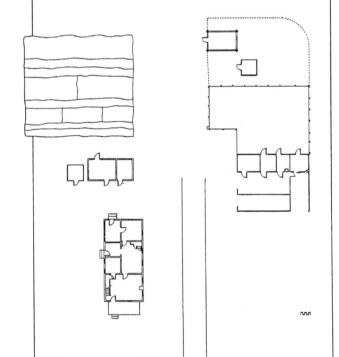

Figure 5.25
Steve Hudson farmyard, Baltimore Hundred, Sussex County,
Delaware. In this typical rural farmyard, the farmhouse (*bottom*) fronts the road across a small yard. Behind the house
are a smokehouse, pump house, storage shed, and garden.
Across from these are the mixed-use barn and adjacent barnyard with corn crib, poultry house, and hog and fowl pens.

provide clear evidence about the care and sophistication with which farmers organized their work.

The Hudson Farm, in Sussex County, Delaware, provides an excellent example of the mixed-use barn and its place in the farmstead. Built in the early twentieth century, the Hudson Barn belongs to the family of gable-fronted barns discussed above (Fig. 5.24). It is sheathed with a mixture of horizontal weatherboard and vertical board siding, covered with metal roofing over wood shingle, and was left unpainted. The Hudson Barn, which achieved its present form through a process of addition, contains an original central earth-floored aisle, which provided access to a storeroom and to the cattle and draft animals housed in stalls ranged along the left side of the building. The stalls opened onto a fenced livestock yard on the left side of the barn. To the right of the aisle stood a long open lean-to addition used for storing farm equipment like wagons and plows. A second added open-fronted shed spanned the back of the barn and provided storage for other items, such as lumber and additional carts, plows, and harrows. Overhead, the original loft sheltered hay, animal feed, and seasonal implements. The entire building extends 37 feet in length and offers a 30-foot-wide three-bay gable front divided into three nearly equal units.

The barn provided the centerpiece for the farmyard. It faced the farmhouse across the lane, its roof ridge running parallel to the public road (Fig. 5.25). Within the fenced livestock yard stood a log corn crib and poultry house as well as hog and fowl pens. Across the farm lane from the barn, behind the house, were ranged several domestic support structures, including the smokehouse and more storage sheds. Behind these was the family garden.

Considerably less pretentious than its bank barn kin, the mixed-use barn, well represented by the Hudson Barn, nonetheless conveys many of the functions of Victorian agriculture, such as the careful definition and segregation of work and storage space within a single structure and its thoughtful siting in a well-ordered farm plan.

Silos

Silos, among the most conspicuous of buildings on many farmsteads, are a relatively recent phenomenon on the rural landscape. The first silos appeared after 1875 and became numerous only in the years just prior to 1900. The most active period of silo building began around the second decade of the twentieth century; by mid-century, they were commonplace. Used for grain and feed storage, the most visible silos are tall, usually cylindrical farm structures (see Fig. 5.14). Unlike bins and similar devices for storing dried grain, silos are designed to preserve green fodder crops in a semimoist condition by excluding air and water. This method of preservation, known as the ensilage process, produces livestock feed—green fodder or silage—that can be used throughout the year. Because silos made loft storage space no longer so necessary for keeping hay, their advent and gradual acceptance in the late nineteenth and early twentieth century shifted prevailing agricultural practices and building use by many farmers.[4]

While experiments with the ensilage process had been undertaken in Europe by the end of the eighteenth century, the practice was never successful enough there to become particularly widespread. American agriculturalists and gentleman farmers, prompted by articles in agricultural publications that explained and illustrated the ensilage process, first began to experiment with silos after 1875. These early efforts generated considerable debate and some criticism in the American agricultural press. As a result, silos and the use of ensilage as livestock feed were slow to gain acceptance in America, and some extremely conservative farmers continued to be wary even as late as the first decade of the twentieth century. Still, the many advantages that silos offered eventually convinced even the most cautious and old-fashioned agriculturalists. Because silos allowed farmers to maintain larger numbers of cattle more economically and less labor-intensively, and because cows that were fed on green fodder produced milk throughout the entire winter season as well as during the rest of the year, silos gradually proliferated in the early twentieth century, especially in dairy regions.[5]

The earliest silos consisted of excavated masonry-lined pits. These pit silos were impractical, however, and soon gave way to upright, or tower, silos. Upright silos were built in several forms—first as rectangular, gable-roofed towers attached to existing barns, and then as cylindrical towers constructed of wooden staves, masonry, poured concrete, tile blocks, or brick. Wooden stave silos began to appear at the end of the nineteenth century (Fig. 5.26). These structures were built of vertical wooden staves that were secured with iron hoops fastened with turnbuckles and usually capped with conical or hipped roofs. Wooden stave silos were relatively inexpensive, but they required interior linings in order to make them more nearly airtight, and the iron bands and turnbuckles that secured them required periodic tightening. Around the 1920s, the popularity of wooden stave silos was gradually eclipsed by masonry, poured-concrete, and tile-block silos, like the one still standing at Fancy Farm in Kent County, Maryland (Fig. 5.27). All of these construction

Figure 5.26
Wood silo, Bucks County, Pennsylvania. Photographed 1975. Wooden stave silos first appeared at the end of the nineteenth century.

Figure 5.27
Tile-block silo, Fancy Farm, Chestertown vicinity, Kent County, Maryland. Photographed by David Ames, HABS, 1994. Construction materials such as tile block and poured concrete replaced wooden staves beginning in the 1920s, allowing construction of taller, larger, and more airtight silos.

materials were more durable than wooden staves; they also permitted farmers to build higher, more airtight silos that had greater capacities. After 1945, further developments in materials and techniques permitted the construction of truly airtight silos.[6]

Other Buildings

SWEET POTATO HOUSES

In parts of southern Delaware and adjacent Maryland as well as southern New Jersey, specialized farm buildings designed exclusively for storing and curing sweet potatoes appear on the landscape. Although they are no longer representative of a dominant crop and are consequently falling into disrepair or being dismantled, numerous sweet potato houses still remain. Few have survived intact; many have been adapted for modern farm use and transformed into barns, storage sheds, stables, and, rarely, houses. While the architectural origins of the sweet potato house remain unclear, interviews with former sweet potato farmers confirm that building designs were frequently copied from farm to farm.[7]

Sweet potato houses on the Eastern Shore are usually tall, two- or three-story, narrow, gable-fronted frame buildings that were originally designed to be heated with a coal- or wood-burning stove (Fig. 5.28). Typical identifying features on the exterior include minimal fenestration and a single chimney. A single window on the first and second floors may occupy the rear gable; small ventilation windows are often found in the attic story of the front and rear gables. The main entry and second-floor loading doors are usually located on the front gable. The second-floor doors were originally designed to accommodate the loading and unloading of wagons filled with baskets of sweet potatoes; in a few instances, a hoisting pulley and projecting platform have been constructed over and under the second-story doorway for the same purpose. The sweet potato houses of southern New Jersey exhibit the additional distinctive feature of partially excavated or embanked lower floors walled with a locally quarried iron-bearing sandstone.

Proper ventilation and careful temperature control are critical to the sweet potato storage and curing process. After the sweet potatoes were harvested, beginning in early October, they were loaded into the potato houses to be cured. Curing involved thoroughly drying the tubers to evaporate excess moisture that might otherwise cause rot during extended storage. During the colder months of storage, sweet potatoes also had to be kept at a constant

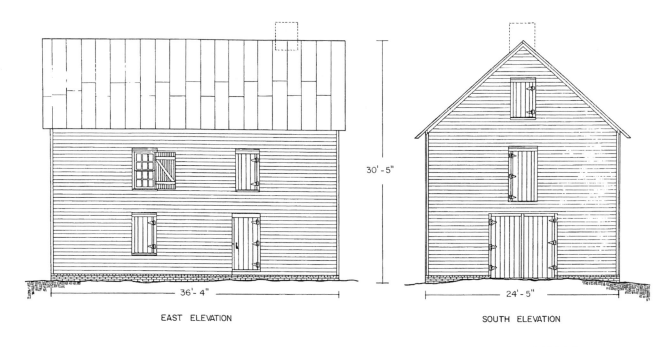

EAST ELEVATION

SOUTH ELEVATION

0 1 2 3 4 5
SCALE 1/4" = 1' - 0"

Figure 5.28
Chipman sweet potato house, Broad Creek Hundred, Sussex County, Delaware. Drawn by Judith Quinn. Sweet potato houses, built for the storing and curing of sweet potatoes, tend to be tall, narrow, and gable fronted. A coal- or wood-burning stove would be located at the center or back of the building. Many sweet potato houses have been adapted to other uses, even occasionally as dwellings.

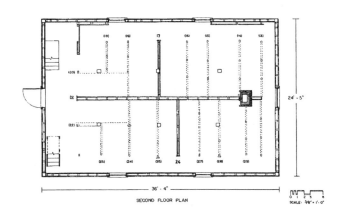

SECOND FLOOR PLAN

0 1 2 3 5
SCALE: 3/8" = 1' - 0"

temperature to prevent freezing and prolong storage life. For these reasons, sweet potato houses were structurally designed to maximize ventilation while providing careful temperature control. Floors and ceilings were sometimes slatted. Interior storage bins were often fitted with pallets to promote air circulation beneath the bins. Hollow walls and deliberate gaps of approximately four inches between the side walls and the ceiling were often incorporated into the original building design. Trap doors or sliding panels were sometimes inserted in the attic floors to allow air from open gable windows to circulate through the lower floors. Finally, a wood- or coal-burning stove was almost always present. From its customary position near the center or back of the house, the stove generated enough heat to maintain a consistent interior temperature. Additional warmth was distributed by the interior chimney and the stove pipe, which usually ran through the center of the first floor under the ceiling. Insulation, often in the form of multiple layers of siding and double doors, helped to maintain consistent temperatures within.

Sweet potato houses were usually constructed on a center aisle plan. Storage bins might be placed in one of two interior arrangements. In the first arrangement, a central hall was flanked by deep, narrow, three-sided bins rising to ceiling height. In the second arrangement, the narrow, three-sided bins were placed back to back in the center of the house, while a two- or three-foot walkway around the bins provided loading access.

MUSHROOM HOUSES

Mushroom houses, specialized agricultural buildings used for cultivating mushrooms, first began to appear in southeastern Pennsylvania and northern Delaware around the turn of the twentieth century and can still be seen throughout Kennett Square and Avondale, Pennsylvania, and Hockessin, Delaware, today. Unlike sweet potato houses, which were intended to store and cure a fully harvested, field-grown crop, mushroom houses were designed to accommodate every aspect of the growing process, from soil preparation and sowing to cultivation and harvest. In the 1890s, mushroom culture was introduced in the neighborhood of Kennett Square, Pennsylvania. By the second decade of the twentieth century, northern Delaware and southeastern Pennsylvania had become significant mushroom producers, accounting for more than 80 percent of the total U.S. crop.

The basic requirements for growing mushrooms are controlled temperature and air flow, darkness, humidity, and space to fill and remove compost. At first, mushrooms were cultivated in basements of other buildings. As mushroom culture became an increasingly significant local industry, wood

Figure 5.29
Mushroom houses, Hockessin vicinity, New Castle County, Delaware. Photographed 1995. Mushroom houses are typically constructed in joined pairs called doubles.

frame houses especially designed for growing mushrooms were constructed. These frame houses were eventually abandoned, because of problems with dampness and hygiene. More sanitary mushroom houses, built of concrete block, replaced the earlier forms; these are the type most commonly seen today. Mushroom houses typically measure about 68 by 20 feet, and there are usually at least two buildings, joined in pairs called doubles (Fig. 5.29). The buildings are designed to permit access to the mushrooms as they grow. Each building is furnished with two tiers of six wooden shelves called beds; each of the beds contains a 6-inch layer of compost that is scattered with mushroom spawn. Growing beds are typically built of a rot-resistant wood such as cedar, cypress, or redwood. Catwalks often run between the tiers so that workers can constantly monitor the growth in the beds. Because it is essential to maintain a constant temperature, mushroom houses are usually insulated and built into a hillside.[8]

Modern Farms, 1920–1950

The last and most recent phase discussed here focuses on some of the later building types developed to meet the requirements of the region's changing agricultural landscape. At the very outset, however, it is important to remember that thousands of farm buildings erected by earlier generations continue to be used. In some cases, older buildings have been altered dramatically; in other instances their flexibility has enabled farmers to use them in new ways with few changes to their fabric and appearance.

Major changes in agricultural economy and practice have stemmed from several sources. First, automobiles and tractors changed the technology and face of farming. Truck transport enabled farmers to ship perishable crops to urban markets even faster than the railroads had permitted. Crops such as bell peppers, tomatoes, green beans, melons, cucumbers, berries, and squash could be harvested in the early morning and arrive in nearby city markets well before noon. Second, the advent of the broiler chicken industry radically changed the farm economy, especially on the lower Eastern Shore of Delaware and Maryland. The first modestly scaled broiler houses quickly gave way to ever larger poultry houses extending hundreds of feet in length. Agricultural engineering and the poultry business promoted one chicken house design after another. The history of chicken house design remains largely undocumented. Third, public standards for hygiene in the dairy industry dramatically changed the interiors of old dairy barns and influenced the appearance of new ones. The two most visible and common mid-twentieth-century farm building types, the chicken house and dairy barn, are considered here.

Broiler Houses

The development of the commercial broiler industry, which involves raising chickens primarily for meat rather than for eggs alone, was one of the most significant events in the evolution of the region's commercial agriculture. The mild weather conditions and sandy soil of the Delmarva Peninsula make it an ideal location for this twentieth-century industry. The broiler business began by accident, when Mrs. Wilmer Steele of Ocean View, Delaware, received a surplus of baby laying chicks, raised the birds, and sold them for meat at sixty-two cents per pound. After she had repeated this process for several years, news of her success in this new venture spread to other farmers, and the commercial broiler industry, now an economic mainstay of the Delmarva Peninsula, had begun.[9]

The first broiler houses were small, shedlike buildings that were a far cry from the ubiquitous long, low chicken factories that are so visible on the Eastern Shore today. Mrs. Steele's 1923 broiler house, now a museum known as the First Broiler House, located at the University of Delaware Experiment Station in Georgetown, Delaware, was a square one-story frame building, 16 feet on each side, capped with a single-pitched shed roof. This small building—known as an individual colony brooder house—sheltered 500 chickens that were warmed by the heat of a coal stove, fed from wooden trough feeders, and watered by hand. Hatching chicks were warmed by an incubator heated with a kerosene lamp. Other early broiler houses were similarly uncomplicated. Modern broiler houses, by contrast, often extend hundreds of feet in length and contain large numbers of birds in a windowless, insulated, and mechanically controlled environment.[10]

Early-twentieth-century agricultural journals urged farmers to place broiler houses in locations with easy access, good drainage, and air circulation, as well as protection from extreme heat or cold. Various designs were promoted, ranging from colony houses—one relatively small, squarish room designed to house 70–150 birds—to multiple-unit houses—many colony houses under one roof, measuring from 20 by 200 feet to 18 by 180 feet and designed to hold up to 1,000 birds—to multiple-story houses, also designed to house large flocks. Recommended roof configurations varied from shed to gable, half-monitor, and combination types. Since ventilation was so important, the open-front design was favored for optimal air circulation.[11]

Like Mrs. Steele's broiler house, the chicken houses of the mid-twentieth century continued a design tradition of being lightly framed buildings with shed or shallow asymmetrical gable-roofs. During the 1930s and 1940s, however, a unique type of chicken house proliferated: long, low, groundhugging buildings with small, two-story structures in the center that included second-story "chicken house apartments." These chicken houses, often ranging between 400 and 500 feet long and 16 to 20 feet wide, could hold between 5,000 and 15,000 birds in the chicken house itself (Fig. 5.30). In the center section, typically gable-roofed and weatherboarded on the exterior, was a first-floor feed room, ventilated with windows, and a second-story caretaker's apartment that was usually more finished than the lower room. The feed room had doors leading to either side of the chicken house. These wings were usually partitioned and extended several hundred feet out from the center section of the building. An exterior stair provided access to the second-story apartment, which most often consisted of three rooms: a living room, kitchen, and bedroom. A bathroom might also be included. These apartments offered chicken farmers a convenient place for their tenants to live without much additional expense; they also provided a viable employment option for many individuals during the 1930s and 1940s.

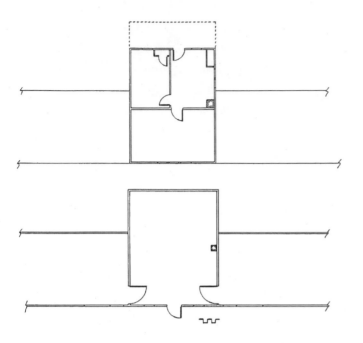

Many such chicken houses were owned by companies such as Townsend
Poultry and Allen Family Foods. Although they were a common sight on the
lower Delaware landscape in the 1930s and 1940s, few remain in use today.
Changes in poultry raising practices coupled with the increasing use of automated feeding and watering gradually altered chicken house design. Many of
the earlier chicken house apartments have since been replaced with wider,
gable-roofed buildings that are more compatible with modern equipment and
techniques (see Fig. 8.10B).[12]

Dairy Barns

Just as improvements in poultry equipment effected changes in chicken
house design, the issues of health and hygiene on the farm became critical
during the early twentieth century and also prompted a shift in dairy barn
design. Between 1890 and 1915, the incidence of cattle diseases peaked. As a
result, newspapers and agricultural journals published increasingly frequent
articles promoting hygienic farming practices, and farm organizations such
as the university extension services and state boards of agriculture intensified
efforts to educate farmers about cow nutrition and cleanliness. By the second
decade of the twentieth century, pasteurization of milk was common; by the
1940s, it was illegal to sell raw or unpasteurized milk in many areas. Archi-

tects, including Alfred Hopkins, began to promote dairy barn designs that emphasized smooth surfaces and easily cleaned building materials, such as steel, concrete, and glass brick. In 1913, Hopkins wrote that "all projections and moldings should be eliminated: the walls and ceilings plastered in cement, and the floors made of concrete, never of wood."[13] He also recommended that the long axis of the barn run roughly northwest-southeast for optimal exposure, that hay and cows be kept in the same building if the floor between them was fireproof, and that the barn be furnished with numerous large windows for proper ventilation. By the second decade of the twentieth century, technological novelties—concrete floors, glass bricks, steel tubing for stall partitions, sliding doors, iron window and door frames, and steel trusses—began to appear on dairy farms, in particular on those of wealthy land owners, who could afford to build and experiment with innovative designs.[14]

Built in 1914 as part of a progressive agricultural estate, during a time when farms in the Pennsylvania and Delaware Piedmont region were growing in size and increasing in value, the A. I. du Pont dairy complex included a separate bank barn and dairy and was surrounded by a stuccoed stone wall over 500 feet long. The dairy barn employed many architectural features that were characteristic of nearby elite country houses—light-colored stucco, slate roofing, coved cornices, sparse detailing, and simple proportional relationships. Constructed of stuccoed stone, steel columns, and iron roof trusses, the main block of the T-plan, two-story bank barn measured 90 feet by 47 feet and could accommodate at least 36 cows. The first floor was divided into two rooms finished with concrete floors, plaster walls, and ventilation holes that ran up to the roof. Each of these rooms was furnished with hay bins, feed chutes, wooden feed troughs, cow stanchions constructed of metal tubing, and concrete manure gutters (Fig. 5.31). The partition doors between the two rooms were built of wood sheathed in metal. The second floor was accessed from the outside by a long tractor ramp that led into the largest of six rooms finished with concrete floors and unpainted stone or steel-and-wallboard walls. These rooms were used for hay, feed, and tool storage. The ventilation shafts opened at this level, where they could be adjusted to the wind.

With its up-to-date construction materials and streamlined design, the A. I. du Pont dairy barn reflected the height of early-twentieth-century dairy technology. Like similar dairy barns that subsequently proliferated in the Piedmont region, and like the scores of chicken houses that are so common

Figure 5.31
A. I. du Pont dairy barn, 1914, Wilmington vicinity, New Castle County, Delaware. Photographed by Susan Brizzolara, 1988. This barn, constructed of stuccoed stone, steel columns, and iron roof trusses, utilized the latest in early-twentieth-century dairy technology. The first-floor rooms were furnished with hay bins, feed chutes, wooden feed troughs, cow stanchions constructed of metal tubing, and concrete manure gutters.

Figure 5.32
Isle of Wight County, Virginia. Photographed 1974. On many farms, the farmyard, barn, and outbuildings were placed to one side of the house.

on the Eastern Shore today, it illustrates how profoundly changes in agricultural practices have altered the architectural landscape.

Farm Plans

Finally, we need to gain a general sense of farmyard plans. The types and placement of buildings on farms relate to a multitude of factors, including the kinds of agriculture historically and currently practiced, regional building preferences, and spatial innovations accompanying various agricultural reform movements. Just as we classify houses by plan, we can group farmsteads by their spatial arrangement of barns and other outbuildings in relationship to each other. For the most part, the placement of farm buildings follows the commonsense aesthetic of function and geometry. Like the house lot, the placement of the farmyard is typically described in relationship to the house. The most common arrangements place the farmyard behind the house, to one side of the dwelling, or across a road or farm lane from the residence (Fig. 5.32).

Whatever the placement of the farmyard relative to the house, the arrangement of the whole complex of buildings tends toward either a courtyard or a range. Henry Glassie recognized two basic farmyard plan types in the Delaware valley, and this is true of much of the region. The courtyard plan is

Figure 5.33
Haycock Township, Bucks
County, Pennsylvania. Photographed 1975. Linear
farm plans, most often seen
in the landscapes of southeastern Pennsylvania and
adjacent portions of Maryland and Delaware, consist
of an arrangement, like the
one on this farm, wherein
the ridges of the house (*far
right*) and barn are aligned
and the buildings placed
end to end.

defined by the house at one end, typically facing the road, and the barn, located behind the house with the farmyard between them. The courtyard is
completed by one or two lines of smaller outbuildings, which extend between
the house and barn and form an open work area. The intervening structures
begin behind the dwelling, with the outbuildings associated with the house
lot, and continue with stables, granaries, pens, cribs, and other buildings related to the farmyard. There are all sorts of variations on the courtyard plan.
In some locales, for example, the courtyard is more implied than real, consisting of the house and barn but few or none of the lesser structures. The absence of other structures may indicate that smaller buildings were lost over
time, that they were planned but never constructed, or simply that no additional buildings were deemed necessary. On the lower Eastern Shore, the
courtyard may be placed in front of the house where a lane leads from the
public road past barns and other farm buildings before terminating in front
of the house.[15]

Glassie's other basic plan is linear. It consists of an arrangement in which
the ridges of the house and barn are aligned and the buildings oriented end
to end. Most closely associated with the landscapes of southeastern Pennsylvania and adjacent Maryland and Delaware, the linear plan typically incorporates a bank barn (Fig. 5.33). The plan often includes other farm buildings.
Farm planners commonly grouped these other buildings (wagon barns, corn
cribs, workshops, and hog houses) into secondary courtyards defined by
their relationship to the barn rather than to the house. As with the court-

Figure 5.34
Noxontown vicinity, New Castle County, Delaware. Photographed 1979. In a farmyard laid out on the range plan, the farm lane extends along the side of the house, and the farm buildings are lined up behind the house, facing the lane.

yard plan, the linear plan is best described by first establishing the overall geometry of the farmyard, and then describing the functional relationships between buildings.[16]

In addition to Glassie's courtyard and linear plans, farmers utilized a third option: a range or extended line of agricultural structures. In a range plan, the house faces the main road, the farm lane runs along the side of the house, and the farm buildings are placed behind the house, each facing the lane, with those related to domestic functions placed nearest the house and the main barn farthest from it (Fig. 5.34).

Still other farmsteads appear to follow no plan at all. Such seemingly random arrangements are particularly common in poorer agricultural districts like those on the margins of the New Jersey Pine Barrens or the Delmarva Peninsula's Cypress Swamp.

When describing a farmstead plan, first establish its overall geometry, then describe the functional relationships between the buildings. Be aware that a lack of obvious geometric order does not necessarily represent disorder. The basis for order may reside wholly in other concerns, such as function or topography. Again, the best advice for rural fieldworkers studying everything from barns to farm plans is to look, describe, consider, and evaluate.

6

COMMERCIAL, INDUSTRIAL, AND INSTITUTIONAL ARCHITECTURE

Rural, village, and urban houses, along with farm buildings, compose much of the Middle Atlantic architectural landscape. While they have been the primary focus of this guide, there are other types of structures that shape the built environment. These include such wide-ranging categories as commercial establishments, institutional buildings, bridges, lighthouses, water towers, and industrial complexes. Although a discussion of all of these building types is not possible here, this chapter will provide a brief introduction to other building types. Following an archaeological model we will look at categories of buildings on the basis of broadly defined functions. The functions housed by each of these building types vary, but the diverse structures illustrated here uniformly represent social and economic processes that link people together in the larger landscape.

Because people employ so many architectural strategies for housing everything from worship to transportation, it is an impossible task to provide a comprehensive guide to all the other sorts of buildings in the region beyond domestic and agricultural ones. What the following chapter does do, however, is present common categories of human activity and some of the often-found building types and associated landscape features identified with those activities. A number of categories, such as transportation, food processing, commerce, and maritime work are already comprehensively covered in other publications. Wherever a detailed text that could serve as a guide to a particular category of building design and function is known, we cite it in the text.

Again, the goal here is one of learning how to look at buildings and, from looking, to discover the ways in which architecture and landscape work together. The theme of landscape introduced here is pursued in greater detail through a single case study in Chapter 7. Here, however, our intent is to lay the groundwork for studying six broad functional classes of architecture—those associated with commerce, industry, maritime enterprises, transportation, government, and religion.

Commercial Buildings

Richard Longstreth, an architectural historian who has studied commercial architecture extensively, has shown that buildings for transacting business, such as public marketplaces and individual shops with attached residences, have always been common and often conspicuous features of many communities. Still, buildings earmarked solely for commercial purposes began to appear only in the early 1800s. At that time, commercial buildings with characteristics distinguishing them from other types of buildings began to be constructed. By the end of the nineteenth century, commercial architecture had become nationally widespread.[1] Throughout this region, concentrations of commercial buildings can be seen, from downtown Wilmington to the Eastern Shore of Virginia (Fig. 6.1). The construction technologies and fashionable treatments found in these buildings respect the same combination of local, regional, and national preferences observed in dwellings and farm buildings.

Throughout the region, development of commercial architecture has been seen as an indicator of each community's achievements and potential. Early commercial buildings were often erected in clusters or districts that eventually became the familiar main streets of many towns. Like the commercial districts of Seaford, Delaware, or Bridgeton, New Jersey, these main streets became increasingly important town focal points (Fig. 6.2). From the early 1800s until the mid-twentieth century, the commercial development of most main streets tended to follow a similar pattern: the main street or primary road formed the spine of the area, while perpendicular and parallel side streets formed lateral extensions of the main street and expanded the district's reach. The main street usually acted as the anchor for the commercial district.[2]

Buildings constructed in these districts tended to abut the street as well as neighboring buildings and often utilized as much lot space as possible.

Figure 6.1
Concentrations of commercial architecture survive through-
out the mid-Atlantic region. (*A*) Mixed commercial block,
Wilmington, New Castle County, Delaware. Photographed
by David Ames, 1984. (*B*) Cape Charles, Northampton
County, Virginia. Photographed 1995.

Figure 6.2

Figure 6.2
Woodstown, Salem County,
New Jersey. Photographed
1995. Commercial build-
ings have often defined a
town's main street and become its focal points.

Development was characteristically dense. As a result, an urban building configuration—narrow but deep—became typical. Space between buildings was usually maintained only to permit access or to provide light and air for the interior. Commercial districts were characterized by a number of features that set them apart from other densely built areas. First, most of these districts consisted solely of commercial buildings, rather than a mixture of commercial and residential architecture. Second, as streets in commercial districts developed, they tended to create wide, straight spaces that were visually and spatially different from streets in residential or mixed commercial and residential areas. Third, by the mid-nineteenth century, commercial districts began to develop their own unique character. While commercial buildings usually clustered in districts, churches and other public structures tended to be constructed as freestanding buildings surrounded by open space. This pattern of development began in the early nineteenth century and continued virtually unchanged through the end of World War II. Thus, commercial districts gradually developed a character that was separate and distinct from the surrounding community.[3]

Commercial buildings developed similarly throughout the country. In most parts of late-nineteenth-century America, despite regional variations, commercial buildings looked alike, in part because most such buildings were based on a national urban ideal rather than a specialized, local notion of what commercial architecture should look like. Because commercial buildings are generally designed to be seen from the street, the front or public facade tends

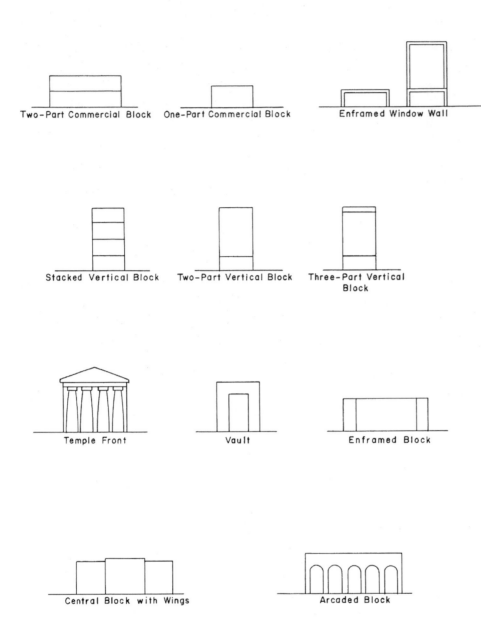

Figure 6.3
Types of commercial buildings. Drawn by Gabrielle Lanier after Longstreth, *The Buildings of Main Street*, and Longstreth, "Compositional Types in American Commercial Architecture." Most commercial buildings constructed between about 1800 and 1950 conform to one of these compositional arrangements, reflected in the visual organization of the facade.

to be their most distinctive feature. Side walls, often contiguous with adjacent buildings, are usually concealed and rarely intended to be seen. Since other characteristics of commercial buildings—such as their massing or their floor plans—vary considerably, they are not useful for creating classification systems. Unlike the floor plans for domestic buildings that are designed as groups of rooms with specialized functions and relationships to other rooms, commercial floor plans are designed to be flexible. Richard Longstreth likens commercial buildings to "vessels, efficient containers of flexible space, their form determined by one set of demands and their internal organization dictated by others."[+]

Because the development of commercial buildings was so similar throughout the country, Longstreth developed a simple classification system, based on extensive field observations. His typology is as applicable to commercial buildings is this region as it is to commercial architecture erected elsewhere in the country. His classification system is based upon the notion that the commercial facade is composed of several key elements. Most commercial buildings constructed between about 1800 and 1950 conform to a few compositional arrangements, which are reflected in the basic pattern of their facades. The compositional types Longstreth outlined provide a useful framework for looking at commercial architecture and can help us describe these buildings more effectively (Fig. 6.3). The most commonly observed compositional types in the mid-Atlantic region are outlined below.[5] Longstreth's study of commercial building types is so thorough and helpful as a field guide that we encourage readers to make use of his book.

The compositional types described here introduce some of the basic elements in the design vocabulary of commercial buildings. Some commercial buildings are combinations of several types and others do not fit into any category. Still, the compositional language of nineteenth- and early-twentieth-century commercial facades rarely varied a great deal. After World War II the range of options utilized for commercial buildings gradually changed. At this point, many of the previously widespread compositional types described below lost popularity and began to be modified. The changes were driven partly by the proliferation of suburban commercial development and partly by a changing approach toward architectural design and land use. The widespread availability of land near population centers and the growing use of automobiles fueled these changes. As a result, old notions of land use gave way to a new aesthetic that emphasized open space. By the mid-1950s, commercial districts characterized by densely clustered buildings oriented to the street and packed into gridded blocks had become outmoded in favor of commercial establishments surrounded by large amounts of open space suitable for automobile parking.[6]

Two-Part Blocks

Two-part commercial blocks, among the most commonly utilized compositions for moderately sized buildings, are usually limited to buildings of two to four stories, although taller examples of this type can be found. The primary identifying characteristic of these buildings is a horizontal division of the facade into two distinct zones. In most cases, these zones are treated separately in terms of decoration. The two zones also reflect differences in use on the interior: the lower zone usually contains public spaces while the upper zone most often houses private spaces. A series of examples of two-part commercial blocks can be seen, for example, on a principal street of Salem, New Jersey (Fig. 6.4). The two-part commercial block became widespread during the early nineteenth century. It evolved in part from the combination of dwelling and shop, examples of which can still be found in older villages, such as Chestertown, Maryland. The shop-house form was gradually abandoned in favor of buildings that were devoted exclusively to commercial purposes. The earliest two-part commercial blocks, while similar to their shop-house ancestors, generally tended to be taller and were built in uniform rows or large blocks.[7]

Built around 1900, the Burton Hardware Store in Seaford, Delaware, illustrates a typical two-part commercial facade (Fig. 6.5). The building, consisting of two identical storefronts facing High Street, has always housed a hardware store on the left side, while the right side has been a movie theatre and a repair shop. The spaces above have been used for a stock room and an apartment. A notable feature of the Burton Hardware Store is the exterior finish of elaborately wrought, galvanized, pressed sheet metal that imitates rusticated concrete blocks. The building provides an excellent example of this type of decorative metal work, which was popular during the late nineteenth century. Cast-iron fronts and woodwork imitating stone had been introduced in the

Figure 6.4
Commercial district, Salem, Salem County, New Jersey. Photographed 1995. Salem's commercial district contains many examples of two-part commercial block buildings.

Figure 6.5
Burton Hardware Store, Seaford, Sussex County, Delaware. Photograph, ca. 1975, courtesy of Delaware State Historic Preservation Office. This typical two-part block commercial facade also exemplifies a type of decorative metalwork that was popular during the late nineteenth century.

mid-nineteenth century. By the 1870s, lighter weight, less expensive pressed sheet metal became available for use in elaborate cornices for parapet walls and roofs. Gradually, pressed sheet metal became available for entire embellished facades, eventually supplanting the heavier and more expensive cast iron.[8]

One-Part Blocks

Generally found only in one-story buildings, the design of the one-part commercial block is treated as if it were simply the lower portion of a two-part commercial block and usually appears as a simple box with a decorated facade. Most buildings of this type that were constructed in the nineteenth century functioned as retail stores, and many were often grouped together along a single street. Because the street facades of these buildings are characteristically narrow and relatively small, the front walls are sometimes extended upward to provide a space for advertising and make the buildings seem larger than they actually are.[9] Numerous examples of one-part commercial blocks can be seen in the towns of the Delaware valley and the Chesapeake Bay country. Among the most distinctive examples of this type are the small early-twentieth-century town banks of Virginia's Eastern Shore (Fig. 6.6).

The one-part commercial block differs from an earlier commercial type, the one-story store, which was an extremely common form during the eighteenth

A

B

Figure 6.6
Small early-twentieth-century town banks are good examples of one-part commercial blocks. The bank near Capeville is a mirror image of the Old Bank of Marion.
(A) Deal Island Bank, 1908, Deal Island, Somerset County, Maryland. Photographed 1995. *(B)* Bank, Capeville vicinity, Northampton County, Virginia. Photographed 1995.
(C) Old Bank of Marion, 1914, Marion Crossroads, Somerset County, Maryland. Photographed 1995.

C

Figure 6.7
Hitchens' Store, early to mid-1800s, Gray's Branch vicinity, Broad Creek Hundred, Sussex County, Delaware. Photographed by David Ames, HABS, 1991. A typical eighteenth- or early-nineteenth-century one-story store was usually freestanding, topped with a gable roof, and often resembled a small house.

and early nineteenth centuries. A typical one-story store, usually a freestanding building topped with a gable roof, often had the appearance of a small house or outbuilding.[10] The Hitchens Store in Sussex County, Delaware, provides an excellent example of this type of building (Fig. 6.7). The store was begun in the early nineteenth century as a one-room, one-story frame building; a frame wing was added on to one gable wall to create a second room some time later in the century. The earlier portion of the building is furnished with an off-center fireplace, counter, display shelves, and benches by the fireplace and door; the later addition is fitted with shelves for storage as well as a stair to the attic. Attic loft space over both rooms provided extra storage space for kegs, barrels, and bulk goods.

Of one-part commercial block designs, one closely associated with the Chesapeake tidewater consists of a one- or two-story gable-fronted structure one room wide and two rooms deep. While the two-story examples seem to break the one-story rule for the one-part commercial block, their layout and use is more consistent with this form than with any of Longstreth's other compositional categories. A typical fully developed two-story example, like the brick store in Accomac, Virginia, shown in Figure 6.8, contained a ground floor retail room with shelving and counters for display and marketing. Often a second heated room stood behind the front one and served as a business or counting room. Upstairs spaces were often set aside for storage and sometimes even a one-room apartment for the proprietors or their staff. Ample storage space was required; rural and village stores supplied goods ranging from necessities to luxuries. Items stocked might include foodstuffs, spices,

A

Figure 6.8
Two-story one-part commercial blocks, like those shown here, contained a
retail room downstairs and storage upstairs. (*A*) Brick store, Accomac, and
(*B*) Hopkins Store, Onancock, Accomack County, Virginia. Photographed
1995.

B

EVERYDAY ARCHITECTURE OF THE MID-ATLANTIC

A

B

Figure 6.9

An enframed window wall has a large glass center section surrounded by a wide, almost continuous border. It is usually seen on retail stores. (*A*) Woodstown, Salem County, New Jersey. Photographed 1995. (*B*) Cape Charles, Northampton County, Virginia. Photographed 1995.

imported and domestic textiles, clothing trims such as buttons and buckles, frying pans, snuff boxes, and rum.[11]

Enframed Window Walls

This type of commercial facade is generally seen in one-story or slightly taller buildings and is most often associated with retail stores. Composed of a large glass center section surrounded on three or four sides by a wide, almost continuous border, the front is visually treated as one compositional unit. Border decoration is usually minimal (Fig. 6.9). When multistory buildings of this type occur, they are characterized by very wide front bays. More frequently associated with urban business districts than smaller towns, this type of commercial building began to appear early in the twentieth century and remained popular through the 1940s.[12]

Two- and Three-Part Vertical Blocks

This type of facade is found in multistoried buildings and is divided into two principal sections: the lower portion of the facade, which is usually two stories high, tends to be the smaller of the two zones and is more heavily ornamented than the upper part. The upper and dominant section presents a

A

Figure 6.10

The two-part vertical block, which became popular in the middle to late nineteenth century, is divided into two distinct zones; unlike the two-part commercial block, however, the two zones of the vertical block are carefully related to one another. The three-part vertical block, illustrated here, is crowned with a third distinct zone. (*A*) 229 Market Street, Wilmington, New Castle County, Delaware. Photographed by David Ames, HABS, 1988. (*B*) Laurel Street, Bridgeton, Cumberland County, New Jersey. Photographed 1995.

B

unified appearance. Like the two-part commercial block, the two-part vertical block is divided into two distinct zones; unlike the former, however, the two zones of the vertical block are carefully related to one another. The upper zone of this type also tends to be much larger, usually towering at least four stories high. The two-part vertical block, most often utilized for office buildings, department stores, and hotels, became popular in the middle to late nineteenth century. Market Street in Wilmington, Delaware, especially the area located between Second and Fifth Streets, contains many good examples of this type. The facade of the three-part vertical block has a distinct third zone at the top of the building which functions as a visual cap to the composition in much the same way that a classical capital completes the design of a column (Fig. 6.10).[13]

Temple Fronts and Vaults

The temple front is usually found in buildings ranging from one to three stories. Characterized by facades embellished with columns, pediments, porticos, and friezes, the decorative organization of temple front buildings is derived from Greek and Roman temples. In the early nineteenth century, this form was popular for various sorts of commercial buildings; but by the time the style was revived in the early twentieth century, it tended to be used predominantly for banks.[14] An example is the Eastern Shore National Bank, erected in Crisfield, Maryland, in 1900, the temple front of which consists of a full pediment carried on engaged flattened Doric pilasters (Fig. 6.11). The classical treatment extends down one side elevation of the building.

The vault composition is usually used in one- to three-story buildings. The organization of the facade consists of a massive front penetrated by a single large opening in the center. Sometimes there are smaller openings on either side of the main opening. Like the enframed window wall, the main facade contains a single large opening, but in contrast to the former, the vault creates a visual effect of massiveness and enclosure. Sometimes there are smaller openings on either side of the main opening. Partly because of their monumental appearance, vault designs were popular for banks in the first three decades of the twentieth century (Fig. 6.12).[15] Another Crisfield bank, this one built in 1937, exemplifies the vault composition (Fig. 6.13); its heavy facade includes a recessed central element, which contains the entry to the public spaces at street level and metal frame windows for the principal boardroom or offices above.

A

B

Figure 6.11
During their early-twentieth-century revival, temple fronts, derived from Greek and Roman temples, became popular for use on banks. (*A*) Eastern Shore National Bank, Crisfield, Somerset County, Maryland. Photographed 1995. (*B*) Farmers Bank, Wilmington, New Castle County, Delaware. Photographed by David Ames, mid-1980s.

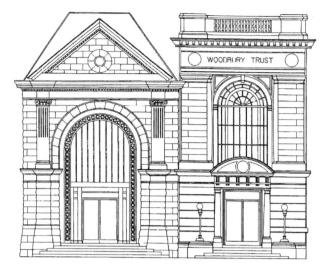

Figure 6.12
Surrogate Court and Woodbury Trust, Woodbury, Gloucester County, New Jersey. Temple front (*left*) and vault designs
(*right*) create a monumental appearance. Both were popular
for public buildings such as banks in the early twentieth
century.

Figure 6.13
Bank of Crisfield, 1937, Crisfield, Somerset County, Maryland. Photographed by Paul Touart. Photograph courtesy of
the Maryland Historical Trust. This vault facade exemplifies
the visual effect of massiveness and enclosure created by
the type.

Roadside Stands

Longstreth's typology for commercial buildings emphasizes structures that exhibit qualities of durable construction and self-conscious design, but there are considerably more ephemeral and less formal types of commercial buildings. In the mid-Atlantic region, the most ubiquitous of these less pretentious commercial structures is the roadside stand. Roadside stands range from the tailgate of a parked truck, displaying a sign which might advertise live crabs or fresh peaches, to a sprawling pole-built shed complete with display stands, refrigerated storage, and checkout counter (Fig. 6.14). Janet's Farm Market, in Salem County, New Jersey, is typical of roadside stands in the region (Fig. 6.15). It consists of a long open-sided, pole-supported shed within which a number of plain wooden counters display fruit and vegetables in loose piles or in baskets. One counter serves as a checkout stand where the proprietors accept payment, make change, and prepare produce for display and sale. Roadside stands not only vary significantly in appearance and quality, but they are seasonal structures as well. The produce stands of southern New Jersey packed with the abundance of late summer and early fall typically stand empty and forlorn through the winter months.

The importance of roadside stands for this discussion is two-fold. First, these often insubstantial structures encourage us to document and record regional architecture of all sorts, particularly those buildings and structures which may not last a single season. Second, roadside stands encourage us to consider what is architectural in the broadest sense of what constitutes a building or structure.

Manufacturing

The industrial heritage of the Middle Atlantic region, like its stock of commercial buildings, is rich and diverse. With its twin geographic assets of location on a fall-line—a major source of water power for early industry—and established ports that offered access to national and international markets, the area was an early and active participant in the industrial revolution. Early industrial development, which varied throughout the region, concentrated where natural power sources, raw materials, transportation networks, and markets were accessible. Grist- and sawmills appeared first, followed by paper mills, iron rolling and slitting mills, and textile, fertilizer, gunpowder, lumber, snuff, and spice mills. The flour and gristmills in the Wilmington and Baltimore hinterlands were especially active in the late

Figure 6.14
Truck-mounted produce stand, Machipungo vicinity, Northampton County, Virginia. Photographed 1995. Roadside stands can range from the tailgate of a parked truck to a comparatively permanent pole-built shed equipped with refrigerated storage and a checkout counter.

Figure 6.15
Janet's Farm Market, Carney's Point Township, Salem County, New Jersey. Photographed 1995. Janet's Farm Market consists mostly of a long, open-sided, pole-supported shed.

1800s. In the early nineteenth century, numerous industrial hamlets and towns developed throughout the area. Good examples of these are communities such as Ellicott City, Maryland, and Coatesville, Pennsylvania. The black powder mills of E. I. Du Pont de Nemours and Company, among the most famous mills in the region, later evolved into the Du Pont Company, one of the nation's largest chemical manufacturers. Continuing maritime commerce on the Chesapeake Bay and the Delaware River fostered an important shipbuilding industry. Wooden shipbuilding in the area began in the eighteenth century, and the shipbuilding industry continued to maintain strength through the 1900s.[16] Ship- and boat-building communities like Bethel, Delaware, Deal Island, Maryland, and Fairton, New Jersey, still exhibit the houses and work buildings associated with this industry.

Changing technology and expanding railroads fueled the development of manufacturing in nineteenth-century cities. Supplies of coal and iron ore shipped from northern Pennsylvania via the new canals and railroads further enhanced the manufacturing assets of cities as large as Baltimore and as small as Downingtown, Pennsylvania. By the third quarter of the nineteenth century, a diversified manufacturing economy founded on machine tools, metal fabrication, tanning, carriagemaking, shipbuilding, and railroad car construction was well established in the region's cities and larger towns. Industrial productivity in and around cities like Wilmington peaked at the turn of the twentieth century.[17]

In the rural tidewater country of the Delaware and Chesapeake bays, the development of agriculture, industry, and transportation networks was closely intertwined. Industry grew as the agricultural economy expanded and transportation networks extended southward. From southern New Jersey to the Eastern Shore of Virginia, the most prominent industrial buildings tended to be structures related to agriculture. Cultivation of grain, especially corn and wheat, was among the most important agricultural activities until the late 1860s. Surviving water-powered gristmills illustrate the former primacy of these crops. The extension of the railroads in the latter part of the nineteenth century allowed farmers to ship produce from inland orchards and seafood from the Chesapeake and Delaware bays to markets as far away as Chicago; as a result, peach cultivation expanded dramatically. Peaches and other delicate fruits and vegetables became important cash crops and their cultivation stimulated the growth and development of a series of industries related to processing, packaging, and transporting the harvest to markets. A significant canning industry developed on the Eastern Shore and in southern New Jersey, and by 1870, canning had become one of the largest and most important industries in the region. Similarly, basketmaking evolved from an agriculture-related craft to a full-fledged industry in the 1870s. When peach production declined in the 1880s because disease attacked the peach crop, the established agriculture-related industries continued to package and process other crops, such as tomatoes. In the twentieth century, the growth of poultry production emerged as the most significant change in the agriculture and related industry on the Eastern Shore. Mass raising of broiler chickens brought growth to other industries, including feed processing and dressing. Smaller local manufacturing activities in the region were characteristically diverse, ranging from forest-based industries, such as sawmills, carriage shops, and tanneries, to coalyards, ice plants, brickyards, paste brush manufacturing, and pearl button shops.[18]

The form, facades, and floor plans of industrial buildings, like those of commercial buildings, vary dramatically, from imposing buildings with exteriors that clearly suggest the processes housed within to relatively unassuming buildings that could serve any of a number of functions. Since the architecture in many industrial buildings is secondary to the process that takes place inside, a classification system based on floor plans or overall form is not a particularly useful way to assess these sites. Industrial buildings, like commercial buildings, are often "efficient containers" for manufacturing processes. Industrial architecture is also often altered or adapted for other processes as economic climates shift or as technology and markets change. Like the Augustine Paper Mill in Wilmington, which was originally built to manufacture snuff but was later converted to a flour and, finally, to a paper-processing mill, multiple layers of adaptation can sometimes exist in a single building. As we look at industrial architecture, then, it is important to consider the technological process that takes place within the building. An industrial survey form developed by the Delaware State Historic Preservation Office has a section for noting the function of the building as well as other features unique to industrial sites: places of access for materials, workers, and locations of offices. The form also includes a section for descriptive architectural information. Similarly, Pennsylvania's industrial survey form includes a section for noting the nature of the power system and the type of machinery present.

Because industrial architecture varies so widely, it is impossible to treat the subject in any depth here. Instead, we will examine a few specific examples that not only represent a broad geographic and chronological range but also illustrate the character and diversity of industrial architecture in the region. For fieldworkers with a particularly strong interest in the architecture and processes of industry—a field known as industrial archaeology—there is an extensive literature of guides, not only to particular industries, but also to more specific field methodologies and documentation techniques. A good starting place for the further exploration of industrial archaeology is David Weitzman's *Traces of the Past: A Field Guide to Industrial Archaeology.* Although Weitzman deals only with a few categories of industrial buildings, he offers useful advice for looking at industrial remains and pursuing further research. Considerably more detailed, and targeted for a more academic and professional audience, is Emory Kemp's book *Industrial Archaeology: Techniques,* which deals specifically with site documentation procedures.

Gristmills and Flour Mills

No single building evokes a greater sense of rural calm than the gristmill. Romantically popularized during the Victorian period, these once-common rural industrial structures processed grain into meal and flour throughout the eastern United States. Gristmills and flour mills represent a general designation that covers all industrial structures where corn, wheat, or other grains are ground into meal and flour. Depending on circumstances of topography, available power sources, local grain cultivation, transportation networks, and marketing, grist- and flour mills ranged from small inefficient operations running one pair of millstones to huge multistory flour factories. Distinctions among mills are drawn in various ways and include clientele, power sources, and grinding technology. Thus, mills grinding grain for an exclusively local trade were known as custom mills, while those engaged in volume production and shipping were designated as merchant mills. Somewhere in the middle were the many rural mills that pursued a dual strategy of grinding for the local trade as well as the distant marketplace. The single best introduction on the mechanical workings of mills remains John Reynolds' *Windmills and Watermills.*

Mills can be classified as those dependent on topography for their power sources and those that are engine-driven. Topographically dependent mills, such as those powered by water, wind, or tide, exhibit the evidence of human intervention in the landscape. Dams, millponds, and raceways, for example, are common landscape features associated with milling and often survive to indicate a mill seat, or site, long after the buildings have vanished from both view and memory. Engine-driven mills, such as those fueled by coal, wood, electricity, or diesel fuel, tended to be free of any topographic constraint for power, but they were dependent on other landscape features for their economic success. Accordingly, engine-driven mills are often found adjacent to railroad lines, canals, rural crossroads, or at the edges of towns. Power source is a descriptive and classification factor not just for grist- and flour mills but for all types of manufactures.

Grinding processes have varied over the years and from one mill to another. In the late 1800s, for example, a distinction was drawn between old process and new process mills. Old process mills, regardless of power source, ground grain between pairs of heavy millstones mounted in the floor. New process mills exploited late-nineteenth-century manufacturing innovations and ground grain between grooved steel or porcelain rollers mounted in upright chests. Generally each chest contained two pairs, or breaks, of rollers. Associated with the new process mills (also known as roller mills) was a wide variety of machinery, including sifters, bolters, barrel packers, and grain elevators and other devices that carried the flour or meal through the process. By the early twentieth century, old and new process millers had incorporated new technologies into "combination" mills intended to satisfy a varied clientele. Mills of this type are by far the most common examples of grist- and flour mills standing in the modern countryside.

The one distinguishing construction feature in mills is the husk frame—a heavy internal timber framework most often associated with water-powered old process mills. The husk frame provided a separate structural system for carrying the gear train attached to the water wheel or water turbines and for supporting the millstones on the floor above. The husk frame absorbed much of the vibration that is generated in the grinding process and would otherwise shake and weaken the overall structure. Except for the husk frame, grist- and flour mills make use of the same construction technologies associated with other local building types, including houses and barns. Mills of log, frame, brick, and stone construction ranging from one to four stories in elevation stand throughout the region. Today we recognize these buildings primarily through their associated landscape features, such as streams, ponds, dams, bridges, and railroad sidings.

Two water-powered examples, a three-story stone mill near Quakertown in Bucks County, and the Exton Mill in Chester County, Pennsylvania, illustrate a number of common features (Fig. 6.16). Both are partially embanked and housed the drive machinery in the lower story. In the Bucks County example, the arched opening near the rear wall indicates that a water wheel or turbine was placed inside the building—a feature confirmed by the stone- and concrete-walled race. Both buildings also possess a roof extension at the gable

A

Figure 6.16
Most water-powered mills are partially embanked, with the lower story containing the drive machinery. (*A*) Grist mill, Haycock Township, Bucks County, Pennsylvania. Photo: graphed 1976. (*B*) Grist mill, Exton vicinity, Chester County, Pennsylvania. Photographed 1981.

B

peak. These extended gables, or cats heads, shelter a beam carrying a block and tackle for hoisting bags of grain. The upper-story doors in both buildings facilitated moving heavy loads in and out of the building to a waiting wagon or loading dock. The covered bridge behind the Bucks County mill illustrates the typical association of grist and flour mills with such other landscape features as bridges, storehouses, workers' housing, and other industrial activities, like sawmilling.

Canneries

The agricultural bounty of the Middle Atlantic region, a shift away from a grain-based farm economy in the last third of the nineteenth century, the development of an extensive railroad shipping network, and the need to reach a year-round market were all factors contributing to the rise of canneries. Canneries for preserving fruit and vegetables were housed in all sorts of buildings, from farmhouse kitchens to long warehouses placed adjacent to railroad sidings, of which the King's Creek Canning Company near Princess Anne, Maryland, is a good example (Fig. 6.17). The best regional overview of canning processes and buildings is found in Dean Doerrfeld's *The Canning Industry in Delaware.*

Doerrfeld notes that "canning factories included not just buildings, but everything that contributed directly to the canning of foodstuffs, from the initial preparation of food after harvesting to the storage of the finished product. Canning factories consisted of labor and process machines as well as buildings." [19] Doerrfeld charts the canning process through a number of steps. First, there was a "preparation stage," which began with the inspection of the produce to be canned, included basic preparations such as peeling, hulling, shucking, and slicing, and concluded with filling the cans. The preparation steps varied with the fruits or vegetables being canned. Tomatoes, for example, had to be inspected, sorted, scalded, peeled, and then prepared either whole, crushed, or pre-cooked as sauce or paste. The "sterilization stage" involved capping and sealing the cans and then heating the cans and their contents—in effect using heat to kill the bacteria inside the can. Other processes associated with canneries included support functions such as making and storing the cans, labeling the finished product, and shipping.

Large-scale canning factories appeared on the rural and town scene at the turn of the twentieth century. Again, Doerrfeld provides the best architectural summary of the canning factory or complex:

The load-bearing elements of the structure supported processing equipment,
and served as a framework for attaching the equipment used to transfer power
throughout the cannery, such as line shafting or electric motors. Cannery
buildings often contained second, even third, levels, that housed can-making
shops, or served as living quarters or storage areas. A canning factory, as a
manufacturing process, could assume an unlimited number of forms depending on the various products and the configuration of the process equipment:
therefore, the simplest way to examine the factory is to think of it as an assemblage of building blocks with each block representing a separate factory activity such as preparation, sterilization, or can-making.[20]

The key elements in Doerrfeld's synthesis are process, adaptability, vari-
ability, and assemblage. The cannery, like the mill, is a building or group of
buildings designed to house a manufacturing process that varies considerably
in response to what is being canned or the physical scale of production. The
architectural building blocks for the factory range from the most basic metal-
sided balloon-frame sheds to sprawling brick factory buildings with distinctive clerestory windows and towering smokestacks. The process aspect of
canning is best documented by the types of machinery found in and around
the buildings. The Isaacs Cannery near Ellendale in Sussex County, Delaware, for example, is a 50-foot by 125-foot, two-story, frame, wire-nailed,
early twentieth-century structure of a type suitable for housing a wide variety
of manufacturing and storage functions (Fig. 6.18). On the interior, however,
the types of machinery and their arrangement enable us to identify the produce being processed—peas and lima beans—and the steps employed in the

Figure 6.18
Isaacs Cannery, Ellendale vicinity, Cedar Creek Hundred,
Sussex County, Delaware. Photographs by David Ames,
HABS, 1994. The early twentieth-century building type
shown here was suitable for a wide variety of manufacturing
and storage functions. The details of its interior furnishings
reveal the type of manufacturing it housed, in this case, canning of peas and lima beans.

canning process, from arrival and sorting to labeling and storage. Our sense of the Issacs Cannery is achieved, as Doerrfeld reminds us, not through the building itself, but by the ways in which the building houses the manufacturing process.

Paper Mills

The same process-based strategy employed in the examination of other industrial buildings carries over into the study of heavy manufactures. As with canneries, boatyards, and flour milling, we are recording the architectural context in which an industrial process takes place. Often the buildings are generic in terms of construction details and form but highly distinctive in the way they accommodate a manufacturing process within their walls and how they relate to their immediate environment. While there are specialty buildings and structures for heavy manufactures like steel, glass, or petroleum production, most of the architectural evidence for heavy industry that we see in the region's common landscapes makes use of building designs and construction techniques that can serve any number of manufacturing purposes. More often than not, the manufacturing process defines the building.

From the early eighteenth century until the present, papermaking has been a significant element in the regional economy of the Philadelphia area. In the middle to late nineteenth century, a number of papermaking concerns upgraded their production systems to become fully automated. Typical of these operations is Auburn Mills in Yorklyn, Delaware. Auburn Mills, situated on the Red Clay Creek, occupies a site that has been used for water-powered manufactures since the early colonial period. By the late nineteenth century, the owners of the site had focused their attentions on rag paper production. The papermaking occurred in a long, low stone building adjacent to a mill race and road. Across the road stood the first millowner's house, workers' housing, and an office. A later manufacturing building and a new owner's mansion were added to the complex around the turn of the twentieth century. The paper mill and its setting do not exhibit architectural characteristics that visually identify the complex as anything more specific than an industrial assemblage. Inside the mill, however, the 1880s machinery (with later improvements) and the process it reveals remain intact. Bales of rags were brought into one end of the buildings, where they were mixed with water and ground in vats. From the vats, the rag slurry was introduced into a continuous mechanical process that converted the wet mixture at one end into huge rolls of finished paper at the other. How that process worked would require a considerably more detailed discussion, but the lesson for fieldworkers in architecture is clear. You may begin with buildings in the study of industrial architecture, but in the end you will need to situate those buildings within a manufacturing process to understand how they worked and why they occupy the landscape the way they do.

Small-Scale Shops

Innumerable entrepreneurs constructed workshops that employed one to a dozen individuals in various aspects of small-scale, often handicraft, production. Backyard sheds were used by boat builders and decoy carvers in nineteenth-century Virginia and Maryland maritime communities. Eighteenth-century residents of Sussex County, Delaware, built loom and weaving houses. Artisans in southeastern Pennsylvania constructed cooperages and blacksmith shops. As with many workaday structures in rural and village settings, there is often little to distinguish these buildings from similarly constructed storehouses, small barns, stables, slave quarters, and modest dwellings. Even with the rise of more specialized manufacturing complexes in the late nineteenth century, small-scale light manufactures continued to be housed in buildings that tended to mirror general local building styles rather than reveal a specific manufacturing process (Fig. 6.19).

The specific use of these buildings is likely to be revealed by the raw materials stored in the yard, under a shed, or indoors and by specialized tools, such as drill presses or other power equipment, as illustrated by the H. W. Hocker Paste Brush Factory in Lewes, Delaware (Fig. 6.20). This business represents one of the first successful small-scale industries in its area that was not related to either agricultural interests or the maritime occupations of Lewes. The factory, which produced tin- and wood-handled mucilage brushes for a limited market, is typical of small-scale, family-owned and -operated firms in the early twentieth century. Brush manufacture involved both hand and machine processes, both of which took place in the small, one-story circa 1910 frame building that also served as office and storage space for the firm. The manufacturing process involved cutting and forming sheet tin into handles, which were filled by hand with goat- or horsehair and then tapped and trimmed on kick presses.

Figure 6.19
Ward Brothers Carving
Shed, Crisfield, Somerset
County, Maryland. Photo-
jgraphed 1977. Buildings
that housed small-scale
light manufactures tended
to reflect local building
styles rather than display
architectural traits particular to a specific industry.

The History of Three Companies

The common industrial buildings and complexes of the region include many sites that are geared to the manufacture of goods from local resources. Some of these, such as brickworks, represent categories of industrial activity found throughout the United States; others, such as basketmaking, depended on more localized raw materials and markets. As with canneries, the manufacturing process may direct the architectural description of the building more than matters of construction and plan. In other situations, the manufacturing process required specifically designed, purpose-built structures such as kilns. The examples of three local industries, the Houston-White Company Mill and Basket Factory, the Day Basket Company, and the J. H. Wilkerson and Son Brickworks, illustrate both the architectural form and diversity of local manufactures throughout the region.

Located in Millsboro, Delaware, the Houston-White Company Mill and Basket Factory illustrates the intertwined relationship between agriculture and some important Delaware valley industries. Established in 1893, the company grew in tandem with the produce industry of Sussex County. By the second decade of the twentieth century, the factory had become the principal employer in Millsboro, as well as the second largest manufacturer of wood veneer produce containers in Delaware.

At its largest, the factory facilities included twenty-four structures. The main mill and basket factory, a frame building that was absorbed by numerous

Figure 6.20

H. W. Hocker Company, ca. 1910, Lewes, Sussex County, Delaware. Photographed by Charles Foote, Historic American Engineering Record, 1975. This little building housed the entirety of the Hocker paste brush factory: manufacturing, storage, and office operations.

Figure 6.21
Houston-White Company
Mill and Basket Factory,
Millsboro, Sussex County,
Delaware. Photographed
by Charles Foote, Historic
American Engineering Rec-
ord, 1975. The original
frame building was ab-
sorbed by several later
additions.

later additions, illustrates the characteristically random growth of the company's production facilities (Fig. 6.21). Various steps in the basket manufacturing process took place at specific locations in the main factory building.
Sawn logs to be converted to veneer were steamed to loosen the bark as well
as to facilitate cutting on the veneer lathe. Once the logs were stripped and
steam-softened, they were then processed into staves. Basket bottoms were
manufactured in a separate section of the mill. Once they were assembled, the
damp baskets were transferred by the dozens to open drying sheds for even-
tual shipment.[21]

The Houston-White Company had begun production at a time when markets for fresh fruits and vegetables were expanding, and its basketmaking operations grew along with regional agriculture. Changes in Delaware agriculture forced the company to cease basketmaking in 1959–60, although lumber
production continued at the company until the mill shut down in 1974.[22]

Like the Houston-White Company, the Day Basket Company, located in
North East, Maryland, began business by producing hand-made splint bas-
kets for a market that was largely regional and dependent upon agriculture.
Unlike the Houston-White Company, however, the Day Basket Company

Figure 6.22
Day Basket Company,
North East, Cecil County,
Maryland. Photographed
1995. The Day Basket
Company, which continues
to produce handmade splint
baskets, began business
serving a market that was
largely regional and dependent upon agriculture.

remains in operation and continues to produce a range of baskets today. Located in an unassuming, concrete-block, gable-roofed building, the company's
manufacturing facility consists of a large, well-lit open work space that ac-
commodates several work stations. At each work station, employees accom-
plish a different step in the basketmaking process—splitting staves, weaving
the basket bottoms, finishing the rims, or attaching the handles stamped with
the company name to the basket rims. The finished baskets are then stacked
in one part of the building to await shipment (Fig. 6.22).

Located on the north side of the Mispillion River, just east of Milford in
Kent County, Delaware, the J. H. Wilkerson and Son Brickworks complex
illustrates a twentieth-century Delaware brickworks as it appeared when
small local brickworks characterized the industry. When brickmaking ceased
here in 1957, J. H. Wilkerson and Sons was among the last of eleven similar
small-scale brickworks in Delaware to close down. The firm was a leading
area supplier of face and common bricks in the early twentieth century. During the years that the factory operated, there were relatively few changes to
the original manufacturing system. Because the raw materials involved in
brick manufacture were bulky and difficult to transport over great distances,
most brick factories were located close to clay deposits and potential markets.
Although clay deposits suitable for brick manufacture are uncommon in Sussex County, the Wilkerson factory is situated upon a prime source of clay
adjacent to the Mispillion River.[23]

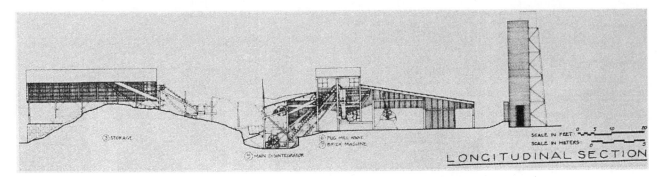

The site originally included sheds, machinery, a kiln, and other structures associated with the brickmaking process (Fig. 6.23). It is now partially ruinous, but the storage shed, the shed over the brickmaking machine, and one of the drying sheds still stand. Because the complex has been undisturbed since the brickmaking operation shut down, the steps in the brickmaking process remain discernible in the layout of the surviving machinery and structures. The standing buildings are wood frame capped with metal roofs. Machinery associated with the brickmaking process included disintegrators, a pug mill for mixing clay, a brickmaking machine, a brick cutter, and an arrangement of belts and cups that transported the clay through the various stages of the process. Other essential tools included drying pallets, metal wagons that carried bricks to the drying shed and kiln, and the wooden wheelbarrow used to empty the kiln. The walls of the brick kiln still stand.[24]

Figure 6.23
J. H. Wilkerson and Son Brickworks, Milford, Kent County, Delaware. Drawn by K. D. Anderson, Historic American Engineering Record, 1975. This drawing of a twentieth-century brick factory illustrates how brickworks were designed when small local brickworks characterized the industry.

Maritime Structures

Tidal rivers, bays, and the Atlantic Ocean define the topography of much of the middle Atlantic region. Activities such as fishing and shipbuilding have left a rich and varied architecture that includes boathouses, wharves, and shipyards. We approach our description of these structures, as we have that of other building types defined by function, through the categories of construction, form, and style. A boathouse such as one recorded on Box Tree Creek in Virginia can be described simply as a one-story, frame, pole-supported building with gable roof and vertical board siding (Fig. 6.24). As with most of the categories covered in this chapter, the factors of siting, use, and associated structures provide the defining elements for our understanding of architectural design and purpose. Thus, the Box Tree Creek boathouse is defined further by its placement on pilings over the water, the narrow plank gangway which leads to the structure itself, and the small dock which provides a moor-

Figure 6.24

Boathouse, Box Tree Creek, Northampton County, Virginia. Photographed 1977. In identifying and describing this boathouse, its architectural form—a one-story, frame, pole-supported building with a gable roof and vertical board siding—and its relationship to nearby environmental features—docks, mooring places, outdoor work spaces—are equally important.

ing place for work boats, open storage for fishing equipment, and a work space for culling, cleaning, and packing the catch. Because the Box Tree Creek boathouse is part of a larger working landscape defined by its relationship to the waters of the vast Virginia seaside marshes, we would also do well to include features such as crabbing grounds and oyster reefs in our evaluation. The seasonal aspect of work on the water further complicates our ability to produce meaningful architectural descriptions. The ways in which a building is used for one aspect of the middle Atlantic fishery, such as crabbing in the summer months, may change significantly during the winter oyster harvest. The following discussion focuses on two maritime activities: shad fishing on the Delaware Bay and oystering on the Chesapeake. The brief explorations of these two industries illustrate the extraordinary architectural diversity of common maritime buildings.

Shad Fishing

Early every spring great schools of shad migrate up the Delaware River to their freshwater spawning grounds. Fishermen from both sides of the Delaware have worked the annual run from prehistoric times to the present. From the late 1700s through the middle of the nineteenth century, nets were pulled across the mouths of tidal tributaries as people sought to capture as many shad as possible. On the open waters of the river, fishermen worked together around the clock laying out their nets across the tide. At night the reflected glare of the metal lamps mounted in the bows of their skiffs could be seen from the river's shorelines. Pollution and overfishing greatly reduced shad fishery in the first half of the twentieth century, but in recent years the shad have returned and shad fishing—both commercial and recreational—has found new vitality. The surviving architecture of the shad fishery dates primarily from the late nineteenth and early twentieth centuries. As a functionally related category, the structures historically associated with shad fishing on the Delaware illustrate the need to view the extraordinarily ordinary and ephemeral with a sensitive eye.

The architecture of the shad fishery consisted primarily of wharves, small frame sheds, drying racks for nets, and floating cabins. When the shad were not in season the same structures found use in other aspects of traditional Delaware River fishing and hunting, including sturgeon fishing, wildfowl gunning, and turtling. Early-twentieth-century photographs of the shad fishery fall into two categories, each documenting a particular environment. The riverside wharves and boathouses represent one environment, which is characterized by lightly constructed frame work buildings. These are typically one story high, supported on posts or poles set in the marsh bottom, gable roofed, roughly sided, and have exposed wall framing and rafters on the interior.[25] Associated with these work structures are lightly built pole-supported wharves and docks, which provided work space for sorting and packing the catch, drying and mending nets, and preparing for the next day's fishing. The second environment was the one of temporary fishing camps, which were composed of floating, scow-bottomed cabins anchored in "scow dives" and temporary docks built of trimmed saplings pushed down into the mud (Fig. 6.25). The floating cabins, with their gable or segmental arch roofs, dimensioned-lumber frames, horizontally sliding sash, and one- or two-room plans divided into a cooking and sitting space at the front and a sleeping area at the back, were the most distinctive architectural element in this maritime landscape (Fig. 6.26).[26]

Taken together as a landscape ensemble (a theme pursued in the following chapter) the architecture of the shad fishery exhibits a number of traits that provide a significant caution about how we look at buildings. The architecture of the shad fishery is seasonal, and the seasonal aspect of the activity makes us realize that the structures and their sites possess the additional qualities of being adaptable and ephemeral. The floating cabins used in the shad season were regularly relocated to other scow dives depending on the nature of marshland work—an action that redefined both function and site. Additionally, constructions such as the sapling wharves and net drying racks were temporarily built to serve a finite use. The fishery also produced environmentally and functionally specific structures, like the floating cabins; and these structures, as seen in the following discussion of the oyster industry, were defined by a host of related objects, such as shad skiffs, live boxes, metal torches, clothing, baskets, and nets. The qualities of ephemerality and functional definition can be seen in other types of architecture. Hog gallows in

Figure 6.25

Southern New Jersey, early 1900s, Clem Sutton photograph collection.
Early twentieth-century photographs of the shad fishery and hunting
camps document an environment composed of floating, scow-bottomed
cabins (like the one *right of center* here) anchored in "scow dives" and temporary docks built of trimmed saplings pushed down into the mud. The
white building behind the floating cabin, with bagged wildfowl nailed to the
gable wall, was a nonfloating gunning and trapping cabin.

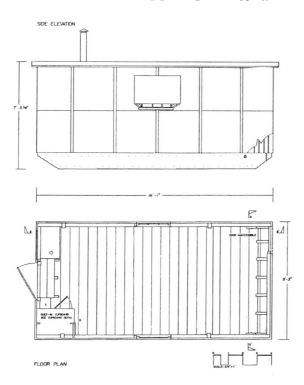

Figure 6.26

Plan and elevation of a floating cabin, Liston Point vicinity,
New Castle County, Delaware. Drawn by Johanna McBrien
and Margaret Watson. Floating cabins, used during shad
season, were typically constructed with gable or segmental
arch roofs, dimensioned-lumber frames, horizontally sliding
sash, and one- or two-room plans divided into a cooking and
sitting space at the front of the cabin and a sleeping area at
the back.

southeastern Virginia, for example, consist of little more than upright poles with a cross bar, a trestle table, and an open fire.

Oystering

Few aspects of maritime material life are so closely tied to a particular place in the popular imagination than oystering is to the Chesapeake Bay. Although oysters have been taken from the Chesapeake for thousands of years, the dramatic rise of a large-scale oyster fishery and its subsequent decline are the products of the last one hundred and fifty years. The architectural field study of the oyster industry can be divided readily into two parts: the fishery and the processing of the harvest. The architecture of the Chesapeake (and Delaware Bay) oyster fishery consists of the same buildings associated with other aspects of maritime material culture. Wharves and wharfside sheds and boathouses, blacksmith shops, chandleries, and sail lofts are all architectural elements in the fishery. The physical character of these structures and buildings is best described using the basic terminology of construction and form laid out in earlier chapters. Like the architecture of factories, though, the buildings of the oyster industry need to be described on the basis of how they work as well as how they look.

An excellent example of the functionally specific architecture of the oyster fishery is found in the processing end of the industry, as discussed in Paula Johnson's *Working the Water: The Commercial Fisheries of Maryland's Patuxent River.* Johnson's work offers two advantages to fieldworkers in traditional maritime architecture. First, she discusses individual buildings, for instance shucking houses, on the basis of how they work from the arrival of the oysters, dredged and tonged out of the murky waters by watermen, to their departure in individual cans. In her examination of the J. C. Lohr and Sons oyster shucking house, built in 1934, Johnson describes the two-story, gable-roof, frame building by explaining how the oysters pass through the structure on their way to market. Built adjacent to Back Creek on the Patuxent near its confluence with the Chesapeake, the Lohr shucking house provided a wharf area with a buying station for purchasing and offloading the oysters from workboats onto a conveyor belt. The oysters' journey from the waterside carried them through an open receiving area, where they were dumped, shoveled into wheelbarrows, and carried to the shuckers standing in wooden stalls in two shucking rooms. Once shucked and sorted by size into buckets, the oysters were carried by the shuckers to a processing room. In the processing room the oysters were rinsed and weighed and the shuckers' quantities posted on a tally board. Following repeated rinsing, draining, skimming, and washing, the oysters were canned for market. From the processing room the cans of oysters went either to a shipping room where they could be trucked out immediately or to cold storage rooms where they awaited later shipment.

Johnson's exploration of oyster processing underscores just how much the archaeology of all architecture depends on the documentation of other objects. Her accompanying catalog of oystering artifacts begins with various forms of tongs and dredges employed for oyster harvesting and then proceeds through all the objects associated with the fishery itself, including bushel measures, culling hammers, and even clothing. Similarly, her overview of the processing end of the industry lays out the full range of objects associated with getting oysters out of their shells and into the marketplace. Oyster knives, shuckers' blocks and stands, aprons, gloves, buckets and measures, tally boards and tokens, dippers, skimmers, blow tanks, paddles, cans, labels, lid "clappers," shipping barrels, and shipping stencils are all objects associated with the way the process operates in its architectural setting. In this descriptive context, Johnson's discussion of oyster houses illustrates a strategy emphasizing process in the understanding of architecture—a strategy that is broadly applicable to everything from steel mills to harness shops.

Transportation

The history and technology of transportation is well represented in the landscape. The growth of the railroad can be discovered in the miles of track that lace the region, as well as in railroad bridges, trestles, sidings, roundhouses, and stations. Maritime transportation is documented in the physical evidence of shipyards, canals, navigational aids, ferries, and wharves. Aerodromes and early runways enable us to discover the architectural history of air travel and transport, just as radar stations and missile silos enable us to better understand the Cold War on the home front. The introduction of the automobile generated the largest number of buildings related to transportation: household garages, gas and service stations, automobile showrooms, junk yards, diners, and other forms of roadside architecture ranging from the vanishing drive-in movie theater to the ever more common minimart. Overall, transportation architecture, particularly in the middle to late twentieth century, paid increasingly little heed to local traditions. With the rise of national oil companies, airlines, and rail networks came a parallel move toward building designs intentionally conceived to stand apart from local practice.

Transportation architecture has generated a large popular literature. Most of these works can serve as field guides in their own right. Typically, these publications consist of a general introductory history, followed by a series of chapters or a gazeteer which categorizes buildings along developmental or stylistic guidelines. Because transportation-related architecture is so well-represented in the literature, we will not treat it in any depth here. Instead, we offer several publications that can be used as starting points for further exploration.

As a guide to aspects of the automobile landscape, Daniel I. Vieyra's *"Fill'er Up": An Architectural History of America's Gas Stations* offers a concise history of service station design and then explores a series of design categories, such as "the Fantastic," "the Respectable," and "the Domestic," based on observed architectural qualities. While Vieyra's categories may prove unsuitable for other interpretations, they do offer a clear framework from which to start. Similarly, Philip Langdon's *Orange Roofs, Golden Arches: The Architecture of American Chain Restaurants* explores the history of buildings associated with fast food. Langdon's work also reveals another aspect of transportation architecture: its fundamentally national character. Richard Gutman's *The American Diner, Then and Now* traces the architectural history of a roadside icon, while Will Anderson's *Mid-Atlantic Roadside Delights* provides a more general overview of drive-ins, motels, gas stations, and diners in the region.

Railroad architecture has produced the most extensive body of histories and guides. Carroll Meeks's 1956 *The Railroad Station, An Architectural History* stands as a thorough introduction to railroad station design in the context of major architectural style periods. A very different approach to the buildings and structures associated with rail transport are the guides and manuals published for the industry itself. Among the most accessible of these is John Droege's *Passenger Terminals and Trains*, published in 1916, which covers a variety of topics, including terminal construction and maintenance, ticket offices, train indicators, and passenger train operation. More recent works, like Lawrence Grow's *Waiting for the 5:05: Terminal, Station and Depot in America*, function as photographic indices to the history of American railroad architecture.

Government and Institutional Buildings

Unlike commercial and industrial buildings, which are "efficient containers" for the processes that are housed within, the primary function of many institutional buildings is often symbolic. For example, government buildings are often substantial, elegantly constructed, and prominently placed. In the following pages we will briefly discuss several common categories of public building and public space, including the courthouse square, schools, and houses of worship.

Every county, town, and city throughout the region possesses a seat of government. By far the most common of these are the courthouse groupings that define the political and public center of every county from southeastern Pennsylvania to the Eastern Shore of Virginia. The most common functional components of the courthouse complex are the courthouse itself, the clerk's office, and the county jail. Additionally, courthouse ensembles may contain attorneys' offices, monuments, administrative annexes, commercial buildings, inns and cafés, post offices, and other buildings. The single function that unifies courthouse groupings throughout the region, however, is that of governance, and the single defining building is the courthouse. Although courthouses vary in appearance and construction depending on when they were built and size of the administrative burdens of county and municipal government, they generally contain one or more courtrooms, judge's chambers, deed and probate offices, tax assessors and licensing offices, and other functions essential to the business of the county or town. Some communities' government enclaves retain their eighteenth-century courthouses, but most often as a museum or ceremonial building. The oldest working courthouses that remain in use date to the early nineteenth century and are typically large, two-story brick structures which have received numerous additions. A good example of this is the courthouse in Sussex County, Delaware. More common are late-nineteenth and early-twentieth-century buildings that house all the functions listed above. In the late twentieth century, there has been increasing pressure to abandon the courthouse square in favor of new administrative complexes, often situated on the outskirts of the county seat.

One of the best preserved county courthouse squares is found in Eastville, Virginia.[27] Located in Northampton County, Eastville has been the county seat since the early colonial period. An early-eighteenth-century plat of the courthouse square shows the courthouse, with the prison and stocks nearby, surrounded by several dwellings, including one labeled "Loghouse" (Fig. 6.27). Today the courthouse square reflects three centuries of architectural activity (Fig. 6.28). The centerpiece of the Eastville complex is the two-story brick courthouse commissioned early in the twentieth century. Elaborated with decorative brickwork, the gable front faces Eastville's main street across a neatly trimmed lawn. At the head of the sidewalk leading up

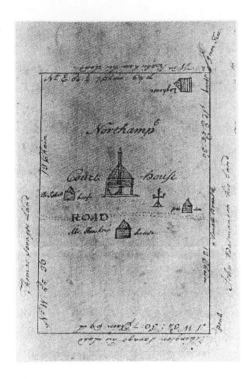

Figure 6.27
Plat of courthouse square, Eastville, Northampton County, Virginia. Eastville is home to one of the best preserved county courthouse squares. This early eighteenth-century plat shows the courthouse, prison and stocks, and several dwellings.

Figure 6.28
Courthouse square, Eastville, Northampton County, Virginia. Photographed 1994. The centerpiece of the Eastville courthouse complex is the two-story brick courthouse, commissioned in the early twentieth century.

Figure 6.29
Old Courthouse, Eastville, Northampton County, Virginia. Photographed 1995. Originally erected in 1795, this building was moved and renovated early in the twentieth century, following the aesthetic of the Colonial Revival.

to the courthouse stands a Confederate monument. To the south a range of nineteenth-century, one-story attorney's offices known as Lawyers Row looks across the open courtyard toward a grouping of restored eighteenth- and early-nineteenth-century brick public buildings including the old courthouse, the clerk's office, and a gaol. The old courthouse, originally erected in 1795, was relocated to its present site when the new courthouse was planned in 1913. The renovation of the old courthouse, which included a completely rebuilt gable front and the addition of a stylish Federal period townhouse doorcase salvaged from a demolition in Norfolk, followed the aesthetic of the Colonial Revival (Fig. 6.29). Behind the northwest corner of the courthouse looms the county jail, executed in a style similar to the new courthouse; to the south extends a mid-twentieth-century administrative wing housing the county's expanded governmental functions within the architectural language of institutional modernism. The Eastville courthouse square extends beyond the county's administrative precinct. To the south stand a two-story, Flemish bond, gable-front commercial building of the early nineteenth-century as well as the rambling expanse of the eighteenth-century Eastville Inn, which continued to serve the role of courthouse tavern and café into the late twentieth century. A mixture of commercial buildings, a gas station, and dwellings completes the setting.

Not all public service buildings were located in the courthouse complex. Closely identified with rural landscapes throughout the United States are country schools. Among the earliest purpose-built schools in the region are one- and two-room schools containing a single space shared by all the students regardless of their academic progress. Nineteenth-century schools differ little in their appearance and construction from other rural public buildings. This fact is noted by Sara Leach and Kimberly Sebold in reference to southern New Jersey: "The majority of country schools are lookalike, modest, gable-roofed frame buildings constructed of commercially produced and dimensioned materials and manufactured hardware, but incorporate provincialized ornamentation. The forms," Leach and Sebold continue, "built from the mid- to late 1800s, are repeated in nearby churches, community centers, granges, and Masonic halls."[28] Thus, fraternal halls, such as the Pride of Virginia Lodge near Eastville, Virginia, or small rural churches, like Otts Chapel near Newark, Delaware, closely parallel school design (Fig. 6.30).

Nineteenth-century rural and town schools were characterized by a one- or two-story gable front typically surmounted by a small cupola containing a bell. Built of frame, brick, and stone, these buildings are particularly common

Figure 6.30

Nineteenth-century fraternal halls and small rural churches closely parallel school design. (*A*) Pride of Virginia Lodge, Eastville, Northampton County, Virginia. Photographed 1995. (*B*) Otts Chapel, Newark, New Castle County, Delaware. Photographed 1995.

A

B

in the Delaware valley (Fig. 6.31). The Goshen Public School in Cumberland County, New Jersey, exemplifies the type. Built in 1872, the two-story frame building features a pedimented gable front with cupola. A round arch with louvered vents in the cupola and Italianate brackets decoratively enhance the overall appearance of the building. Some rural schools, however, adopted plans and massing that differed from other buildings. In some locales, one-story buildings with a shallowly pitched hip roof pierced by a centrally placed stove flue were erected on a square plan. More distinctive and exceptional was the Octagonal Schoolhouse, built in 1831 and once considered the finest district school in Delaware (Fig. 6.32). When it was built, the schoolhouse accommodated eighty-seven pupils and was known as Pleasant Hill Academy. Insurance records from Kent County, Delaware, describe another unusually shaped school building, a twelve-sided dormitory in Laurel that measured 140 feet around the circumference. The building was furnished with twelve communicating rooms that were used as sleeping rooms for students and were heated with a single, centrally placed stove.[29] For more information on the architecture and use of rural schools, the single best source book remains Andrew Gulliford's *America's Country Schools.*

The many churches, chapels, meeting houses, and synagogues found throughout the region testify to a historic diversity of religious faith. From the Quaker meeting houses of the Delaware valley to the Pentecostal Holiness churches of Virginia, the region's landscape yields a rich tradition of religious architecture (Fig. 6.33). One of the best areas in which to view the diversity of religious architecture in the region is the countryside of southern New Jersey between Salem and Bridgeton.[30]

The Quaker meeting houses of southern New Jersey, like those elsewhere in the Delaware valley, are typically sparely ornamented rectangular brick structures with gable roofs and a balanced principal elevation containing two entries. The Greenwich Friends Meeting, with its plain Flemish bond brickwork, interior galleries, and gender-divided seating area, epitomizes the meeting house form as it emerged at the close of the eighteenth century (Fig. 6.34). The Greenwich Friends Meeting also presents a uniformity of style that unites meeting houses throughout the region on both sides of the Delaware River and Bay. The uniformity extends to a surprising level of detail, such as the profiles of meeting house benches.

The emergence of a regional culture represented in houses of worship is not limited to Quaker meeting houses. The Old Broad Street Presbyterian Church in Bridgeton, the Old Stone Church at Fairton, Cohansey Baptist Church near Roadstown, and Emmanuel Lutheran Church near Friesburg in

Figure 6.31
Mauricetown Academy,
1860, Mauricetown, Cum-
berland County, New Jer-
sey. Photographed by
David Ames, HABS, 1991.
Rural and town schools
in the Delaware valley are
characterized by a one- or
two-story gable front, often
surmounted by a small cu-
pola containing a bell.

Figure 6.32
Octagonal School House,
1831, Leipsic vicinity, Kent
County, Delaware. Photo-
graphed by W. G. White,
HABS, 1936. An excep-
tional type of schoolhouse
architecturally, the building
accommodated eighty-
seven pupils. It was once
considered the finest district school in Delaware.

A

B

Figure 6.33

The Delaware valley landscape yields a rich tradition of religious architecture. (*A*) Barratt's Chapel, 1780, Frederica vicinity, Kent County, Delaware. Photographed by David Ames, HABS, 1982. (*B*) First Presbyterian Church, 1856, Salem, Salem County, New Jersey. Photographed by David Ames, HABS, 1991. The designer of this building, Philadelphia architect John McArthur, Jr., acted as chief architect of Philadelphia's City Hall in 1869. (*C*) John Wesley Methodist Episcopal Church, 1889, 1914, Deal Island, Somerset County, Maryland. Photographed 1995. This Gothic Revival T-plan church is similar to several others in Somerset County.

C

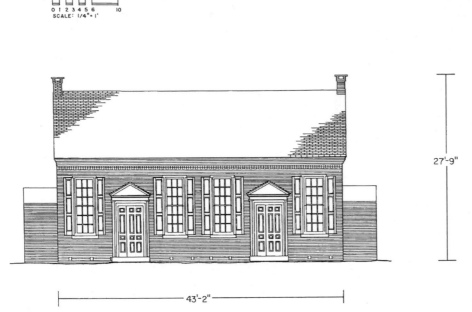

SCALE: 1/4"= 1'
0 1 2 3 4 5 6   10

27'-9"

43'-2"

FRONT ELEVATION

Figure 6.34
Greenwich Friends Meeting House, Greenwich, Cumberland County, New Jersey. Drawn by Catherine Anderson, HABS. The Quaker meeting houses throughout the Delaware valley are typically sparsely ornamented rectangular brick structures with gable roofs and a balanced principal elevation containing two entries.

Salem County exhibit a consistent use of locally manufactured brick, relatively plain exteriors, and well-finished interiors. Methodist and African Methodist Episcopal congregations were founded in the same time period, but the surviving churches associated with those denominations tend to date to the mid-nineteenth century. With their Italianate detailing, structures like the Goshen Methodist Church and Mt. Pisgah African Methodist Episcopal Church reflect local building traditions overlaid with nationally popular design elements (Fig. 6.35).

As emblems of an emerging regional culture, the meeting houses and churches of southern New Jersey function in three ways. First, in their construction and detail, houses of worship continue the same local building traditions that are found in the earliest dwellings. Builders of churches and meeting houses drew on an existing regional architectural vocabulary and from that range of options created a body of functionally related buildings that visually unify the landscape. For example, Quaker meeting houses such as the Salem Friends Meeting (Fig. 6.36) often contain glazed brick dates in their gable ends in a style that connects them to local domestic architectural practice. Interestingly, all the meeting houses dated in this fashion were erected in the years after the practice of dating houses had begun to wane. Second, if houses represented one type of visual organization of the landscape, houses of worship provided another common architectural point of reference that

Figure 6.35
Mt. Pisgah African Methodist Episcopal Church, 1878, Salem, Salem County, New Jersey. Photographed by David Ames, HABS, 1991. Surviving Methodist and African Methodist Episcopal churches in New Jersey tend to date from the mid-nineteenth century or later.

strengthened and communicated a regional landscape character. At the level of religious belief and practice, we see communities coalesce around shared philosophical and spiritual values; at the material level, we see communities of buildings that celebrate the virtues of local design and construction. Third, the churches also connect across denominational lines and visually express common values. In the fabric and fixtures of the landscape, we see the workings of a shared architectural language that suggests a level of cultural connection conveyed across diverse views of the world.

While the creeds and modes of worship practiced by individual congregations differed, there was a remarkable architectural unity to places of worship throughout the region. Certainly, however, the Quaker meeting houses of southern New Jersey represent a distinctive body of buildings, with their exterior appearance and interior design representing an outward show of Quaker values. Places of worship belonging to other Protestant congregations more closely respect vernacular and popular architectural styles rather than liturgically specific expressions of faith. In Somerset County, Maryland, for example, almost all the late-nineteenth- and early-twentieth-century churches make use of the same design vocabulary, albeit in different ways. Springing from a popular acceptance of Gothic Revival decorative motifs, the

Figure 6.36
Gable detail, Salem Friends Meeting, Salem, Salem County, New Jersey. Photographed 1995. In their construction and detail, the meeting houses and churches of southern New Jersey continue the same local building traditions that are found in the area's earliest dwellings. Quaker meeting houses often contain glazed brick dates in their gable ends in a style that connects them to local domestic architectural practice.

churches of Somerset make use of architectural elements such as lancet windows, bell towers with dramatic spires, quatrefoil windows, and sawnwork Victorian trim. While the majority of recorded Somerset County churches house Methodist congregations, the same architectural iconography is found on Episcopal, Catholic, and African Methodist Episcopal churches.[31] Similarly, the mid-nineteenth-century congregations of New Castle County, Delaware, and Salem County, New Jersey, drew on a hybridized Italianate–Greek Revival stylistic vocabulary.

Among the oldest institutions in the Methodist Church, camp meetings date to a time when itinerant ministers preached outdoors to large congregations. These first outdoor meetings were located in temporary shelters constructed of boughs lashed together. Once these "brush arbor" meetings became annual events, camp meeting grounds were established, complete with permanent tabernacles and living accommodations. Methodist Camp Meetings were located throughout Delaware and the Maryland Eastern Shore. To-

Figure 6.37
Figure 6.37
Carey's Camp Meeting
Ground, Philips Hill vi-
cinity, Sussex County,
Delaware. Photograph
courtesy of Delaware State
Historic Preservation Of-
fice. Photographed 1972.
Methodist camp meetings
date to a time when itinerant ministers preached outdoors to large congrega-
tions. This is one of three
Methodist camp meetings
that remain active in Delaware today.

day Carey's Camp Meeting Ground is one of only three active camp meetings in Delaware (Fig. 6.37).[32]

The campground, defined by a circle of forty-seven cabins, is situated in a grove of oak trees adjacent to Carey's United Methodist Church, near Philips Hill, Delaware. The cabins, which are called tents, face inward. The center of the circle is occupied by a large, open frame structure called the tabernacle. The tents are two-story frame buildings with two rooms on the first floor and a single sleeping room on the second. A stair, located between the two first-floor rooms, provides access to the upper story. The oldest tents at this site were built up to eighty years ago; the most recent was erected in 1972. Tents are usually owned by individual families, but the camp committee owns the boarding tent, where the food is served, the preacher's tent, and a few others. The tabernacle is a cruciform frame structure set on posts; it was originally built as a long shed and was subsequently enlarged with additions. The first tabernacle was a temporary structure of oak boughs, lighted by burning pine knots. A horse pound originally stood near the rear of the site; it has since been replaced by a parking lot. Some families bring camper trailers to the meetings, but the atmosphere of the camp meeting has not been appreciably altered by modern improvements.[33]

Figure 6.38
New Jerusalem Holiness Church, Exmore, Northampton
County, Virginia. Photographed 1986. Storefront churches,
such as the New Jerusalem Holiness Church, exemplify one
of the many ways in which people alter the meaning of their
environment through use.

Figure 6.39
Willis Wharf, Northampton County, Virginia. Photographed 1977. Sacred buildings can also be transformed into secular spaces. Moved from its original foundation onto pilings by the water's edge, this chapel began a new working life as a boathouse.

Not all places of worship are defined by purpose-built churches, chapels, and meeting houses. Small congregations operating on the margins of larger denominations often capture their sanctuaries from buildings constructed for other purposes. The most common example of this process is the storefront church. Found in cities and in the countryside, storefront churches take the open sales rooms of commercial buildings and convert them into worship spaces. The process often involves only the placement of bench pews or folding chairs before a podium or lectern which serves as pulpit. In some instances the congregation may add an altar rail. The storefront church tradition is an excellent example of how people alter the meanings of their environments through use. The New Jerusalem Holiness Church in Exmore, Virginia, exemplifies this process (Fig. 6.38). Built as a one-part block commercial building and provided with a false front gable, shed porch, and display windows with heavy wood security shutters, the building still displays its retail character. The conversion from store to church was a simple one. The interior of the building was refurnished, but not refurbished, and its new use proclaimed by new hand-lettered signs. The process of transforming secular buildings into sacred spaces has sometimes been reversed, as illustrated by a boathouse at Willis Wharf, Virginia (Fig. 6.39). Here a deconsecrated chapel was uprooted from its foundation, moved onto pilings by the water's edge, and given a new working life. As with industrial and commercial buildings, the documentation and analysis of secular and sacred buildings depends as much on the history of function as that of construction and style.

Still, even the most thorough and integrated examination of function, form, construction, and stylistic features is not always enough to unravel the most complex building histories. No building can be studied in isolation. All buildings, from meeting houses to muskrat-skinning sheds, exist within and derive much of their significance from a much broader landscape context. Just as an understanding of process and function becomes especially important in analyzing commercial, industrial, and institutional architecture, a consideration of physical and historical contexts allows us to comprehend buildings, not only as isolated artifacts, but as significant, functioning parts of complex landscape ensembles.

7   LANDSCAPE ENSEMBLES

The Example of Port Penn, Delaware

Landscape, from an archaeological point of view, is both artifact and site, place and space. Like other objects made or modified by humans, the spaces between buildings and communities—what archaeologist James Deetz calls the "connective tissue that gives houses and communities their proper context"— are material manifestations of individual or community values. Roads, field patterns, and fences serve specific needs, but they also define the environment in accordance with the ideas and cultural rules of their creators. As the geographer W. G. Hoskins has remarked, "the landscape, if we know how to read it, is the richest historical record we possess." [1]

Defining landscape has been a major activity (and point of contention) for geographers, historians, folklorists, and others with an eye to understanding people and places. Here, however, we want to define landscape as the range of human relationships expressed in the physical environment—as made, seen, experienced, understood, and imagined by people both as individuals and as members of a larger society. This definition focuses the object of landscape studies on the environmental understanding of human relationships. Attention to the physical environment as the source of evidence for both documenting and illustrating these relationships lends our definition two advantages. First, the knowledge of historic landscapes comes from objects recorded in the field. We can best know the sum and significance of historic landscape relations on the basis of the buildings, field patterns, earth works, decorative plantings, street plans, and other tangible, visible features left behind. Second, emphasizing human relationships concentrates our attention on the dynamic aspects of landscape, where buildings, plantings, and topographical features provide the means of discovering how people in the past thought about and ordered their environments.

Almost all landscapes have been shaped or modified in some way. From burgeoning suburban subdivisions to the marshes bordering the Delaware and Chesapeake bays, no portion of the region's landscape has remained unmanipulated. Roads have been cut through fields and forests, trees have been harvested, streams have been rechanneled, and acres of fill have been moved from one part of the region to another. One of the most important and significant changes to the Delaware valley landscape, the Chesapeake and Delaware Canal, was dug to connect the Delaware River to the Chesapeake Bay, thereby reinforcing what has become an important cultural divide between North and South. On a smaller scale, living fences and hedgerows have been planted, land earmarked for subdivision has been regraded, and entire farmsteads, replete with all of the evidence of past occupation, have been bulldozed. Even the most heavily forested areas show evidence of change, for the acres of woodland that survive in many locales today consist almost entirely of second-growth timber that has matured in areas that were once given over to cultivated fields.

People have altered the land for reasons that range from marking and maintaining boundaries or increasing soil productivity to providing a contemplative and quiet place to enjoy nature. Changes to the land may be limited to a single locale or extend across an entire region. While some modifications have proceeded from intentions that at first seem to have been purely utilitarian—fencing land to keep livestock from wandering, for example, or transforming forests into cultivated fields—each modification bears the stamp of deeper cultural values that have left their mark on the fabric of the larger landscape. Whether the reasons for shaping the land are economic, social, or aesthetic, each change creates a powerful statement of prevailing, often conflicted, cultural ideals. Landscape, then, is the largest but perhaps the most frequently overlooked cultural artifact.

Buildings are intimately connected to their surrounding landscape of house lots, farmyards, roads, and fields. Landscapes, like buildings, also have their own stratigraphy. Just as a single building can contain many different layers of occupation embedded in its structure, a single expanse of land often shows evidence of multiple changes. By determining when and why these changes occurred, we can sometimes reconstruct the appearance of the landscape at various points in its history. What we are really looking for as we read the landscape, then, is evidence for processes of continuity and change. We find that evidence, not just in the material character of individual buildings, but in the relationships among buildings, their settings, and the people who experience these environments.

Before we begin to examine specific kinds of landscapes, it would be well to consider the idea of an archaeological assemblage. The concept of an assemblage acknowledges that there are often many objects associated with a particular building or site. While we may begin with the individual objects recovered from the site, we ultimately find ourselves describing the larger context from which the objects came and the types of possible relationships that existed between objects unified by specific spatial and chronological circumstances. The underlying principle of the archaeological assemblage as a tool for looking at landscape is its explicit emphasis on establishing functional, aesthetic, symbolic, social, and other connections between objects and people. The concept of the landscape ensemble closely parallels the archaeological assemblage.[2] The landscape ensemble is composed of many discrete elements, like houses, barns, and fences, and it is best understood by examining how those parts work together and contribute to a larger whole. Archaeological assemblage and landscape ensemble are ideas further linked by the recognition that buildings and their current and historic relationship to the countryside reflect a process of landscape formation. The idea of a landscape ensemble also conveys the experiences of movement and human interaction. An approach to looking at landscape that draws on the idea of ensemble clearly prevents the false complacency that stems from discussing individual buildings in isolation. The concept of the ensemble also provides the framework for introducing the many types of buildings not included in our outlines of dwelling types, house lots, farm buildings, and architectural styles. To read the architectural environment, you must begin with individual buildings and types of buildings and then move on to establishing the relationships between structures within a category as well as between categories. Thus, the ideas of archaeological assemblage and landscape ensemble underscore our obligation to understand landscape as a system of connected artifacts and human actions. The kinds of connections we seek to identify and describe include siting, setting, function, ownership, occupancy, and chronology. Together these connections describe the complex process of landscape formation.[3]

This chapter, through a specific example, illustrates ways to read the landscape from an archaeological perspective. The following example offers several different approaches to landscape study, but all retain the common goal of describing and interpreting the human relationships that exist between buildings and landscape over time. The example chosen does not pretend to define the range of possible landscapes but instead attempts to suggest the complexity of the historic environment in one particular area. As in other chapters, our intention is to provide an approach for looking—not an encyclopedia of building types. Finally, this chapter is very different from the preceding discussions of form, construction, and building types. Our goal is to describe a way to look at and think about the historic landscape. Our concern is less for "what is" than "how to." The buildings, structures, and landscape features singled out in the following pages are intended as key examples that help us think about architectural connections in the landscape. Because this is not a history of one particular area, but a discussion of that area as an example for looking at the landscape, we have made our choices on the basis of their illustrative effectiveness.

There are many valid ways to begin the study of an historic landscape, but our example begins with the way most of us actually encounter historic buildings and their settings—an approach by automobile.

Three roads converge on the tiny Delaware River village of Port Penn. From the north, Route 9 skirts huge petrochemical complexes and the western edge of the old canal town of Delaware City. On the south side of Delaware City, two bridges carry the road first across the last surviving stretch of the Chesapeake and Delaware Canal, excavated in the 1820s, and second over the new deep water cut for the canal, which links the shipping channels of the Delaware with those of the Chesapeake Bay to the west. From the summit of the second bridge, we gain our first glimpse of Port Penn in the distance (Fig. 7.1). The steeple of the Presbyterian church and the rooftops of the village houses protrude between the trees planted along village streets and in backyards. The view from the bridge also affords a sense of Port Penn's watery setting. Between the bridge and the town stretch over a thousand acres of marsh and wetlands. The tidal marshes to the east of the two-lane road, which leads straight from the bridge into town, are crowded with tall stands of feathery grass rooted in the clearly visible muck of tidal ditches and flats. The same grass dominates the fringes of the freshwater wetlands west of the road, but these marshes are visually more expansive, with greater stretches of open shallow water.

West of the freshwater marshes stand the ragged silhouettes of tree lines:

Figure 7.1
View of Port Penn from the bridge, New Castle County, Delaware. Photographed 1995. The tiny Delaware River village of Port Penn is bordered by over a thousand acres of marsh and wetlands.

dark green in summer, progressively red and gold and then brown in autumn, bare gray branches in winter. Fields lie between the stands of trees, and like those of the trees, their colors and textures vary with the seasons. Houses and barns furnish this landscape vista. In the middle ground, on a slight rise, stands a two-story white dwelling with a long two-story gable wing. Additional houses and outbuildings occupy other plots of land, some standing at water's edge, others pedestaled on gentle rises surrounded by fields. In recent years the houses have multiplied with the development of new commuter suburbs, some of which are distantly visible to the west. Route 9 continues along the river shore south of town, and the road can be seen on a clear day, particularly in the winter when the air is clearer and the leaves have fallen. Similarly discernible is the principal westward-leading road that connects Port Penn to Route 13, Delaware's primary north-south highway roughly five miles away.

Still, our first impression from the bridge is incomplete. The broad waters of the Delaware, to the east, define Port Penn's setting just as effectively as do the surrounding marshes and countryside. The single dominant architectural feature in that landscape today is the nuclear reactor cooling tower of the electric generating plant across the river in southern New Jersey. The distinctively shaped structure looms over the shoreline and is of such immense scale that it alters the very way in which we first comprehend the river and the village. But a second look reveals a long narrow island in the river just offshore, as well as distantly glimpsed buildings on the opposite shore. The river itself is not an empty expanse of water. Ocean-going freighters and tankers churn up and down the waterway. Channel markers and buoys broadcast their cautions. Small commercial and recreational fishing boats scoot in and out of the breakwater, visible as a thin dark line on the river's surface south of town. We see all this in the space of a few moments as we descend from the heights of the bridge down to the low road which runs straight to the village. But what is it we have seen? And, as fieldworkers in traditional architecture and landscape, what questions do we ask about the landscape and where do we begin our explorations?

Our initial step is one of discovery and of sorting out what we see in the field. Because this book is a guide to everyday architecture, we begin with buildings and then move on to the ways in which those buildings define and are defined by the countryside they occupy. An inventory of all the buildings in Port Penn and the surrounding area involves several fieldwork techniques. First, we survey all the existing buildings within our research area. Surveying includes mapping the location of each site, shooting some basic photographs, and writing a brief description. The photography should address each building individually as well as yield an overall view of the way the buildings relate to one another within a farm complex, on a village street, or in another larger setting. The written description should always proceed building by building and begin with the basics before working toward greater levels of detail. Characteristics of physical setting, material, shape, height, size, and function together provide a starting place which can be elaborated with more detailed observations regarding building techniques, decorative finishes, and other diagnostic details. The earlier sections of this book, as well as other sources, provide information that helps in describing and dating buildings of all sorts. A sketch plan of the building and of its relationship to the overall physical setting provides additional information for later evaluation. The goals of this first step are quite specific: we seek to know what we are looking at and attempt to situate what we see geographically and chronologically.

With a basic survey in hand we can pursue the second step in our fieldwork project. Sorting through our inventory, we determine several categories for further investigation. Functional categories based on building use include dwellings, barns, granaries, churches, commercial buildings, and other specific building types. Within a given functional type, such as dwellings, we can organize our initial survey findings by other typological considerations such as plan types (hall-parlor, center-passage, bungalow, etc.) or styles (Greek Revival, Italianate, Georgian, etc.). We can also sort our survey findings according to spatial relationships—for example the placement of structures in a farm complex—and chronological considerations, in which buildings are assigned general dates of construction and subsequent alteration.

The first two steps of a fieldwork project are important to landscape study and evaluation in several key ways. First, we learn what is standing in the countryside in very general terms. Second, we sort and organize what we have seen according to a number of variables, such as time, form, and function. The sorting process allows us to identify and pursue specific historic and architectural themes in the landscape. Third, the identification of landscape themes enables us to begin the exploration of landscape relations—the spatial and chronological relationships between buildings, historic processes—and, finally, the ways that people historically viewed, valued, used, and moved in the landscapes they experienced. Answering this last group of questions requires us to take our fieldwork into the library and the archives. There, we can assess what standing buildings actually represent in terms of historic realities, individual lives, and community structures—all intangible elements necessary for understanding buildings in terms of landscape.

In a sense, the study of Port Penn and other landscapes is the study of the sum of human experience reflected in the material world of house, farm, town, river, marsh, and wood—all landscape elements clearly visible from our first vantage point atop the bridge. We should bear in mind, though, that the buildings and other cultural features which compose the landscape do not carry a single set of absolute meanings. The significance of houses depends in great measure on the relative social and economic standing of the people who experience the architecture. One of the goals of architectural fieldwork is the definition of overlapping frameworks for the social interpretation of buildings. Overall, the unifying thread in the preceding discussion and throughout this book is the strategy of beginning with, and returning to, buildings. Let us turn to the buildings of Port Penn.

Situated just south of Thousand Acre Marsh and on the first high ground near the Delaware River, Port Penn consists primarily of houses. These are interspersed with other structures, including two churches, an old schoolhouse used as a community museum, a modern concrete-block tavern, a post office, work sheds, and two or three shops. These buildings stand along the four principal streets that define the single city block of the town (Fig. 7.2).

Figure 7.2
View of main block, Port Penn, New Castle County, Delaware. Photographed 1995. In the village of Port Penn, all of the public buildings stand within a single city block.

The first task in assessing the Port Penn landscape is to inventory and map the buildings in the village. The problem with Port Penn, though, is the difficulty we encounter everywhere in the surrounding region: the common buildings of the Port Penn landscape exhibit only vague gestures to historic styles even as they mask often complicated individual building histories. Our step-by-step strategy is to sort out these building histories as accurately as field techniques allow us, place the architectural evidence in a documentary context, and then connect the individual building and site histories to the larger landscape. The subtleties of everyday buildings are not just limited to Port Penn: similarly nuanced landscapes are the essence of the region.

Port Penn, founded in 1763 by David Stewart, survives today as a community reflecting more than 250 years of architectural activity. The earliest standing building in the village is the Stewart family house, which predates the town's founding by approximately twenty-five years (Fig. 7.3). The two-story brick dwelling exhibits the balanced five-bay front with a central entry usually associated with a center-passage plan. Interior gable chimneys at either end of the dwelling confirm the likely plan of the house. The decorative brickwork includes glazed header Flemish bond, a decorative water table, and a belt course designed to flash the peak of an earlier pent roof. Evidence in the form of plain English and common bond brickwork and sawn-off joist ends indicate the exact height of the missing pent. Similar indicators suggest

Figure 7.3
Stewart House, Port Penn, New Castle County, Delaware. Photographed 1995. The earliest standing building in the village, the Stewart family house was built around 1740 to 1750 and predates the town's founding by approximately twenty-five years.

the former presence of a cove cornice at the base of the roof. A one-story brick kitchen wing extends from the rear of the house. Finally, the Stewart house stands slightly skewed to the street, which passes in front of the building.

Taken together, the architectural features and siting of the house reveal a first insight into the original landscape of Port Penn—an insight confirmed by the documentary record. The use of glazed header Flemish bond, pent roof, cove cornice, and stepped water table suggest a circa 1730–1740 construction date, and all are features associated with the mid-eighteenth century in the lower Delaware valley. The off-line placement of the house relative to Stewart Street also suggests that the house may predate the town plan, in which all the other houses face squarely on the street. Architecture, in this case the earliest surviving building in the community, thus provides us with a first framework of landscape relations. The position of the house relative to the town indicates that the town grid was laid over a preexisting agricultural landscape. Several questions arise from this first connection: How does the Stewart House compare to other colonial dwellings in the surrounding landscape? Why did Stewart found a town on this site? What was Stewart's vision for his town, and how did the town appear in its early years? All these questions both carry us out into the landscape of countryside and village and require us to look at buildings in the context of their relationships to other buildings. The former process is geographical or proxemic; the latter entails an archaeological perspective; together they suggest techniques for landscape archaeology. The landscape archaeology of Port Penn begins with the natural topography and the three interconnected landscapes of river, marsh, and upland.

The Delaware River dominates the landscape in which the Stewart House stands. The tidal flow, with its roughly six-foot rise and fall, sweeps by the marshes that bridge open water and high ground. Offshore stretches the low eroding outline of Reedy Island, formerly the site of an early-twentieth-century U.S. government quarantine station. The space between the island and the river shore offers one of the last naturally formed sheltered anchorages on the lower Delaware River. Inland, the terrain rises rapidly into well-drained fields intercut with shallow streams that empty into the marshes. Second-growth woodlands, consisting of mixed hardwoods like oak and maple, line the banks of a creek that cuts through farmland, woods, and marsh. The fertile and stone-free soils have supported profitable market agriculture for over three centuries. Overall, the topography surrounding the Stewart House suggests relationships to the neighboring countryside. The problem before us is to make the historical connections between buildings and environment.

Our first step is to assess the Stewart House in relation to other Port Penn vicinity buildings that predate the town's founding. The Stewart House is not the only colonial building standing in the Port Penn vicinity. Field surveys have identified at least a dozen other structures that date from roughly 1700 to 1775. All are houses, and all but three are built of brick. The earliest brick houses (those dating from before 1750) typically make use of pent eaves and glazed header Flemish bond masonry—two diagnostic features observed on the Stewart House—but they are far from uniform in plan. Several dwellings, among them the Dilworth House (Fig. 7.4A), were built as one- to two-story, one-room houses. More elaborate dwellings, such as the Ashton House (Fig. 7.4B) of circa 1705, featured hall-parlor plans. In quality of construction and detailing, these open-plan dwellings represent the best of the early colonial housing in the area. Only three wooden houses (one of sawn plank, two of frame) survive to represent the majority of early buildings. The wooden buildings, all built as single-room dwellings one or two stories in height, are exceptional survivals from an area where the average eighteenth-century house contained less than 400 square feet of living space and was in constant need of repair. In this architectural landscape, the Stewart House looms large. The early date of the house and its fully developed closed stair-passage plan

A

B

Figure 7.4
The earliest brick houses in Port Penn vary in plan. Simpler dwellings, such as the Dilworth House, were built as one- to two-story one-room houses, while more elaborate dwellings, such as the Ashton House, featured hall-parlor plans. (*A*) Dilworth House, ca. 1700, Port Penn, New Castle County, Delaware (see also Fig. 2.2A). Photographed 1995. (*B*) Ashton House, ca. 1705, Port Penn, New Castle County, Delaware (see also Fig. 2.4A). Photographed by David Ames, HABS, 1986.

distinguish this building from its surviving contemporaries. Not until the 1760s did the local builders commissioning new mansion houses begin to embrace the various Georgian plans, and when they did, they quickly moved away from visually distinctive local detailing. Windsor (see Fig. 3.4), built by the Van Dyke family outside Port Penn in the 1760s, abandoned the glazed header brickwork, pent eaves, and cove cornice observed in the Stewart House. Instead, Windsor displays plain Flemish bond masonry with a box cornice. Thus, the Stewart House and Windsor are united by form but separated by finish, even as the Stewart House is identified with its early brick contemporaries on the basis of finish but distinguished by form.

Our second step is to evaluate the information gained through architectural comparison. What we are seeing and describing in these early buildings are relationships between houses within a larger landscape. The use of brick (a material historically associated with greater individual affluence) in so many dwellings in such a small area suggests a general degree of prosperity. The combination of a Georgian plan and locally distinctive construction details in the Stewart House, especially when compared with other contemporary houses in the area, further suggests a landscape in transition—a landscape shifting from building traditions implying shared values to those charting emerging social divisions with the community. Thus, the Stewart House stands at a crossroads between the older local architectural traditions of the early colonial period and the development of broader regional trends in the pre-Revolutionary decade.

Our knowledge of the Port Penn landscape during the colonial period would be significantly limited if we relied exclusively on surviving architecture. Written descriptions compiled for the county orphans' court during the 1760s and 1770s suggest just how much of that landscape we have lost. When Samuel Carpenter died in the mid-1770s, his heirs acquired his farm, just outside of the Stewarts' fledgling village. The appraisers recorded "one logg dwelling house two stories high wants some repairs such as two hearths layed and twelve sash lights in the windows, one logg kitchen in good repair one draw well a pailed garden in middling order one meathouse in good repair one smith's shop in repair one logg stable and hen house in midling repair one corn crib one large frame barn wants some repairs on the southend struck with thunder . . . one logg house not tenantable." Of all the functional building types listed in addition to the main dwelling—kitchen, meat house, smith's shop, stable, hen house, corn crib, barn, and tenant house—only one, the meat house, is illustrated by a surviving contemporary example in the Port Penn vicinity. Yet it is these minor buildings which define the setting. Clearly, one requirement in the archaeology of historic architecture and landscape is the cultivation of a historical imagination, leading to plausible documentary reconstruction and interpretation.

As we have learned, the Stewart family house was already standing when the Stewarts purchased the property on which they intended to lay out the city of Port Penn. The house's early date, which we have deduced from visible architectural details and its skewed orientation, confirms its existence prior to the founding of the town. But it is more from the first generations of Port Penn's post-Revolutionary development that we begin to gain a larger sense of what the landscape looked like and how much the native terrain shaped the development of village and countryside.

The next step in interpreting Port Penn's architecture is the description of the total town plan, both as projected and as built. Beside the road leading into Port Penn, a sign proclaims the founding of the village in the 1760s. The town itself consists of a single fully-formed city block and the suggestion of continuing streets, which were either built and abandoned or, more likely, never extended. The town plan, consisting of Congress, Merchant, Market, and Stewart streets, is a landscape feature in its own right and can be read in terms of its relationships to buildings as well as to the topography of river, marsh, and upland. Before turning to the documentary evidence for the Stewart family's urban ambitions, let us "read" the architectural plan of the landscape itself.

Although Port Penn is only a single square block, we quickly recognize that the plan is a fragment of an urban grid not unlike Philadelphia's. Furthermore, the grid is oriented to face directly onto the river, as if the river itself were one of the streets in the town plan. The street names testify to the Stewarts' aspirations: "Market" and "Merchant" reflect commerce; "Congress" reflects republican governance; and "Stewart" glorifies the town founders. An urban grid crisscrossed with streets celebrating economic and political power suggests that the Stewarts' vision was of a Port Penn considerably grander than a backcountry agricultural town. The documentary record reveals the real scale of the Stewarts' dream. In newspaper advertisements, they promoted their city-to-be as the future rival to Philadelphia. The sheltered anchorage provided by Reedy Island, the productive countryside, the city site considerably downriver from Philadelphia and therefore closer to the sea were all hailed as important advantages. The Stewarts also left plans of Port Penn's projected early growth. Far from the four streets that describe the village today, Port Penn as planned extended a block and a half through the

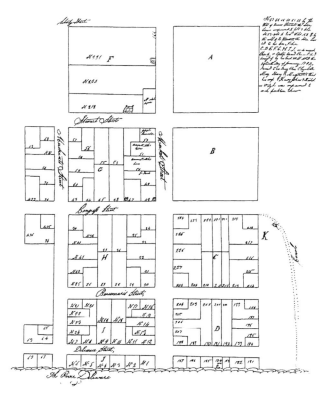

A

Figure 7.5

As originally planned, Port Penn would have extended a block and a half to the river's edge and inland roughly a third of a mile. (*A*) Dr. David Stewart's plan for Port Penn, from an original plat, ca. 1790. Drawn by Gabrielle Lanier after manuscript original in Stewart family papers, Delaware State Archives. (*B*) Port Penn in 1868. From *Beer's Atlas,* 1868.

B

marsh to the river's edge and in the other direction ran inland roughly a third of a mile (Fig. 7.5). The marshes and creeks that created an uneven and irregular complex of low ground, woodlots, and fields were secondary considerations. Wetlands could be filled and urban spaces allocated before they were built on.

The next question that confronts us is whether or not there are landscape features visible today that reflect the Stewarts' lofty goals of two centuries ago. Consequently, we turn our attention to the discovery of landscape features like dikes and drainage ditches that would document the process of land reclamation. In their various deeds, wills, and surveys, the Stewarts focused on developing two elements of their city plan. First, they projected Port Penn to the water's edge; second, they planned a town which ran westward at least a quarter of a mile to a square designed to contain a church, school, and burying ground. The expansion of the town to the east necessitated the reclamation of considerable tidal wetlands; the expansion to the west was intended to incorporate other Stewart family properties, including the family cemetery, into the town plan. The former endeavor was part of a larger late-eighteenth- and nineteenth-century regional process of marsh management through extensive diking and drainage systems; the latter goal simply represented a strategy for including preexisting landscape features in the projected town plan.

Extending their town to the river's marshy bank required building an earthen dike rising nearly ten feet above the marsh floor, as well as ditching and draining the marsh bottom to create firm ground. When this dike was built is uncertain, but according to early maps it was in place at least by the mid-1800s. The Port Penn dike, however, is a landscape feature which tells us much more about the countryside than just the founding of Port Penn. The remnants of dikes appear all along both sides of the Delaware River north and south of Port Penn (Fig. 7.6). In construction and silhouette, all the dikes are similarly configured earthen embankments rising above the marsh. When we look at the Port Penn dike, we need to consider these other landscape features in the same way that we placed the Stewart House in the comparative context of its neighbors. Thus, a brief look at the early history of marshland reclamation and management enables us to put the Stewarts' city-building efforts into a larger perspective.

One of the most dramatic changes to the Delaware landscape occurred early in the nineteenth century when large areas of marshland in the coastal region were reclaimed for building and farming, through ditching, diking, and draining. The intricate system of ditches and drains that is so visible today is a relatively recent alteration of the wetlands. Marsh reclamation yielded acres of "new" land along the entire coast. As a result, towns could utilize this land by extending street grids and waterfronts onto previously unusable wetlands.[4]

Marshes in their native state, according to early-nineteenth-century observers, remained "wild and worthless." To agricultural reformers bent upon maximizing the productivity of the earth, the agricultural potential of Delaware's marshland—the deep, dormant deposits of rotting, nutrient-rich vegetation—would remain untapped without extensive draining and ditching. Marsh improvement also offered other advantages. The proponents of marsh reclamation argued that it would boost the economy, permit direct access to distant stands of timber, and protect residents from summer drought, "mosquitoes and putrefecation," and the "stagnated fogs" and "miasmatic vapors" that were thought to emanate from the marshes, exposing nearby residents to disease. During the early nineteenth century, reclamation of the vast marshes in central and southern Delaware, like marsh improvement projects elsewhere in the country, increasingly became a priority. The ultimate goal was to transform what some viewed as a "fruitless, loathsome waste into a healthful, fertile soil."[5]

Draining any marsh was a labor-intensive affair. Drainage systems usually consisted of a network of hand-dug ditches and earthen embankments similar to the dike that survives near Port Penn. Embankments were built first, to prevent further flooding. Then a network of ditches was dug to drain excess surface water and lower the water table. Once embankments and ditches were constructed, they had to be maintained. Rainstorms, tidal flow, and muskrat burrows could all take their toll.[6] Marsh reclamation was so costly that no landowner was wealthy enough to attempt the job alone. Consequently, individual landowners banded together to form marsh or ditch companies— private organizations which the state legislature authorized to levy their own taxes to support the draining of the wetlands. Opposition to marsh improvement was acute in the first two decades of the nineteenth century but then declined; most marsh improvement companies encountered little resistance after their first few years of existence.[7]

Ditching and draining continued throughout the 1800s and into the early twentieth century. While the first efforts at marsh reclamation involved individuals banding together into corporations in the interest of land improvement, twentieth-century efforts were geared toward civic enhancement and were especially designed for mosquito and drainage control. Still, the most

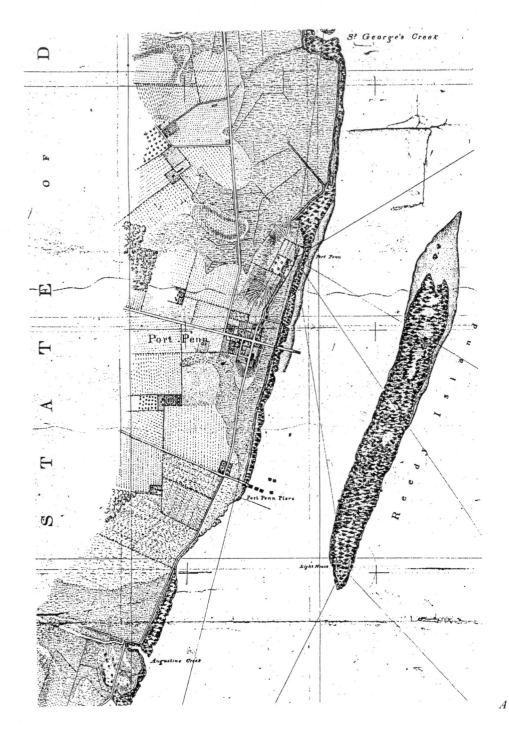

St George's Creek

Port Penn

Reedy Island

Port Penn

STATE OF D

Port Penn Piers

Light House

Augustine Creek

A

Figure 7.6
An elaborate system of dikes was already in place by the mid-nineteenth century. In *A*, the dikes are visible along the coastline on the inland edge of the marshland, terminating at the Port Penn Piers. The remnants of dikes are common along the Delaware River north and south of Port Penn. (*A*) Survey of the coast of Delaware, no. 140, F. R. Hassler, superintendent, July and August, 1841, National Archives. (*B*) Remnant of dike. Photographed 1995.

B

significant changes to the wetlands occurred in the earliest years of the nineteenth century and were made in the interest of agricultural reform. Thus we see that the Port Penn dike, like the networks of ditches and drains that are such familiar sights in the Delaware marshes today, was a product of a large-scale landscape manipulation that began over one hundred fifty years ago.

The Stewarts' eyeing of the river included more than just marsh reclamation. From the very beginning, they intended to build wharves, canals, and other landscape features that would enable the townspeople to transport goods to and from river vessels. Several landscape features survive today that illustrate the early physical link between land and water: the Market Street wharf, the pilings of old piers that are exposed at low tide, and the trace of the Stewarts' eighteenth-century canal.

The measure of Port Penn's fate as a new seaport city on the Delaware is revealed in the houses built prior to 1820. The town was founded in the 1760s; only the Stewart House remains to document colonial Port Penn. The landscape features suggesting the textures of Port Penn's earliest history and its great ambition are both borne out and belied by the first generation of village houses built after the Revolution. All of those houses have received later overlays of fashionable trim and extensive additions, but sufficient detail survives below the surface to enable us to assess Port Penn's earlier character. A walk down the village streets reveals a scattering of freestanding houses. Other than the Stewart and Cleaver houses and the Presbyterian Church, all the dwellings in town are built of wood, stand two or two-and-a-half stories tall, and face directly onto the street. Like the vast majority of traditional buildings that fieldworkers encounter, the houses of Port Penn offer only the slightest nod to different stylistic periods. Porches with sawnwork brackets and turned posts hint at the Eastlake style of the late Victorian period. Elsewhere, dormer windows may be trimmed out with stylized classical pilasters and cornices finished with Italianate brackets. In Port Penn, however, we cannot rely on a vocabulary of style to help us place the buildings in a stylistic continuum. Visible details of construction and massing, such as beaded weatherboard, flush vergeboards, rubble stone foundations, and recognizable original plan types, provide some help in separating the earliest houses from later ones. Our ability to date these buildings is enhanced when we include the careful reading of the historic documents that describe the town, its founding, and its earliest residents. While a dozen or more of the village's early houses remain standing today, we will focus on a single example here.

Few houses are more unassuming in their exterior appearance than the Eakin House at 103 South Congress Street (Fig. 7.7). The two-story wood house covered with buff-colored, brick pattern composition siding offers few exterior hints regarding its age or architectural character. Only the flush vergeboards, chimney stacks, and foundation masonry suggest a construction date earlier than the mid-1800s. However, the house is one of the earliest dwellings in the town. Built by John Eakin on a lot he rented and then purchased from the Stewart family, the dwelling under the siding is a frame and log building.

Dr. David Stewart, the son of Port Penn's founder, conveyed the lot to John Eakin in 1804. Eakin, however, appears to have built at least this log house

Figure 7.7
Eakin House, Port Penn,
New Castle County, Dela-
ware. Photographed 1995.
Although it offers few exterior hints regarding its age,
the Eakin House is one of
the earliest dwellings in
Port Penn.

around 1800, prior to his land purchase, when he was still occupying the lot on ground rent paid to the Stewarts. The manuscript census records for Port Penn in 1800 report that John Eakin was living in his house with seven other individuals, including a free African American. John Eakin's residence is confirmed in the 1797 tax lists, where he was assessed for a lot containing a total of three houses; in 1816 his tax assessment included two lots: one was improved with a house, tavern, and stables, and the other with a tenement in the occupation of Josiah March.

The Eakin House faces Congress Street on lot number 77 in the old Stewart plan and has a 26-foot, three-bay, center-door front. Extending back 18½ feet, the house was built of regularly sized 8½-inch by 3½-inch, pit-sawn logs joined at the corners with full dovetail notching. Wooden pins driven into the upper and lower surfaces of the logs stabilized the wall as it was raised. The interstices between the logs are infilled with riven construction scrap packed with clay mortar. The exterior surfaces of the logs were left exposed to the elements. Interior finishes are masked on the ground floor by a more recent layer of wallboard, but on the second floor, original surfaces, including vertical beaded partition walls and fireplace paneling, survive. The house was covered with a gable roof seated on a raising plate secured to joists that projected beyond the face of the building to form a box cornice. As built, the Eakin House had a two-room plan with a 17½-foot by 12½-foot common room and 17½-foot by 11-foot "inner room" or parlor. In the early 1800s the Eakin family enlarged their building with a two-story braced-frame wing appended to the south gable of the original house. The wing, as built, consisted of heavy principal post construction. The posts, wall plates, and roof plates all jutted into the interior and were either finished or cased. In terms of materials, plan, and finish, the Eakin House represents the typical townhouse of early Port Penn.

We can read the Eakin House as an individual structure or as an element in a larger landscape ensemble. Compared to the Stewart House, the Eakin residence lacks the distinguishing characteristics of decorative brick construction and Georgian plan. Today our attention remains drawn to the Stewart House—the obvious architectural symbol of wealth and prestige. The character of the Stewart House is clearly communicated through its brick construction, balanced five-bay Georgian front, skewed relationship to the street, and central location behind the Presbyterian Church. But the distinctiveness of the Stewart House is achieved only by the visual and physical relationships established by this dwelling and its less elaborate wooden neighbors. Thus, the Eakin House sheds greater light on the middling architecture that would have been inhabited by the majority of Port Penn residents, while the Stewart House documents a village hierarchy of proprietors, householders, and renters. Just as the clues in the landscape enable us to see the town plan laid over the Stewart House, the architecture of the entire town allows us to see differences between town residents in ways that suggest social and economic distinctions. Compared to the Stewart House, the Eakin dwelling is an ordinary building in a town of seemingly ordinary architecture.

The documentary record, however, enables us to push our analysis of the early Port Penn landscape a little further. Today the Eakin House is occupied as a dwelling, but can we accept present use as evidence for a continuous history of use? An inventory of Eakin's personal estate taken in 1816 suggests several possibilities about the history of the building. One possibility includes multiple functions of the structure as a combination tavern, retail store, and residence. The inventory begins by listing the contents of a small retail store (likely the ground floor of the south gable wing), where Eakin sold a variety of textiles, cheap ceramics, and sundries. Then the inventory specifically mentions the contents of a bar, along with thirteen chairs and at least three tables, apparently located on the ground floor of the two-story portion of the house. Third, the upper story of the plank house contained a variety of beds and bedding, tables, and other equipment. The large number of beds and associated household objects suggests that while some of the upstairs rooms were set aside for family occupation, other spaces provided accommodations for travelers. The inventory and a later orphans' court property valuation also identify numerous outbuildings that would have related to the three functions of retail, entertainment, and domestic life. They include a kitchen, "out cellar," and "a stable & meat house thatched all of wood." Thus, the store contents, reference to a bar, and extensive listing of beds, chairs, tables, and numerous outbuildings suggest a building that contained a ground floor store and tavern with upstairs provisions for accommodating overnight guests. What remains difficult to determine is the question of whether or not the family lived in the building. The fact that the inventory does not suggest a second household in another building and that the upstairs rooms housed a well-defined group of domestic artifacts further suggests that the family probably occupied the second-floor front rooms over the principal ground-floor room of the log building.

Looking at houses and other buildings in light of landscape issues always carries us back to discussions of landscape ensembles and relationships defined by setting and human interaction. The town plan, the Stewart and Eakin houses, the earthen dike and other features are all elements in the larger landscape. Individually we describe them by function, form, and ap-

Figure 7.8
Cleaver House, ca. 1835,
Port Penn, New Castle
County, Delaware. Photo-
graphed 1977. The Cleaver
House is now the largest,
most visible private dwell-
ing in Port Penn.

pearance; as an ensemble of related landscape features we begin to describe the same objects in terms of relationships that reflect patterns of human interaction and cultural process. The relationships we discover among objects in the landscape enable us to talk about much more than just architecture— they inspire us to talk about the lives and actions of people in the past. Through study of these objects and actions, we seek to recover some sense of how people conceptualized the world they occupied. Landscape studies are as archaeological as building studies. The Stewarts' vision of Port Penn and the actions they took emerge shardlike from our landscape excavation. Cross-mended and compared, they offer a fragmentary vision of urban aspiration and failure in the late eighteenth and early nineteenth centuries. Overlaying Port Penn's early strata, however, are nearly two centuries of subsequent shaping and reshaping of the landscape.

The Stewart and Eakin houses, and indeed the projected plan for the city-to-be that Port Penn failed to realize, describe an initial period of economic enthusiasm. By the 1820s, however, the Stewarts' vision had failed. Looking at buildings enables us to postulate dates for construction and, by extension, larger landscape changes. Following the construction of the Stewart House in the mid-1700s and the first generation of frame and log buildings, the next major period of architectural development was signaled by the construction of the Cleaver House and the subsequent building of two churches.

The Cleaver House is a two-and-a-half-story brick structure sited on the northeast corner of Congress and Market streets (Fig. 7.8). Built of brick laid

in a tightly joined Flemish bond, finished with doorways capped with elliptical fanlights and similarly arched dormer windows, and enlarged with a long
service ell extending backward toward the edge of the reclaimed marsh, the
Cleaver House is now the largest, most visible private dwelling in the village.
In our interpretation of landscape ensembles, both the topographical location
and the chronological position of the Cleaver House in the Port Penn social
and economic landscape concern us. The plan of the Cleaver House draws on
the older, formal image of the Georgian house, but with some significant
variations. First, one first-floor room was purpose-built as an office. Second,
the two northern rooms on the ground floor were designed to be utilized as a
single, visually unified entertainment space. With three-quarters of the main
floor given over to formal entertainment and commerce, the Cleaver House
communicated its inhabitant's connections, indeed dominance, of the social
and business life of the village.

The construction and decorative detailing of the Cleaver House suggest a

Figure 7.9
A View at Appoquinimink,
State of Delaware, attributed
to George Washington Jan-
vier (1784–1865), ca. 1805,
watercolor on paper. Re-
produced courtesy of the
Henry Francis du Pont
Winterthur Museum. The
picket and rail fencing,
shown here adjacent to the
house, were two of the most
common types of fencing in
the colonial and early national periods.

building date between 1830 and 1840. The same fully developed center-passage plans with extensive service wings and late Federal detailing emerged in
the mid-nineteenth century as the most popular architectural elements for the
wealthy farmers and townsfolk of the lower Delaware valley. Houses similar
to the Cleavers' townhouse were commissioned throughout the area in the
mid-1800s, with the result that the countryside around Port Penn experienced a period of intensive remodeling and replacing of houses and also construction of new farm buildings, such as bank barns, granaries, stables, and
threshing barns. The evidence for this period of architectural transformation
comes from the buildings that stand in the landscape, because of our ability
to evaluate and date them. We discover that the chronological context for the
Cleaver House is one of widespread architectural change, which includes the
design and construction of a new generation of large stair-passage plan
houses incorporating service functions in extensive wings and making use of
nationally popular architectural styles—all aspects of building design discussed in earlier chapters. These architectural changes can be linked in turn
to the local agricultural prosperity of a landed minority and to changing sensibilities about domestic life that included the careful segregation of household work such as cooking from more refined domestic behavior. We can see
this same process at work in the Stewart House, where the family added a
one-story kitchen ell to their old mid-eighteenth-century dwelling. The increasingly precise definition of household space also found its expression in
other areas of the landscape. Certainly, the changes in agricultural building
and farmstead design discussed earlier are one place to look, but we can also
look at more subtle landscape features, such as fencing, hedging, and plantings, for additional evidence about buildings and how people saw and valued
their countryside.

Traveling down the country roads around Port Penn and throughout the
region, we often encounter roads bordered by thick-growing Osage orange
hedgerows. Easily recognized by their distinctive large green fruit, these
plantings are remnants of "live fencing" popular in the middle to late 1800s.
The Osage orange hedgerows, however, represent only one of the many
means historically employed to divide fields and define property. In the colonial period, the most common forms of fencing used wood in a variety of
designs (Fig. 7.9). Nearest the dwelling, the householder enclosed the family
garden with a fence consisting of boards or palings nailed to rails supported
by posts set in the earth. Builders of rougher garden fences dispensed with
the boards, preferring instead to weave their fences with brush wattles. Ranging from 4 to 6 feet in height, garden enclosures, like all early fences, were

designed to keep marauding animals, especially free-ranging swine, away from the plants inside. The enclosures for the barnyard and the fields nearest the house consisted of post-and-rail fences: mortised posts were sunk into the earth every 8 to 10 feet, and the pointed ends of horizontal rails were then inserted into the mortises. Post-and-rail fences could be six or seven rails high. "Virginia" or "worm" fences were five to eight rails high and topped with cross pieces or "stakes" carrying an additional two or three rails called riders. Worm fences surrounded fields farthest from the house but were not limited to field enclosures. Archaeological investigation at Thompson's Loss and Gain in Sussex County, for example (see Fig. 3.3B), indicated that a rough fence of this sort encircled the house and yard.

All fencing was not of wood. In the Delaware, Maryland, and Pennsylvania Piedmont, we can still find evidence of fieldstone fences snaking their way through woods and along the margins of pastures. Archaeologists in Kent County, Delaware, have excavated ditch fences, formed by digging ditches three to four feet deep and piling the lost earth to one side in an embankment of similar height. Farmers often stabilized the S-shaped profile of ditch and bank with plantings of thorn bushes. The resulting fence supposedly deterred scavenging animals and reduced the use of rail timber—an increasingly scarce and costly commodity from the early 1800s onward. By the mid-1800s, the craze for Osage orange and other fencing plants, like Newcastle thorn, was well entrenched. In the later decades of the nineteenth century, Delaware farmers began to string their fields with metal wire. Evidence of wire fences, from early examples of barbed wire to modern electrified wire, can be found throughout the state. Often these newer fences mark long-established barnyards and field patterns. Finally, the history of fences includes the removal of fence lines and hedgerows during the early- to mid-twentieth century. Modern tractors and cultivation equipment made it easier for farmers to cultivate large fields. As a result, the fences and plantings defining the old 10- to 25-acre lots of the 1800s were ripped out. Still, a sharp eye can discern the remnants of these old divisions within and along the edge of larger fields.

Other landscape remnants are frequently visible on or around many early house sites. Sometimes, the only surviving features of an early dwelling site are shade trees, old overgrown gardens, and ornamental plantings. For example, one common hallmark of early dwelling sites is a set of "bride and groom trees"—a pair of trees, typically buttonwoods, which were traditionally planted close to the main entrance of eighteenth- and nineteenth-century houses. Although such plantings have failed to survive in Port Penn, they remain elsewhere in the neighborhood. Fairview, built in the 1760s, for example, retains its buttonwood trees. One also finds seemingly stranded clumps of double-headed daffodils, periwinkle, and hosta along the edges of modern fields and woodland, indicating old house sites. But while bride and groom trees and other types of plantings were once fashionable and commonplace, they are rarely planted today. Types of ornamental plantings wax and wane in popularity over the years, and, because modern hybrid plants often outgrow and outperform earlier varieties, some older varieties are no longer as widely available as they once were. Finally, environmental factors and changes in horticultural practices—the advent of plant hybridization, changes in insect populations, and subtle climatic shifts—have also affected the choice of landscaping plants. Precisely because of these variations over time, the plants found in a landscape can offer useful archaeological evidence.

Although the Cleaver House has lost its historic plantings, it continues to reflect a very specific chronological period in the physical topography of the village. Whereas the Stewarts sited the proposed Port Penn market square adjacent to their house, the Cleavers positioned their house at the principal intersection of town near the town wharf. The wharf, consisting of a long earthen dike terminating in a timber dock, was one of the first improvements the Stewarts implemented in establishing the infrastructure of their proposed town. By the time the Cleavers commissioned their house, the urban ambition for Port Penn had diminished into a village reality. The Port Penn of the 1840s functioned as little more than a backcountry landing to which farmers brought their produce for shipment into the local river market, which served Wilmington and Philadelphia. In a village economy of such small scale there was room for only one major entrepreneurial family—and the Cleavers willingly assumed that role from the Stewarts. The location they chose for their house describes a shift in Port Penn's perceived commercial center from the market square, to be centrally located two-and-one-half blocks away from the waterfront, to a commercial center at the point where the village wharf met the street. The design of the Cleaver House reinforces its place in the landscape. The southwest corner of the house—the corner of the dwelling directly on the intersection—was dedicated to business use. Two fanlit doorways—one facing the wharf and one facing Congress Street—opened into the corner room, which was heated by a stove. The orientation of the office in the Cleaver House speaks directly to the owners' view of their environment. Neither the house nor its business space fronted on the reclaimed marshland to the river. Instead, both the house as a whole and its commercial room faced inland, architecturally privileging Port Penn's backcountry orientation over its original trans-Atlantic vision.

The office of the Cleaver House occupied the southwest corner of a center-passage, double-pile dwelling. On the other side of the broad center passage, which contained the stair to the upper stories, were two parlors standing front to back. Architectural details such as twin marble mantels, neatly executed door and window surrounds, and a large double door opening that connected the two rooms indicate that the two spaces were designed to be opened up as a single large formal room for specific social activities such as fancy dinners. Moreover, when we look closely we find that the door surrounds between the passage and the two parlors on one side and the office opposite not only differ visually, but also suggest different construction periods from the office door, which likely dates to the twentieth century. Thus, we discover that the office originally did not open into the passage but connected instead to a back room, which was in turn connected to the passage by a door under the stair landing. The overall result was a plan that carefully segregated business space from domestic space under a common roof. Taken as a whole, the Cleaver House describes a process of functional distinction within consolidation. The same process was at work in the countryside around Port Penn, where mid-nineteenth-century farmers commissioned large bank barns and surrounded them with other farm buildings, such as drive-through granaries. Like William and Catherine Cleaver, these builders erected a structure that symbolized the consolidation of agricultural functions; at the same time, these farmers continued the old eighteenth-century practice of farmstead planning using many functionally specific and physically separated outbuildings. In this larger landscape context, the Cleaver House plan expresses and illustrates the growing complexity and conflicting values in mid-nineteenth-century vernacular building design.

As exemplified by the Cleaver House, the changing landscape of Port Penn, which shifted from an orientation that looked outward with great commercial optimism to one that turned inward with a more pragmatic eye, is also borne out by the two principal public buildings in the village, the Port Penn Presbyterian Church (1834, replaced in 1856) and St. Daniel's Methodist Church (1843, rebuilt 1891). Sited less than a block from each other, the two churches served not only different Protestant congregations but also two social communities within the village and its immediate neighborhood. Both churches also relate to the fortunes and the houses of the two principal families in Port Penn.

Figure 7.10

Port Penn Presbyterian
Church, 1856, Port Penn,
New Castle County, Dela-
ware. Photographed 1995.
With its brick construction
and Italianate and Roman-
esque Revival detailing, the
church stands as the grandest public building in Port
Penn today.

The present Port Penn Presbyterian Church, built in 1856, faces north and overlooks Market Street from its site adjacent to the Stewart House (Fig. 7.10). Built of brick laid in stretcher bond, the two-story church consists of a ground-level community hall and Sunday school and an upstairs sanctuary. The gable front, with its round and segmental arch gable-end windows and door, quatrefoil rose window, and sawnwork brackets, represents a free borrowing of popular Italianate and Romanesque Revival detailing. The considerably plainer side elevations have brick paneled surfaces that provide recesses for square-headed windows. Only the cornice brackets extend from the stylish front to the less assuming sides. With its brick construction and use of nationally popular mid-nineteenth-century architectural elements, the Port Penn Presbyterian Church is the most visible and pretentious public building in the village. The steeple's dramatically pointed spire insures that the visual presence of the church can be appreciated from afar. In fact, the steeple of the church is one of the first landscape features recognizable in our original view from the bridge.

Although the Port Penn Presbyterian Church today stands as the grandest and most public building in Port Penn, it was not always so. Basic historical information enables us to understand the physical and chronological context of the church in the community. First of all, the original church erected on the site was built more than twenty years earlier, in 1834. In the larger landscape history of Port Penn, that date falls at the point when the Stewarts' urban dream had failed and the Cleavers' more pragmatic vision for a small river landing and market village had taken hold. The site of the 1834 church—adjacent to the Stewart House and on the lot originally set aside for a market square—describes the complete abandonment of Port Penn's original promise. A proposed market square—the secular hub of a commercial community—had been replaced with a church—the new congregational focus for the village. The true commercial center, as exemplified by the Cleaver House, had shifted closer to the river where the Port Penn wharf met Market Street.

Second, the earlier church had been a very different structure: one story in height, considerably smaller (24 by 36 feet), and built of wood, the 1834 church consisted of rows of bench pews facing an altar and low pulpit built against one gable end. The overall impression was one of a plain meeting house lacking architectural pretensions any greater than those of the town's timber frame houses. Thus, the replacement of the 1834 frame meeting house with the stylish brick church of 1856 also suggests a change in the congregation's representation of itself in the landscape. No longer drawing on the

Figure 7.11
St. Daniel's Methodist Church, Port Penn, New Castle County, Delaware. Photographed 1995. Founded in 1843 by both black and white Port Penn citizens, the St. Daniel's congregation has been solely African American since early in the twentieth century.

plain architectural language associated with a "nonconformist" religion, the new church employed architectural fashion to link itself with an established and popular national culture. Both the transition from market square to sacred site and from plain meeting house to fashionable church represent changes in the landscape as a whole that we have been able to connect to both the principal houses in the village and the larger countryside.

St. Daniel's Methodist Church, begun in 1843 and significantly reworked in 1891, stands a block to the north of the Presbyterian church on the edge of the town abutting the marsh (Fig. 7.11). Oriented with its gable front facing west, the tall, single-story frame church consists of a rectangular sanctuary with a bell tower on the west gable. Like the Presbyterian church, the siting and architectural character of the Methodist church suggests a number of thoughts about the social organization of the landscape. In terms of siting, the Methodist church sits away from the center of the town. It borders the marsh. St. Daniel's also sits lower in the landscape than the Presbyterian church. The placement of the Methodist church both away from and below the village center immediately suggests a hierarchy of congregations within the community. This hierarchical division is reinforced by the simply finished weatherboard exterior of the Methodist church as compared to the much more fashionable trim and decorative brickwork sponsored by the Presbyterian congregation. Thus, the architectural hierarchy suggested by church siting, building materials, and finishes may mirror another division—that of congregational wealth.

Although founded by both white and black citizens, St. Daniel's became a solely African-American congregation early in the twentieth century. The original Methodist congregation purchased the building site from the Cleaver family and commissioned the church as a permanent place of worship intended to replace the impromptu sites of local revival meetings. For various reasons, though, the congregation failed to flourish and the church was shut in the late nineteenth century. In 1922 the old Port Penn Methodist congregation sold the church and lot to the African-American congregation, which rededicated the building as St. Daniel's. Because St. Daniel's has been an African-American congregation for most of living memory, the local assumption is that the church has always been associated with Port Penn's black community. In modern eyes, where a history of racial prejudice coupled with economic marginalization by a dominant white society is well understood, St. Daniel's can be misread by fieldworkers in architecture as evidence of racial struggle and ethnic identity. Again, the documentary record, which in this case disproves the assumption, is vital to understanding landscape ensembles, particularly where changing circumstances render meanings in the landscape ambiguous.

Standing on the western edge of town, the Port Penn School, built in the late nineteenth century, illustrates the way a single public building can remain vital and retain similar meanings through changing circumstances. The one-story frame building, sheathed with plain weatherboard and capped with a small bell cupola over its gable entry, faces south, overlooking the road into town and a broad empty lot. The interior of the building consists of two rooms: the front one served as the primary classroom space for all the grades, and the back room was set aside for storage. The undifferentiated classroom space must have required all of the teacher's instructional and disciplinary skills for both education and order. Heated by a wood-burning stove, finished with plaster surfaces above narrow board wainscot, and provided with separate privies for girls and boys situated in the back corners of the schoolyard, the Port Penn School provided a visible and public community statement. Even after the county school system abandoned the school, the old building continued to symbolize the value of community education. In the mid-1970s,

several community members joined forces to refurbish and furnish the old school as a local museum. In the 1990s, the museum was renovated as a community-sponsored and state-supported natural and historical interpretive center with a clearly stated public education mission (Fig. 7.12). The history of the Port Penn School suggests the value in seeking continuity of use in the landscape. Although the schoolhouse no longer served its original educational purpose, its place in the landscape and the public consciousness of the community remained intact and vital. Continuity of use, as we shall see in our concluding discussion of the Port Penn marsh, presents both insights and problems in the documentation and interpretation of the historic built environment.

In some instances, landscape features are almost invisible, and only oral history and documentary evidence reveal details of use and appearance. Still, architectural fieldworkers need to be as aware of what has vanished as of what remains. Chief among the lost buildings and landscape features of Port Penn are those associated with life and work on the marsh and river. For example,

Figure 7.12
Port Penn Museum, formerly the Port Penn School, Port Penn, New Castle County, Delaware. Photographed 1995. Built in the late nineteenth century and refurnished as a local museum in the mid-1970s, the Port Penn School illustrates the way a single public building can remain vital and retain similar meanings despite changing circumstances.

on the northern extension of Congress Street and adjacent to the last house in town stand a small brick storage building and four concrete pads in which arc embedded rusting iron bolts. Each pad once supported one leg of an iron navigational beacon, while the brick building held the oil that fueled the beacon's lamp (Fig. 7.13). Several lighthouses with similar construction and settings survive along the shorelines of the Delaware River and other waterways throughout the region. A few miles to the west of Port Penn stands the Reedy Island Rear Range Light, a tall slender iron navigational aid, accompanied by a lighthouse keeper's cottage and oil house. Like the Port Penn Lighthouse, the Reedy Island Rear Range Light physically links the countryside to the river in a landscape of movement. Without the navigational beacons, ships and boats on the Delaware would be imperiled by the river's often treacherous waters.

A more subtle architectural remnant than the lighthouse footings is the large level vacant lot across the road from the old Port Penn School (now the village museum) on the western edge of the village. The only trace of activity here is the lack of any visible architectural remains on a site so close to town. Historic photographs in the village museum, however, reveal that the lot was the site of the Port Penn cannery—one of those long, low, rambling one-story structures once common in the region's landscape—that processed tomatoes and other local produce. The Port Penn cannery and the lighthouse, both early-twentieth-century constructions, represent two additional dimensions to the architectural landscape: industry and transportation. Both activities can be described in terms of the specific structures associated with them, but both can only be understood and interpreted through their relationships to the larger community defined by the town, its agricultural backcountry, and the river. Still, we have yet to address the more ephemeral landscape of the marsh.

The Port Penn landscape of the mid-nineteenth century, characterized by diminished commercial expectations and an increasingly local character, continued (and continues) to develop through the twentieth century. In the closing discussion we turn our attention to the natural landscape feature which now most thoroughly dominates Port Penn—the marsh. The marshlands around the town appear at first glance to present a vast natural vista. As we look closer, however, we discover that this natural setting is also a cultural landscape and that it defines the community in the present and, in large measure, will direct its future.

The marshes that extend around Port Penn on three sides consist of several

Figure 7.13
Port Penn Lighthouse re-
mains, Port Penn, New
Castle County, Delaware.
Photographed 1995. A
small brick storage building and four concrete pads
with rusting iron bolts pro-
truding from them are the
only features remaining
from the Port Penn Light-
house. Several lighthouses
remain along the shorelines
of the Delaware River and
other area waterways.

different wetland environments. To the east, the marsh is tidal and brackish,
with dense stands of the tall feathery marsh reed called phragmides choking
the banks and blocking the view of the town from the river. On the north side
of the village stretch recently restored freshwater marshes. With their borders protected by earthen dikes and their water levels regulated by flood
gates, these freshwater wetlands present more open vistas of ponds bordered
with stands of cattails and phragmides. Different fauna are drawn to each type
of marsh habitat. Wood ducks and American mergansers prefer the freshwater environment with its abundance of wild grains; other wildfowl, such
as black ducks, mallards, and puddle ducks, are drawn to the more saline, tidal topography of the river's edge; broadbills, redheads, and diving ducks
frequent the open river. Plant and animal habitats represent a very different
aspect of Port Penn's landscape ensemble, and they are reflected in two
structures—the muskrat skinning shed and the fisherman's floating cabin.
An example of each of these has been placed on display along newly developed
hiking trails designed to educate visitors to the natural and cultural ecology
of the marsh.

The muskrat skinning shed is a roughly 12-foot square, braced-frame,
gable-roofed structure sheathed with vertical board siding attached with cut
nails (Fig. 7.14). Like most older skinning sheds in the area, the Port Penn
example was converted from its prior use as a smokehouse. The interior walls
and ceiling are boarded, and an old work table stands in one corner. The

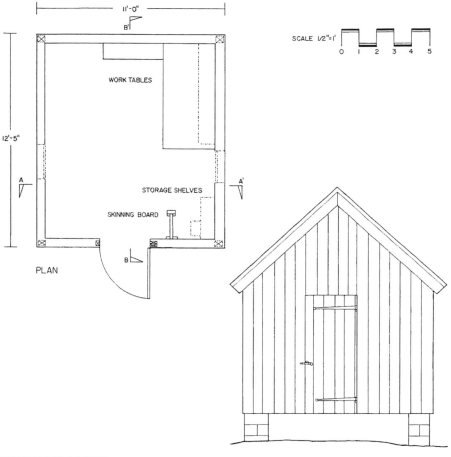

11'-0"

12'-5"

B'

WORK TABLES

STORAGE SHELVES

SKINNING BOARD

A

A'

B

PLAN

SCALE 1/2"=1'

0 1 2 3 4 5

SOUTH ELEVATION

Figure 7.14
Port Penn area muskrat skinning shed, Port Penn vicinity,
New Castle County, Delaware. Drawn by Caroline Fisher.
Like most older skinning sheds in the area, this one previ-
ously functioned as a smokehouse.

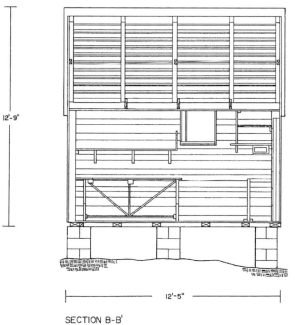

12'-9"

12'-5"

SECTION B-B'

Figure 7.15
Skinning sheds are increasingly rare remnants of the trapping industry of Delaware's tidal marshes and repositories of watermen's material culture. (*A*) Ike Cleaver's muskrat shed, Odessa vicinity, New Castle County, Delaware. Photographed by David Ames, HABS, 1987. (*B*) Ike Cleaver with harvest from his muskrat trapping ground, mid-1900s. Photograph courtesy of Port Penn Interpretive Center Collection. The name and role of the individual to the left of Cleaver is unknown.

building presently stands on the edge of the marsh and serves as part of a larger educational program administered by the Port Penn Museum, but its original physical context was behind a farmhouse located near the banks of the Delaware River, where it functioned as an integral part of an agricultural economy. The historic landscape relations suggested by the architectural character of this shed are more fully represented in the nearby Ike Cleaver muskrat skinning shed, which retains its functional setting.

Skinning sheds represent an increasingly rare survival of a building type associated with the trapping industry of Delaware's tidal marshes, as well as a nearly vanished repository of watermen's material culture (Fig. 7.15). Ike Cleaver's muskrat shed, a roughly 16-foot-square hewn-timber frame building constructed in the mid-1800s as a smokehouse, was slightly revised on the interior when it was converted for skinning muskrats and processing the skins and meat. The interior contains a work table, stretching boards used for curing pelts, a skinning bench and board, and other tools used for trapping and dressing both muskrats and snapping turtles. Like other area trappers, Ike Cleaver set his mechanical traps along the many muskrat runs crisscrossing the marshes. Every day of the season he walked his trap line to collect his catch. Returning to the skinning shed with the carcasses, Cleaver dressed the muskrats by first hanging them hind feet up and abdomen out on the skinning board and then stripping them of their hide with handmade knives. The pelts were then pulled over curing boards made from shingles and hung to air dry inside the shed.

Other landscape ensemble features essential to trapping include the marsh itself. Ike Cleaver carefully gridded his small portion of marsh and mapped the locations of all the muskrat houses during the winter of 1938–39 (Fig. 7.16). Cleaver's actions, mapping and trapping, claimed the natural habitat as part of a cultural landscape, but with some very significant ramifications, such as the problem of ephemeral or fleeting landscapes. Looking at buildings as material markers of the past focuses our attention on what is lasting and monumental in the countryside. Looking at landscape features, some with uses lasting only hours and leaving no physical trace, encourages us to think in terms of action and experience as well as architecture. Ike Cleaver's trapping marsh is not an artifact so much as a place defined by its use. In the seasonal round of the farm family's and waterman's year, muskrat trapping represented only one category of environmentally dependent work. At other times of the year, the marshes and the nearby river and its tributaries were used for hunting wildfowl, catching snapping turtles, cutting marsh hay, and fishing (Fig. 7.17).

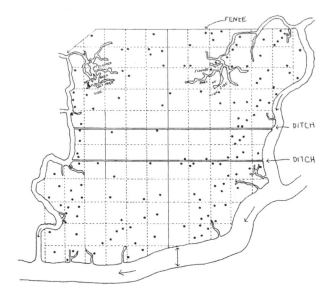

Figure 7.16
Marsh map for winter 1938–39, Odessa vicinity, New Castle County, Delaware. Drawn by Gabrielle Lanier after original on canvas. Ike Cleaver's map of his muskrat hunting grounds is a valuable document of local landscape history.

Figure 7.17
Shad skiffs moored at Port Penn. Photograph, ca. 1920, courtesy of Port Penn Interpretive Center Collection. In Port Penn, the marshes and the nearby river and its tributaries were used for hunting wildfowl, catching snapping turtles, cutting marsh hay, and fishing. In addition to four shad skiffs, this photograph also shows a bateau (*lower left*), used for fishing, trapping, hunting, and recreation, and what appears to be a floating cabin with temporary dock (*lower left*).

We have seen how Port Penn, with its overlapping layers of architecture, intentions, and actions, illustrates the intertwined notions of archaeological assemblage and landscape ensemble. Similarly complex and nuanced landscapes, many with even more startling juxtapositions of historic and current features, can be found everywhere in the mid-Atlantic region. Learning to look with care and read those landscapes for evidence of continuity and change allows us, as house historians, not only to understand the connections among people, buildings, objects, and their surroundings, but to place the architecture that we study into a broader and far more meaningful historical and cultural context.

8 RECORDING HISTORIC BUILDINGS

Architectural documentation serves a number of objectives. While the primary goal is to gather information about the building being examined, these observations ultimately help to illuminate larger issues of social change and cultural transformation. Field recording—drawing, photographing, and verbally describing a building—is one of the most effective methods for learning about or "reading" architecture. Yet fieldwork that focuses on how a building has been put together, used, and changed through time often raises as many questions as it answers. Specific questions about when and how a building was altered eventually lead to broader issues, such as why those changes occurred and what they meant to the people who effected them. People are constantly remaking their environments. The choices they make, often most clearly reflected in their architecture and their landscapes, are sometimes telling indicators of their individual and community values. Thus, while field recording documents a building at a specific point in time, it also identifies sequences of historical change and raises questions about the social values that motivated those changes. Architectural documentation constitutes a lasting record of ideas, as well as of buildings, and it provides future generations with important information about structures that may by then have been altered or demolished.

The historic built environment in much of the Delaware valley has changed dramatically and irreversibly over the past decade. Abandonment, neglect, and increasing pressure from development have contributed to the loss of many early structures. In addition, a widespread lack of public recognition that such buildings have value—both as part of our cultural inheritance and as economic assets—has resulted in a high rate of loss for cultural resources and the destruction of whole historic landscapes. Although the goal of historic preservation is to prevent excessive loss of historic resources, circumstances often prevent the preservation of actual structures. Sometimes "preservation on paper"—field recording through scaled architectural field drawings, archival photography, and architectural descriptions—provides what amounts to the only permanent record of historic structures.

Preliminaries: Mapping and Reconnaissance-level Surveying

Before undertaking field recording of any kind, it is important to locate the building or structure in question both geographically and historically. A sense of geographic location—the physical context in which the building stands, its relationship to its surrounding environment, topography, and to similar buildings in the area, and its historic and current accessibility to transportation routes—can clarify many subsequent issues and suggest further ones. For example, many of the eighteenth-century pattern-end brick dwellings that are so well known in Salem County, New Jersey, were originally built near landings on the Delaware River, with their front or "public" sides facing the water. The orientation of these dwellings suggests the historical primacy of the river as a major transportation route. While many of these earlier river inlets have since silted over, and subsequent overlays of settlement and land-based transportation systems in the area have followed different patterns, the original orientations of these early buildings remain today as cultural artifacts embedded in a twentieth-century landscape.

Questions about geographic location, orientation, and siting can often be readily answered by consulting maps, which can help to determine a building's current and historic geographic context as well as its actual physical location. Although historic buildings can sometimes be identified visually in the course of fieldwork, they must often be located without any prior visual familiarity. Detailed highway maps that show minor roads are good places to start. Once the location of the building has been established, United States Geological Survey (USGS) quadrangle maps, which are discussed in greater detail later in this chapter, can be very helpful. Because they are printed at a scale that is large enough to show every building, they can help you to determine the density of settlement and to see relationships between the building and surrounding geographic features. USGS quads are also updated with enough regularity to make them fairly current, especially in rural areas, where the rate of change can be slow. Although route numbers for more minor roads are not typically marked on USGS quads, they are useful navigational tools when undertaking a basic field survey. For instance, if you wanted to gain a sense of the extent to which the historic built environment survives in a particular area, one way to start would be to drive over every road in that area, noting the earliest buildings, their location, and any historic landscape features. Mapping an area in this way not only provides you with a sense of the physical locations of buildings, but also reveals patterns that might not be apparent otherwise. Early maps, which are discussed in more depth below, can be just as useful as contemporary maps for determining historic information such as the chronology of settlement in a given area, the names of prior property owners, or the former locations of landscape features that have long since disappeared.

Survey Techniques

Field examinations at any level of intensiveness are likely to be most instructive if they are undertaken systematically. A consistent technique for looking at and recording buildings helps to retrieve information efficiently and insures that no parts of a building are overlooked. For this reason, field surveyors generally use a standardized form that lists all of the component parts of a building, from the foundation to the roof, in turn. These forms usually call for construction details (building material, construction techniques, and ornament), site information, and a sketch of the first-floor plan. Site information might include the relationship of the building to the road or to surrounding buildings as well as distinguishing natural or man-made landscape features, such as hedges, fences, foundations, or evidence for old property lines.

Most state historic preservation offices use their own standardized survey forms for recording information about historic architecture, but the various formats require essentially the same types of information. The Delaware State Historic Preservation Office's survey form (Fig. 8.1) can be used as a general checklist for observing buildings. The survey forms used throughout the region request different levels of information. Maryland, for example, uses a fairly open-ended format that is essentially a blank National Register of Historic Places form and relies on the surveyor's knowledge of what information to include, whereas Delaware's form utilizes more of a checklist approach.

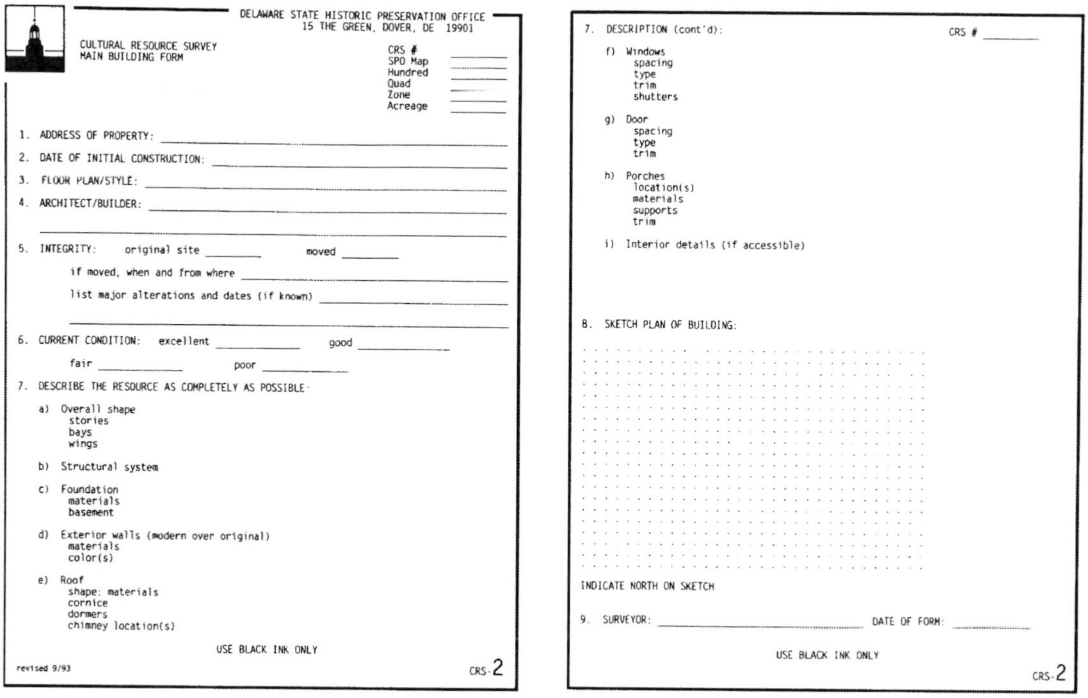

DELAWARE STATE HISTORIC PRESERVATION OFFICE
15 THE GREEN, DOVER, DE 19901

CULTURAL RESOURCE SURVEY
MAIN BUILDING FORM

CRS #
SPO Map
Hundred
Quad
Zone
Acreage

1. ADDRESS OF PROPERTY: _____

2. DATE OF INITIAL CONSTRUCTION: _____

3. FLOOR PLAN/STYLE: _____

4. ARCHITECT/BUILDER: _____

5. INTEGRITY: original site _____   moved _____

    if moved, when and from where _____

    list major alterations and dates (if known) _____

6. CURRENT CONDITION: excellent _____   good _____

    fair _____   poor _____

7. DESCRIBE THE RESOURCE AS COMPLETELY AS POSSIBLE:

    a) Overall shape
        stories
        bays
        wings

    b) Structural system

    c) Foundation
        materials
        basement

    d) Exterior walls (modern over original)
        materials
        color(s)

    e) Roof
        shape: materials
        cornice
        dormers
        chimney location(s)

    USE BLACK INK ONLY

    revised 9/93   CRS-2

---

7. DESCRIPTION (cont'd):   CRS # _____

    f) Windows
        spacing
        type
        trim
        shutters

    g) Door
        spacing
        type
        trim

    h) Porches
        location(s)
        materials
        supports
        trim

    i) Interior details (if accessible)

8. SKETCH PLAN OF BUILDING:

INDICATE NORTH ON SKETCH

9. SURVEYOR: _____   DATE OF FORM: _____

    USE BLACK INK ONLY   CRS-2

Figure 8.1

Cultural Resource Survey, Main Building Form, Delaware State Historic Preservation Office. Most state historic preservation offices use standardized survey forms, such as this one, for recording information about historic architecture.

For the Delaware form, a surveyor would typically collect the following information:

1. *Address:* This should include both the street address and if possible a geographic location, such as "east side of Road 710, north of its intersection with Road 709." Also include county, township or hundred, and town or vicinity.

2. *Description of the structure:*

    a. *Overall shape:* Describe the overall shape and massing of the building as visible from outside. Note whether it is of single- or double-pile construction. Also note the number of stories and bays, the presence of wings, and the overall measurements of the structure. Include a sketch of the floor plan, showing window and door openings and additions. Be sure to note the direction the building faces, by placing a north arrow on the plan drawing.

    b. *Structural system:* Note building material (such as brick, stone, log, or braced frame). Also note material shifts: if parts of the building are constructed of different materials, note differences in structural systems from one portion of the building to another.

    c. *Foundation:* Describe building materials as well as construction methods; note whether a partial or full cellar is present and where it is located.

d. *Exterior walls:* Describe walling materials and wall coverings (such as stone, frame, or brick, and weatherboard, aluminum siding, or stucco). If the building is stone, record the type of stone (such as field or rubble stone) and its treatment (whether the stone is dressed or finished) and the way in which it is laid (coursed, roughly coursed, or uncoursed). If the building is brick, record the type of brick bond used, noting any differences in brick bond patterns from one elevation to another. Also note such exterior features as paint color and the presence of water tables or gable decoration.

e. *Roof:* Describe type (such as gambrel, hipped, or gable) and construction materials. Also note any detail at verge, eaves, or ridge, whether cornice details are present and what they are, whether dormers are present, and the location and number of chimneys. Note any corbeling at chimney tops.

f. *Windows:* Note the number and placement of windows, their shape, whether windows consist of fixed or moveable sash, and whether they are double hung. Also note the number of panes in each sash. Include the style of all window frames and trim, and if shutters are present and where they are placed.

g. *Doors:* Note the number and type of doors and their spacing. If door surrounds are present, describe them.

h. *Porches (if present):* Describe their location and building materials. Record information about any supports, trim, and roof.

i. *Interior details:* Note presence and style of woodwork, hardware, mantels, and significant construction details to which you have access. Any details of interior finish should be noted here.

3. *Condition:* Assess and describe the overall condition of the building.

4. *Integrity:* Record any apparent alterations and your best assessment of their dates. Note whether or not the structure has been moved from its original site.

5. *Date:* Try to estimate the date of initial construction.

6. *Architect/Builder:* Record this information if it is available.

7. *Site:* Describe the general setting. Is the building surrounded by other closely spaced buildings, or does it border on woodland or cultivated fields? Record any related outbuildings and gardens. Describe the relationship between farm buildings, farmhouse, and gardens. Also note uses of specific outbuildings if known. Sketch a general site plan showing the building and its relationship to other structures, driveways, and roads. Note the direction the building faces with a north arrow on the site plan. Pay attention to the building in its larger context: is it similar to other

buildings in the general area, or is it substantially different in terms of style or construction date?

8. *Use:* Describe the original and subsequent uses of the structure, as well as any possible associations with historic events or persons.

9. *References:* Explain the source of your information about the site, such as oral tradition, family papers, or public documents. Include where you found the reference.

10. *Owner's name, address, and telephone number:* Include as much of this information as is available.

Alterations are just as significant as the current appearance of the structure. Pay special attention to clues suggesting changes or additions. Some alterations are obvious, such as a telltale seam in a brick or masonry facade, a filled window or door opening, or a cellar relieving arch with no fireplace above (Fig. 8.2). Other changes are more subtle. A row of nail holes in an overhead joist may be all that remains of an early room partition; the header for a relocated stair may be represented by a faint whitewash "ghost" on the surrounding timbers; the subterranean remnants of a long-demolished kitchen may be visible only as yellowed patches in the grass.

Evidence of structural alterations often exists throughout the building. On the exterior, look for seams or irregularities that might indicate alterations to windows or doors. In eighteenth- and nineteenth-century brick buildings, for example, the perimeters of window and door openings were often finished with closers. When these openings are subsequently filled, the closers remain embedded in the wall. By looking carefully at the brick bonding for such evidence, you can sometimes determine whether the existing openings are original. Likewise, look for indications of subsequent additions. Evidence for additions might include material shifts—changes in mortar joints, or the type or treatment of masonry or framing lumber, for example—or moved or altered interior openings. Other evidence might consist of timbers cut in inappropriate places or subtle differences in joinery from one part of the building to another. Foundation remnants or imprints of earlier structures on the existing exterior walls—sometimes visible through differences in surface weathering, discrepancies in mortar pointing, or whitewash "ghosts"—can also imply that the building once had an addition.

Indications of changes in orientation and traffic patterns may also be visible. As buildings pass through different owners and room uses change, shifts in access patterns sometimes leave evidence behind—reworked stairs, moved door openings, or altered heating arrangements. Changes in transportation

A

B

EVERYDAY ARCHITECTURE OF THE MID-ATLANTIC

Figure 8.2
"Ghosts" on brickwork and plaster scars often reveal much
about a building's history. Evidence of earlier chimneys and
of roof raising is visible on the Parson Thorne Mansion,
heavily altered in 1879. Faint ghosts of a pedimented door
surround with flanking columns can be seen on the Crossan
House. And the original contours of a mantel in the Mendenhall House are clearly revealed. (*A*) Parson Thorne Mansion, mid-1700s, Milford vicinity, Kent County, Delaware.
Photographed by James C. Massey, HABS, 1982. (*B*) Crossan House, 1798–1804, Bear vicinity, New Castle County,
Delaware. Photographed by David Ames, HABS, 1989. (*C*)
Captain Thomas Mendenhall House, third floor front chamber, Wilmington, New Castle County, Delaware. Photographed by David Ames, HABS, 1981.

C

networks can also effect changes in adjacent buildings. Streets and river
routes that were once primary modes of access are often superseded by subsequent roads.

In timber-framed buildings, reused framing members are common and can
provide subtle clues to a building's earlier lives. Roofs and interior walls in
early buildings were frequently reworked; consequently, timbers that were
originally designed for one purpose often reappeared later in another guise.
Floor joists, rafters, and braces could all be reappropriated whole or piece-
meal and functionally transformed. Reused timbers might come from any
source but were often derived from earlier portions of the same building or
from demolished or reworked buildings nearby. If enough of these timbers
remain largely intact, they can provide sufficient evidence to reconstruct the
earlier appearance of the building in which they are used or even the one from
which they came. For example, original rafters are sometimes used in reworked roofs; if the earlier rafters are whole, or even if a complete, uncut
original rafter can be located elsewhere, the original roof pitch, height, and
type of roof covering can often be determined simply from measurements and
nailing patterns. Whole or partial timbers, weatherboards, or other materials

Figure 8.3
Wheatland Granary, Claytons Corner vicinity, St. George's Hundred, New Castle County, Delaware. Photographed 1982. In timber-framed buildings, reused framing timbers are common and can provide subtle clues to a building's earlier lives. These recycled floor joists once functioned elsewhere as principal posts, as evidenced by the tenons visible here.

salvaged from earlier building periods might also be stored and forgotten in attics, crawl spaces, cellars, and nearby outbuildings and can provide additional clues (Fig. 8.3).

When buildings are partially or completely ruinous, careful observation and field documentation can sometimes enable you to reconstruct the original appearance of the building with great accuracy. This type of field recording—which is true "preservation on paper," because it involves nearly total reconstruction drawings of structures that have disappeared—involves methodically gathering enough information from existing materials to produce measured drawings (Fig. 8.4).

Graphic Documentation

One of the best ways to understand a building is to draw it. Architectural drawings can be as simple as a quickly sketched floor plan or as complex as a series of measured drawings showing different views of the building, such as front, back, or side walls (elevations) or cross sections. Drawing floor plans and construction details requires careful and methodical observation and focuses one's attention on the components of a building and on the way they interrelate. Field drawing also helps to explain spatial relationships that might not be readily apparent in photographs or written descriptions. Generally, short of certain types of construction and architectural information, we draw what cannot be readily photographed or described (Fig. 8.5).

The process of taking good architectural field notes is seldom seamless. Even experienced fieldworkers spend as much time looking, reassessing, and

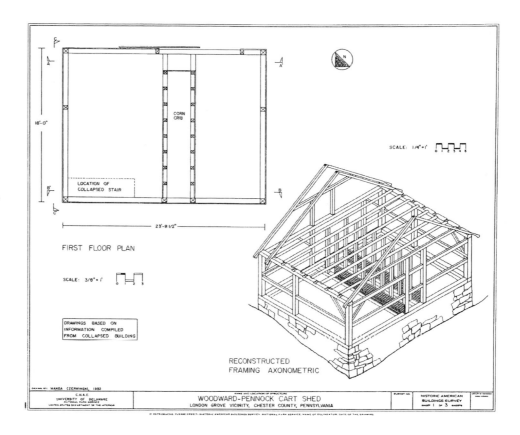

Figure 8.4
Woodward-Pennock cart shed, London Grove vicinity, Chester County, Pennsylvania. Drawn by Wanda Czerwinski, HABS. This nineteenth-century cart shed was completely ruinous, but careful observation and field documentation enabled the delineator to reconstruct quite accurately the original framing of the building.

erasing as they do drawing. The most instructive field drawings are analytical rather than merely illustrative in their approach and attempt to ask questions of the building, engaging in a dialogue with the structure instead of simply describing it. For example, building alterations are important indicators of changing uses and intentions and when visible they should be noted. The physical history of most buildings is very disorderly; to be effective, fieldwork should respond to the complexity of the building and its surroundings. Questions—and answers—about room function, movement patterns, and construction sequences emerge naturally from the process of drawing.

You will eventually develop your own system for taking field notes, but you should aim to produce notes that are as legible and comprehensible to someone else as they are to you. While some fieldworkers choose first to produce a rough sketch of the view they plan to draw, then add measurements later, it is usually preferable to take the extra time and effort to draw field notes roughly to scale on site. Drawing to scale in the field demands that you examine the building very carefully while it is in front of you. This method eliminates many later questions at the drafting table and immediately clarifies

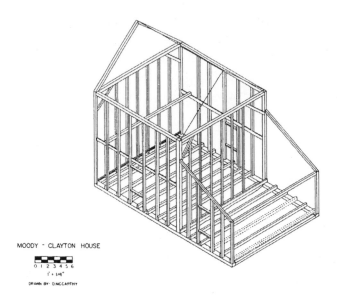

MOODY - CLAYTON HOUSE
0 1 2 3 4 5 6
1' = 1/4"
DRAWN BY: D.MCCARTHY

Figure 8.5
Axonometric drawing of Moody-Clayton House, Clayton's Corner vicinity, St. George's Hundred, New Castle County, Delaware. Drawn by Deidre McCarthy. Drawings can be used to communicate information that photographs cannot possibly capture. This axonometric drawings shows a cutaway view of the construction of a two-story dwelling with one-story lean-to. The delineator has stripped away the exterior walls as well as the rafters and roofs so that the framing members are more clearly visible.

relationships that might remain hidden until you translate your rough field notes into finished pencil drawings.

Equipment

For reasons of portability and storage, many fieldworkers like to use graph paper, either in loose sheets or bound in 8½ by 11 inch laboratory notebooks. This method is inexpensive but requires compressing a lot of written information into a small area. For this reason, some fieldworkers prefer to record their notes in a larger format such as 18 by 24 inch sheets of graph paper taped to a piece of masonite, heavy cardboard, or a large portable drawing board. These sheets come gridded at four squares to the inch or eight squares to the inch. This size paper is useful for taking field notes with lots of annotations, but it tends to be more expensive and a bit more unwieldy in the field. No matter what size paper you choose, you will also need inexpensive mechanical pencils, an eraser, masking or drafting tape, and a tape measure or two. A combination of two tape measures usually works best: a stiff, retractable 25- or 30-foot tape and a flexible 50-foot tape.

Recording

To allow enough room for notations and details, use the largest possible scale that will allow you to fit your drawings on the page. Field notes are most commonly drawn at a scale of ¼ inch = 1 foot. On standard-sized graph paper, this would mean that one block would equal one foot. If the building you are recording is small, you may be able to use a larger scale—½ inch = 1 foot would be suitable. This larger scale is especially helpful when you need to fit a lot of information on a single page. To prevent confusion later, note the name of the building, its location, the date, the view you are drawing (first-floor plan, cellar plan, etc.) and, if you are working with others, the members of your field team on each page of field notes. Indicate the scale of measurement you are using and include a north directional arrow on your floor plan.

Although it is possible and sometimes necessary to work alone, it is always best to undertake field recording with at least one other person, for expediency as well as safety. Three people is an ideal number for a field team; one person can draw and record dimensions while the other two take measurements. Because old buildings are sometimes unstable and poorly lit in places, safety should be your first consideration whenever you pursue fieldwork. When recording buildings that are in badly deteriorated or ruinous condition, take extra safety precautions. In such circumstances, bring along flashlights and hard hats if necessary, always wear shoes with hard soles, and always work with another person.

Before starting to draw, walk around and through the building to get a sense of its construction and to determine which views of the building will provide the most information. For general recording purposes, and especially if field time is limited, a scaled, annotated floor plan alone is probably sufficient. Plans are often the most useful form of field notation and yield the greatest amount of information about the building in the least amount of time. Floor plans can suggest interpretations about the history of the building, such as changes in room use or function over time. A first-floor plan will generally contain the most significant information. If the building has undergone extensive interior alterations on the first floor, sometimes a cellar plan will disclose features such as the location of original fireplaces or stairs.

Other types of drawings (such as elevations, sections, and details) might occasionally be used to supplement the information contained in the floor plan, but they are not usually necessary for basic field recording (Fig. 8.6). *Elevations* are drawings that show the three dimensions of a wall of the building as if they were collapsed into two dimensions. Projecting features like window and door moldings, window sills, steps, and eaves are all rendered

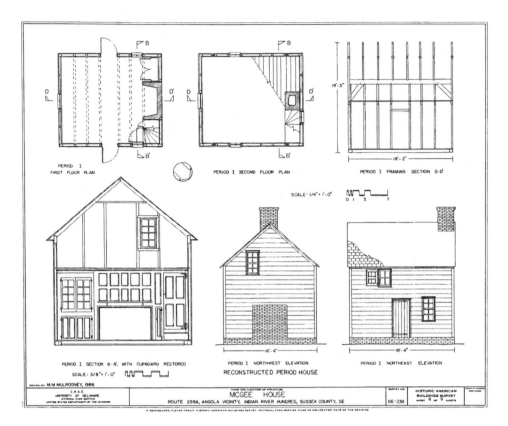

Figure 8.6
These plan, section, and
elevation drawings show
the McGee House as it was
originally built. Section
drawings are keyed to the
floor plans with lettered
section flags pointing in the
direction that the section
projects (B-B′ and D-D′).
Drawn by Meg Mulrooney.

as if they were totally flat. Elevations are most useful for showing surface
organization and detail and often reveal less about interior layout and construction than plans or cross-sections; they are also relatively easy to record
photographically. Consequently, it is not always necessary to go to the trouble
of recording elevations with scaled field notes. *Section* drawings show the
building as if it had been cut open, revealing construction details which would
not be apparent in a plan or elevation. A section is drawn as if the building
were cut on one specific axis, and the drawing is projected forward from that
point. There are different types of section drawings. A longitudinal section is
cut through the ridge of the building and includes a view of one of the long
interior walls; a gable or transverse section slices through the building at
some point perpendicular to the ridge and includes a view of one of the interior gable walls. A framing section is sometimes useful for revealing details in a timber-framed building and is usually drawn to show the framing
only. Sections are used to show structural relationships between different
levels of the building. *Detail* drawings of door and window hardware, moldings, mantels, and other items are also occasionally used. Unlike sections,
elevations, and plans, detail drawings are usually straightforward repre-

sentations of architectural features rendered at a larger scale or even at actual size.

Building Plans

To begin drawing your floor plan, start by recording the overall measurements of the building (Fig. 8.7). Not every building is square on the exterior, so accurate measurements are important. Once you have blocked out the overall building dimensions on the page, the next step is to measure the exterior openings—windows, doors, etc. Plans usually reflect measurements taken at 3 feet above floor level, so be consistent about the height at which you take measurements. It is also important to keep tapes taut while measuring. Running or cumulative measurements (taken along a given dimension by reading each measurement as a point along a continuous extension of the tape) are generally more accurate than incremental or consecutive measurements (taken by adding a series of separate measurements) and should be used whenever possible. Running measurements minimize errors, because a measurement along a given dimension is taken only once. Incremental measurements tend to compound many tiny measurement discrepancies into larger errors and are often difficult to calculate accurately in the field.

Work your way around the building, measuring and drawing features and noting measurements as you go. When recording interior room measurements, keep in mind that, like buildings, all rooms are not necessarily square. By taking the time to draw the building roughly to scale now, you will help to avoid mistakes later. A standardized system of notation helps to maintain coherence. Many fieldworkers find that a superscript notation system is the easiest and clearest to use. This system simply means writing the measurement two feet three inches, for example, as 2^3 instead of $2'\ 3''$. By using this type of notation system, you will eliminate confusion and minimize errors in the field. Record your measurements to the nearest quarter-inch, rounding up when necessary.

Remember to include wall thicknesses when drawing your floor plan. Determine wall thicknesses by measuring through opened windows and doors. A brick building will have thicker exterior walls than a frame building. As you measure a masonry building that has a later addition tacked on to it, you might find that one of the interior walls is much thicker than the others; this is an original exterior wall, which in the enlarged structure has become an interior wall (Fig. 8.8). Shifts in the thickness of interior walls, which may not be readily apparent until you actually measure and draw the building, may

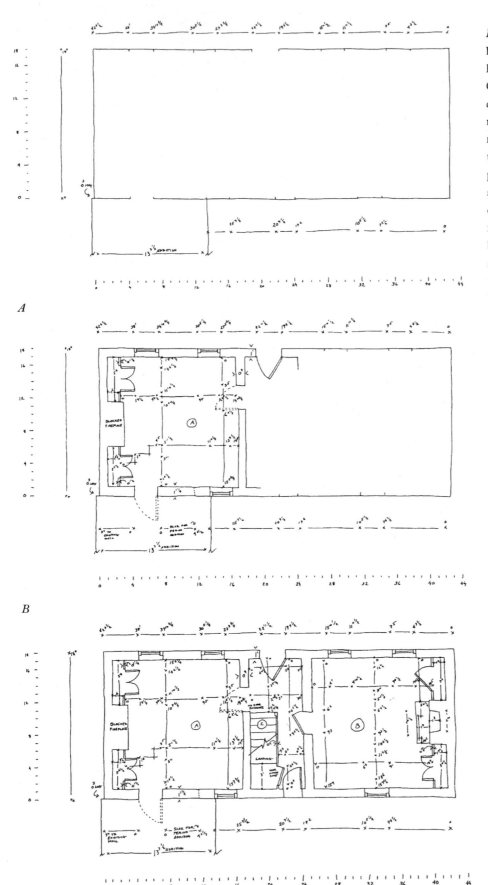

A

B

C

Figure 8.7

Field notes of Crossan House, Bear vicinity, New Castle County, Delaware. When drawing field notes, begin by recording the overall measurements and exterior openings of the building (*A*). Note the placement and overall dimensions of any additions. Next, establish wall thicknesses in as many places as possible and begin to record interior dimensions (*B*). It is generally easiest to work from one side of the building to the other and from a known toward an unknown point. Clearly drawn and carefully annotated field notes (*C*) provide the most comprehensive visual record of a building, and often they must serve as the final form of graphic documentation for some buildings. Note the use of dashed lines to indicate missing building fabric (in this case, the two missing doors at left.)

Figure 8.8

Greenmeadow, Odessa, New Castle County, Delaware. From Herman et al., *National Register of Historic Places: Dwellings of the Rural Elite in Central Delaware, 1770–1830.* December, 1989. Differences in wall thicknesses distinctly show separate building periods as well as different materials. This house was constructed in three phases, two of which are indicated on the bottom section. When the newest wing was built, the old house, which then became the rear wing of the structure, was relegated to kitchen and other service functions. The reconstructed first period floor plan is shown at upper left.

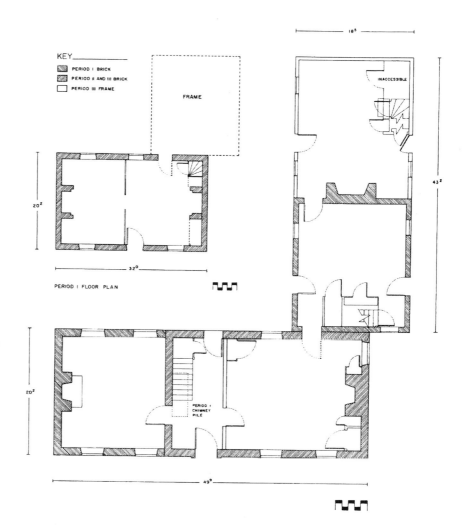

also suggest structural additions or changes, such as moved openings or later room divisions. Even in a building which appears to be quite regular, all walls do not necessarily have equal thicknesses. Note wall thicknesses for every wall if possible.

When recording interior dimensions, it is generally easiest to work from one side of the building to the other, from a known toward an unknown point. Record everything necessary in one room before moving on to the next. Be sure to record all interior measurements that would be reflected in your floor plan, such as overall room dimensions, closet widths and depths, interior wall thicknesses, fireplace jamb widths and depths, and hearth lengths and widths. As you work, note the direction of each door swing. Draw all doors as if they were wide open, at 90 degrees; if they would be obscured by another feature in that position, draw them halfway open, about 45 degrees. Look for evidence of structural changes. Altered parts of the building might include moved

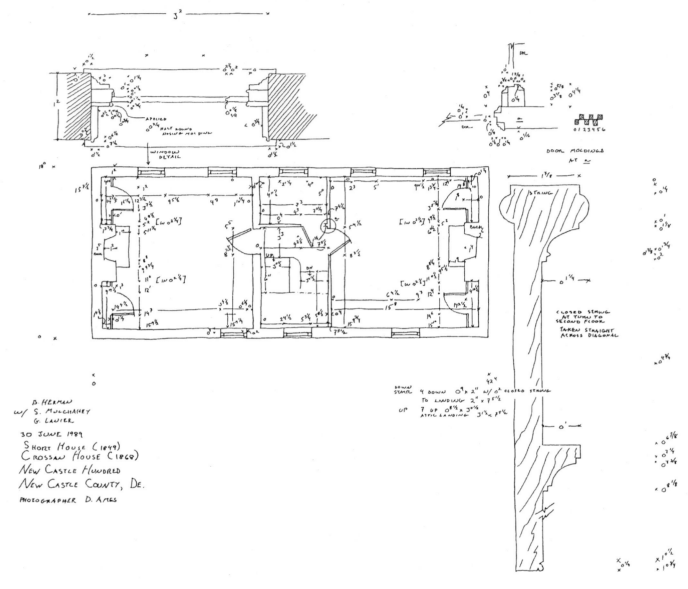

doors or walls, missing hearths, missing doors, or blocked openings. Many fieldworkers use a drawing convention of dashed lines on their field notes to indicate building parts that are altered or missing. As you draw missing or altered sections, include any explanatory notations you feel are necessary to enable you to interpret the changes later. If a door is missing but evidence of its original placement is present on the jambs, draw the door and the direction of its swing with dashed lines. Draw inaccessible features with dashed lines as well. Features that are overhead, such as joists or bearing beams, are usually drawn with dotted and dashed lines. In stone or brick buildings, pay special attention to the window openings. If the interiors of window openings

Figure 8.9

Crossan House, Bear vicinity, New Castle County, Delaware. This second floor plan was originally drawn at a scale of ¼ inch to 1 foot, but some details, including molding profiles and a detail of the window sash construction (*top left*), were drawn at a much larger scale for clarity.

are intentionally angled or splayed, record the depth of the window as well as the difference between interior and exterior dimensions. When recording stairs, note the length, width, and number of stair treads as well as the overall direction of the stair. It is often helpful to draw enlarged versions of some details, such as molding profiles or complicated construction features, to maintain the clarity and legibility of your drawing (Fig. 8.9). Because field notes frequently end up being the only record of buildings that are subsequently demolished, it is always best, from the outset, to draw your notes clearly and thoroughly enough that someone who has never seen the building can understand your drawings easily.

Site Plans

Site plans are essentially scaled maps of a site and usually include buildings and other major features, such as roads, driveways, and visible wells. By showing a bird's-eye view, site plans help to clarify traffic patterns and establish the relationships between buildings and other significant features. They are particularly useful on sites like farmsteads and industrial complexes that have multiple structures. Site plans are also used to plot landscape features, including retaining walls, trees, gardens, and other botanical material.

The easiest way to record site information is to use a measuring technique known as triangulation, a method which allows you to determine any point on a site by first establishing its distance from two other points. To triangulate, begin by establishing a constant set of points, such as the exterior dimensions of a building. To draw a site plan of a farm complex, for example, first establish the exterior dimensions of one of the larger structures on the site, such as a house or barn. Using this building as your anchor, measure the distance from each corner of this building to the other site features, using the sides of the building as sides to your triangles and plotting a series of interlocked triangles as you go. Write your measurements on the lines that connect each set of points. Be sure to create triangles as you measure by plotting each feature from two separate points. To maintain accuracy, keep tapes taut when measuring and run several measurements from different points back to your original starting points. In this way, you can rapidly measure an entire site. You can translate the field notes for your site plan into a more finished pencil drawing by drawing the triangulated measurements to scale and following the same procedure you used to draw the original field notes (Fig. 8.10).

A

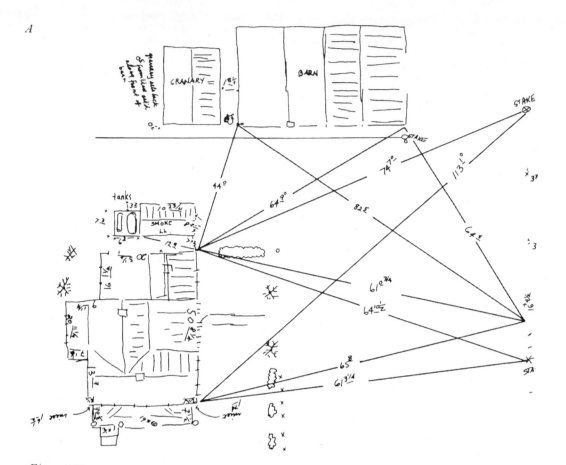

Figure 8.10
Cullen Farm complex, Roxana vicinity, Sussex County, Delaware. Drawn
by Carolyn Torma and Susan Chase. (*A*) Triangulation allows you to locate
any point on a site in terms of its distance from two other points. Using
this technique, you can rapidly measure an entire site. These field notes
show one portion of the farm complex. (*B*) The complete site plan drawn
from the triangulated field notes clearly shows the relationship between
buildings and landscape features, including roads, farm lanes, and fields.

B

FIELD   FIELD

FIELD

PUBLIC ROAD

FIELD

N

0   40   80   120
SCALE 1"=40'

CULLEN FARM SITE PLAN

KEY

A - CHICKEN HOUSE   F - CHICKEN HOUSE   K - SWIMMING POOL
B - FEEDER   G - DOG HOUSE   L - PUMP HOUSE
C - GRANARY   H - SMOKE HOUSE   M - STRAWBERRY PICKERS' HOUSE
D - BARN   I - DWELLING   N - CLOTHES LINE
E - GRAPE ARBOR   J - SUMMER PORCH

Drawing from Field Notes

Carefully measured scaled field notes require a minimum amount of equipment and provide the most comprehensive record of your building. If your notes are clearly drawn and annotated, they should communicate visually as well. Since time and resources are sometimes limited, field notes often must serve as the final form of graphic documentation for a building. In fact, some architectural historians prefer using clear, annotated field notes rather than finished pencil or ink drawings for illustrative purposes. If you have the time and have access to drafting equipment, you may choose to translate your field notes into hard-line pencil or ink drawings. There are good reference sources that explain techniques for drafting. If you decide to produce more finished drawings from your field notes, try to draw soon after you have visited the site, while your memory of the building is still fresh.

Photography

Photographic field documentation is a fast, inexpensive, and easy method of obtaining a visual record of a building; it can be used alone or to supplement graphic recording and documentary site research. Photographs are most useful for conveying the kinds of information that are not as clearly expressed by graphic documentation or written descriptions: environmental context, spatial relationships, condition, and three-dimensional qualities. Photographs are also helpful for quickly communicating information that would be too time-consuming to draw.

Approaches to architectural photography vary enormously. Some photographs are intended as representational images that are descriptive, factual equivalents to architectural drawings. Overall views in this tradition are often composed so that a floor plan can be inferred from them. Other photographs eschew this comprehensive approach and focus instead upon a specific aspect or detail of the building. Atmosphere and evocative power often receive primary emphasis in these latter images, sometimes at the expense of descriptive content.

When planning photographs, it is helpful to think of a building in terms of the three primary organizing features of form, plan, and ornament. The most eloquent documentary photography often involves expressing all three of these features while exploring the tension and negotiation between them. Still, it is important to remember that each building is also a complex series of accretions. Overlays of time, use, and change can mask original features and add their own subtle inflections to the intended design. Even the simplest and most unprepossessing of buildings has its own individual style, and part of the challenge of documentary photography is to capture that style on film.

Also, think carefully about your total documentation program and the way that your photographs can best augment any field drawings or written descriptions. For instance, if you are able to photograph a building but will not have enough time to draw floor plans, try to communicate as much as possible about the interior through your photographs. When shooting exterior views, think about the ways in which the surface of a building can express something of its interior, and plan your interior photographs carefully so that the most significant features of the plan and interior finish are recorded. Still, while the primary purpose of photographic documentation is to record information, aspects of composition, line, weight, and color must also come into play. Photographs, after all, are abstractions of reality, and pure documentation and aesthetics do not necessarily have to be mutually exclusive.

For general field photography, a 35-mm camera equipped with a 50-mm lens is a good choice. A slightly wider-angle lens, such as a 35-mm or perhaps a 28-mm lens, is almost indispensible if your fieldwork takes you into more constrained urban settings. Black-and-white film is best, because it is archivally stable and is often relatively inexpensive to use when processed as contact prints. Contact prints are so named because they are made by grouping the film negatives together and placing them under a sheet of glass, in direct contact with photographic paper. The photographic paper is then exposed to light briefly to produce the prints, which are the same size as the negatives. Although the printed images are small, contact prints enable the photographer to choose only the most suitable shots for enlargement without paying for an entire roll of separate prints, and this usually proves an effective and economical method for processing field photographs. If more than one camera is available, you can also shoot color slides for presentation purposes. Color slides are not archivally stable, however, and usually fade after twenty years or so. Also, you can always produce a good slide from a black-and-white print, but you can rarely get a particularly good quality black-and-white print from a color slide. Still, color slides are commonly used in lectures and public presentations, and, because of their size when projected, can sometimes offer a more immediate and compelling photographic experience for the viewer than standard-sized black-and-white prints. Color is a completely different medium, however, and introduces an entirely new set of possibilities—and problems—to documentary architectural photography.

A

B

Figure 8.11
Making good use of lighting conditions when photographing subjects can greatly enhance the documentary usefulness of a photograph. In *A*, raking light emphasized the textures on the door and three-dimensional qualities of the surround. In *B*, the framing and open vertical slats are displayed much more vividly because of the angle of the light. (*A*) Corbit Sharp House, Odessa, New Castle County, Delaware. Photographed 1979. (*B*) Achmester frame granary, Armstrong Corner vicinity, St. George's Hundred, New Castle County, Delaware. Photographed by David Ames, HABS, 1985.

When photographing buildings and their sites, aim to secure the best photographic coverage with the least amount of film. Plan photographs in advance, by walking around and through the building to determine which combination of shots will convey the most information. Lighting is an important consideration (Fig. 8.11). If you have the luxury of extra field time, pay attention to the way the sun illuminates the building throughout the day and plan your photographing schedule accordingly. If time is limited, of course, your photographs will be governed by existing climatic and lighting conditions. To capture as much detail as possible, shoot photographs with the light behind you. Try to avoid shooting backlit photographs.

A

B

Figure 8.12
Careful framing of a shot can create a rhythmic photographic composition. (*A*) Greenlawn, Middletown vicinity, St. George's Hundred, New Castle County, Delaware. Photographed by David Ames, HABS, 1983. (*B*) Rockwood, Wilmington vicinity, New Castle County, Delaware. Photographed by David Ames, HABS, 1983.

Composition is just as important as proper lighting (Fig. 8.12). When framing overall exterior shots, for instance, avoid cropping portions of the building from the picture. Stand close enough to the building to fill in the camera frame, but far enough away to include all corners, roof peaks, and chimney tops. Differing perspectives will affect your images dramatically (Fig. 8.13). Photographs shot from an especially high or low vantage point can be particularly revealing. Plan the shots carefully, trying to minimize or avoid distracting intrusions that block essential structural details.

While each building presents different photographic opportunities and challenges, it is important to aim for the most comprehensive photographic coverage that your time and budget will allow. The following checklist of views can serve as a guide:

1. Perspective view or corner shot showing the front elevation on one side and establishing the depth and three-dimensional quality of the building

2. Perspective view or corner shot showing the rear elevation and opposing side

3. Exterior views showing significant exterior details, such as front entrances, door surrounds, typical windows, brackets, and cornices

4. Overall environmental view of the site establishing the relationship of the building to the site or to adjacent buildings and including significant landscaping features if present

5. Elevation shot of the main facade showing the style and integrity of the building

6. Significant interior views showing information on the scale and massing of the building

7. Interior details, such as stair halls, fireplace or mantel details, or unusual attic construction

Some photographers write out in advance a photodocumentation plan—a written schedule of planned photographic views that may include specific information such as the best time of day for the photographs, correct camera placement, and possibly even notations of additional equipment that will be needed, such as special lenses or tripods—in order to make the time spent at the site as efficient as possible. Regardless of what you decide to photograph, try to keep a record or log of all of the photographs that you actually shoot. Keeping a photo log becomes especially important if you shoot multiple rolls of film during a short time, or if you wait for a while before having the film processed. Even if you only shoot a single roll of film, it is surprisingly easy to forget even key details about the buildings you have just photographed—

A

B

Figure 8.13
When photographing a site, varying the perspective can create more informative and dramatic photographs. By capturing a series of door openings in a single shot (*A*), the photographer has clearly indicated spatial relationships. In *B*, the photographer's low camera angle emphasized the textures on this cobbled barn floor. (*A*) W. H. Robinson house, Mechanicsville vicinity, White Clay Creek Hundred, New Castle County, Delaware. Photographed by David Ames, HABS, 1983. (*B*) Fahnestock Barn, Waynesboro vicinity, Franklin County, Pennsylvania. Photographed by David Ames, HABS, 1985.

the name of the building, its street address, or the camera orientation—unless you write them down. It may not be necessary or feasible to shoot very many photographs. Sometimes you may be limited to one or two views of a building. In this case, you will have to assess photographic views in order of their importance and make your choices accordingly. If you could shoot only one or two photographs, which views would reveal the most about the building? And what is most important to convey in a photograph? Of the many aspects of a building—its design, use, context, style, or the changes it has undergone through time—which deserve the most emphasis? For example, one criterion for assessing importance might be the degree of architectural finish present throughout the structure. Stylistic embellishments such as door and window surrounds call attention to specific elevations or spaces, designate certain spaces as public rather than private, distinguish one space from another, and subtly direct movement through a building. By noting the level of finish present throughout the building, you can often determine the intended importance of specific spaces or elevations. Other criteria for assessing importance might be a building's current or historic use or its relationship to its site and to surrounding structures. These features may be far more revealing than its overall design and thus may be more worthy of photographic treatment (Fig. 8.14).

Documentary Research

While careful examination of a building's physical fabric reveals a great deal, documentary research is an indispensable complement to field observations. Documentary research uncovers information that is usually not readily apparent during fieldwork. For example, the date of a building may be difficult to establish precisely with architectural clues alone. By searching through written documents such as deeds, probate inventories, tax lists, and maps, you can often establish a solid date or range of dates for the building. You can also learn more about the inhabitants and possibly the builders of the structure. Documentary research can help you to determine the identities of the original property owners and occupants, what their relative socioeconomic status was, and when they lived on the property. Finally, some documents offer historical descriptions of the property and can suggest a great deal about original room layout and use as well as changes through time.

Because different types of documents contain different types of information, each is most helpful when used in conjunction with other written

A

B

C

D

Figure 8.14

Oliphant House, early 1800s, Laurel vicinity, Sussex County, Delaware. Photographed by David Ames, HABS, 1986. This short photographic sequence was designed to complement a set of measured drawings. Note the inclusion of an environmental shot establishing the relationship of the building to the site, as well as front elevations, perspective shots, and significant interior details. (*A*) Environmental view looking northeast, showing front and west gable elevations. (*B*) Front elevation. (*C*) Perspective of front and west gable elevations. (*D*) Perspective of back and west gable elevations. (*E*) East gable elevation. (*F*) Front door detail. (*G*) First floor interior showing corner stair. (*H*) Second floor interior showing partition wall.

E

F

G

H

records rather than in isolation. What follows is a list and brief description of the kinds of documents that are useful for architectural research. A list of selected repositories of documentary materials in the Delaware valley follows this chapter as an appendix. In most states in the region, documentary materials of interest to the architectural historian, such as deeds, wills, and inventories, are archived in county courthouses; in Delaware, however, such documents are centralized in the Delaware State Archives in Dover. In order to avoid duplication of effort, it is wise to check thoroughly for prior research before undertaking in-depth documentary research. Every state archive maintains a list of active historical societies and manuscript collections. Local historical societies and state or county historic preservation offices are good places to start; both are likely to know of or have copies of many existing architectural research reports. Museum, college, and university libraries may also contain useful secondary sources as well as fine collections of primary source materials.

Deeds are among the most useful documents for researching a property. They are signed by the seller or grantor and name the buyer or grantee. They are most constructive for providing physical descriptions and establishing a chain of title that reveals who the property owners were at various points in time. They also include the price the land was sold for, the size of the property, and sometimes whether or not there was a mortgage. To locate deeds, you will need to work with the grantor-grantee indexes. These indexes reference deeds in two ways: by the name of the seller (grantor) and that of the buyer (grantee). Consequently, you can trace a title as long as you know the name of either party. To begin a title search, you will need to know the name of the current property owner. Tax parcel maps can refer you to this information. These maps contain the tax parcel number as well as the name, address, and deed reference for the current property owner and are helpful at the beginning of a deed trace. Each deed for a given property refers to the previous deed by deed book volume, page number, and the year the deed was recorded. By following the property backward through the deeds and indexes in this way, you can establish a chain of title.

When they exist, probate inventories can help to determine original house and yard layout and use. Usually used by the courts as a way of documenting and transferring property when a property owner has died intestate (without a will), inventories list the contents of a dwelling at a particular point in time and are sometimes enumerated one room at a time. Even if the inventoried goods are not listed under specific room headings, the rooms the inventory refers to—and sometimes even the floor plan of the house—can often be determined by careful attention to the types of goods listed and the order in which they are enumerated. Inventories can be extremely detailed or maddeningly brief; in the best of all cases, they can provide very specific information, such as the titles of books, the arrangement of rooms, or the color and condition of furnishings. No matter what the level of detail, inventories provide valuable information about historic values and room use as well as the textures and nuances of everyday life.

Wills can reveal vital statistics that include the birth, death, and marriage dates of property owners and other family members, as well as the names of parties who are absent from the chain of title. Because they sometimes contain partial property descriptions, wills can supplement other historical information about a house. They are especially helpful when the property in question has remained in the same family for a long period of time, and they can be productively used in conjunction with deeds and inventories to flesh out the total documentary description.

Orphans' court descriptions, which are available everywhere but are particularly detailed resources in Delaware and Maryland, enumerate the holdings of every real property owner who died survived by minor children. They provide detailed information about land, buildings, and landscape features (such as fences and orchards) and are particularly rich in descriptive information about property size and condition, dwellings, and outbuildings. They can also be used to uncover information about land and property divisions and tenants. Property descriptions and divisions are especially visible in the maps, plats, and verbal descriptions that are often included in orphans' court records; these plats often show the placement of buildings on the property in question. Orphans' court descriptions can also be used for identifying the names of family members, since they will generally list the name of the mother, the names of all minor children, and the guardian's name. This data can also help to clarify property information.

Census listings contain vital statistics such as age, race, and gender for property owners. The Federal Manuscript Census, which began in 1790 and is available on microfilm, contains a listing of each household. It records the age, race, and gender of every occupant and sometimes provides detail about occupation, birthplace, and degree of literacy. Published indexes to many of the censuses are often available in archives and larger university libraries. These indexes, compiled by the Bureau of the Census, typically contain all available information for each census year, such as totals for state, county, and municipal populations. The types of summaries contained therein vary depending on the year. Other census documents, such as the agricultural and manufacturing censuses, may also be useful. The agricultural census, which began around 1850, contains information such as farm size, number and value of livestock, property valuation, and agricultural produce. The manufacturing census began in the early nineteenth century.

Court records sometimes include information pertaining to specific properties. Most court records deal with issues of property and debt. The records of the Court of Common Pleas generally contain minor claims, such as debt cases and property disputes, and occasionally contain property descriptions that can be helpful in solidifying a chain of title. Cases tried in the Court of Common Pleas are sometimes referenced in property deeds. Architectural descriptions are also found in court cases not related to property issues. Divorce proceedings and coroner's inquests, for example, devote considerable effort to describing the physical circumstances of specific events.

Legislative petitions are documents filed in the state legislature requesting improvements such as fences, roads, and marsh reclamations. They can be helpful in tying a house to a specific property. Road papers, compiled whenever a new road was planned, are similarly useful. Usually organized by county, they contain accurate illustrations of proposed road locations and may include sketches of buildings that stood near intended roadways.

Maps, plats, and atlases are used to determine the names of original property owners or the original layout of roads. They can also help you to determine the construction date of a building. Atlases, published with some regularity starting in the early to mid-nineteenth century, are available for most parts of the Delaware valley, usually from state and local historical societies as well as in county and town libraries. Atlases routinely identify the location and ownership of individual properties, and, in some locales, include farm names, town plans, and engraved views of notable houses, farms, industries, and commercial establishments. Useful reference maps also include the Sanborn Fire Insurance Company maps, which represent predominantly urban sites and have been produced periodically since the 1880s. These maps include street names and show buildings. Other maps are tied directly to architectural surveys and are often available at your state historic preservation office. For example, the Delaware State Historic Preservation Office uses aerial maps to record Cultural Resource Survey inventory information. All surveyed sites are marked on these maps with their Cultural Resource Survey number, so if you can identify a particular site on the map and if it contains a survey number, you can then research the property by looking up the survey number at the State Historic Preservation Office in Dover. United States Geological Survey quadrangle maps are used for initial survey work and are helpful tools for pinpointing building locations. USGS maps can be purchased in some locations; complete sets of USGS maps for the entire United States are available in some large libraries. Other maps may be filed in county archives or historical societies.

Some insurance records contain detailed descriptions of buildings. Because they were generated for insurance purposes, these records focus special attention on the location of heat and water sources and the safety and solidity of construction materials and may provide a site plan that shows building location and orientation. These records can reveal whether the property owner was also the occupant or if there was a separate tenant. Information about building alterations may be contained in additional volumes compiled after the policy was initiated. The Insurance Company of North America records, housed at the Cigna Archives in Philadelphia, and the Kent County, Delaware Mutual Insurance records, located at the Delaware State Archives, are particularly useful record groups.

Tax assessments enumerate individual properties and include listings of dwellings, outbuildings, tenants, and livestock. Assessments in most locations vary through time and across county, township, and hundred boundaries. They also vary in the degree of detail they contain—some tax lists provide only very brief building descriptions, while others provide more detailed information about building materials and condition. In some areas they include itemizations of individual land holdings and describe the amount and type of acreage and its value. They may also describe numbers and valuations of livestock, slaves, and silver plate and often include a poll tax based on a man's ability to work or produce income. In general, males over the age of 16 were taxed for all of these items through the late nineteenth century, while women and minor children were assessed only for real estate, livestock, and slaves. County and state archives often have complete collections, as well as microfilmed copies, of original documents. Many local tax lists, such as the triennial assessments recorded in the late eighteenth and early nineteenth centuries for parts of Chester County, Pennsylvania, reveal information about the condition of buildings and provide astonishing levels of detail. One document that house historians find useful is the 1798 Direct Tax, also sometimes known as the "glass tax" or "window tax." This tax was a one-time assessment that enumerated dwellings, outbuildings, tenants, livestock, acreage, and assessed valuation for all property owners and usually contained more detailed information, such as building materials and measurements, number of windows, and number of glass panes, or lights, per window (hence the nickname). Sadly, the records of the 1798 tax have not survived for any part of Delaware or Virginia and only survive in a few areas of New Jersey, but detailed assessments for almost all of Maryland and much of Pennsylvania do exist.

Local histories and other secondary works can provide context and help to round out the information contained in other documents. Historical societies and county, municipal, and college libraries are usually good places to start. Consult individual nominations to the National Register of Historic Places, which are usually available at state historic preservation offices, for bibliographies tailored to specific properties or types of buildings.

You may find useful information in periodicals and technical reports. State- and county-based history magazines, such as *Delaware History*, a quarterly periodical published by the Historical Society of Delaware, or *The Pennsylvania Magazine of History and Biography*, published by the Historical Society of Pennsylvania, occasionally contain articles that reference specific sites. Past copies are usually available at larger libraries and historical societies. There are many site-specific architectural and archaeological reports, many of which are issued by state transportation departments, cultural resource management firms, or independent architectural historians. These reports are usually on file at the preservation office in each state and include information about standing structures as well as archaeological data.

The files of properties recorded for the Historic American Buildings Survey (HABS) and the Historic American Engineering Record (HAER) contain photographs, architectural data sheets, and, occasionally, measured drawings. The original documentation materials for properties recorded for HABS or HAER are located in the Library of Congress in Washington, D.C., but copies of state-specific HABS and HAER files can also sometimes be located elsewhere. Check to see if your state historic preservation office maintains files of properties that have been documented for HABS or HAER.

Many area museums contain excellent photographic collections that offer assistance in determining architectural and site changes. For example, both the Hagley Museum and Library and the Historical Society of Delaware maintain extensive photographic collections. In addition, the Delaware State Archives has a fine collection of agricultural photographs that were taken in the 1930s as well as a series of highway department photographs that often include buildings. The Purnell Collection of photographs at the Delaware State Archives includes Sussex County materials. Similar collections exist in other historical societies and local repositories. The Thomas Yorke photographs of Salem County, New Jersey, for example, were made in the 1880s, in an effort to record the houses identified with the county's earliest English-speaking settlers. Similarly useful photographic collections are housed in the Pennsylvania State Archives.

Newspaper articles are sometimes used to confirm the dates of building alterations. Real estate advertisements are helpful for determining when a property changed hands as well as what was on the property at the time of sale. Collections of newspapers, which sometimes exist as files of clippings, are also likely to be available on microfilm.

Architectural survey forms, usually located at state historic preservation offices, can provide essential information about specific sites at the time they were surveyed. While early survey forms contain less precise property descriptions than more recent forms, they all contain some level of useful information about property owners as well as the physical structures on the site. Survey forms contain references to aerial and USGS quad maps. They also contain Cultural Resource Survey numbers that tie surveyed properties to National Register nominations. The survey collections also include the original 35-mm black and white photographs or contact sheets that were taken at the time of the survey.

An Archaeological Approach

This book offers an archaeological approach to the field study of buildings and landscapes. The advantage of this approach lies in how it enables us to see individual houses, barns, outbuildings, industrial structures, and landscapes as integral elements in a constantly changing countryside. An archaeological approach recognizes the basic fact that buildings are sites where significance is found in the material evidence that charts change over time. We are not looking at buildings and landscapes in the monumental sense of objects frozen in time but as vivid reflections of how people have historically perceived, organized, reorganized, and valued the world around them. From this perspective, in studying architecture we seek not only to comprehend the histories of specific buildings but also to link those histories to one another in a way that lets us see individual architectural expression as part of larger historic patterns in the cultural landscape. The first step on the path to understanding historic landscapes and the people who made and occupied them, however, is always the detective work that discovers the history of individual buildings.

The archaeological approach provides a way of looking at buildings that enlivens architectural fabric with the human agency of those who made and experienced those spaces and places. Our goal from the outset has been to give readers the tools to undertake this study and interpretation on their own. Architectural guides to stylistic periods and knowledge of building technologies and functional typologies can augment this book; but their reliance on promoting chronological sequences for fashion, construction, and function robs us of the very life of buildings and landscapes. Certainly, a sound knowledge of dating techniques and style periods is essential for looking at and evaluating historic buildings, but it is simply not enough. We need to remind ourselves constantly of why we study buildings. The answer is simple. We study everyday architecture and landscape because we want to know about people—about how they saw themselves, their neighbors, their workaday world in all its complexity—and how they projected that sense of self and society into the substance of their environment.

APPENDIX

Directory of Resources

The following directory is necessarily brief but provides a starting point for documentary research into Delaware valley architecture and landscapes. The best places to begin your architectural research are usually state historic preservation offices, county historical societies, and libraries.

Preservation Offices, Organizations, and Assistance

Brandywine Conservancy
Box 141
Chadds Ford, Pa. 19317

Center for Archaeological Research
101 Ewing Hall
University of Delaware
Newark, Del. 19716

Center for Historic Architecture and Design
Alison Hall
University of Delaware
Newark, Del. 19716
(*formerly the Center for
Historic Architecture
and Engineering*)

Chester County Parks and Recreation Department
Heritage Preservation Officer
Government Services Center, 160
601 Westtown Road
West Chester, Pa. 19382-4534

Delaware State Historic Preservation Office
15 The Green
Dover, Del. 19901

Heritage Conservancy
35 Old Dublin Pike
Doylestown, Pa. 18901

Historic Preservation Trust of Lancaster County
123 North Prince Street
Lancaster, Pa. 17603

Kent County Preservation Office
County Administration Building
414 Federal Street
Dover, Del. 19901

Maryland Historical Trust
Division of Historical and Cultural Programs
Department of Housing and Community Development
100 Community Place
Crownsville, Md. 21032-2023

National Conference of State Historic Preservation Officers
Suite 332
Hall of the States
444 North Capitol Street, N.W.
Washington, D.C. 20001

National Park Service
Mid-Atlantic Regional Office
Custom House
2nd and Chestnut Streets, Room 251
Philadelphia, Pa. 19106

National Trust for Historic Preservation
Mid-Atlantic Regional Office
6401 Germantown Avenue
Philadelphia, Pa. 19144

National Trust for Historic Preservation
1785 Massachusetts Avenue, N.W.
Washington, D.C. 20036

New Castle County Preservation Office
Department of Planning
2701 Capitol Trail
Newark, Del. 19711

Office of New Jersey Heritage
Division of Parks and Forestry
Department of Environmental Protection
501 East State Street
Station Plaza #5, Second Floor
Trenton, N.J. 08625

Pennsylvania Historical and Museum Commission
Bureau for Historic Preservation
Box 1026
Harrisburg, Pa. 17120

Philadelphia Historical Commission
1313 City Hall Annex
Philadelphia, Pa. 19107

Preservation Pennsylvania
2470 Kissel Hill Road
Lancaster, Pa. 17601

Preservation Salem, Inc.
P. O. Box 693
Salem, N.J. 08079

Vernacular Architecture Forum
P.O. Box 962
Newark, Del. 19715-0962

Wilmington Preservation Office
Wilmington Office of Planning
City/County Building
800 French Street
Wilmington, Del. 19801-3537

Historical Societies, Libraries, and Archives

American Philosophical Society
105 South Fifth Street
Philadelphia, Pa. 19106

Bucks County Historical Society
Pine and Ashland Streets
Doylestown, Pa. 18901

Chester County Archives
601 Westtown Road, Suite 80
West Chester, Pa. 19382-4527

Chester County Historical Society
225 North High Street
West Chester, Pa. 19380

Cigna Corporation Archives
2 Liberty Place
1601 Chestnut Street
Floor TLP05
Philadelphia, Pa. 19192

Cumberland County Historical Society
Box 16
Greenwich, N.J. 08323

Delaware County Historical Society
Wolfgram Memorial Library at Widener College
Chester, Pa. 19013

Delaware State Archives
Hall of Records
Court Street at Legislative Avenue
P. O. Box 1401
Dover, Del. 19903

Free Library of Philadelphia
Logan Square
Philadelphia, Pa. 19103

Hagley Museum and Library
P. O. Box 3630
Greenville
Wilmington, Del. 19807

Historical Society of Delaware
505 Market Street
Wilmington, Del. 19801

Historical Society of Montgomery County Library
1654 DeKalb Street
Norristown, Pa. 19401

Historical Society of Pennsylvania
1300 Locust Street
Philadelphia, Pa. 19107

Historical Society of York County
250 East Market Street
York, Pa. 17403

Lancaster County Historical Society
230 North President Avenue
Lancaster, Pa. 17603-3125

Library Company of Philadelphia
1314 Locust Street
Philadelphia, Pa. 19107

Maryland Historical Society
201 West Monument Street
Baltimore, Md. 21201

Maryland State Archives
350 Rowe Boulevard
Annapolis, Md. 21401

Morris Library
The University of Delaware
Academy Street
Newark, Del. 19716

National Archives
Regional Office
9th and Market
Room 1350
Philadelphia, Pa. 19106

New Jersey Historical Society
230 Broadway
Newark, N.J. 07104

Pennsylvania State Archives
Division of Archives
P. O. Box 1026
Harrisburg, Pa. 17108-1026

Philadelphia Athenaeum
219 South Sixth Street
Philadelphia, Pa. 19106

Salem County Historical Society
79–83 Market Street
Salem, N.J. 08079

Winterthur Museum and Library
Winterthur, Del. 19735

NOTES

Chapter 1   Introduction

1. James Deetz, *Invitation to Archaeology* (New York: Natural History Press, 1967), 45–46. James Deetz, *In Small Things Forgotten: The Archaeology of Early American Life* (New York: Anchor Press/Doubleday, 1977), 24.

2. For a solid introduction to the techniques and terminology of historical archaeology, see Ivor Noël Hume, *Historical Archaeology: A Comprehensive Guide* (New York: Alfred A. Knopf, 1972).

3. James Deetz, *In Small Things Forgotten*, 40–41. See also Deetz, *Invitation to Archaeology*, 59, 61; Stanley South, *Method and Theory in Historical Archaeology* (New York: Academic Press, 1977; and Gordon R. Willey and Philip Phillips, *Method and Theory in American Archaeology* (Chicago: University of Chicago Press, 1958).

Chapter 2   House Forms and House Lots

1. Henry Glassie, "Eighteenth-Century Cultural Process in Delaware Valley Folk Building," in *Common Places: Readings in American Vernacular Architecture*, edited by Dell Upton and John Michael Vlach (Athens: University of Georgia Press, 1986), 394–425.

2. Sussex County, Delaware Orphans' Court manuscript case file, Delaware State Archives.

3. Ibid.

4. John A. H. Sweeney, *Grandeur on the Appoquinimink: The House of William Corbit at Odessa, Delaware* (Newark: University of Delaware Press, 1989).

5. John Michael Vlach, "The Shotgun House: An African Architectural Legacy," in *Common Places: Readings in American Vernacular Architecture*, edited by Dell Upton and John Michael Vlach (Athens: University of Georgia Press, 1986), 58–78.

6. Susan Mulchahey Chase, "Rural Adaptations of Suburban Bungalows, Sussex County, Delaware," in *Gender, Class, and Shelter: Perspectives in Vernacular Architecture, V,* edited by Elizabeth Collins Cromley and Carter L. Hudgins (Knoxville, University of Tennessee Press, 1995), 179–89.

7. Alan Gowans, *The Comfortable House: North American Suburban Architecture 1890–1930.* (Cambridge: MIT Press, 1986), 84.

8. Rebecca J. Siders et al., *Agricultural Tenancy in Central Delaware, 1770–1900 ± : A Historic Context* (Newark: Center for Historic Architecture and Engineering, University of Delaware, for the Delaware State Historic Preservation Office, 1991). Siders and Anna Andrzejewski, "The House and Garden in Central Delaware, 1780–1930," in *Perspectives in Vernacular Architecture VII*, edited by Annmarie Adams and Sally McMurry (Knoxville: University of Tennessee Press, forthcoming). Lucy Simler, "The Landless Laborer in Perspective: Part 2. Inmates and Freemen: A Landless Labor Force in Colonial Chester County" (paper presented to the Philadelphia Center for Early American Studies, April 18, 1986), p. 3.

9. Siders et al., *Agricultural Tenancy in Central Delaware*, 41–47.

Chapter 3 Construction

1. Hume, *Historical Archaeology*, 115–19.

2. Cary Carson, Norman F. Barka, William M. Kelso, Garry Wheeler Stone, and Dell Upton, "Impermanent Architecture in the Southern American Colonies," *Winterthur Portfolio* 16, no. 2/3 (summer–autumn 1981), 135–96.

3. Carson et al., "Impermanent Architecture"; Dell Upton, "Traditional Timber Framing," in *Material Culture of the Wooden Age*, edited by Brooke Hindle (Tarrytown, N.Y.: Sleepy Hollow Press, 1981), 55–61.

4. For a discussion of the regionally distinctive architectural traditions of lower Delaware, see Bernard L. Herman, *The Stolen House* (Charlottesville: University of Virginia Press, 1992), 166–222, esp. 182–83.

5. Bernard L. Herman, *Architecture and Rural Life in Central Delaware, 1700–1900* (Knoxville: University of Tennessee Press, 1987), 90.

6. Subcellars, or cellars excavated below cellar level, were also used for storage purposes and, although rare in the mid-Atlantic region, are sometimes found in northern Delaware and southeastern Pennsylvania.

7. Wade P. Catts and Jay F. Custer, *Tenant Farmers, Stone Masons, and Black Laborers: Final Archaeological Investigations of the Thomas Williams Site, Glasgow, New Castle County, Delaware*, DelDOT Archaeology Series No. 82 (Newark: Center for Archaeological Research, Department of Anthropology, University of Delaware, 1990), 101–3, 118–24.

8. Ibid.

9. Ronald W. Brunskill, *Illustrated Handbook of Vernacular Architecture* (London: Faber and Faber, 1987), 34–35.

10. New Castle, Kent, and Sussex County, Delaware, Tax Assessments, Delaware State Archives.

11. Fred B. Kniffen and Henry Glassie, "Building in Wood in the Eastern United States: A Time-Place Perspective," in *Common Places: Readings in American Vernacular Architecture*, edited by Dell Upton and John Michael Vlach (Athens: University of Georgia Press, 1986), 159–81.

12. Ibid. Herman, *Architecture and Rural Life*, 92–93.

13. This finish treatment was described by one nineteenth-century traveler as "Wilmington stripes." "The taste is to white-wash the smooth mortar between the logs," he remarked, "but not the logs themselves, thus making the house in stripes of alternate white, and dusky wood color." John Fanning Watson, *Annals of Philadelphia, and Pennsylvania, in the Olden Time*, vol. 2 (Philadelphia: J. B. Lippincott, 1870), 529. Quoted in Scott T. Swank, "The Architectural Landscape," in *The Arts of the Pennsylvania Germans* (New York: Norton, for the Henry Francis du Pont Winterthur Museum, 1983), 29.

14. Herman, *Architecture and Rural Life*, 88–92. Kniffen and Glassie, "Building in Wood," 165–66.

15. Clifford W. Zink, "Dutch Framed Houses in New York and New Jersey," *Winterthur Portfolio* 22, no. 4 (winter 1987), 265–94.

16. Fred W. Peterson, *Homes in the Heartland: Balloon-Frame Farmhouses of the Upper Midwest, 1850–1920* (Lawrence: University Press of Kansas, 1992).

17. Tracy Kidder, *House* (Boston: Houghton Mifflin, 1985), 133–35. Carl W. Condit, *American Building Art: The Nineteenth Century,* (New York: Oxford University Press, 1960), 22–24.

18. Lee H. Nelson, "Nail Chronology as an Aid to Dating Old Buildings: American Association for State and Local History Technical Leaflet 48," *History News* 24, no. 11 (November 1968).

19. Ibid.

20. Harley J. McKee, *Introduction to Early American Masonry: Stone, Brick, Mortar, and Plaster* (Washington, D.C.: Preservation Press, 1973), 9–39.

21. Alan Gowans, "The Mansions of Alloways Creek," in *Common Places: Readings in American Vernacular Architecture*, edited by Dell Upton and John Michael Vlach (Athens: University of Georgia Press, 1986), 368. 1798 Direct Tax for Lower Alloways Creek, Salem County, N.J., A and B schedules.

22. Michael J. Chiarappa, "The First and Best Sort: Quakerism, Brick Artisanry, and the Vernacular Aesthetics of Eighteenth-Century West New Jersey Pattern Brickwork Architecture" (Ph.D. diss., University of Pennsylvania, 1992).

23. Herman, *Architecture and Rural Life*, 85, 95–96. McKee, *Introduction to Early American Masonry*, 41–46.

24. McKee, *Introduction to Early American Masonry*, 44–46.

25. For a discussion of the use of rockfaced concrete block, see Pamela H. Simpson, "Cheap, Quick, and Easy: The Early History of Rockfaced Concrete Block Building," in *Perspectives in Vernacular Architecture III*, edited by Thomas Carter and Bernard L. Herman (Columbia: University of Missouri Press, 1989), 108–18.

26. McKee, *Introduction to Early American Masonry*, 61–79.

27. Ibid.

28. Herman, *Architecture and Rural Life*, 87–88.

29. Joseph W. Glass, *The Pennsylvania Culture Region: A View from the Barn* (Ann Arbor, Mich.: UMI Research Press, 1986, 1971), 170–71.

30. Jan Jennings and Herbert Gottfried, *American Vernacular Interior Architecture, 1870–1940* (New York: Van Nostrand Reinhold, 1988), 64–67, 90, 100–101. Pamela H. Simpson, "Cheap, Quick, and Easy, Part II: Pressed Metal Ceilings, 1880–

1930," in *Gender, Class, and Shelter: Perspectives in Vernacular Architecture, V,* edited by Elizabeth Collins Cromley and Carter L. Hudgins (Knoxville: University of Tennessee Press, 1995), 152–63.

31. Upton, "Traditional Timber Framing," 57–59. Herman, *Architecture and Rural Life,* 99–104.

32. Herman, *Architecture and Rural Life,* 101–3.

33. Ibid., 104.

34. Cedar shingles were cut and riven in the forest by gangs of workers who excavated the logs from the swamp, cut the timber into workable lengths, split the wood blocks into shingles, smoothed and shaped the shingles, and hauled the finished products out of the swamp. Herman, *The Stolen House,* 67–69, 71–72.

Chapter 4   Popular Architectural Styles

1. Deetz, *In Small Things Forgotten,* 64–90; and Deetz, *Invitation to Archaeology,* 26–37.

2. Dell Upton, *Holy Things and Profane: Anglican Parish Churches in Colonial Virginia* (New York: Architectural History Foundation; Cambridge: MIT Press, 1986).

3. Deetz, *In Small Things Forgotten,* 39–43, 110–17.

4. Richard Webster, *Philadelphia Preserved: Catalogue of the Historic American Buildings Survey* (Philadelphia: Temple University Press, 1976).

5. Vincent J. Scully, *The Shingle Style and the Stick Style: Architectural Theory and Design from Richardson to the Origins of Wright* (New Haven: Yale University Press, 1971), 99.

6. Gowans, *The Comfortable House,* 202–3.

7. Sandra L. Tatman and Roger W. Moss, *Biographical Dictionary of Philadelphia Architects: 1700–1930.* (Boston: G. K. Hall, 1985), 583–85.

8. Alice Kent Schooler's forthcoming study of R. Brognard Okie and his work explores many of these issues in greater detail. Telephone interview with Alice Kent Schooler, 21 September 1994.

9. Scott Steven Erbes, "The Readi-Cut Dream: The Mail-Order House Catalogs of the Aladdin Company, 1906–1920" (Master's thesis, University of Delaware, 1991). Katherine Cole Stevenson and H. Ward Jandl, *Houses by Mail: A Guide to Houses from Sears, Roebuck and Company* (Washington, D.C.: Preservation Press, 1986).

Chapter 5   Farm Outbuildings and Plans

1. *The Farmer's Cabinet: Devoted to Agriculture, Horticulture, and Rural Economy. Volume III-August, 1838 to July, 1839.* (Philadelphia: Prouty and Libby, 1839), illustration ("Farm Buildings . . .) 56–57.

2. In a recent study, Robert Ensminger argues that the Pennsylvania forebay barn originated directly from the log forebay bank barns of Prätigau, Switzerland. Robert F. Ensminger, *The Pennsylvania Barn: Its Origin, Evolution, and Distribution in North America.* (Baltimore: Johns Hopkins University Press, 1992), 15–17.

3. John Fitchen, *The New World Dutch Barn: A Study of Its Characteristics, Its Structural System, and Its Probable Erectional Procedures* (Syracuse, N.Y.: Syracuse University Press, 1968).

4. Allen G. Noble, *Wood, Brick, and Stone: The North American Settlement Landscape*, vol. 2, *Barns and Farm Structures.* (Amherst: University of Massachusetts Press, 1984), 69. Telephone interview with Dr. George Haenlein, 24 August 1992.

5. Noble, *Wood, Brick, and Stone*, 70–72.

6. Ibid., 73–80.

7. Judith A. Quinn and Bernard L. Herman, *National Register of Historic Places: Sweet Potato Houses of Sussex County, Delaware.* Newark: Center for Historic Architecture and Engineering, College of Urban Affairs and Public Policy, University of Delaware, 1988.

8. Frank J. McKelvey and Bruce E. Seely, *Industrial Archaeology of Wilmington, Delaware, and Vicinity: Site Guide for the Sixth Annual Conference of the Society for Industrial Archaeology* (Wilmington, Del.: Society for Industrial Archaeology, April 1977), site #70.

9. J. Frank Gordy, *National Register of Historic Places: The First Broiler House*, S-151 (Georgetown, Sussex County, Delaware), August 1972.

10. Ibid.

11. Kimberley R. Sebold, "Chicken-House Apartments on the Delmarva Peninsula," *Delaware History* 25, no. 4 (fall–winter 1993): 253–63.

12. Ibid.

13. Alfred Hopkins, *Modern Farm Buildings* (1913). Rev. ed. (New York: Robert M. McBride, 1920), 98. Quoted in Susan Brizzolara, *National Register Nomination for the A. I. du Pont Dairy Farm Complex* (Georgetown, Wilmington, New Castle County, Delaware), December 1989.

14. Brizzolara, *National Register Nomination.*

15. Glassie, "Eighteenth-Century Cultural Process," 394–425.

16. Ibid.

Chapter 6   Commercial, Industrial, and Institutional Architecture

1. Richard Longstreth, *The Buildings of Main Street: A Guide to American Commercial Architecture.* (Washington, D.C.: Preservation Press, for the National Trust for Historic Preservation, 1987), 12–13. Richard Longstreth, "Compositional Types in American Commercial Architecture," in *Perspectives in Vernacular Architecture II*, edited by Camille Wells (Columbia: University of Missouri Press, 1986), 12–23.

2. Longstreth, *Buildings of Main Street*, 12–23.

3. Ibid.

4. Ibid.

5. Ibid.

6. Ibid., 120–31.

7. Ibid., 24–53. Longstreth, "Compositional Types," 17–19.

8. Edward F. Heite, *National Register of Historic Places: The Burton Hardware Store*, S-385 (Seaford, Sussex County, Delaware), May 1977.

9. Longstreth, *Buildings of Main Street*, 54–67. Longstreth, "Compositional Types," 17–21.

10. Longstreth, *Buildings of Main Street*, 54.

11. Herman, *The Stolen House*, 112–13.

12. Longstreth, *Buildings of Main Street*, 68–75. Longstreth, "Compositional Types," 17.

13. Longstreth, *Buildings of Main Street*, 82–99. Longstreth, "Compositional Types," 17.

14. Longstreth, *Buildings of Main Street*, 100–107. Longstreth, "Compositional Types," 17–18.

15. Longstreth, *Buildings of Main Street*, 108–13. Longstreth, "Compositional Types," 18.

16. McKelvey and Seely, *Industrial Archaeology of Wilmington*.

17. Carol Hoffecker, *Wilmington, Delaware: Portrait of an Industrial City 1830–1910*. (Charlottesville: University Press of Virginia, for the Eleutherian Mills–Hagley Foundation), 174; McKelvey and Seely, *Industrial Archaeology of Wilmington*.

18. McKelvey and Seely, *Industrial Archaeology of Wilmington*.

19. Dean A. Doerrfeld, with David L. Ames and Rebecca J. Siders, *The Canning Industry in Delaware, 1860 to 1940 ±: A Historic Context* (Newark: The Center for Historic Architecture and Engineering, University of Delaware, for the Delaware State Historic Preservation Office, 1993), 71.

20. Ibid., 87.

21. Historic American Engineering Record #DE-6.

22. Ibid.

23. Joan Norton and Dean E. Nelson, *National Register of Historic Places: The J. H. Wilkerson and Son Brickworks*, K-360 (Milford, Kent County, Delaware), October 1977.

24. Ibid.

25. Natalie Peters, "Floating Cabins on the Delaware River" (B.A. honors thesis, University of Delaware, 1993).

26. Ibid.

27. Ralph T. Whitelaw, *Virginia's Eastern Shore: A History of Northampton and Accomack Counties* (Richmond: Virginia Historical Society, 1951), 241–70.

28. Kimberly R. Sebold and Sara Amy Leach, *Historic Themes and Resources within the New Jersey Coastal Heritage Trail: Southern New Jersey and the Delaware Bay: Cape May, Cumberland, and Salem Counties* (Washington, D.C.: Historic American Buildings Survey/Historic American Engineering Record, National Park Service, 1991), 136.

29. Kent County Mutual Insurance Co., 1847–1962. Reel 2. 1 January 1868. Policy #2707: Sidney B. Frost, Laurel vicinity, Kent County, Delaware.

30. Sebold and Leach, *Historic Themes and Resources*, 141–53.

31. Paul Baker Touart, *Somerset: An Architectural History* (Annapolis, Md.: Maryland Historical Trust; Princess Anne, Md.: Somerset County Historical Trust, 1990).

32. Edward F. Heite, *National Register Nomination for Carey's Camp Meeting Ground*, S-180 (Philips Hill, Sussex County, Delaware), August 1972.

33. Ibid.

Chapter 7   Landscape Ensembles

1. James Deetz, "Landscapes as Cultural Statements," in *Earth Patterns: Essays in Landscape Archaeology*, edited by William M. Kelso and Rachel M. Most (Charlottesville: University Press of Virginia, 1990), 1. W. G. Hoskins, *The Making of the English Landscape* (London: Hodder and Stoughten, 1955).

2. John Michael Vlach, *Back of the Big House: The Architecture of Plantation Slavery*. (Chapel Hill: University of North Carolina Press, 1993), 183–94.

3. Ibid.

4. David L. Ames, Mary Helen Callahan, Bernard L. Herman, and Rebecca J. Siders, *Delaware Comprehensive Historic Preservation Plan*, (Newark: Center for Historic Architecture and Engineering, University of Delaware, 1989), 48–49.

5. David Grettler, "The Landscape of Reform: Society, Environment, and Agricultural Reform in Central Delaware, 1790–1840" (Ph.D. diss., University of Delaware, 1990), 157, 167–70, 178–83.

6. Grettler, "The Landscape of Reform," 166–67.

7. Ibid., 160.

GLOSSARY

Adamesque style. See Federal style.

adze. An axelike tool with a curved blade set at a right angle to the handle. Used for dressing wood.

agricultural census. Record of population enumeration begun around 1850. Included also farm size, number and value of livestock, property valuation, and measure of agricultural production.

alternating Flemish bond. Bricklaying pattern produced by laying alternating courses of Flemish bond (alternating headers and stretchers) and common or stretcher bond.

arcade. A line or row of arches.

architrave. The trim, often molded, surrounding openings such as doors and windows.

ashlar. Stone masonry of regularly shaped and finished blocks laid in even courses.

axonometric drawing. A measured drawing that shows three dimensions. (See Fig. 3.23.)

balloon frame. A type of wooden building frame that utilizes light, thin, closely set studs and nails instead of the complicated wooden joints and pegs characteristic of timber framing. The studs extend in a single piece from the sill to the plate, and floor boards are nailed to the studs and supported by horizontal boards called ledgers. Introduced in the 1830s, it eventually replaced timber framing as a construction method. (See Fig. 3.30.)

baluster. A small upright post that supports a railing, such as those found on a staircase or porch. Can be turned on a lathe or left square.

balustrade. A row of balusters, usually connected at the top, and sometimes at the bottom, by a rail.

bank barn. A two- or three-story multipurpose barn generally sited with one wall built into a natural or manmade embankment.

bargeboard. A board, sometimes ornamented, placed just under the gable ends of a roof, parallel to the gable side of a building. Also known as a vergeboard.

baseboard. A plank used to finish the juncture of an interior wall and the floor, providing a tight and even seal between wall and floor. Can be decorative as well.

batten door. A door formed of parallel vertical boards held together by horizontal or sometimes diagonal boards.

bay. 1. The portion of a structure located between sections of framing or bents. 2. Any window or door opening in a structure. Thus, a building with one door and two windows on the first floor can be described as a three-bay building.

bead. A rounded molding shaped by pulling a plane along the edge of a timber or board.

bearing beam. Heavy supporting timber.

bearing wall. Supporting wall that usually begins in the cellar and extends to the top of the first story. Often constructed of masonry.

bed molding. The decorative molding applied to the uppermost area of the frieze below the drip and crown molding in an entablature.

belt course. A projecting, sometimes decorative, band of exterior masonry that visually defines an internal division between stories or serves as flashing for a pent or porch roof.

bent. Transverse structural unit consisting of at least two principal posts joined by a tie beam; also defines one side of a bay.

birdmouth. Notched joint often found at the base of a rafter, where it is fitted over the plate.

block. 1. A heavy piece of unworked timber (such as a section of tree trunk) averaging two to three feet in height and employed as a foundation supporting the underframe of a building. 2. A term used to describe discrete portions of a building; the main section of a building with an adjoining ell is often described as the main block.

board false plate. A single thin board that is placed above the true wall plate and supports the weight of the roof. The rafter feet rest on the false plate. (See Fig. 3.19.)

bolection molding. A molding or combination of moldings that projects beyond the surface or surfaces that it decorates. Often used to conceal and decorate joints in which two surfaces come together at different levels.

bonding. The pattern in which bricks are laid.

bond shifts. Changes in the pattern in which bricks are laid.

bowfat, beaufet, beaufette. A built-in cupboard, typically ornamental, used for display and storage of china and plate. Can also refer to a freestanding sideboard or side table used as display area.

bow-roofed barn. Large barn with a curved roof.

boxed stair. A staircase concealed behind a wall or within a stairbox.

brace. In timber framing, a diagonally set timber stiffening the frame and preventing twisting and other distortion. (See Figs. 3.19 and 3.25.)

braced frame. A building frame characterized by the use of timbers stabilized with diagonal braces and joined together with specially fitted joints and wooden pins. Also called *joined timber frame.*

bracket. Projecting, often decorative, support member located under an eave or other overhang.

brickbat. A small piece of brick.

brick bonds. The patterns employed in laying brick in courses.

bridle joint. Timber framing joint formed when the end of one timber is forked and fitted over a simple tenon cut into the end of another timber. (See Fig. 3.18.)

broadaxe. An axe with a wide, offset blade. Used for hewing logs into square building timbers.

broken arch pediment. A triangular decorative element in which the two sloping sides do not meet at the apex. (See Fig. 4.3.)

builder's trench. Ditch dug for the purpose of seating the foundation of a building. (See Fig. 3.1.)

bungalow. A housing style usually characterized by a low silhouette, a low-pitched, overhanging roof, an encircling porch, naturally colored exterior walls, fine craftsmanship, and materials left as close as possible to their natural state. Bungalows began to appear around the turn of the twentieth century and remained popular throughout the 1930s. (See Figs. 2.27 and 4.37.)

butterfly shelves. Carved, curving shelves; sometimes found in display cupboards flanking fireplaces in mid-eighteenth century dwellings.

butt joint. A joint in which two pieces of wood are joined end to end without overlapping.

carriage house, chair house. Outbuilding used to garage carriages.

cart shed. Building designed to garage farm equipment. Most commonly a low frame structure with an asymmetrical gable roof, open front, and sided back and gables.

casement window. A window with a sash or sashes that open on hinges usually fixed to a vertical edge. When there are two sashes they are separated by a thin vertical partition called a mullion.

ceiling medallion. Ornament for the center of a ceiling, often made of cast plaster.

center-hall plan, center-passage plan. Floor plan characterized by a center hall or passage that provides access to the surrounding rooms.

chair house. See *carriage house.*

chair rail. A strip of decorative and protective molding running around the walls of a room at about three feet above the floor. Known as a chair board in the eighteenth century.

chamber. Period term for a bedroom. Each chamber was designated by the space beneath it; thus the parlor chamber was the bedroom located directly over the parlor.

chambered hall. Two-story, one-room house plan. House built on such a plan.

chamfer. A decorative beveled-edge molding, cut along the exposed corners of framing members. Chamfers often terminate in decorative designs called stops.

Chesapeake building traditions. Building traditions that are associated with the Chesapeake region, characterized in part by earthfast construction and the use of downbraces and false plates. (See Figs. 3.24 and 3.25.)

chimney breast. The part of a fireplace and its walls that projects forward into a room.

chimney stack. The entire vertical masonry mass, including fireplaces, flues, and chimneys. (See Fig. 3.5.)

chinking. The material used to fill the space between members in a log or plank wall.

cinder block. A hollow rectangular building block made of cement and coal cinders.

cistern. A below-grade water storage space.

clamp. A temporary kiln designed for firing bricks on a building site.

closed plan. A floor plan characterized by a lack of direct access into the heated living spaces of the dwelling. (See Fig. 2.14.)

closed string stair. A stair in which the ends of the treads and risers are concealed by the sloping side board (the string) that supports the ends of the risers and treads.

closer. A brick that has been specially cut so that its header is about half the size of a standard header (in which case it is called a *queen closer*) or half the length of a stretcher (*king closer*). Closers are often used to finish the perimeters of window and door openings. (See Fig. 3.40.)

collar, collar tie, collar beam. A roof-framing member serving as a tie between opposing pairs of rafters. The earliest examples are fixed to the rafters with half-dovetailed lap joints and pinned in place, while in late nineteenth-century structures they are nailed to the sides of the rafters. (See Fig. 3.19.)

combination frame. Wood framing that uses a combination of joined timber-framing and balloon-framing techniques.

common bond. Bricklaying pattern composed of multiple courses of stretchers interspersed with single rows of headers. (See Fig. 3.37, bottom.)

common rafter. One of a series of equal-sized rafters, usually placed about 2 feet apart, carrying the roof covering. (See Fig. 3.47.)

contact print. Photographic print made by sandwiching the film negative between a sheet of glass (above) and a piece of photographic paper (below). Prints made using this method are the same size as the negatives that were used to produce them.

continuous foundation. A fully excavated masonry supporting wall located at the base of a building.

corbeled cornice. Cornice that has been finished with several stepped, cantilevered masonry courses. (See Fig. 3.9.)

corbeling. Courses of masonry cantilevered outward so that the vertical surfaces remain parallel but are not aligned; each course is secured by the weight of the masonry above it. (See Figs. 3.9 and 3.38.)

Corinthian order. A classical architectural order characterized by plain columns topped with ornately decorated capitals.

corn crib, stack, corn stack, corn house. Long, narrow log or frame gable roofed structures designed to store corn.

corner block. Ornamental blocks at the corners of door or window surrounds.

corner passage plan. Floor plan in which the stair passage is located in a corner and separated from the rest of the living space on the first floor.

corner post. Vertical framing member located at the corner of a building. (See Fig. 3.19.)

cornice. A molding of wood, plaster, or other material located at the intersection of the base of the roof and the top of the lateral surface of an exterior wall or at the juncture of an interior wall and the ceiling.

course, coursing. A horizontal row of bricks in a wall or shingles on a roof or wall.

coved cornice. A cornice with a concave molding.

crawl space. The shallow space between the first floor and the ground where there is no cellar. Crawl spaces are also often found in combination with full partial cellars.

crenelation. Ornamentation with regular rectangular indentations similar to a battlement.

cresting. Ornamental railing, sometimes perforated, running along the ridge of a roof. (See Fig. 4.35B.)

crib barn. A one-story, gable front farm building, typically with double doors at each end, the interior of which is subdivided into compartments called cribs or pens.

crosseted surround. Molded surround for a door, window, or overmantel; its squared corners project a few inches beyond the top, bottom, and sides. (See Fig. 4.3.)

cross gable. Gable perpendicular to the ridge of the main roof. (See Fig. 4.27.)

crossmending. The process of piecing and reconstructing archaeological remains.

cross passage plan. A customary or traditional floor plan in which the first floor is divided into three rooms, the largest of which usually contains the stair passage in one corner. The first floor plan is divided by two partition walls, one located near the middle of the house and the other placed at right angles to the first, further subdividing half of the dwelling into two smaller rooms.

crown molding. Molding located at the junction between wall and ceiling or at the very top of an exterior wall.

cruciform plan. Cross-shaped floor plan.

customary form. A term used in this guide to describe the earliest houses in the Delaware valley, most of which do not easily fit into a particular style category but can be grouped together on the basis of several identifying features, including exposed structural members, heavy bolection moldings, and raised-panel architectural furniture.

cut nails. Machine-made nails sheared in quantity from flattened plates of steel. (Fig. 3.31.)

cyma. A double or S-shaped curve formed by the junction of a concave and a convex curve. Also, a projecting molding with the profile of a double S-shaped curve.

dairy, milk house. Outbuilding designed for keeping milk and processing butter and/or cheese.

dentilated. Decorated with small, projecting rectangular blocks, or dentils.

dentils. Small rectangular projecting blocks, usually arranged in a row, used to form an ornamental pattern. (See Fig. 3.38.)

dimension-sawn lumber. Wood sawn to standardized measurements, such as 2 inches by 4 inches.

dog-toothed. Characterized by architectural ornament that usually consists of four leaves radiating from a raised central point.

Doric order. A classical order characterized by fluted columns with no ornament at the base and with plain capitals.

dormer. A vertical window flanked by walls that project from a sloped roof; usually has its own roof.

double-cell plan. Hall-parlor floor plan in which the two rooms are located back to back rather than end to end. (See Fig. 2.5.)

double-hung sash. Window with two separate, usually moveable, units, each of which contains framework holding window panes.

double pile. Two rooms deep.

dovetail. Timber framing joint consisting of a flared tenon and a complementarily shaped mortise into which it fits tightly. (See Fig 3.13B.)

downbrace. Brace that extends downward from the corner post to the sill. (See Figs. 3.24 and 3.25.)

dressed stone. Stone that has been specially cut into any of a variety of ornamental finishes on one or more exterior surfaces.

drop-away hay mow. Barn arrangement in which the hay mow is located on a lower level than the threshing floor.

drop mortise joint. Mortise-and-tenon joint often used for joining floor joists to plates; one side of the mortise is left open so that the tenon can be dropped into it.

Dutch doors. Doors divided horizontally into separately hinged upper and lower sections.

earthfast construction, impermanent architecture. A method of building in which, in lieu of an excavated masonry foundation, the posts of the building frame were simply set into holes in the ground; generally quicker and less labor-intensive than constructing a more durable foundation.

eave. The part of a roof that projects beyond the walls.

eclectic style. A style of architecture, popular in the late nineteenth century and early twentieth century, that drew upon a mixture of styles. (See Fig. 4.36.)

elevation. 1. One face, or side, of a building. 2. A graphic or photographic view of one face, or side, of a building.

ell. A wing or addition built at right angles to one side or at one end of a structure, creating usually an L shape, sometimes a T shape.

engaged column. A column that is in direct contact with a wall and projects outward to at least half of the depth of the column.

English barn; feed barn; runway, three-bay, or Yankee barn. A barn with a central runway and two flanking spaces. These barns are typically entered by tall double doors on either end of the runway.

English bond. Bricklaying pattern composed of alternating courses of headers and stretchers. (See Fig. 3.37, middle.)

entablature. The part of a classical facade carried by the columns; consists of the architrave, frieze, and cornice.

facade. Front or principal exterior face of a building.

false plate. A timber or plank set into or across the upper sides of ceiling joists; provides a seat for the rafter feet. Also known as a *raising plate*. (See Figs. 3.19 and 3.48.)

fanlight. Semicircular or fan-shaped window, usually used over a door. (See Fig. 4.8.)

fanning. Process of winnowing chaff from grain kernels.

Federal Manuscript Census. Record of periodic population enumeration begun in 1790; contains a listing of each household enumerating the age, race, and gender of every occupant and sometimes contains information such as occupation, birthplace, and degree of literacy.

Federal style, Adamesque style. An architectural style that was popular from the years just following the Revolution until around 1830. The Federal style emphasized verticality, symmetry, delicate and restrained ornamentation, carefully controlled proportions, and smooth surfaces. (See Fig. 4.8.)

feed barn. See *English barn.*

felling axe. An axe with a small, wedge-shaped blade; used for felling trees and scoring the surfaces of logs in preparation for hewing.

fenestration. The arrangement of windows on an exterior wall.

field notes. Roughly scaled drawings produced on site. Field notes usually contain notations for measurements as well as descriptive information.

fillet. A small, flat, decorative band, often used between curved or fluted moldings.

firebox. The open chamber of a fireplace.

flat arch, jack arch. A course of bricks laid in a radiating pattern and spanning the head of an opening.

Flemish bond. Bricklaying pattern in which headers and stretchers alternate within each course and vertically. (See Fig. 3.37, top.)

flutes, fluting. Parallel, closely spaced vertical, concave grooves or channels; usually used for ornamenting pilasters, columns, or other surfaces.

footing. The base or lowest portion of a foundation.

forebay. A second-story overhang; in barns it is designed to provide storage space on the second floor and protection for farm animals in the yard below.

foundation. The part of the building that is in direct contact with the ground and serves to transmit the weight of the walls and roof to the earth.

four-room plan. Floor plan with four rooms, usually characterized by direct access from the outside into a heated room containing a stair. (See Fig. 2.9.)

frame construction. Method of construction in which the walls carry the load of the roof and floors to the foundation, but the "skin" of the building exists independently of the frame and is not load-bearing.

framing. The wooden structure of a building, including such elements as sills, posts, rails, plates, braces, tie beams, girts, rafters, and collars.

framing section. A cross-section drawing that shows framing elements only.

frieze. The plain or decorative band on the top of a wall immediately below the cornice.

froe. A heavy, thick, dull-edged tool used for riving or splitting wood along the length of its grain.

gable. In a building with a ridged roof, the triangle created on the end walls by the roof.

gable-shedded plan. Double-cell floor plan in which one room is often a one-story shed with a gable roof. The shed is usually inferior to the main living area in terms of space, finish, and construction.

gambrel roof. A gable roof in which each side has two slopes, usually a shallower slope above a steeper one, and is constructed with two separate sets of rafters. (See Fig. 3.49.)

Georgian plan. A floor plan featuring a central hall flanked by one or two rooms on each side.

Georgian style. An architectural style, popular in the middle to late eighteenth century, characterized by a formal symmetry embellished with robust classical detail and a floor plan that emphasizes the specialized functions of rooms. (See Fig. 2.16.)

girt. In framed buildings, a horizontal member in a bent supporting ceilings or floors. (See Fig. 3.19.)

glazed header. Brick with a dark, glassy surface on one short end.

Gothic Revival, Gothic style. Architectural style, popular in the mid-nineteenth century, characterized by picturesque, asymmetrical massing, varied building heights, multiple gables, and elaborate ornamentation. (See Figs. 4.22 and 4.23.)

graining. Decorative painting technique that imitates and often elaborates on the look of wood grain.

granary. Agricultural building designed for storage of grain.

grantee. The property buyer in a deed transaction.

grantor. The property seller in a deed transaction.

Greek Revival style. Architectural style, popular in the early to middle nineteenth century, characterized by low-pitched roofs, pedimented gables, heavy cornices with unadorned friezes, and porches supported by prominent columns. (See Fig. 4.19.)

half-dovetail joint. A timber framing joint consisting of a tenon with one flared and one straight side and a mortise, cut to match, into which it fits tightly. (See Fig. 3.18.)

half-header. Brick that has been specially cut down to a fraction of the width on one short end.

half-passage plan. Side-passage plan in which the entry and stair penetrate only half the depth of the house.

hall. The all-purpose, primary room in early buildings.

hall-parlor plan. Two-room dwelling plan in which the hall and parlor are placed side by side under a continuous ridge line.

hall plan. One-room dwelling plan which in its simplest form contains a single door opening directly into the living space.

hay track. Track along the ridge line of a barn designed to facilitate hauling and moving of hay from one part of the barn to another.

H-bent construction. Timber framing method employing transverse, H-shaped structural units consisting of upper story floor joists tenoned into principal posts. In this method of construction, individual bents rather than walls are preassembled on the ground and raised one by one. (See Fig. 3.28).

header. The short face or butt end of a brick, usually measuring 1¼ inches high by 2¼ inches wide.

header bond. Bricklaying pattern in which all the bricks are laid with the short end, or header, out.

herringbone brickwork. Bricks laid diagonally in a zig-zag or herringbone pattern.

hewing. Method of preparing logs for building by squaring the rounded surfaces with a felling axe and broadaxe.

hipped roof. Roof that is formed of four pitched surfaces.

Historic American Buildings Survey (HABS). Branch of the National Park Service that oversees the production and collection of documentation of historic architecture. Documentation consists of measured drawings, photographs, and written data. HABS documentation materials are permanently housed in the Library of Congress.

Historic American Engineering Record (HAER). A companion program to the Historic American Buildings Survey, designed to record historic engineering and industrial sites.

hog gallows. Seasonal farmyard structure designed for hanging hog carcasses during gutting, scraping, and butchering.

horizon. In archaeological terminology, the broad geographic distribution of a set of cultural traits that last a relatively short period of time.

hyphen. In architectural terminology, a short connecting wing between two larger buildings.

impermanent buildings, impermanent architecture. See *earthfast construction.*

intermediate posts. Vertical posts that are smaller than principal posts.

interrupted foundation. Foundation consisting of individual piers or pilings.

intestate. Without a will.

inventory, probate inventory. Enumeration of cash and household possessions following the death of an individual who has left no will.

Ionic order. A classical order characterized by columns topped with scroll-shaped forms called volutes.

Italianate style. Architectural style, popular in the middle to late nineteenth century, characterized by wide, overhanging eaves supported by large brackets, flat or low-pitched hipped roofs, and tall, attenuated windows. (See Fig. 4.28.)

jack arch. See *flat arch.*

jamb. Side portion of a fireplace opening or doorframe.

joist. A timber that spans the width of a building and supports the floors and, at the attic level, the base of the roof framing.

kerb plate. Framing timber used to support the upper, more shallowly pitched set of rafters in a gambrel roof.

keystone. Wedge-shaped stone located at the top center of an arch.

lamb's tongue stop. Cyma or S-shaped terminal ornament on a chamfer.

lap joint. Wood framing joint formed by making an L-shaped cut into the ends of two timbers to about half their thickness and overlapping the cut portions. (See Fig. 3.18.)

lath. Strip of riven or sawn wood to which shingles or plaster are applied.

laying houses. Agricultural buildings designed to house laying hens.

lean-to. A shed addition, usually no more than one room deep and one story in elevation, with a single-pitched roof.

lean-to plan. Double-cell floor plan in which one room is topped by a single-pitched roof, the other typically by a gable roof. The lean-to room is usually left with exposed framing and is used for purposes such as storage or sleeping.

light. A period term for each pane of glass in a window.

lintel. A horizontal architectural element that spans an opening such as that for a door or window and carries the load of the wall above the opening.

little room over the entry. A term, frequently found in early documents, that was used to describe the room located on the second floor over the main entry. Such rooms were often found in center-passage, single-pile houses.

loft. An upper floor or gallery at attic level.

log sag. A sag that characteristically develops through the middle of a log building as it ages.

longitudinal section. An architectural drawing that shows a building's structure as if it had been cut open lengthwise along or parallel to the ridge line.

main block. The larger or main portion of a building that has an addition.

mansard roof. A double-pitched roof with a steeply pitched lower section and a low, shallowly pitched and hipped upper section that often appears flat. Mansard roofs are often pierced with dormers. (See Fig. 4.31.)

mansion house. In eighteenth-century and early-nineteenth-century documents, the term for the principal dwelling on a tract of land.

mantel. Decorative fireplace surround, often topped with a projecting shelf.

mantel cornice. The part of a mantel that forms a projecting shelf.

manufacturing census. A census, begun early in the nineteenth century, that contains information such as the name of a manufacturing establishment, the number of people it employs, the value of the product produced per year, and the value of the stock on hand.

marbleizing. Decorative painting technique that aims to imitate masonry materials, most typically marble.

mass construction. Method of construction in which the masonry walls carry the load of roof and floors to the foundation and also protect the interior of the building from the weather.

measured drawings. Accurately scaled architectural drawings.

milk house. See *dairy*.

mixed-use barn. A barn designed for multiple agricultural purposes, such as grain storage, crop processing, housing of farm animals, and dairying activities.

modillion block. An ornamental block or bracket under the overhang, or corona, of a cornice.

molding. A decorative recessed or relieved surface used for finishing or purely as ornamentation.

molding plane. A type of woodworking plane with a knife that is specially shaped for creating a specific type of ornamentation, such as beads, fillets, ogees, or flutes.

mortar. Masonry bonding cement usually composed of lime and sand and, in the late nineteenth and twentieth centuries, of Portland cement.

mortise and tenon. A timber framing joint formed by cutting the end of a timber back to form a rectangular projection, called a tenon, and fitting it into an equal-sized hole, called a mortise. Mortise-and-tenon joints are usually locked together with wooden pins or nails. (See Fig. 3.18.)

mullion. The principal vertical member between the lights in a window with two or more lights.

muntin. A thin strip of wood used for holding panes of glass within a window sash. (See Fig. 4.9.)

nailer. 1. A narrow board that is attached perpendicular to rafters and to which roofing shingles are nailed. Also called shingle lath. 2. A block or length of timber set into a masonry surface, such as a chimney pile or brick wall, and to which mantels, paneling, or other trim can be nailed.

nogging. A filling for the spaces between timbers in the walls of frame buildings, usually consisting of soft bricks or rubble masonry.

notching. Also called cornering. In log construction the basic technique used for joining logs at the corners of a building.

oakum. Hemp fiber used for chinking spaces between logs in log buildings; also used for packing the seams of boats.

ogee. A molding with an S-shaped profile.

one-room plan. Floor plan in which the ground floor consists of a single room.

open plan. Floor plan laid out with direct access from the outside into the heated living areas of the dwelling. (See Figs. 2.4 and 2.7.)

open-string. A stair in which the ends of the treads and risers extend beyond the side board (the "string") that supports the ends of the risers and treads.

orphans' court records. Legal documents of a court that had jurisdiction over the affairs of minors and the administration of estates. Orphans' court records in Delaware and Maryland enumerate the holdings of everyone owning real property who died survived by minor children.

outbuilding. Functionally specific building that is separate from the main dwelling.

outfield. Small field designed for rough usage that is located as much as a mile away from the main home lot. Outfields sometimes consisted of enclosed clearings surrounded by woodland and were often the location of the plantation tenant's house.

overmantel. A section of paneling or plaster work circumscribed by a molding and located above the mantel surrounding a fireplace opening. (See Fig. 4.3.)

packing shed. Agricultural building designed for packing farm produce.

Palladian window. A window consisting of a central arched sash flanked by smaller side lights.

parlor. The most formal room in a house, usually intended for receiving or entertaining guests.

passage. A hall, corridor, or entry, often an unheated space and often containing a stair. The passage connected other rooms and provided access between floors and/or to the outside.

patera, paterae. Round or oval medallion(s), sometimes simply finished but often embellished with carved ornamentation such as leaves and fluting.

pattern books. Architectural guides illustrated with patterns designed to aid builders and architects. (See Fig. 2.24.)

pediment. A triangular decorative element consisting of two opposing raked sides and a horizontal molding at the base. Pediments often crown doors, windows, and overmantels. (See Fig. 4.3.)

pendant. A hanging decorative element projecting from eaves, the bottoms of staircases, or bargeboards.

Penn plan. See *Quaker plan.*

pent. In Delaware valley architecture, a shallow roof, framed on extended joists between floors or at the base of the gable.

periodization. Division of the construction history of a building into periods.

perspective photographic view. Photograph that shows more than one wall of a building, often taken from one corner.

piazza. An arcaded and roofed gallery or a large porch along one or more sides of a house. In reference to buildings in Philadelphia, piazza denoted the room linking the main house and the kitchen and containing the principal stair.

piers. Individual foundation supports, forming, in effect, an interrupted foundation. May be stumps, concrete blocks, cast cement pilings, or be constructed of stacked bricks, stones, or combined materials.

pilaster. A rectangular column attached to a wall, often resembling a classical column.

pile. 1. Term of measurement used to describe the depth of a building. One pile is equivalent to the depth of one room; thus, a single-pile building is one room deep, a double-pile building two rooms deep. 2. The mass of an entire chimney stack.

piling. Pier or individual foundation support.

pit-sawing. An early hand sawing process that utilized a pit dug into the ground and a long, double-handled saw operated by two people, one of whom stood above the pit while the other stood in the pit.

plan. 1. The arrangement of architectural space at floor level. 2. A drawing of the arrangement of architectural space at floor level.

plank. Generally, a heavy thick board; in log building technology, a log that has been finished on two sides and is usually fixed and pinned into grooved corner posts.

plat. A plan, map, or chart of a piece of land, delineating features such as lots and boundaries.

plate. The horizontal framing member extending across the tops of the framing posts or placed at the top of a masonry wall, providing the base for the attic and roof framing. (See Fig. 3.19.)

platform framing. A modification of balloon framing techniques in which each floor is built as a separate component or platform. Floor platforms are supported by vertical studs, corner posts, and partition walls that are only a single story high.

pointed arch. Arch with a pointed top, associated with Gothic architecture and in the Delaware valley often seen in Gothic Revival buildings.

pointing. The finish treatment for mortared joints. (See Fig. 3.46.) *Repointing* is a process of applying a second layer of mortar to masonry joints after the initial layer has hardened. Repointing may be undertaken to increase durability, to improve weather resistance, to repair deteriorating masonry joints, or to achieve a particular surface appearance.

pole-built. Built of slender, usually unbarked logs or poles.

pole joist. Joist made of a slender, usually unbarked log or pole.

portico. A covered porch, usually over an entry, often supported by columns or pillars.

Portland cement. A type of cement that hardens under water, made from a mixture of limestone and clay.

post. 1. A principal vertical support for a timber-framed building. (See Fig. 3.19.) 2. A timber set vertically into the ground as a support for the base of a structure.

post-and-plank. A combination of log and frame walling in which logs are laid horizontally and joined to corner posts.

post-and-rail. A framing system in which upright members carry horizontal members to which vertical siding is attached. Also a type of log fencing.

post-set. Erected on posts set into the ground rather than on partially or fully excavated foundations. See *earthfast construction.*

potato pit, root pit. Below-grade semifinished rectangular storage space common to the Chesapeake region and designed to keep root crops from freezing; excavated beneath the floor, usually just in front of the cooking hearth.

pound. Outdoor paddock or enclosure for animals.

principal rafter. Major load-bearing rafter, usually larger in size than intermediate or common rafters.

principal rafter roof. Roof that is constructed of a mixture of principal and common rafters.

principals. In braced-frame construction, major load-bearing members, usually arranged as opposing pairs.

privy. A small outbuilding used as a toilet; usually contains a bench, with one or more holes cut in it, built over a pit.

probate inventory. See *inventory.*

punch-and-gouge. Type of ornamental woodwork characterized by grooved and punched carving.

purlin. A roofing timber that runs parallel to the roof ridge under or between the rafters.

Quaker plan, three-room plan, Penn plan. Floor plan composed of a large common room and two adjacent and usually smaller rooms. The common room typically contains a cooking fireplace and stair, and the adjacent rooms usually each contain a corner fireplace and a single window. (See Fig. 2.8B.)

quatrefoil. A four-lobed shape, often utilized in Gothic Revival style architecture.

Queen Anne style. Architectural style popular in the United States between 1880 and 1910, characterized by varied surface textures and colors, irregular floor plans, irregular projecting shapes that include towers and bay windows, and multiple steep roofs. (See Fig. 4.35.)

queen posts. Paired vertical posts utilized with a system of trusses.

rafter. The sloping framing element that is seated on a plate or a false plate and supports the roof covering. (See Fig. 3.19.)

rafter foot. The bottom end of a rafter.

rail. A section of timber framing running at right angles between two posts and providing a nailing surface for vertical board siding.

raised joint. In masonry construction, a type of joint in which the mortar projects beyond the wall surface. (See Fig. 3.46, bottom.)

raised-panel. A type of finish utilized on doors and fireplace walls that consists of projecting rectangular panels surrounded by a decorative molding.

reeding. Molding consisting of a series of closely spaced parallel convex strips.

relieving arch. Large masonry arch located in the cellar of a building and designed to carry the weight of the fireplaces, hearths, and chimneys above. (See Fig. 3.5.)

ridge, ridge line. The line of intersection of the opposite slopes of a roof.

riven. Split along the length of the wood grain, usually by means of a heavy, thick, dull-edged splitting tool called a froe.

road papers. Documents compiled whenever a new road was planned. Road papers frequently contain accurate illustrations of proposed road locations and sketches of buildings that stood near intended roadways.

robbed mortise. The mortised portion of a dismantled mortise-and-tenon joint, often found in timbers that have been reused.

rockfaced or rusticated concrete block. Concrete block that has been roughly textured (rusticated) on the exterior face.

roofing board. A broad board that is placed over the rafters, parallel to the ridge of the roof.

root pit. See *potato pit.*

round. An eighteenth-century term denoting an individual horizontal layer of logs in a wall, equivalent to a course in a brick wall.

round-head windows. Windows with round-arched tops.

rowlock arch. A brick arch in which the bricks are laid in an arch shape with the headers outward.

rubble, rubble stone. Rough fieldstone, usually undressed, typically uncoursed.

running measurements. Cumulative measurements that are taken along a given dimension by stretching the tape measure across it and reading each measurement as a specific point along the tape.

runway. The primary passageway in a barn.

runway barn. See *English barn.*

rusticated Flemish bond. Bricklaying pattern in which plain stretchers and roughly textured headers alternate within each course and vertically.

rustication. Roughening, beveling, or distressing of a surface to create a textured appearance.

sammel bricks. Softer, underfired bricks, usually used in places where they would seldom be seen, such as the interior surfaces of cellar walls.

sawn-plank construction. Log construction that utilizes three- to four-inch-thick logs sawn or hewn into planks and tenoned into square, grooved corner posts.

scooped stop. A curved, spoon-shaped chamfer terminal.

scroll saw. A saw designed for cutting elaborately curved decorative shapes. A jigsaw.

Second Empire style. Architectural style, popular in United States approximately from 1860 to 1890, characterized by mansard roofs, projecting and receding surfaces, and varied textures and colors. (See Fig. 4.31.)

section. An architectural drawing that shows a building's structure as if it had been cut open; reveals construction details that would not be apparent in a plan or elevation.

segmental arch. Masonry arch forming a portion of a circle.

service wing, service ell. A house addition that concentrates housekeeping functions, including kitchens, food storage areas, and servants' quarters, under one roof.

shingle lath. Narrow, lightweight strips of wood that are attached to the rafters parallel to the ridge line and onto which shingles are nailed. Also called *nailers*.

shingle style. A style of architecture, popular in the late nineteenth century, characterized by a uniform, monochromatic covering of wood shingle siding, multiple gables, and sash and casement windows with multiple lights.

shouldered corner post. Corner post with wide, projecting upper portions called shoulders.

sidelight. Window located to one side of a door opening.

side-passage plan. Floor plan characterized by a side corridor providing access to two adjacent rooms and the second floor.

sill. In timber framing, the bottom-most member, carrying the first-floor joists, seating posts, and studs. (See Fig. 3.19.)

single pile. One room deep.

site plan. A scaled map of a site; usually includes buildings and other major features, such as roads, driveways, and wells. (See Fig. 8.10B.)

sitting room. Small room, less formal than a parlor, designated for quiet pursuits and reception of guests.

skinning shed. Outbuilding used for skinning and processing muskrats. Skinning sheds were often converted smokehouses.

smokehouse. Outbuilding designed for smoking meats.

soldier arch. A flat arch of bricks laid vertically.

springhouse. Outbuilding built over a spring and used for cool storage of foods such as dairy products.

stack. See *corn crib*.

standing-seam metal roof. Roof finish consisting of metal plates joined with raised seams that usually run perpendicular to the ridge line of the building.

stairbox. Stair enclosure, usually for a winding or corner stair.

stick style. Style of architecture popular during the 1860s and 1870s; derives its name from the "stickwork" decoration applied to exterior surfaces.

stickwork. Applied decoration exaggerating or simulating structural features, such as posts and braces.

story. The space in a building between two adjacent floor levels.

stratigraphy. The layering of archaeological remains through time; based on the notion that, archaeological remains accumulate over time in layers, with the oldest layers lying deepest in the ground.

stretcher. The long side of a brick, usually measuring 8¼ inches long by 2¼ inches high.

stretcher bond. Bricklaying pattern composed entirely of stretchers laid end to end.

struck joint. A mortar joint that is finished by impressing it with a mason's trowel to achieve a concave or angled surface. (See Fig. 3.46.)

strut. A structural timber, usually associated with roofing systems, that is used as a brace between two timbers, such as tie beams and rafters or plates and purlins.

stucco. An exterior wall coating usually made of cement, sand, lime, and water.

stud. A vertical framing member running between sill and plate or sill and girt. In braced-frame construction, these are not necessarily load-bearing members but serve as nailing surfaces for lath and siding. (See Fig. 3.19.)

subcellar. An underground space excavated below cellar level.

summer kitchen. A small kitchen or cooking shed, near or adjacent to the main dwelling, used as a kitchen in warm weather.

superscript notation. Form of writing measurements, in which the abbreviations for feet and inches are not used; instead, the measurement for inches is written as a superscript to the measurement for feet: two feet nine inches or $2'9''$ would be written as 2^9.

surround (door surround, fireplace surround). Architrave or molded trim encircling door or window openings.

survey forms. Standardized architectural documentation forms that list all the component parts of a building, from the foundation to the roof, in sequence, and are designed to provide a consistent technique for looking at and recording buildings. (See Fig. 8.1.)

sweet potato house. Specialized agricultural building designed exclusively for storing and curing sweet potatoes. (See Fig. 5.28.)

tax list, tax assessment. Document that enumerates and assesses an individual's taxable property.

tax parcel map. Map that indicates property boundaries and numbers each property for tax purposes.

temple front. In Greek Revival architecture, a facade that includes elements derived from classical buildings including porches supported by prominent columns, pedimented gables, and heavy cornices with unadorned friezes. (See Fig. 4.20.)

tenant house. A dwelling inhabited by or designed to be occupied by tenants or renters.

tenon. The rectangular projection designed to fit into a matching cavity, or mortise, in a mortise-and-tenon joint. (See Fig. 3.18.)

terminus post quem. An archaeological principle, translated as "the date after which."

terra cotta. Brownish-orange earthenware made of fired clay. Used to make tiles, sometimes glazed, carved, or molded, that are used to ornament the exteriors of buildings.

three-bay barn. See *English barn.*

three-room plan. See *Quaker plan.*

threshing floor. The area of a barn floor designated for threshing, the process of separating the grain from the harvested plant.

tie beam. A framing timber binding two opposing framing members or units together; for example, a collar beam acting as a tension member between two opposing rafters. (See Fig. 3.19).

timber framing. A framing system that uses wooden timbers fitted together with specially cut joints and wooden pins.

title search. A process of tracing the chain of ownership of, or title to, a given piece of property through deed transactions.

tooled joint. A concave mortar joint that has been grooved with a curved jointing tool. (See Fig. 3.46.)

townhouse. In modern parlance, a rowhouse or a house that is connected to another, usually similar, house by a common sidewall. In the eighteenth and early nineteenth centuries, simply a house in a town.

tracery. Decorative openwork, usually consisting of a pattern with branching lines. Used, among other places, in the ribbing of Gothic windows.

transom. A small window directly above a door. Transoms can be fixed or movable and can consist of single or multiple panes. (See Fig. 4.18B.)

triangulation. A method of measuring a site that allows you to locate any point on the site by first establishing its distance from two other points. (See Fig. 8.10A.)

trimmer. Framing member placed on the side of an opening in a floor, such as that for a stair or hearth.

truss. A framing member that, by its placement, forms a triangle in a rigid roof framework designed to span two load-bearing walls.

typology. A system of classification based on types.

underpinning. The foundation or supporting portions of a building.

upbrace. Brace that extends from the corner post to the plate. (See Fig. 3.19.)

verge. The edge of the roof where it projects over the gable.

vergeboard. See *bargeboard.*

vernacular architecture. A term used to describe common or everyday architecture.

Victorian. A catchall term used to describe a number of styles of architecture that were popular during the mid-nineteenth century, including Queen Anne, Gothic Revival, stick, and shingle.

V-notching. Type of notching used in log construction in which the notches are cut in a V shape. (See Fig. 3.13A.)

wagon barn. Agricultural building designed for vehicle storage and other purposes; often combines the functions of crib barns, carriage houses, workshops, and cart sheds.

wainscoting. Decorative and protective finish of wood paneling on the lower three or four feet of a wall.

water table. In masonry structures, a ledge, projection, or plinth on an external wall, usually at the first floor level, that protects the foundation from rainwater. On brick structures, the water table may be finished with beveled or molded bricks. (See Fig. 3.35.)

well sweep. A lifting device designed for drawing water from a well; usually consists of a long timber pivoted on tall posts. (See Fig. 2.35.)

winder stair. Stair composed of steps that are carried around curves or angles.

wing. Ell or addition.

wire nail. Modern machine-made nail characterized by a round shank.

wrought nail. Hand-forged nail.

Yankee barn. See *English barn.*

BIBLIOGRAPHY

Ames, David L., Mary Helen Callahan, Bernard L. Herman, and Rebecca J. Siders. *Delaware Comprehensive Historic Preservation Plan.* Newark: Center for Historic Architecture and Engineering, University of Delaware, 1989.

Bennett, George Fletcher. *Early Architecture of Delaware.* New York: Bonanza Books, 1932.

———. *The Perennial Apprentice: Sixty-Year Scrapbook: Architecture 1916 to 1976.* Wilmington, Del.: TriMark, 1977.

Blumenson, John J. G. *Identifying American Architecture.* Rev. ed. Nashville, Tenn.: American Association for State and Local History, 1981.

Bonta, Juan Pablo. *Architecture and Its Interpretation: A Study of Expressive Systems in Architecture.* New York: Rizzoli International, 1979.

Bourcier, Paul G. "'In Excellent Order'; The Gentleman Farmer Views His Fences, 1790–1860." *Agricultural History* 58, no. 4 (1984): 546–64.

Brandywine Conservancy. *Protecting Historic Properties: A Guide to Research and Preservation.* Chadds Ford, Pa.: Brandywine Conservancy, 1984.

Brunskill, R. W. *Illustrated Handbook of Vernacular Architecture.* New York: Universe Books, 1971.

Brunskill, Ronald, and Alec Clifton-Taylor. *Brickwork.* New York: Van Nostrand Reinhold, 1977.

Buck, William J. *History of Bucks County: From Its Earliest Period of Settlement to the Close of the Eighteenth Century.* Doylestown, Pa.: printed by John S. Brown, 1855.

Buck, William Joseph. *Local Sketches and Legends Pertaining to Bucks and Montgomery Counties, Pennsylvania.* Philadelphia: privately printed, 1887.

Burns, John A., and the staff of the Historic American Buildings Survey and the Historic American Engineering Record. *Recording Historic Structures.* Washington, D.C.: American Institute of Architects Press, 1989.

Candee, Richard. *Building Portsmouth: The Neighborhoods and Architecture of New Hampshire's Oldest City.* Portsmouth, N.H.: Portsmouth Advocates, 1992.

Carson, Cary, Norman F. Barka, William M. Kelso, Garry Wheeler Stone, and Dell Upton. "Impermanent Architecture in the Southern American Colonies." *Winterthur Portfolio* 16, no. 2/3 (summer–autumn 1981): 135–96.

Carson, Cary. "Doing History with Material Culture." In *Material Culture and the Study of American Life*, edited by Ian M. G. Quimby. New York: W. W. Norton, 1978.

Carter, Thomas, and Peter Goss. *Utah's Historic Arcitecture, 1847–1940*. Salt Lake City: University of Utah Press, 1988.

Carter, Thomas, and Bernard L. Herman, eds. *Perspectives in Vernacular Architecture, III*. Columbia: University of Missouri Press for the Vernacular Architecture Forum, 1989.

———. *Perspectives in Vernacular Architecture, IV*. Columbia: University of Missouri Press for the Vernacular Architecture Forum, 1991.

Catts, Wade P., and Jay F. Custer. *Tenant Farmers, Stone Masons, and Black Laborers: Final Archaeological Investigations of the Thomas Williams Site, Glasgow, New Castle County, Delaware: DelDOT Archaeology Series No. 82*. Newark: Center for Archaeological Research, Department of Anthropology, University of Delaware, 1990.

Chappel, Edward A. "Architectural Recording and the Open-Air Museum: A View from the Field." In *Perspectives in Vernacular Architecture, II*, edited by Camille Wells, 24–36. Columbia: University of Missouri Press, 1986.

———. "Looking at Buildings." *Fresh Advices: A Research Supplement* (November 1984): i–vi.

Chase, Susan M., and David Ames. *A Historic Context for Suburbanization in Delaware*. Newark: Center for Historic Architecture and Engineering, College of Urban Affairs and Public Policy, University of Delaware, 1992.

Chiarappa, Michael J. "The First and Best Sort: Quakerism, Brick Artisanry, and the Vernacular Aesthetics of Eighteenth-Century West New Jersey Pattern Brickwork Architecture." Ph.D. diss., University of Pennsylvania, 1992.

Ching, Frank. *Architectural Graphics*. 2nd ed. New York: Van Nostrand Reinhold, 1985.

Condit, Carl W. *American Building Art: The Nineteenth Century*. New York: Oxford University Press, 1960.

Cromley, Elizabeth Collins, and Carter L. Hudgins, eds. *Gender, Class, and Shelter: Perspectives in Vernacular Architecture, V*. Knoxville: University of Tennessee Press, 1995.

Cummings, Abbott Lowell. *The Framed Houses of Massachusetts Bay, 1625–1725*. Cambridge: Harvard University Press, 1979.

Cushing, Thomas. *History of the Counties of Gloucester, Salem, and Cumberland New Jersey: With Biographical Sketches of their Prominent Citizens*. Philadelphia: Everts and Peck, 1883.

Davis, W. W. H. *History of Bucks County, Pennsylvania from the Discovery of the Delaware to the Present Time*. New York: Lewis Publishing, 1905.

Deetz, James. *In Small Things Forgotten: The Archaeology of Early American Life*. Garden City, N.Y.: Anchor Press/Doubleday, 1977.

————. *Invitation to Archaeology*. Garden City, N.Y.: Natural History Press for the American Museum of Natural History, 1967.

Delaware Bureau of Archaeology and Historic Preservation. Cultural Resource Survey. Dover: Delaware Division of Historical and Cultural Affairs. Ongoing project frequently updated.

Doerrfeld, Dean A., with David L. Ames and Rebecca J. Siders. *The Canning Industry in Delaware, 1860 to 1940: A Historic Context*. Newark: Center for Historic Architecture and Engineering, University of Delaware, 1993.

Downing, A. J. *Cottage Residences, Rural Architecture and Landscape Gardening*. 1842. Reprint, Watkins Glen, N.Y.: American Life Foundation, 1967.

————. *The Architecture of Country Houses; including designs for cottages, and farmhouses, and villas, with remarks on interiors, furniture, and the best modes of warming and ventilating*. 1850. Reprint, New York: Dover Publications, 1969.

Downing, Frances, and Hubka, Thomas C. "Diagramming: A Visual Language." In *Perspectives in Vernacular Architecture, II*, edited by Camille Wells, 44–52. Columbia· University of Missouri Press, 1986.

Eberlein, Harold Donaldson, and Cortlandt V. D. Hubbard. *Historic Houses and Buildings of Delaware*. Dover, Del.: Public Archives Commission, 1962.

Ensminger, Robert F. *The Pennsylvania Barn: Its Origin, Evolution, and Distribution in North America*. (Baltimore: Johns Hopkins University Press, 1992).

Erbes, Scott Steven. "The Readi-Cut Dream: The Mail-Order House Catalogs of the Aladdin Company, 1906–1920." Master's thesis, University of Delaware, 1991.

The Farmer's Cabinet: Devoted to Agriculture, Horticulture, and Rural Economy, Volume III —August, 1838 to July, 1839. Philadelphia: Prouty and Libby, 1839.

Favretti, Rudy J. *For Every House a Garden: A Guide for Reproducing Period Gardens*. Hanover, N.H.: University Press of New England, 1990.

————. *Landscapes and Gardens for Historic Buildings: A Handbook for Reproducing and Creating Authentic Landscape Settings*. Nashville, Tenn.: American Association for State and Local History, 1978.

Fitchen, John. *The New World Dutch Barn: A Study of Its Characteristics, Its Structural System, and Its Probable Erectional Procedures*. Syracuse, N.Y.: Syracuse University Press, 1968.

Forman, Henry Chandlee. *Early Buildings and Historic Artifacts in Tidewater Maryland: 1. The Eastern Shore*. Easton, Md.: Eastern Shore Publishers' Associates, 1989.

————. *Maryland Architecture: A Short History from 1634 through the Civil War*. Cambridge, Md.: Tidewater Publishers, 1968.

Futhey, John Smith. *History of Chester County, Pennsylvania with Genealogical and Biographical Sketches*. Philadelphia: L. H. Everts, 1881.

Garrison, J. Ritchie, Bernard L. Herman, and Barbara McLean Ward, eds. *After Ratification: Material Life in Delaware, 1789–1820*. Newark: Museum Studies Program, University of Delaware, 1988.

Garvin, James L. "Mail-Order House Plans and American Victorian Architecture." *Winterthur Portfolio* 16 (1981): 309–34.

Glass, Joseph W. *The Pennsylvania Culture Region: A View from the Barn.* Ann Arbor, Mich.: UMI Research Press, 1986.

Glassie, Henry. "Eighteenth Century Cultural Process in Delaware Valley Folk Building." In *Winterthur Portfolio 7,* edited by Ian M. G. Quimby, 29–57. Charlottesville: University Press of Virginia, 1972. Also reprinted in *Common Places: Readings in American Vernacular Architecture,* edited by Dell Upton and John Michael Vlach, 394–425. Athens: University of Georgia Press, 1986.

————. *Folk Housing in Middle Virginia: A Structural Analysis of Historic Artifacts.* Knoxville: University of Tennessee Press, 1975.

————. *Pattern in the Material Folk Culture of the Eastern United States.* Philadelphia: University of Pennsylvania Press, 1968.

Gordy, J. Frank. *National Register of Historic Places: The First Broiler House,* S-151 (Georgetown, Sussex County, Delaware). August 1972.

Gottfried, Herbert, and Jan Jennings. *American Vernacular Design, 1870–1940.* New York: Van Nostrand Reinhold, 1985.

Gowans, Alan. *Architecture in New Jersey: A Record of American Civilization.* Princeton, N.J.: D. Van Nostrand, 1964.

————. *The Comfortable House: North American Suburban Architecture, 1890–1930.* Cambridge: MIT Press, 1986.

Grettler, David. "The Landscape of Reform: Society, Environment, and Agricultural Reform in Central Delaware, 1790–1840." Ph.D. diss., University of Delaware, 1990.

Grow, Lawrence. *Waiting for the 5:05: Terminal, Station, and Depot in America.* New York: Main Street/Universe Books, 1977.

Hamlin, Talbot. *Greek Revival Architecture in America.* 1944. Reprint, New York: Dover, 1964.

Harris, Richard. *Discovering Timber-Framed Buildings.* Aylesbury, U.K.: Shire Publications, 1978.

Heite, Edward F. *National Register of Historic Places: The Burton Hardware Store,* S-385 (Seaford, Sussex County, Delaware). May 1977.

Herman, Bernard L. *Architecture and Rural Life in Central Delaware, 1700–1900.* Knoxville: University of Tennessee Press, 1987.

————. "Delaware Vernacular: Folk Housing in Three Counties," in *Perspectives in Vernacular Architecture I,* edited by Camille Wells. Columbia: University of Missouri Press, 1982.

————. "Multiple Materials/Multiple Meanings: The Fortunes of Thomas Mendenhall." *Winterthur Portfolio* 19, no. 1 (spring 1984): 67–86.

————. "The Archaeology of Architecture: Reading a Building and Historic Architectural Technology." Paper delivered at the Historic Architectural Research Conference sponsored by the National Park Service, Society of Architectural Historians, American Institute of Architects, and the Association of Collegiate Schools of Architecture, Washington, D.C., April 1986.

————. *The Stolen House.* Charlottesville: University Press of Virginia, 1992.

Herman, Bernard L., Gabrielle M. Lanier, Rebecca J. Siders, and Max Van Balgooy. *National Register of Historic Places: Dwellings of the Rural Elite in Central Delaware, 1770–1830.* Newark: Center for Historic Architecture and Engineering, College of Urban Affairs and Public Policy, University of Delaware, 1989.

Hoffecker, Carol E. *Delaware: A Bicentennial History.* New York: W. W. Norton, 1977.

Hopkins, Alfred. *Modern Farm Buildings.* 1913. Rev. ed., New York: Robert M. McBride, 1920.

Hoskins, W. G. *The Making of the English Landscape.* London: Hodder and Stoughten, 1955.

Hubka, Thomas C. *Big House, Little House, Back House, Barn: The Connected Farm Buildings of New England.* Hanover, N.H.: University Press of New England, 1984.

Hume, Ivor Noel. *Historical Archaeology.* New York: Alfred A. Knopf, 1969.

Isaac, Rhys. *The Transformation of Virginia, 1740–1790.* Chapel Hill: University of North Carolina Press, 1982.

Jackson, John Brinckerhoff. *Discovering the Vernacular Landscape.* New Haven: Yale University Press, 1984.

Jandl, H. Ward, ed. *The Technology of Historic American Buildings: Studies of the Materials, Craft Processes, and the Mechanization of Building Construction.* Washington, D.C.: Foundation for Preservation Technology, for the Association for Preservation Technology, 1983.

Jennings, Jan, and Herbert Gottfried. *American Vernacular Interior Architecture, 1870–1940.* New York: Van Nostrand Reinhold, 1988.

Jicha, Hubert F. "Bank Barns in Mill Creek Hundred, Delaware." Honors thesis, University of Delaware, 1984.

Johnson, Matthew. *Housing Culture: Traditional Architecture in an English Landscape.* Washington, D.C.: Smithsonian Institution Press, 1993.

Kalm, Peter. *The America of 1750: Peter Kalm's Travels in North America, The English Version of 1770.* 1937, revised from the original Swedish. Reprint edited by Adolph B. Benson. New York: Dover Publications, 1966.

Kelso, William M., and Rachel Most, eds. *Earth Patterns: Essays in Landscape Archaeology.* Charlottesville: University Press of Virginia, 1990.

Kidder, Tracy. *House.* Boston: Houghton-Mifflin, 1985.

Kniffen, Fred. "Folk Housing: Key to Diffusion." *Annals of the Association of American Geographers* 55, no. 4 (December 1965): 549–77.

Kniffen, Fred, and Henry Glassie. "Building in Wood in the Eastern United States: A Time-Place Perspective." *Geographical Review* 56 (1966): 40–66.

Lamme, Ary. *America's Historic Landscapes: Community Power and the Preservation of Four National Historic Sites.* Knoxville: University of Tennessee Press, 1989.

Lancaster, Clay. *The American Bungalow, 1880s–1920s.* New York: Abbeville, 1983.

Lawrence, Roderick J. "'The Interpretation of Vernacular Architecture." *Vernacular Architecture* 14 (1983): 19–28.

Leighton, Ann. *American Gardens of the Nineteenth Century: "For Comfort and Affluence."* Amherst: University of Massachusetts Press, 1987.

———. *Early American Gardens: For Meate or Medicine.* Boston: Houghton Mifflin, 1970.

Lemon, James T. *The Best Poor Man's Country: A Geographical Study of Early Southeastern Pennsylvania.* New York: W. W. Norton, 1972.

Liebs, Chester. *Main Street to Miracle Mile: American Roadside Architecture.* Boston: Little, Brown, 1985.

Longstreth, Richard. "Compositional Types in American Commercial Architecture." In *Perspectives in Vernacular Architecture, II,* edited by Camille Wells, 12–23. Columbia: University of Missouri Press, 1986.

———. *The Buildings of Main Street: A Guide to American Commercial Architecture.* Washington, D.C.: Preservation Press for the National Trust for Historic Preservation, 1987.

Lounsbury, Carl. *An Illustrated Dictionary of Early Southern Architecture and Landscape.* New York: Oxford University Press, 1994.

Lowenthal, David. *The Past Is a Foreign Country,* Cambridge: Cambridge University Press, 1985.

McAlester, Virginia, and Lee McAlester. *A Field Guide to American Houses.* New York: Alfred A. Knopf, 1991.

McKee, Harley J. "Brick and Stone: Handicraft to Machine." In *Building Early America: Contributions toward the History of a Great Industry,* edited by Charles Peterson. Radnor, Pa.: Chilton, 1976.

———. *Introduction to Early American Masonry: Stone, Brick, Mortar, and Plaster.* Washington, D.C.: Preservation Press, 1973.

McKelvey, Frank J., and Bruce E. Seely. *Industrial Archaeology of Wilmington, Delaware, and Vicinity: Site Guide for the Sixth Annual Conference of the Society for Industrial Archaeology.* Wilmington, Del.: Society for Industrial Archaeology, 1977.

Meinig, D. W. *The Interpretation of Ordinary Landscapes: Geographical Essays.* New York: Oxford University Press, 1979.

Michel, H. John, Jr. "A Typology of Delaware Farms, 1850." Paper delivered at the Organization of American Historians annual meeting, Los Angeles, April, 1984.

Mombert, Jacob Isidor. *An Authentic History of Lancaster County, in the State of Pennsylvania.* Lancaster, Pa.: J. E. Barr, 1869.

Mulchahey, Susan A., Rebecca J. Siders, Gabrielle M. Lanier, Nancy K. Zeigler, and Bernard L. Herman. *National Register of Historic Places: Adaptations of Bungalows in the Lower Peninsula/Cypress Swamp Zone of Delaware, 1880–1940±.* Newark: Center for Historic Architecture and Engineering, College of Urban Affairs and Public Policy, University of Delaware, 1990.

Munroe, John A. *History of Delaware.* Newark: University of Delaware Press, 1979.

Nelson, Lee H. "Nail Chronology as an Aid to Dating Old Buildings: American Association for State and Local History Technical Leaflet 48." *History News* 24, no. 11 (November 1968).

Noble, Allen G. *Wood, Brick, and Stone: The North American Settlement Landscape.* Vol. 2, *Barns and Farm Structures.* Amherst: University of Massachusetts Press, 1984.

Nolan, J. Bennett. *Southeastern Pennsylvania, A History of the Counties of Berks, Bucks, Chester, Delaware, Montgomery, Philadelphia, and Schuylkill.* Philadelphia: Lewis Historical Publishing, 1943.

Norkunas, Martha. *The Politics of Public Memory: Tourism, History, and Ethnicity in Monterey, California.* Albany: State University of New York Press, 1993.

Norton, Joan, and Dean E. Nelson. *National Register of Historic Places: The J. H. Wilkerson and Son Brickworks, K-360 (Milford, Kent County, Delaware).* October 1977.

Passmore, Joanne O., Charles Maske, and Daniel E. Harris. *Three Centuries of Delaware Agriculture.* Delaware State Grange and the Delaware American Revolution Bicentennial Commission, 1978.

Pendleton, Philip E. *Oley Valley Heritage, The Colonial Years: 1700–1775.* Birdsboro, Pa.: Pennsylvania German Society and Oley Valley Heritage Association, 1994.

Phillips, Steven J. *Old House Dictionary: An Illustrated Guide to American Domestic Architecture 1600 to 1940.* Lakewood, Colo.: American Source Books, 1989.

Peterson, Fred W. *Homes in the Heartland: Balloon Frame Farmhouses of the Upper Midwest, 1850–1920.* Lawrence: University Press of Kansas, 1992.

Pierson, William H., Jr. *American Buildings and Their Architects: The Colonial and Neoclassical Styles.* Garden City, N.Y.: Doubleday, 1970.

Pocius, Gerald L. *A Place to Belong: Community Order and Everyday Space in Calvert, Newfoundland.* Athens: University of Georgia Press, 1991.

Poppeliers, John, S. Allen Chambers, and Nancy B. Schwartz. *What Style Is It?* Rev. ed. Washington, D.C.: Preservation Press, 1983.

Quinn, Judith A., and Bernard L. Herman. *National Registre of Historic Places: Sweet Potato Houses of Sussex County, Delaware.* Newark: Center for Historic Architecture and Engineering, University of Delaware, 1988.

Rapoport, Amos. *House Form and Culture.* Foundations of Cultural Geography Series. Englewood Cliffs, N.J.: Prentice-Hall, 1969.

Raymond, Eleanor. *Early Domestic Architecture of Pennsylvania.* Exton, Pa.: Schiffer Limited, 1977.

Salem County Historical Society. "Colonial Roof Trees" and "Candle Ends." Collected by Salem County Historical Society. Salem, N.J.: Salem County Historical Society, 1934.

Salvadori, Mario George. *Why Buildings Stand Up: The Strength of Architecture.* New York: Norton, 1980.

Schiffer, Margaret Berwind. *Survey of Chester County Architecture: Seventeenth, Eighteenth, and Nineteenth Centuries.* Exton, Pa.: Schiffer, 1976.

Schlereth, Thomas J. *Cultural History and Material Culture: Everyday Life, Landscapes, Museums.* Ann Arbor, Mich.: UMI Research Press, 1990.

Schwartz, Helen. *The New Jersey House.* New Brunswick, N.J.: Rutgers University Press, 1983.

Scully, Vincent J., Jr. *The Shingle Style and the Stick Style.* Rev. ed. New Haven, Conn.: Yale University Press, 1971.

Sebold, Kimberly R. "Chicken-House Apartments on the Delmarva Peninsula." *Delaware History* 25, no. 4 (1993): 253–63.

Sebold, Kimberly R., and Sara Amy Leach. *Historic Themes and Resources within the New Jersey Coastal Heritage Trail: Southern New Jersey and the Delaware Bay: Cape May, Cumberland, and Salem Counties.* Washington, D.C.: Historic American Buildings Survey/Historic American Engineering Record, National Park Service, 1991.

Shannon, Fred A. *The Farmer's Last Frontier: Agriculture, 1860–1897.* New York: Harper Torchbooks, 1945.

Sharf, Thomas. *History of Delaware, 1609–1888.* Philadelphia: J. Richards, 1888.

Sickler, Joseph S. *The Old Houses of Salem County.* Salem, N.J.: Sunbeam, 1949.

Siders, Rebecca J. et al. *Agricultural Tenancy in Central Delaware, 1770–1900 ±: A Historic Context.* Newark: Center for Historic Architecture and Engineering, University of Delaware, for the Delaware State Historic Preservation Office, 1991.

Simler, Lucy. "The Landless Laborer in Perspective. Part 2. Inmates and Freemen: A Landless Labor Force in Colonial Chester County." Paper presented to the Philadelphia Center for Early American Studies, April 18, 1986.

Simpson, Pamela H. "Cheap, Quick, and Easy: The Early History of Rockfaced Concrete Block Building." In *Perspectives in Vernacular Architecture, III,* edited by Thomas Carter and Bernard L. Herman, 108–18. Columbia: University of Missouri Press, 1989.

Snyder, John J., Jr. *Handbook of Lancaster County Architecture Styles and Terms.* Lancaster, Pa.: Historic Preservation Trust of Lancaster County, 1979.

South, Stanley. *Method and Theory in Historical Archaeology.* New York: Academic Press, 1977.

Spurrier, John. *The Practical Farmer: Being a New and Compendious System of Husbandry, Adapted to the Different Soils and Climates of America.* Wilmington, Del.: Brynberg and Andrews, 1793.

Stevenson, Katherine Cole, and H. Ward Jandl. *Houses by Mail: A Guide to Houses from Sears, Roebuck and Company.* Washington D.C.: Preservation Press, 1986.

Stickley, Gustav. *Craftsman Homes* [pattern book]. 1909. Reprint, New York: Dover, 1979.

Stilgoe, John R. *Common Landscape of America, 1580 to 1845.* New Haven: Yale University Press, 1977.

Stutz, Bruce. *Natural Lives, Modern Times: People and Places of the Delaware River.* New York: Crown, 1992.

Swank, Scott T., Benno M. Forman, Frank H. Sommer, Arlene Palmer Schwind, Frederick S. Weiser, Donald H. Fennimore, and Susan Burrows Swan. *Arts of the Pennsylvania Germans.* New York: W. W. Norton, 1983.

Sweeney, John A. H., *Grandeur on the Appoquinimink: The House of William Corbit at Odessa, Delaware.* Newark: University of Delaware Press, 1989.

Tatman, Sandra L., and Roger W. Moss. *Biographical Dictionary of Philadelphia Architects: 1700–1930.* Boston: G. K. Hall, 1985.

Thomas, Selma, ed. *Delaware: An Inventory of Historic Engineering and Industrial Sites.* Washington, D.C.: U.S. Department of the Interior, 1975.

Touart, Paul Baker. *Somerset: An Architectural History.* Annapolis, Md.: Maryland Historical Trust; Princess Anne, Md.: Somerset County Historical Trust, 1990.

Tuan, Yi-Fu. *Landscapes of Fear.* New York: Pantheon Books, 1979.

———. *Segmented Worlds and Self: Group Life and Individual Consciousness.* Minneapolis: University of Minnesota Press, 1982.

———. *Space and Place: The Perspective of Experience.* Minneapolis: University of Minnesota Press, 1977.

———. *Topophilia: A Study of Environmental Perception, Attitudes, and Values.* Englewood Cliffs, N.J.: Prentice-Hall, 1974.

Upton, Dell. *Holy Things and Profane: Anglican Parish Churches in Colonial Virginia.* New York: Architectural History Foundation; Cambridge: MIT Press, 1986.

———. "Traditional Timber Framing." In *Material Culture of the Wooden Age*, edited by Brooke Hindle, 35–93. Tarrytown, N.Y.: Sleepy Hollow Press, 1981.

Upton, Dell, and John Michael Vlach, eds. *Common Places: Readings in American Vernacular Architecture.* Athens: University of Georgia Press, 1986.

Van Dolsen, Nancy. *Cumberland County: An Architectural Survey.* Carlisle, Pa.: Cumberland County Historical Society, 1990.

Vlach, John Michael. *Back of the Big House: The Architecture of Plantation Slavery.* Chapel Hill: University of North Carolina Press, 1993.

———. "The Shotgun House: An African Architectural Legacy." In *Common Places: Readings in American Vernacular Architecture*, edited by Dell Upton and John Michael Vlach. Athens: University of Georgia Press, 1986.

Watson, John Fanning. *Annals of Philadelphia, and Pennsylvania, in the Olden Time.* Vol. 2. Philadelphia: J. B. Lippincott, 1870.

Webster, Richard. *Philadelphia Preserved: Catalogue of the Historic American Buildings Survey.* Philadelphia: Temple University Press, 1976.

Weeks, Christopher. *Where Land and Water Intertwine: An Architectural History of Talbot County, Maryland.* Baltimore: Johns Hopkins University Press, 1984.

———, ed. *Maryland Historical Trust Inventory of Historic Sites in Caroline County.* Annapolis, Md.: Maryland Historical Trust, 1980.

Wells, Camille, ed. *Perspectives in Vernacular Architecture, I.* Columbia: University of Missouri Press, 1982.

Whitelaw, Ralph T. *Virginia's Eastern Shore: A History of Northampton and Accomack Counties.* 2 vols. Gloucester, Mass.: Peter Smith, 1968.

Willey, Gordon R., and Philip Phillips. *Method and Theory in American Archaeology.* Chicago: University of Chicago Press, 1958.

Wright, Gwendolyn. *Building the Dream: A Social History of Housing in America.* New York: Pantheon Books, 1981.

Zink, Clifford W. "Dutch Framed Houses in New York and New Jersey." *Winterthur Portfolio* 22, no. 4 (winter 1987), 265–94.

INDEX

gravestone styles, as example of seriation, 119–20
Greek Revival style, 31, 138–39, *142, 143, 144,* 153, 167; porches, 138, *143, 154;* temple fronts, 138, *144*
Greenlawn, 127, 147–49, *148, 149, 338;* Farm Manager's House, *3*
Greenmeadow, *331;* barn, *182*
Greenwich Friends Meeting House, 269, *272*
gristmills. *See* mills
Grow, Lawrence, 264
Gulliford, Andrew, 269
Gutman, Richard, 264

Hagley Museum and Library, 348
Hale-Byrnes House, *69*
half-dovetail joints, 79
half-passage plan, 38–39, *39, 44*
hall, 12, 21
hall-parlor plan, 8, 16–19, *17,* 147, 287, *288,* 296–97
hall plan, 8, 12–16, *13, 14, 15,* 288
hay stacks, 196
hay tracks, 205
H-bent construction, 83, 86, *86,* 90–91, *91,* 189
hearth trimmers, 67
hedging, 301–2
Heller House, 132, *137*
hewing, 77
hierarchy of finish, 18, 20–21, 28–32, *29,* 38, *43,* 52
hierarchy of siting and materials, 307
Historical Society of Delaware, 348
Historical Society of Pennsylvania, 348
Historic American Buildings Survey (HABS), 348
Historic American Engineering Record (HAER), 348
Hitchens' Store, *235*
Hocker Factory, H. W., *253, 255*
hog gallows, 196, 260
Holland House, *163*
Hopkins, Alfred, 221
Hopkins, Robert B., 58
Hopkins Store, *236*
horizon, 5, 7
Hoskins, W. G., 278
"house and garden" dwellings, 52
house form, 10–11
house lots, 51–59, *56;* organization of, *58*
house styles, traditional mid-Atlantic, 122–24, *123, 125*
Houston-White Company Mill and Basket Factory, 254–56, *256*
Hudson Farm, 58, 210–11, *210;* barn, 210–11, *210*
Hunter Farm: cider barn, *64;* dairy, *54;* house, 18, *18,* 43–44, *44*

husk frame: in mills, 247
hyphen, 53

Illustrated Annual Register of Rural Affairs, 45, *46*
impermanent architecture, 62–63, 65–66, *65*
industrial archaeology, 245
industrial buildings, 242–64; alterations of, 245; canneries, 249–52, *250, 251, 309;* forms of, 245; gristmills, 246–49; for local manufactures, 254–58, *254, 255, 256, 257, 258;* maritime, 258–63, *259, 261;* paper mills, 252–53; process in, 245, 249–58, 262–63; small-scale shops, 253–55, *254, 255;* surveying, 245
industrial development, 242–46; basketmaking, 245; canning, 244; manufacturing, 244; mills, 242, 244; poultry production, 245; relationship to agriculture and transportation, 244, 254–57; shipbuilding, 244; small manufactures, 245
industrial hamlets and towns, 244
Ingram House, John, *53*
institutional buildings, 264–77, churches, 268–69, *271, 271, 273, 273,* 276–77, *276,* 304–7, *304, 306;* courthouse complexes, 265–67, *266;* fraternal halls, *268;* meeting houses, 272–74, *272, 274;* schools, 267–70, *270,* 307–9, *308*
insurance records as source of information, 346, *347*
interiors, construction and finish of, 111–13
Isaacs Cannery, 250–51, *251*
Italianate style, 31, 147, 152–54, *152, 154, 162, 164,* 296, 304–5; in Delaware valley, *153*

Janet's Farm Market, 242–43, *243*
Johns House, Kensey, 24, 32, 36–37, *36, 37,* 40, 129, *138*
Johnson, Paula, 262–63
joints: bridle, 79–81, *80;* dovetail, 73, *75;* half-dovetail, 79; lap, 79, *80;* mortise-and-tenon, 73, *75,* 79–81, *80;* V-notch, 73, *75*
joists, 77, 80–81, *80,* 90; log, 67
Joshua Pyle Wagon Barn, *209*

Kammer, 24
Kemp, Emory, 246
King's Creek Canning Company, 249, *250*
Kingston-Upon-Hull, *102, 104, 107*
kitchens, 52–53, *53,* 59
Küche, 24

La Grange, 203
Lamb House, Thomas, *142*
land reclamation, 290–93

ABOUT THE AUTHORS

Gabrielle M. Lanier was born and raised in Baltimore. She earned her B.A. in fine arts at the University of Pennsylvania, completed an M.A. in the Winterthur Program in Early American Culture at the University of Delaware, and is currently a Ph.D. candidate in American civilization at the University of Delaware. She has taught historic preservation at Mary Washington College, Rutgers University, and Millersville University, and previously she was a research assistant at the Center for Historic Architecture and Design at the University of Delaware.

Bernard L. Herman was born in Boston and raised in Virginia. He received his B.A. in English literature from the College of William and Mary and completed his Ph.D. in folklore and folklife at the University of Pennsylvania. He is associate director of the Center for Historic Architecture and Design at the Unversity of Delaware, where he is also an associate professor in the departments of art history and history and in the College of Urban Affairs and Public Policy. His books include *Architecture and Rural Life in Central Delaware: 1700–1900*, 1987, *A Land and Life Remembered: Americo-Liberian Folk Architecture*, with Svend Holsoe and Max Belcher, and *The Stolen House*. He has twice, in 1987–88 and 1992–93, received the Abbott Lowell Cummings Award, which recognizes the best book on North American vernacular architecture, and is also a recipient of the Fred Kniffen Award, given by the Pioneer America Society for the best edited book in material culture studies overall.

RELATED BOOKS

IN THE SERIES

The American Backwoods Frontier: An Ethnic and Ecological Interpretation   Terry G. Jordan and Matti Kaups

Apostle of Taste: Andrew Jackson Downing, 1815–1852   David Schuyler

Cities and Buildings: Skyscrapers, Skid Rows, and Suburbs   Larry R. Ford

The Gas Station in America   John A. Jakle and Keith A. Sculle

Jens Jensen: Maker of Natural Parks and Gardens   Robert E. Grese

The Last Great Necessity: Cemeteries in American History   David Charles Sloane

Local Attachments: The Making of an American Urban Neighborhood, 1850 to 1920
Alexander von Hoffman

Measure of Emptiness: Grain Elevators in the American Landscape   Frank Gohlke, with a concluding essay by John C. Hudson

The Mountain West: Interpreting the Folk Landscape   Terry G. Jordan, Jon T. Kilpinen, and Charles F. Gritzner

The Pennsylvania Barn: Its Origin, Evolution, and Distribution in North America
Robert F. Ensminger

The Spanish-American Homeland: Four Centuries in New Mexico's Rio Arriba
Alvar W. Carlson

To Build in a New Land: Ethnic Landscapes in North America   Edited by Allen G. Noble

Unplanned Suburbs: Toronto's American Tragedy, 1900 to 1950   Richard Harris

Library of Congress Cataloging-in-Publication Data

Lanier, Gabrielle M.
   Everyday architecture of the Mid-Atlantic : looking at buildings
and landscapes / Gabrielle M. Lanier and Bernard L. Herman.
   . p.   cm. — (Creating the North American landscape)
Includes bibliographical references and index.
ISBN 0-8018-5324-9 (hc : alk. paper). — ISBN 0-8018-5325-7
(pbk. : alk. paper)
   1. Architecture—Middle Atlantic States. 2. Regionalism in
architecture—Middle Atlantic States. I. Herman, Bernard L.,
1951–   . II. Title. III. Series.
NA717.L36   1996
720′.974—dc20   96-17883